a passion for

FREEDOM

a passion for
FREEDOM

my encounters with
extraordinary people

LEONARD R. SUSSMAN

Prometheus Books
59 John Glenn Drive
Amherst, New York 14228-2197

Published 2004 by Prometheus Books

Inquiries should be addressed to
Prometheus Books
59 John Glenn Drive
Amherst, New York 14228–2197
VOICE: 716–691–0133, ext. 207
FAX: 716–564–2711
WWW.PROMETHEUSBOOKS.COM

08 07 06 05 04   5 4 3 2 1

Library of Congress Cataloging-in Publication Data

Sussman, Leonard R.
   A passion for freedom : my encounters with extraordinary people / Leonard R. Sussman.
      p.cm.
   Includes bibliographical references.
   ISBN 1–59102–142–1
   1. Sussman, Leonard R.—Friends and associates. 2. Sussman, Leonard R.—Political and social views. 3. Intellectuals—United States—Biography. 4. Scholars—United States—Biography. 5. Biography—20th century. 6. Liberty. 7. Freedom House (U.S.) I. Title.

CT3990.S87A3 2004
920.073'09'04—dc22

                                                      2004001174

FOR LYNNE, IN MEMORY

CONTENTS

APPENDICES

INTRODUCTION

WALK ON THE MIDWAY

MIDWAY: (1) The middle . . . way; or (2) a place, as at a fair, on or along which side shows and similar amusements are located.

—Random House Dictionary

"LUCKY"

Never start a book with a cliché like "talk the talk *and* walk the walk"—unless you do both, and not just occasionally; *walk* with fighting reformers, don't just *talk* the good struggle. I walk an average five miles a day. I have talked a lot in some fifty-nine countries. Talk-with-walk is in my blood.

Many of the people in this book have shed *their* blood for the talking they did. So far, I have not. But it is my duty to record their words and deeds.

I am, you see, extraordinarily lucky. Lynne, David, and Mark, my three children, gave me a milestone birthday party. I was asked to say "a few words." I did—very few. It was getting late, and the grandchildren had to leave for bed. I said I had been "lucky," and I left it at that. Mark smiled understandingly. Lynne looked teary. (She did not live to see this book.) Others seemed eager to leave. Understandably—it had been a long week.

So I have written this book to explain "lucky." And to provide for those grandchildren, then seven, eight, and nine years of age, what they couldn't fully understand but may later—at least, by browsing this introduction.

Lucky? Yes, in what *didn't* happen to me. I wasn't born in the dark ages of Europe in either the sixteenth or twentieth centuries. I wasn't the son of a Zulu or Kurd with unbearable hurdles. Nazi submarines missed me at sea just after

11

war started in 1941. I was not aboard the westbound *Andrea Doria* when it sank in July 1956, killing fifty-one people. Instead, my wife, Fran, Lynne, and had I sailed on her shortly before. I saw fighting in the South Atlantic and Vietnam, as well as guerrilla attacks in several countries, but was never a direct target. I was not aboard NASA's *Challenger* when it exploded, though I had asked to be. I was in the street just yards from the World Trade Center between the attacks of the first and second planes on September 11, 2001, and ran unhurt from the first cloud of burning ash.

I was lucky in the timing of my birth. Marking my arrival, 1920 was a great news year. The Nineteenth Amendment gave women the right to vote; the first radio broadcasting license was issued; the Senate barred America from entering the League of Nations; and airmail service began between New York and California. Oh, yes, Coney Island banned socks on women; liquor was made illegal across the United States; and the Cleveland Indians, not the Yankees, won the World Series.

That year, the average income was $2,160, a new car cost $525, and a gallon of milk was sixty-seven cents. On Wall Street, the Dow Jones averaged 90! Life expectancy was 54.1 years. I beat that one! The great new invention was the electric hair dryer. Not yet invented were refrigerators, televisions, dial telephones, dishwashers, antibiotic medicines, copier machines, air conditioning, frozen foods, oral contraceptives, ballpoint pens, FM and transistor radios, and a host of computer-related and satellite-enhanced technologies. I was lucky. At that place and time in history, inventiveness was explosive as never before. I could share its bounty and learn to project still greater technological advances just ahead.

I was lucky, most of all, for what *did* happen. My parents were modestly well-off but taught me the danger of poverty, the value of work, and the flavor of wealth. I learned early that there are several sides to every argument. And that a good way often is the midway.

I was lucky, too, for finding my second wife, Marianne, and for the men and woman my children became—and for their children, following similar values.

Mainly, I have had the best of many worlds. Not least, few knew how young I was when I became press secretary to a governor at twenty-three; or how old when I was teaching and still traveling worldwide at eighty. My passport has been stamped in some fifty-nine countries, to many of which I have returned frequently. What a satisfaction for that travel-minded child whose first dream was to become a cross-country truck driver! My second aspiration, briefly, was the rabbinate. In religious school, I wrote a "March of Time" dramatization, edited several publications, and won prizes there and, as a debater, citywide. But by thirteen I formally announced I would be a newspaperman. My father, a dentist, was relieved. "Anything but dentistry," he beamed.

I have played some of all these roles. I traveled widely but always for a purpose: to discover a fact and report it, or to state a belief and sustain it. In every new place I was accepted, but as an odd man out. I worked in Puerto Rico's social revolution though I was not of Puerto Rican descent, and I was briefly reviled for that lapse. I created religious schools in Judaism, though I never became a rabbi. I challenged the politicization of Jewish institutions when the tide raced the other way. During press-freedom struggles, I addressed international media conferences, though I was no longer a working journalist. I was regarded suspiciously by human-rights groups for taking strong stands in the Cold War. I represented the United States government at international conferences but broke publicly with Washington over its intergovernmental policy. Early on, I described the gains and hazards of the new communication technologies, though I was not an electronics buff. And I managed a late, gratifying career teaching at universities, though I never earned a doctorate. (My children earned three, making me feel like a dropout.)

My education has been derived mainly from the people I have known. This book introduces men and women whose influence I have observed firsthand. I am not sure, though, whether something more than luck brought me to such people. Was it not an underlying belief? I think so.

Judaism influenced me as a child and young adult. Not by active adherence to ritual—my parents were Reform Jews who seldom entered a house of worship except to mark births and deaths. They observed Passover and Chanukah but little else. I brought to them from religious school other practices and symbols that had passed out of my family's religious repertoire a generation earlier. They regarded themselves as little-observant Jews but made certain that I attended temple classes and services until I was confirmed at fourteen.

The Judaism I absorbed in those formative years provided a fundamental commitment to tolerance and, in most things, the middle way. Almost instinctively, I regarded Judaism as a millenarian conveyor of an ethical system for a largely unethical world. The history, traditions, and symbols of Judaism, however, were not entirely otherworldly. Even belief in God could be seen in Reform Judaism as an indwelling force, a spirit, a conscience, without anthropomorphic form.

Judaism for me was a freeing faith, one that could be practiced with equal influence anywhere, in solitude or in company with others. The history of Judaism embodied in religious texts and symbols provides a rich variety of traditions. One person cannot adhere to all, because they differ markedly. There are the liberalizing utterances of the Prophets, who warned against defiling the religion by certain materialistic or nationalistic practices. There are also narrow, even tribal restrictions—and the mystical codes as well. All are part of the historic flow of Judaism as its adherents adapted to the oppression and, later, the emancipation by the non-Jewish world. Clearly, without emancipation in the long history of Judaism, there would be no Jews living today. It required more than survivalism for Jews to withstand the desecration of the temples in Palestine and the Holocaust in Europe. Ultimately, Jewish existence—as, indeed, all democratic existence—depends upon the functioning of a civil society.

Such a society provides more than tolerance for diverse religions, races, and nationalities; it requires active participation in the forms and institutions of democracy. This is what Judaism taught me at an early age. I learned it, ironically, at the very moment when Hitler's Nazi hordes were desecrating every Jewish house of worship in Germany, and planning the "Final Solution," the death of all Jews. Years later, I realized that the very horror of Nazism and its virulent anti-Semitism were the ultimate proof that even a nation's democratic structure—free and fair elections, and the like—could not deter abysmal tragedy in the absence of a viable civil society. In the German Weimar Republic after the First World War there were democratic forms of governance. There was also a vibrant satiric theater and political dissent. But the society was still traumatized by defeat in war and horrendous inflation that produced economic desperation. A truly civil mentality had not developed. There were inadequate restraints on political extremism, increasing social and political violence, and intolerance derived from the perceived need to scapegoat minorities for the failure of the politicoeconomic system.

My wife Marianne's family, among the Jewish aristocracy of Berlin, enjoyed its unsurpassed cultural offerings but suffered under skyrocketing inflation. It was incredible that this seemingly high point of Western civilization would end in the Holocaust. It did, in the absence of adequate civil-society restraints.

In 1962, before the Union League Club of San Francisco, I began a forty-two-year campaign to spell out the responsibilities of the mass news media. I recognized the intimate relationship between responsible journalism and a stable, civil society. I offered guidelines for the press. Later, I appeared on Harry Reasoner's half-hour interview program on the CBS-TV network. In return, Reasoner—one of the most reasonable correspondents in American journalism—sat for an interview with me via a leased wire from a radio station in St. Louis. We discussed "problems in reporting controversial issues." This, four decades before the quality of U.S. journalism dropped in the esteem of most Americans, and before critiquing news products became a cottage industry.

And lest we forget, as I have recorded for thirty years, journalism has become the world's most dangerous craft.

Advancing a civil society should be an objective of everyone, not only the news media and organized religion. The people I recall in this book—journalists by trade, Muslims, Christians, and Jews by religion—act out their commitment to a civil society. They do so by trodding the middle road. Together, we walk the midway.

PLACES, BUT MOSTLY PEOPLE

This book is primarily about people I have known, admired, tried to help: in Africa, Asia, Latin America, the Caribbean, the Pacific, and the Soviet bloc; my good friend Kow Bonzie Brown, called "the best journalist in sub-Saharan

Africa," dead after twelve years in the torture chambers of Ghana's military dictator; Yuri Baturin, with whom I shared ideas for the first Soviet press law before he became Boris Yeltsin's security adviser in the Kremlin; the Dalai Lama, who gave me a shawl for setting up his first visit to the United States; Milovan Djilas, the Communist vice-president of Yugoslavia, who renounced the Party, denounced Stalin, wrote landmark books in prison, and greeted Marianne and me in a moving visit to him under house arrest in Belgrade; a brief encounter with Dr. Isaam Sartawi, a courageous moderate Arab in the murderous Middle East, assassinated for his courage; Inga Arvad, a Danish classmate at Columbia, interviewer of Hitler and Goebbels, under FBI surveillance as a spy, and the only woman whom future president Jack Kennedy repeatedly asked to marry him— and who repeatedly refused him; Jonas Savimbi, the charismatic and regretfully bloodied Angolan guerrilla, whose visits to the United States I arranged; Kim Sang-Man, KBE, who invited Marianne and me to Seoul, South Korea, for helping when the government harassed his newspaper and threatened imprisonment; Leopold Labedz, a hero of the Cold War, who found a publisher for Alexander Solzhenitsyn and whose own extraordinarily valuable East-West journal I helped fund; Humberto and Gloria Rubin, who invited me to Paraguay to defend their radio station, banned by Dictator Stroessner, whose military then detained me . . .

The list goes on. Mohammad Gawad, head of the Middle East News Agency, who conferred with Yasir Arafat (then the Palestinian terrorist leader) while Mohammad and I traveled to Oslo, where he secretly began to arrange Anwar Sadat's historic visit to Israel and the Egyptian-Israeli peace accord; Sergei Grigoryants, wan, nervous, and paranoid after ten years in the Soviet gulag, who handed me his first typewritten copy of the new periodical *Glasnost* for publication in the United States, which would test the liberalization of censorship under Mikhail Gorbachev; Percy Qoboza, beside whom I sat in South Africa as he edited a black newspaper restricted by heartless apartheid laws (the stress soon killed Percy; his heart gave out); my associate Eugene Wigner, the self-effacing Nobel laureate in physics, who helped persuade Albert Einstein to implore President Franklin D. Roosevelt to build the American atomic weapon before Nazi Germany constructed one; and Aristedes Katoppo, the "ghost" in an Indonesian city room, allowed to share his considerable journalistic talent with colleagues, but whose name the government banned from the masthead or bylines, threatened with arrest, he spent a year on a Fulbright scholarship at Harvard; together, we climbed the Roman ruins at Petra, Jordan.

This book is about people whose own striving, sometimes successful, sometimes tragic, reinforces my early attachment to the golden or philosophic mean, the Center. To advance human progress, however defined, the democratic Center must hold.

That is often derided as compromise or shilly-shally. Yet, in the long run (if there is to be one) human interaction, whether in a medical tradeoff for a patient, in democratic policymaking or election, in labor negotiation, or in the murderous confrontation of enemy states—in every human interaction, the moment of truth comes when the extremes give way to the center, however defined.

This is not a book of historic record, but an account of one man's travel through diverse politics and cultures, observing the harm done to the human spirit by intent or, worse, inattention. On a sunny day in New York in 2002 I met for the first time Ambassador Sichan Siv, the American representative on the Economic and Social Council of the United Nations. I was startled when he pressed my hand warmly and recalled that he had been a refugee in Cambodia in 1975 during the genocidal murders by the Khmer Rouge. Most of his family perished. Silenced and marked for death, Siv survived starvation and the worst abuses of human rights. At that moment in history, I publicized Freedom House pleas for international assistance to Cambodians. When we spoke out, no one else raised a voice, and millions died; Ambassador Siv remembered. I was flustered but welcomed his acknowledgment of Freedom House's role in his life.

One person cannot change the world, as even presidents and dictators discover. But *anyone* can help diminish outrages and inhumanities. One does that by talking *and* walking in the right places. New York is my springboard to those places.

WALK IN NEW YORK

Over the years, flying into New York from any of fifty-nine countries I have visited, I feel nerves tingle as I see a view of the skyline that almost brings me to tears. "New York, New York" is my national anthem; I love the place, especially at ground level.

Most days, I walk five miles from home to office, down the Midway, the center of Manhattan. I observe the diversity of New Yorkers and ruminate on the city's history. I sense the presence of Dutch and British settlers along the wharves of lower Manhattan, as well as the recently uncovered bones of black slaves where ground was broken for a new federal building.

New York is also a vibrant fragment of peoples and places across the oceans; on other walks, I visit them in their homelands. New York throbs because *its* people ceaselessly move in, about—and out. Most middle-class New Yorkers leave for the suburbs when the first child looms; others cross to Brooklyn or Queens. Flooding into the city come new generations of upwardly mobile Americans from beyond the Hudson, and Asian and Latino immigrants from several countries. Few New Yorkers—particularly Manhattanites—were born in New York and remain, as have I. Fewer still have a father and a grandfather (born in New York 130 years ago) who led their full lives here. I am a full-bred New Yorker, and glory in it. New York is my world. (My recently born grandson is a sixth-generation New Yorker.) And after sixty years of travel abroad, the world—for me—is revisited in New York.

I visit the "sideshows" of history that illuminate the larger scene: past Washington Square Park (once an execution site, then a potter's field) where, as an NYU undergraduate, I mobilized students and the press to "Save Garibaldi," the statue still standing, then scheduled for obliteration for a bus route; past the Chrysler Building, which I first publicized as winner of the "building race" with a Wall Street edifice (now owned by Donald Trump), the two buildings under construction simultaneously; past the site of my family's tie to Tammany Hall, first empowered by Aaron Burr; past an old poster in a Third Avenue window: "Alexander H. Cohen presents Marlene Dietrich, a Nine O'Clock Theatre Production"—Alex Cohen, Broadway producer-to-be of more than one hundred plays (Arthur Miller's classics among them) and my teenage coauthor of an amateur musical; past historic Gramercy Park, privately owned, where I played as a child and scraped knees on gravel paths not friendly to children; past the Bridge Cafe, the city's oldest saloon, formerly home of a brothel "filled with river pirates and Water Street hags," just two blocks from the Fulton Fish market, where I end my daily five-mile walk. (The market prolongs my passage to Wall Street, but I must view the hyperactive waterfront.)

I also favor the "middle way" in *politics*, at home and abroad; in the divisive Vietnam War; in the aftermath of Watergate scandals; promoting overseas academic exchanges pressed by my mentor Charles Frankel, before he was murdered; in balancing journalism and fighting for decades the censorious "cures" for free-flowing news that were finally defeated at UNESCO; proposing in 1967 the continuing evaluation of the U.S. press and broadcast media—intended to avoid governmental interference in free journalism in the face of growing public dissatisfaction with the quality of reporting; in struggling to restore the humanities in education, from kindergarten to PhD, presented as midway between education solely for employable skill or only as esoterica; and supporting academic freedom that rejects "political correctness" as well as "hate speech" penalties. I worry that concentration on democracy's legalisms, important as they are, has corroded the citizen's commitment to a civil society in which everyone plays a role.

I recall my own mixed role: as a six-year-old my entrance to Tammany Hall politics with my great-uncle, the sheriff; my Jewish father and his relationship with the first American canonized by the Vatican; and growing up somewhere between rich and poor on both sides of the Third Avenue elevated tracks. A middle way.

My synapses tingle when I walk the press-freedom paths of eighteenth-century Manhattan: where some of the nation's first newspapers were printed on a primitive press like that in Federal Hall, the site on Broad Street where George Washington took the oath as first president; past the seventeenth-century Jewish cemetery over whose modern congregation my friend's father presided as rabbi; the friend, Ithiel de Sola Pool of MIT, my guide in melding futurist telecommunications with First Amendment freedom for the electronic "new press"; past a milestone of press freedom, the spot where John Peter Zenger, challenging the colonial governor, won a momentous court trial that first accepted truth as a defense in libel cases; and past the cluster of buildings still standing on Park Row, across from City Hall, where Joseph Pulitzer published the *World*, James Gordon Bennett produced the *Herald*, and Horace Greeley put out the *Tribune*. Greeley put his faith and his paper in the service of "the unshackled mind." For balance, I walk the side streets where Bennett ran to a nearby brothel to observe the body of a murdered prostitute, slain by a notorious man about town, the subject of sensational coverage in the *Herald*. Great newspapers, great newspapermen.

On daily walks, Manhattan is my "fair," not always amusing but always fascinating, always stirring memories of other times and other places.

ACKNOWLEDGMENTS

As the reader will discover, this book is my personal account. It is not a publication of Freedom House, though the organization's themes run through this volume—which is understandable, because I have been associated for thirty-seven years with Freedom House.

Consequently, I owe its board of trustees, past and present, a deep bow and limitless gratitude for the opportunities I have had to roam the world. During those years, but particularly during the last decade, Freedom House has become a major actor in the prodemocracy movement. My twenty-one-year run as executive director was devoted to holding the fort during the contentious Cold War years, while developing programs that later, under successors, are among the signature operations of the organization.

I shall not "name names" of trustees or colleagues on the staff who have been profoundly supportive. Several hundred, not just some, deserve my warm acknowledgment.

The people whose stories I recount in the book reflect my deep empathy or sympathy; their trials are often models of courage and comprise a warning and challenge for everyone who does not face such tribulations. Their passion for freedom has inspired me on the long road I have walked in many lands. I hope their stories will inspire others as well.

For a quarter-century, I labored side-by-side with the officers and staff of the World Press Freedom Committee. The freedom of the press is a prime indicator of the freedom of the human condition anywhere. The WPFC has my great admiration as well as my thanks for that welcome association in a noble cause.

While I was assembling this book, Dorothy Arnsten, a friend who happens to be a psychologist, served as a nonprofessional nudge. Now that the challenge is ended, I thank her for her persistence.

And, of course, my limitless appreciation to Marianne for *not* nudging, but accepting periods of moodiness while new chapters were forming. And for countless other assistances and, above all, understanding and love. She is also a good trouper: just two weeks after suffering a concussion, when a truck struck her as she was crossing a street in Manhattan, she accompanied me to Korea on a trip with a grueling schedule and two thirteen-hour flights. And that is but a small fraction of my appreciation for our forty-five years together—and counting.

Finally, I am deeply grateful to Prometheus Books and its moving spirit, Dr. Paul Kurtz, for the warm understanding of this book's objective. For many years, I have admired Paul's own writing as well as his editorial standards and selections, not the least of which was the work of our great common friend Sidney Hook. I am delighted to appear under the Prometheus banner.

I owe a special debt to Benjamin Keller, the manuscript editor, who improved my product and saved me embarrassment. Christine Kramer, production manager, wondrously kept the manuscript moving through several stages. To Grace Zilsberger I am indebted for her deft handling of the photographs and the very attractive jacket.

Some will find parts of this book intensely controversial. In the spirit of free discourse, I welcome such reactions with the understanding that these views are solely mine, long held.

New York City and Craftsbury, Vermont
January 2004

PART ONE

WALKS AT HOME

1

MY FATHER
AND THE SAINT

I was fifty years old before I realized what a defining influence my father was in my life. I had long felt my mother's presence: she was loving in private but undemonstrative in public. She was an efficient manager of all the family's needs. She had a ready, broad smile, and when her hair turned gray she still looked twenty years younger, and trim (not prim).

My father was strapping, smoked pre-Castro cigars, and learned to swim as a teenager by being tossed into the East River at Fulton Street. Thereafter he swam the "East River stroke"—a hard slapping of the water. He had strong arms and legs and stayed afloat by sheer willpower. As a youth, he and a friend frequently walked a six-mile circuit of Central Park. In the summer they bicycled many miles from Manhattan to Coney Island, swam, and returned home before dark.

Father had a great love of New York City and a gut comradeship for its diverse population. Strangely, he felt elitist yet reveled in being a regular guy, part of the hoi polloi, as he would say. He had eclectic interests. The East Sixty-ninth Street brownstone in which he grew up was in a rough neighborhood. He learned to defend himself. A neighbor was Harry Houdini, the world-renowned magician and escape artist. Houdini was born Ehrich Weiss, son of a Hungarian rabbi. On the tenement roof he practiced escaping from tightly bound ropes. Later, he perfected a theatrical act in which he emerged from chains and a coffin. He played the greatest theaters of his time. His last act was to have been his return from the grave; he has not yet managed that. He is buried beneath a massive monument in Macpelah Cemetery in Glendale, Queens—just a few yards from the grave of my father and the older Sussman family.

Reflecting Father's upscale side, on Sunday he wore a derby and carried a "walking stick." He owned—my earliest recollection—a red Chevrolet convertible, which Mother drove to buy fresh eggs on Long Island, then "the country." (My Walker-Gordon bottled milk came daily from a farm in New Jersey.) The coupe was followed in leaner times by a black, boxlike Essex; later Dad acquired a large, sleek Hudson—the last car he owned. I was not allowed to drive it . . . until he died, and Mother had me deliver it to a buyer. Dad was more than the neighborhood dentist; he was a conversationalist with a broad agenda. He also provided patients with odd dividends—fresh fish. As a teenager, I would catch many porgies, fluke, or sea bass after an early-morning foray from Sheepshead Bay with Uncle Charlie. I would haul the fish-filled, bloody potato sack onto a subway and discover that Dad had promised most of the fish to his patients. But they would accept them only after I had scaled and cleaned the carcasses!

Mother was the moderator between my father and me on those rare occasions when there was disagreement, usually over politics. My father was an old-time Democrat. He grew up in the physical shadow of Tammany Hall, whose headquarters was just a few blocks away. His uncle was a Tammany district captain. Uncle Charlie knew how to get out the vote for the Democrats, no matter who was running or what the platform. My great-uncle was also a full-time sheriff in New York County. This post was obviously a party plum.

Tammany, since the mid-nineteenth century, tightly controlled New York City's police, courts, and public schools. There was graft at low and high levels. Tammany took care of its own—and the voters who supported it. A poor person could see a Tammany leader, my uncle for example, and get coal for fuel in the winter, a job for his son out of school, and applications for diverse city and state assistance. There was no bureaucracy to overcome, no welfare system to buck. Need or desire for help and voting "right" were the requisites. Since New Yorkers voted overwhelmingly for the Democratic Party, there were few rejections. The system worked, and Democrats were consistently maintained in power.

My father and I argued about this. I was becoming a Franklin Roosevelt Democrat. My uncle and my father were wary of this man who spoke of a New Deal and then drafted legislation to nationalize social security, create a welfare system, fund agrarian camps for the unemployed, and further regulate banks and stock exchanges. All that smacked of socialism. My father and I argued at dinner. Mother never participated, though her father had been a Republican district leader in Philadelphia. The Republican machine ran that city just as did Tammany, but with far less national attention. My mother was ready to halt the dinner table proceedings if they got out of hand. They never did: my father held to his ideas but didn't insist that I accept them. That was my first lesson in honest debate and civil discourse. It came at an early age, say twelve or thirteen.

Mother played a behind-the-scenes force in my childhood. She persuaded Father in my thirteenth year to explain to me what was then known not as sex education but the lesson of the "birds and the bees." I can imagine their conversation; Father would have been reluctant to discuss this sensitive subject. Nothing I ever heard him talk about before or after touched on the relationship between men and women. The entire subject was off-limits in our house. Mother probably said that this was a man's job to deal with a son. Father liked to give the impression of being, in today's terminology, macho—but he really was not. He had been in the U.S. Navy during World War I and never lost that feeling of military comradeship, as well as a sense of shared danger at sea. He was a mild-mannered man who pretended at times to be tough.

He would demonstrate this when rowing with me on Lake George. We pulled oars for several hours on that beautiful, long lake. When we returned, Mother noticed that I had huge blisters on both hands. She was concerned and looked accusingly at Dad. He, however, was proud that I had not said a word to him about the pain while we rowed together so ardently on that unforgettable day.

Bearing up was always a strong force in our family. So was *not* speaking of what now may be considered psychologically related physical issues. As mentioned, sex education was an example. Dad probably reluctantly accepted the assignment as a duty. Early one Saturday morning, he invited me to walk with him. I felt this was unusual but I agreed. We went down the four flights that led from our apartment and began walking west on Seventeenth Street, past Tammany Hall, just forty feet from our house. My father began haltingly, "Your mother asked me to talk to you about how babies are made."

"Oh that," I said. "I know all about that."

"You do?"

"Yes, from Henry Blum, in school." Henry was a fellow student about two years older in Wingate Junior High.

"You do?" Dad repeated with obvious relief. And with that, my father turned sharply on his heel, military bearing and all. We both walked home to Mother, assignment completed.

Today, of course, sex education would begin at an early age in the classroom, while fellow students would already have been testing it for themselves; some having babies at thirteen, some depending on welfare to keep their offspring alive.

Around the same time, Dad's quiet and unspoken but obvious command of our household was played out on another brief street encounter. It was Halloween 1930, the scary depths of the Depression. I heard about trick-or-treating. As an only child, however, I had no model in our family or even among my few childhood friends. I simply decided that saying the magic words "trick or treat" would produce some adult response. I walked alone on Eighteenth Street, the block that included our house. I wasn't allowed to cross streets then. I held out my hand to passersby and said the magic words. I had no costume or any other holiday symbol. Several men nevertheless put coins in my hand. After a half-hour, I had $1.15 in coins. Suddenly, I spied my father walking toward me; he was coming home to Mother's full-course lunch, as he did every day of his life. I was overwhelmed with fear. I felt he would not only berate me, but worse than that, think less of me—for begging in the street. I did what seemed the proper thing to do: I stopped a young man and gave him all the coins. At first, he resisted, but then he accepted without further questioning and went on his way. I ran toward my father and greeted him, happily. I asked him what Halloween was all about.

Around that time, Dad asked me the usual what-do-you-want-to-be-when-you-grow-up? question.

"A newspaperman," I replied. I had already written articles for my junior high magazine.

"That's fine," he said, "as long as you don't want to be a dentist."

Until I was about eight, Father's dental office was in a four-story walkup owned by my grandfather. This was the third building owned by my family, later sold with a total of $353 coming to me after my father's death. The check represented one-third of the liquidation of a bank trust fund. The money had been willed to three male descendents, of whom I was one. Today, all three buildings are expensive property—either the bank or the family made some bad judgments.

The site at 208 Third Avenue still brings a nostalgic twinge as I pass the newer building on my walks to work. On the ground floor, my grandfather David ran a large pool parlor and cigar store, with a wooden Indian out front. He died when I was about four. I remember his gray mustache and warm smile. Suddenly, one day he disappeared from my life without explanation or sadness. David's brothers, Ben and Sam, ran a glazier service. The fourth brother, Charlie, was the politician of the family. These three brothers were reclusive and never married. The cigar-and-pool store served both as a community center for the men of the neighborhood and a political headquarters for Charlie. I was the favored boy of this male congregation. At Christmas, after my grandfather died, one of the men dressed as Santa Claus and called at our apartment, a block south on Third Avenue. He would ho-ho-ho and give me small presents until I began asking suspicious questions at age six. (Christmas was regarded simply as a secular holiday in this Jewish household.) Mother told me the depressing fact that Santa Claus was not what I had been led to believe. The beginning of disbelief and skepticism was an epiphany I have never forgotten.

Above the pool parlor was my father's dental office. He had opened it after returning from naval service in 1919. He married Mother, and I was born ten months later. His father rented the space to him at about $25 a month. Grandmother Mamie was furious that father was charged anything. She believed "my son, the dentist" should not be burdened with added expense. My father didn't seem to mind, but his charge to patients was in line with his rent. Most visits brought him ten dollars. He was an "all service" dentist, practicing some forms of dentistry now performed only by specialists. He was proud of particularly difficult extractions of teeth. He had muscular arms, strong hands, and a generally well-proportioned physique. He kept in excellent condition by walking, bicycling, and ice skating until his sixties.

He never forgot one patient who complained of a severe toothache. The guilty tooth had to be extracted. My father made the usual preparation and tugged and twisted. The tooth didn't move. He tried again and again. No response. After a half-hour, my father had made no progress. He was not quite ready to admit his first defeat. In trying to keep the patient somewhat unconcerned, my father began an innocuous conversation. This included a question about the man's occupation. (These were the days before you filled out a life history before seeing a doctor or dentist.)

"I work in the circus," the man replied.

"What do you do?"

"I'm an acrobat. I hang by my teeth from the high bar."

Dad put down the forceps and wrote the name of an extraction specialist who would remove the tooth under complete anesthesia.

I barely remember that office above the pool parlor. I do recall, clearly, the odor as I walked up the rickety stair. The aroma was a combination of dental antiseptics, a faint mustiness, and an overlay of pipe smoke from Dad's tobacco. I would turn left along the dark, narrow hallway and enter my father's operating room. It was suddenly light and cheerful, the sound of the whirring drill punctuated by the Third Avenue elevated trains. They ground to a halt at the Eighteenth Street station just out the front window.

That was the station I would mount on Saturdays with Uncle Charlie. He would take me for rides on the El. We would travel to the end of the lines in all directions. This was my first view of New York. I would memorize the station stops and marvel at the spectacular turns of the train as we reached South Ferry. I would look in the windows of the tenements along the way and see sights not much different from those reported by journalist-muckrakers Lincoln Steffens and Ida Tarbell at the turn of the century. They wrote about mass transit and the people seen along the way, because they believed that reform of transportation would diminish overcrowding and undermine economic monopolies.

At the end of each Saturday journey my uncle would take me to his apartment, next door to mine. Charlie lived with my grandmother after his brother David died. Mamie would make my favorite food after train rides: boiled tongue, creamed spinach, and mashed potatoes. The spinach and potatoes are delicious when mixed together.

Often on Friday evening, Charlie and Mamie would take me to a movie after dinner. We would go to the Jefferson Theater or to the Academy of Music on Fourteenth Street. (Both have recently been demolished.) These theaters in the Depression years would present two feature films, a "short subject" and a news-reel—and then give away a set of dishes or even put on live amateur performances, with a prize to the best contestant. All for fifty cents admission.

Down the street from our apartment was a controversial building that taught me at an early age about conflict and long-remembered bitterness. As a child, I was often awakened at night by loud singing and band-playing from Schieffel

Hall, a well-known German barroom. I knew there was something to dislike, not only about the noise but about the content of the singing and music. It was not long after World War I. During the war, the hall had been closed down as an "enemy." After the war it reopened as Ellaire's but was still German-American in style. After World War II, the restaurant was renamed Tuesday's and became a popular disco haunt until it closed in 1995.

My parents and my mother's half-sister Gussie Marks lived on the same floor of the large five-story walkup as Mamie and Charlie. Our building was next to the Stuyvesant Apartments, the first apartment house built in the United States. It was the marvel of its time. Many famous artists of the day lived there. The lobby was dimly lit, the mahogany staircases grand, and each apartment had four wood-burning fireplaces, including one in the large kitchen. Apartments were light, with a parlor and two chambers in front, a dining room and a third chamber leading to the kitchen, and a maid's room and a bath in the rear. The Stuyvesant was the first example in New York of the "French flats." The architecture was modeled after the *maisons de rapport* in Paris, with its facade altered to match New York's distinctive row houses. There was space on the ground floor for a concierge and distinctive rooms at the top for artists.

Among the first tenants of the Stuyvesant were the mother of the famous actor Edwin Booth; General Custer's widow, who moved there after the battle of Little Bighorn; and Mrs. Burton Harrison, great-grandniece of Thomas Jefferson. Our neighbor-building also housed prominent painters, writers, and editors of the day. Social historian Elizabeth Hawes notes that these dwellers in the Stuyvesant were "on the cutting edge of a new society." They were a "highly respectable and rather impressive assembly of 'bohemians.'"[1]

They were attracted by the gracious accommodations, including twenty-foot ceilings, brass doorknobs, and mahogany staircases. And, strangely enough, reasonable rents—probably compensation for taking the risk of living in that first of a new kind of urban dwelling, the apartment house. The first home I remember, our apartment at 198 Third Avenue, abutting the Stuyvesant, was more modest. It, too, had a long (but not spiral) staircase leading from the street through a dimly lit lobby to our second-floor landing, shared by my grandmother's apartment and ours. We, too, had dark mahogany fittings, and one fireplace. No brass doorknobs that I can recall.

The year I came along, 1920, ushered in both the Jazz Age and the apartment rage in New York. Lewis Mumford, the prime recorder of city culture, said "the city never wore a brighter look." He would write about buildings as a primary reflector of modern culture. "The mind of the 1920s could be seen very clearly in its buildings," writes Hawes.[2] She notes that the population of the city in 1920 was nearly six million people, six times the density of any other American city, and five times that of Paris or London. Some 350 new citizens arrived each day, and new buildings appeared every fifty-one minutes, says Hawes. Old buildings came down at an equally dramatic rate. My father would say, "This city is never completed." New construction fascinated me. I strained at boarded worksites to watch new facades forming.

Years later, I was no less fascinated by the history of the Chrysler Building. For my daughter Lynne, I wrote *The Building Race*, a children's book, to tell the story of urban architecture. In the last gasp of pre-Depression splendor, New York witnessed the simultaneous rise of two tall buildings: the tower at 40 Wall Street and the Chrysler Building at Forty-second Street. Each wanted to claim the title as "the world's tallest." For many months, it seemed certain that 40 Wall would win. But then, as both buildings neared completion, the Chrysler builders mounted an enormous surprise. Under cover of night, they raised the 185-foot spire above the last story. Up, up it went clearly above the topmost point of 40 Wall. For a brief time, until the Empire State Building was completed a year later, the Chrysler Building was the world's tallest.

There was another chapter many years later. Forty Wall fell upon hard times. Most of the giant structure was vacant. Wall Street brokerage houses needed more modern space to accommodate twenty-four-hour electronic communication. In 1996, Donald Trump purchased 40 Wall and announced triumphantly that he would renovate the troubled structure. He said he would restore this formerly "tallest building" to its old glory. I bridled at this revising of history—and so told Mr. Trump in a letter to the *New York Times*.[3]

There was a reply from Mr. Trump—sort of. Within weeks, a fence a third the length of a football field went up along 40 Wall, down the street from the New York Stock Exchange. In two-story-high letters the Trump organization proclaimed, "This 72-story building will be the finest and most beautiful office building anywhere in New York when completed. The great tower, *once the tallest in the world*, will again take its place as the crown jewel of downtown Manhattan" (emphasis added). I suppose it can be said that 40 Wall was "tallest," for a few hours back in the 1920s before the Chrysler spire went through the roof into the night sky. Chrysler is still the epitome of art deco architecture, as well as the end of both the Jazz Age and the seemingly limitless, pre-Depression dreams of 40 Wall's broker-tenants.

In the 1920s, my family had a taste of local luxury. We did, after all, live next door to the grand Stuyvesant Apartments. From our windows we could see the tree-lined courtyard shared with the historic building. From those windows I saw the Graf Zeppelin just after it crossed the Atlantic Ocean, on its way to Lakehurst, New Jersey, and its flaming disaster. It was out of our window facing the gardens that our cleaning woman, a recent Polish émigré, caused a momentary panic. Mother had come home and discovered that Pete, my white-spotted black cat, was missing. "Oh," said Tillie, "I mistake. I pushed him out the window." We recaptured Pete, who was no worse for the one-story fall.

Here, where I spent my childhood, our apartment was large and similar to the French flats. An important presence was my aunt Gussie. She was a second mother to me until she died at the age of eighty. She had retired at sixty-five from the administrative staff of Mt. Sinai Hospital. At seventy-five she retired from a job at Dover Publishers. When New York's citywide blackout came in her seventies, Gussie walked to work on the fiftieth floor of the Empire State Building. She was working at another new job when she died in her sleep at home.

Gussie, Mother's half-sister, lived with my parents from the time Mother and Dad were married. Gussie was related to both my parents. She was a cousin of my maternal grandmother and the daughter of Samuel Marks, a Philadelphia businessman-politician and owner of a hotel in Atlantic City. I remember my maternal grandfather only from photographs, because he died before I was born. He was a tall, slender man with pince-nez glasses. He had come to Philadelphia from Germany as a youth, probably soon after the 1848 revolutions. When his wife died young, Sam did not feel capable of caring for Gussie, though he did manage to keep her younger brother with him. Gussie was sent west; as a young girl, she crossed the country on her own to stay with relatives in Spokane, Washington. The city was a small frontier-like place in the late nineteenth century. Gussie became a tall, attractive, and hardworking but emotionally restricted young lady.

She returned to Philadelphia and worked in a responsible position at a leading woolen manufacturer. Relatives were the Lorsches, Saluses, and Kupenheims, who worked as bankers, a judge, and prominent businessmen. We would visit Philadelphia once a year when I was between ten and fifteen. We would make the rounds of relatives; each had a house in a four-block radius in North Philly. Herman Kupenheim, the elderly uncle of Ruth, my nearest contemporary, was a family character. When he died in his late seventies, Ruth opened several large barrels in the cellar. They were filled with thousands of metal caps Uncle Herman had made and patented. They were milk-bottle caps with a movable part for pouring. Milk was delivered then in bottles with paper caps, which quickly became slimy and unhealthful. Uncle Herman had a good idea but never marketed it.

Though Gussie moved in the affluent German-Jewish society of the city, she had no serious romantic attachment. Except, perhaps, for Sigmund Romberg, the composer of operettas and light music such as *The Student Prince* and *The Desert Song*. Gussie lived in New York and dated Romberg, but their relationship did not flower. Just before World War I, Gussie introduced to my father her half-sister Carrie, her father's daughter by his second wife, whom he married twenty years earlier. My parents-to-be visited in my grandfather's hotel in Atlantic City, which Gussie helped manage. The hotel was on the site where the Convention Hall now stands. Jack and Carrie decided to marry as soon as Jack returned from the war. My father's family was not pleased—they berated Gussie for bringing their Jack together with a daughter of that questionable Sam Marks who had treated his first daughter so miserably.

Gussie and my parents lived together as long as they survived. They shared living expenses and the cost of a house in the country, and Gussie helped sustain my father late in life when he was ill and had extraordinary expenses. Until she died, my maternal grandmother lived with us and was cared for by her step-daughter, Gussie. I was about five at the time she died and remember only that this frail, smiling woman spoke only German and patted me on the head. One day, the house darkened; I discovered that she was carried out and did not reap-pear. Death was never discussed. A few years later my paternal grandmother, sixty, died. She had always said she never fully recovered from giving birth to my father, who was enormous at birth. He, too, was an "only child." And her death, for me, was another disappearance and little more.

All of this took place in our Third Avenue apartment. About that time, other great changes were occurring. I had been sent to a small, red-brick public school just two blocks away on twentieth street, east of Third Avenue. The school had been built when Abe Lincoln was a youth. Teachers were patient, classes were small, and even the principal, Miss Foley, knew many of the students. In the classic mode, she was the sister of an Irish politician. Mother would chat with her before the three o'clock bell released me. Public School 50 seemed like a second home with a caring relative, Miss Foley, in charge.

The other children came from Second and First Avenues and the streets in-between. They were mainly first-generation kids of Polish, Italian, German, and other recent European extraction. No blacks and no Hispanics; there simply were none living in the neighborhood. My self-image was shaped rather deeply at P. S. 50 and probably is still influenced by that time.

I was always dressed in clean clothes and was delivered and picked up by mother. Most other kids made their own way to and from school and were not as neatly dressed. Their conversations often included words and ideas that were for-eign to me. I sensed some gaps and felt the need to explain or even apologize. That need surfaced clearly one day when a little girl asked me, "What does your middle initial stand for?" My mother had insisted that I use the "R" when writing my name. I told the girl, "The 'R' stands for Richard."

"Oh," she said, "you must be rich."

I felt that was a damning thing, and I denied it. But I was hurt. Why should I be considered *that* different? I had no idea what being rich meant. But I knew that in this setting it was not good. I would try *not* to act rich, whatever that meant and whatever it would take.

At the same time, Miss Foley told my mother that I would skip one grade. Mother was delighted. I felt strange in a new class, just as I was coming to terms with being "rich" and the only Jewish boy in class. At the end of that term, Miss Foley made a similar announcement, and I was placed another grade ahead. Mother was joyous. I felt still more out of place. This happened a third time, and then I was graduated a year and a half ahead of my peers and sent to P. S. 40, a junior high—where I was placed in a rapid advancement class and skipped another year. That left me two and a half years ahead of kids with normal social develop-ment (let along skipping grammar and some math instruction). But P. S. 40 did introduce me to "elder" student Henry Blum and his colorful sex instruction.

At eight, my parents enrolled me in the Sunday School of Congregation Emanu-El, the world's leading Reform congregation. Suddenly, I was catapulted uptown into a class with private-school kids from Park and Fifth avenues. I had to make weekend adjustments no less daunting, it seemed, than my weekday accommodations as the "rich" boy. I was well aware of the challenges to play widely different roles, dictated by religious and economic differences. I seemed to live in several worlds.

There were other big changes at this time. Father moved his dental office to Irving Place and Seventeenth Street, across from the brownstone still standing where O. Henry wrote important stories. Across the avenue was Pete's, the famous saloon where O. Henry also wrote. Pete was a patient of my father's. Then, too, we left the Third Avenue apartment and moved into a duplex on Seventeenth Street, two doors east of Tammany Hall. I had my own room for the first time, as well as two gray cats who ran madly up and down our carpeted stair that separated the bedrooms on the top floor from the dining and living rooms on the floor below. I had a window in the penthouse, set back from the main structure, that led onto the roof of the downstairs area. I could climb onto that roof and feel absolutely alone—and free. I would read for hours or just contemplate. Or pet my favorite cat, a wiry, sometimes ill animal I had named Tiny Maimonides Acidophilus Oscar Sussman. I even created a birth certificate with Tiny's full name on it.

These moves of the office and the living quarters were regarded as steps up the social ladder. We were almost in the Gramercy Park set. Was that approaching "rich"? The thought crossed my mind. I would have to watch myself. It wasn't fitting, I thought, for a teenager living so well to be espousing "socialist" views. Little did I know that Norman Thomas, the perennial leader of the Socialist Party and one of the world's foremost Socialists, lived just a few blocks away in his personal brownstone on Nineteenth Street, east of Irving Place. His street was indeed called, "The Street Beautiful." His son Evan Thomas, the publisher, inherited the building. I came to know Norman Thomas years later and arranged for him to speak on Mideast issues. On his eightieth birthday in 1964 I recalled to Norman that "forty years earlier my father interrupted my play at Gramercy Park to say, 'There goes Norman Thomas.' At ten, I knew someone important, walking alone, had just passed by." I acknowledged "the great stature [he] gave to individuality in an age of impersonality."

In my early teens, I was impressed by Father's dental practice and the acceptance our family merited because of his role in the neighborhood. He was known as a conversationalist and a friendly adviser on many subjects, personal, political, and especially naval. His friend and our neighbor, Hezekiah Carroll, was a graduate of the Naval Academy at Annapolis. He was younger than Dad and had been a middle-ranking officer in the navy. But my father never forgot his wartime experience. He enlisted as a lieutenant in the dental corps and served on the battleship USS *Virginia*. He was the only Jewish naval officer aboard. The *Virginia* carried more than a thousand men and made numerous crossings of the

Atlantic supporting convoys during the worst years of submarine warfare. Dad would land at Brest, France, spend a few days ashore, and then return to sea. But those short visits provided Father with years of conversation about France, the French, and the navy. Hezekiah would encourage such conversation. I remember Dad stepping off the sidewalk while a stream of cars passed in front of him. Hezekiah asked, "Would you venture so close if a torpedo was streaming just three feet in front of you?"

One of my clearest recollections of Dad was his ability to win the friendship and confidence of men and women in many occupations, of different classes, and national and religious backgrounds. To all, he was a "regular guy," his favorite test of simple humanity. He was proud of his American Legion membership and, in uniform, carried the American flag in a small-town Fourth of July parade near our country house. But he never went drinking with "the boys." He was unbigoted long before it became a national objective, generally observed in the breach.

I discovered this most dramatically when I was about thirteen. I walked into Dad's office and was suddenly surprised by a sea of black capes spread throughout the waiting room. I could hear chatter and laughter coming from the operating room. The capes were worn by seven nuns, all patients of my father. They were nurses at Columbus Hospital, some five blocks east. Nuns of Columbus had been patients of my father for many years; he was in fact their house dentist. They knew he was Jewish and often joked about it. In quiet ways, I think, they tried to convert him. But it never went beyond banter.

That day, not only these nuns were present, but their mother superior as well. I had met her once before. She was soft-spoken with an infectious smile, immediately likeable. Sometimes she would personally bring a young nun to my father because the new patient would be fearful of the dental drill. Dad and the mother superior would calm her. At Christmas and sometimes in between, the nuns would send my father small gifts they made.

As years passed, I would come to hear more about that mother superior. She had been a young nun when Frances Xavier Cabrini came to New York in 1899 at the request of Pope Leo XIII. Mother Cabrini founded sixty-seven hospitals, orphanages, and charitable institutions in New York. She died in 1917. One day in 1938, when the nuns visited my father, they announced that Mother Cabrini—their spiritual mentor—had just been beatified by Pope Pius XI. One of "ours" would become the first American saint. She was canonized by Pope Pius XII in 1946. The nuns of Columbus Hospital paid a special visit to my father to present him with a small piece of Saint Cabrini's cloak. Dad was deeply moved. The sanctity that Mother Cabrini had conveyed to the successor mother superior was recognized by my father. When he died in 1970 at sixty-six, my mother found the saintly relic still in his wallet.

NOTES

1. Elizabeth Hawes, *New York, New York: How the Apartment House Transformed the Life of the City, 1869–1930* (New York: Knopf, 1993), p. 27.

2. Hawes, *New York, New York*, p. 217.

3. Leonard R. Sussman, letter to the editor, *New York Times*, July 17, 1995.

2

AL SALT
Growing Up on the Seventh Floor

S econd only to my parents, Al Salt most helped shape my life at an early age. Together, we roamed New York, savored its offbeat neighborhoods, and tested our lifelong interests.

We lived in a sparsely populated neighborhood of Manhattan. That is, there were few children our age in the Union Square-Gramercy Park area. The few school-age kids who did live there were shipped off to private schools and seldom ventured on the streets where Al and I played. We skated with hockey sticks and puck, or we would bat stickballs on largely untraveled, two-block-long Rutherford Place alongside Stuyvesant Park (on Second Avenue between Sixteenth and Seventeenth streets). The street was paved with smooth macadam, great for skating—until young gangs from across Second Avenue came to attack us. We moved away fast.

Al was shorter than I, and wiry. We were both good runners. But roller skating was our prime outdoor sport. We would meet early Saturday mornings and skate wherever in New York the luck of the draw would take us. Our trip was directed by the fall of a coin every half-hour. That would determine our course of discovery for the next period. We would search new avenues, new neighborhoods each Saturday. Either by design or sheer luck, we would often skate to the tip of Manhattan, at Battery Park. There we would deposit five cents in the ferry turnstile and ride across the harbor, past the Statue of Liberty, to Staten Island. Al's uncle was a captain on one of the ferries. We felt special at each sailing, but we paid our way. That same nickel would provide a return sail, but not before we walked through part of Staten Island—a vast new country to us.

Al and I did far more than travel the city together. At eight, we also explored our separate interests and how they might be tested together. It was clear that we came from quite different family backgrounds. We both found that appealing, not at all threatening. Perhaps so because our families encouraged our friendship and even came together once or twice a year to put their imprimatur on our friendship. My parents were intrigued by the Salt family's origins. They were first-generation Scots, avid members of historic St. George's Episcopal Church on Stuyvesant Square. They sang Scottish songs, told Scottish tales, and displayed a warm humor that bonded us.

The families would meet at the Salts' unique homestead. Al's father was the superintendent-engineer of a nineteenth-century, seven-story office building at Broadway and Thirteenth Street. The Salts lived in a detached, freestanding house set on the roof of the office structure. Their porch looked out on the broad, block-long graveled roof and, in the distance, the towers of other downtown structures. On an opposite corner of their roof was a metal shed that served Al and me as a hideaway on rainy days. That very shed, unchanged through the years, had been used by Thomas Alva Edison for his experiments with the "peep-show" machine, the forerunner of motion pictures. That shed was part of Edison's Biograph Studio. It did not occur to us that Edison at eighty-one was still alive as we did our own experiments in 1928.

The spirit of Edison may well have inspired Al and me. He had created an experimental electric railroad in 1880. We had our own rail line, among other explorations. This was the Great Depression, and the seventh floor of the building was not rented. That became for Al and me *our* seventh floor. Wondrous things went on there: with Al's father's help we built tracks mounted on boards that ran the whole length of that half-block-long floor with no dividing walls or doors. Our electric train shining a tiny headlight would travel the entire distance and return, covering the unlighted space at night. Not even Lionel, maker of model trains, or any department store selling them had such an extensive track bed. The space was so expansive we could ride bicycles and roller skate beside the train as it made its way around our seventh floor.

That was not all. Edison diversified—not just electric power, but phonographs, movies, and thirteen hundred other patents.

We would try photography. We thought we understood the processing of pictures. We took my Brownie box camera to the high roof of the adjoining building. For two children standing in the heavy wind of a fall day, an amazing vista suddenly appeared below: the grand design of Union Square park. This first "aerial" view probably stirred me always thereafter to climb the next Rocky Mountain peak, ride the highest Alpine cablecar, drive the curviest Corniche to shoot that all-embracing photograph of tiny figures and crowded landmarks below.

We shot the roll and returned expectantly to the seventh floor. We had converted a toilet into a photographic darkroom. With our skimpy weekly allowances we purchased two professional-looking trays for water and fixer. And we had an envelope of photographic paper. Al's father had provided a red light, and his mother lent us her kitchen timer. We managed to produce negatives. We placed one atop the printing paper, covered with glass; turned on the light for two minutes; and waited for a picture. Nothing came. We were frustrated. We tried a five-minute exposure. Nothing. Ten minutes. Nothing. We went back to the camera store and then learned the trick Edison had discovered long ago: you need developing fluid as well as fixer to produce an image on photographic paper! Light alone will not do it.

After that, we had the audacity to persuade one of Dad's patients to allow us to develop his film. We managed somehow and charged less than the going rate. Those first pictures were of two beautiful young women hugging a man on a beach, probably my father's patient. We were in business, sort of.

That was not all we did on the seventh floor. As with Edison, the phonograph and radio interested us; each of us for quite different reasons. Al, even then, was an aspiring technologist. I liked to describe new sights. We combined to create a "broadcast" system. It was hardly more than a primitive PA setup, but we called it "radio." On the seventh floor, we took apart a telephone, rewired the mouthpiece, and ran some wire up a shaft to the Salts' rooftop living room. There we connected it to their radio's speaker. To provide programming, we fed an old phonograph onto the "broadcast" line. Edison would have been proud. We had exactly one recording. Neither the Salts nor the Sussmans would trust us with their best records. The only song we had was "When You Come to the End of a Perfect Day."

That tune suited our need perfectly. We would put on our show only after both families had finished dinner, and the day was ending. We would insist that they gather around the radio upstairs while we put on our program. It would begin with the music, and then my sober announcement: "This is the Trebla and Dranoel broadcasting station." What followed was of small moment. Al had succeeded in making the technical connections. I had done my brief intros and "news." Al and I both gratified early instincts for paths we would later pursue.

That memory came to me fleetingly, years later, in a darkened ABC studio as I awaited a cue for an interview on *Nightline*.

In the intervening years, except for a meeting of families twenty years before that interview, we had barely exchanged annual greetings. Al, his wife, and two sons lived in a small town in North Carolina, where he built a plant to process lumber for utility companies. Al acquired those skills at a technical college after returning from the army. Clearly, our paths had diverged since we were best friends from eight to twelve.

Al returned from World War II with gory memories. He had rumbled across Europe as a tank lieutenant with Gen. George Patton. Al's unit had suffered heavy casualties; some of Al's buddies died beside him, but he escaped physically unharmed, though psychologically shaken for the rest of his life. He died of natural causes at the age of sixty.

3

MURIEL RUKEYSER
Poet in the Family

B efore my morning walk, breakfast includes orange juice from a container whose machine-applied spout defies fingernails. I keep handy a five-inch-long, black-and-white metal bottle opener in the shape of a stylized feline of indeterminate species. The cat was the gift years earlier of Muriel Rukeyser. This tool is my only physical reminder of a talented, sometimes wondrous woman— my late sister-in-law.

That is not quite accurate. There are Muriel's books on our shelves. She began publishing poetry at twenty-one, just out of Vassar. By the time I took college literature courses, Muriel's poetry was in the anthologies. She had been instantly acknowledged by critics. The *London Times Literary Supplement* called Muriel Rukeyser "one of America's greatest living poets." She would later write prose biographies of physicist Willard Gibbs and political leader Wendell L. Willkie (see chap. 15). She also wrote the extraordinary *Life of Poetry*, translations of Octavio Paz and Gunnar Ekelof, four children's books, a documentary screenplay, three plays for the stage, and seventeen books of poetry.

Of Muriel, Louise Kertesz wrote, "No woman poet makes the successful fusion of personal and social themes in a modern prosody before Rukeyser."[1] In her earliest poetry, Muriel wrote of her family and its high position in the socioeconomic structure of the 1920s. She had all the advantages my father-in-law, Lawrence, could provide. He had created and was head of the city's most prominent sand and gravel company, which helped build the city's subways. Laurie started as a young salesman who met an Italian immigrant with a horse and wagon; from a sand quarry on Long Island they quickly developed a trucking fleet that delivered concrete to the city's subways under construction. The immigrant was Generoso Pope.

Pope became a multimillionaire who owned newspapers as well as cement and other companies. He was the most powerful political figure among New York's Italian population and thus played a major role in the city's turbulent political scene. Laurie sold his interest in Colonial Sand and Stone for many millions of dollars while still in his thirties. He sold out, he told me, because the mafia had become thoroughly involved, and Laurie did not want to end at the bottom of the East River in a slab of his own cement. Among his purchasers was sitting mayor James J. Walker, apparently little disturbed by the obvious conflict of interest. Later, Jimmy Walker was forced out of office and fled to France.

While the millions were there, Muriel rode in chauffeured limousines to the family's large apartment on Riverside Drive. On a visit to the sand quarry, her father said, "We'll own the countryside, you'll see how soon I will, you'll have acres to play in." Muriel records that conversation in an early poem, "Sand-Quarry with Moving Figures." Her father expected her to join him in golf at the Long Island club, and in due time she become a socially acknowledged matron.

Much later, Muriel wrote, "To a child . . . whose family was coming up with the building of New York and who felt the astonishing ambition and pride that went with the building, to that child the [concrete] pouring and its terms became a part of life. . . . I remember [at school] being asked what grit was, and I said 'Number 4 Gravel' when I was supposed to say 'courage.'"

Muriel as a child "fused personal and social themes." She would leave behind her exalted living style and secretly play with poor children in the basements and tunnels beneath the apartment buildings. She began writing poetry in high school and noted "the terrible, murderous differences between the ways people lived." Across the street from her house, along the Hudson River, ran the cattle cars that carried live animals to slaughter on lower Manhattan. Another reality for a sensitive girl.

Fran, Muriel's sister, and I—both fourteen when Muriel's first book was published—had attended religious school together since we were eight. At twenty-one we married. Fran's admiration for Muriel was tinged with some hesitancy: Muriel was following a "radical" lifestyle, which her father despised. Yet Muriel had enviable literary success, which Fran's young friends admired.

The family fortune evaporated when Fran was nine years old. For her, the loss was only a might-have-been. Her father had taken the millions of dollars from the sale of Colonial Sand and Stone and purchased many buildings throughout New York. But each one was thinly capitalized, each building supplying another with collateral. Following the 1929 stock market crash, Laurie Rukeyser's debts were called, and he lost all but two small buildings. One was a five-story apartment house on Tremont Avenue in the Bronx; ironically, he had placed that building in his wife's name, a wife he thoroughly belittled at every opportunity.

When she died many years later, she willed the building to her daughters. They asked me to manage it in my spare time. I did for about two years with great irritation: tenants complained of water, power, roofing, and other problems. I would speed repairs. The building, if properly maintained, was clearly not profitable. It had provided my late mother-in-law with reasons for day-long chats over coffee with her superintendent, mainly to devise ways to avoid or minimize repairs. I sold the building, and Muriel and Fran that year took a small tax loss. That ended the multimillion-dollar run of Laurie Rukeyser.

As a result of the sudden change in the Rukeyser family fortune, Muriel was unable to complete her studies at Vassar. Nevertheless, she later taught at Vassar, Sarah Lawrence, and the California Labor School. Fran went to public schools. She had never known luxury, but had been told of it glowingly by her parents. Perhaps it would have been unnatural for Fran to avoid resentment. Yet in her teens and beyond, Fran served as an intermediary between her parents and Muriel. Increasingly in her writing and her lifestyle, Muriel thoroughly rejected the materialistic and political convictions of her father; indeed, she evoked her childhood and young womanhood, including the family, to criticize the larger social and cultural setting in America.

As time passed, Muriel used prose and poetry to write of the anarchists Sacco and Vanzetti, the Depression, the Roosevelt social reforms, the Spanish Civil War, the Holocaust, the Vietnam War, the Cold War, and the women's liberation movement. This was the "successful fusion of personal and social themes" she had been praised for.

But Laurie Rukeyser never understood. He was thoroughly embarrassed by Muriel's subjectivity—almost as much as by her lifestyle in Greenwich Village and her reputation as a Communist. I doubt Muriel was a card-carrying party member, but she appeared often enough on lists of "fellow-travelers" to arouse the enmity of Communist-hunters. In leftist circles she was also, on occasion, a distressing dissident from their causes.

Fran tried to explain Muriel to her father, but Laurie did little more than pat Fran on the head and continue sneering at his older daughter. He would tell me he thought her "crazy." A different reaction came from cousin Merryle Stanley Rukeyser, father of TV star Louis Rukeyser and other sons prominent today in dispensing information. Merryle was a widely syndicated financial columnist for the politically conservative Hearst newspapers and personal adviser to William Randolph Hearst. Merryle also had access to the Roosevelt White House, where he sometimes showed up in the pantry for sandwiches with the president. Muriel said Merryle came to her one day and asked her to change her name because it might lead to confusion with his widely publicized conservative image. Angered, she refused.

But Myra, the sisters' mother, was different. She had little formal education and had been a bookkeeper in Yonkers before her marriage. She was shattered by the family's financial loss and for long periods took to her bed—and to religion. Most of her friends disappeared when the Rukeysers could no longer afford the country and city clubs. Myra met frequently with the rabbis at Congregation

Emanu-El. The temple organizations provided social intercourse, a sense of retribution for past sins, and some religious experience. Myra had long believed that she was a direct descendent of Rabbi Joseph ben Akiba, who lived in Palestine around the year 100 C.E. Akiba was one of the first Jewish scholars to compile the oral laws into the *Mishna* of the Talmud. Akiba resisted the Romans and was tortured to death. Myra found considerable solace in this belief of her tie to Akiba. Her husband scoffed; Fran gave it little thought. Said Muriel, "This is an extraordinary gift to give a child."

There were great differences between Muriel and Fran. Muriel had long broken away from her parents. Fran could never bring herself to do so, yet she clearly wanted the freedom Muriel had found. The distance between the sisters, as well as the gap setting off Muriel from the parents, is described in Muriel's early poem "Four in a Family":*

The father and mother sat, and the sister beside her.
I faced the two women across the table's width,
speaking, and all the time he looked at me.
sorrowing, saying nothing, with his hard, tired breath.

Their faces said : This is your home, and I :
I never come home, I never go away.
And they all answered : Stay.

*   *   *

My sister, I wished upon you those delights
time never buries.
more precious than heroes.

Strange father, strange mother, who are you, who are you?
Where have I come?
how shall I prosper home?

In midlife, there was little contact between the sisters. Sometimes there would be brief, bitter disputes and, much later, embarrassed reconciliation. After a tiff, Muriel would phone Fran at four o'clock in the morning and then hang up without speaking. I angered Muriel when I sent to Monica McCall the manuscript of a children's book I had written. Monica was not only Muriel's agent but a close friend and apartmentmate. Muriel was furious because I hadn't cleared with her first. Perhaps she was right, though I had reasoned that this was a professional matter, not a family affair. Yet when Muriel was about to undergo

*"Four in a Family" by and © Muriel Rukeyser from *The Collected Poems of Muriel Rukeyser*, 1979, McGraw Hill, New York, by permission of William L. Rukeyser.

serious surgery she asked Fran and me, if she died, to adopt her young son Bill. Muriel lived another forty years, though, and Bill, a worthy heir in every respect, provided her with four grandchildren.

If Muriel hadn't been a great poet she might have been a great journalist. Perhaps she was both. She believed there are two kinds of poems. One of "unverifiable facts, based in dreams, in sex, in everything that can be given to other people only through the skill and strength by which it was given; the other kind being the document, the poem that rests on material evidence."[2] Muriel went to extraordinary lengths to provide "material evidence" for poems. She traveled to the Scottsboro and Sacco-Vanzetti trials as well as to the Spanish Civil War, and she learned to fly an airplane before writing her first book, *Theory of Flight*, which won the Yale Younger Poets Prize. This volume revealed Muriel's fusion of scientific theory with social and political interaction—themes that would consistently reappear in her prose as well as poetry.

Toward the end of her life, Muriel said, "I used to talk a great deal about communication. I don't anymore. I communicated badly with the people I was closest to, so I won't talk about it any longer." Muriel communicated orally by measuring words carefully, as if for a poem. One word might stand for a large idea; one pause might signal a great unspoken thought; one bold uplifted eyebrow, a challenge or harsh criticism. One had to watch and listen very carefully; it could be intimidating. One might come away from a talk with Muriel wondering, "What did she mean?" And the answer could be several quite disparate ideas. They might require the careful exegesis of Scripture—or of her poetry.

I often see Muriel these days in the telecasts of Louis Rukeyser on *Wall Street Week*. He has that great Rukeyser hair that Muriel had all her life—and that large, almost oval head. Muriel, too, was a large person, though set on rather spindly legs. Her body alone could seem overpowering; her words, more so. That may have led to faulty communication, as well as her impatience with those who were not already on her ideological or linguistic wavelength. To be so, you had to have merited prior approval for your social, political, or humanistic outlook. That provided a common vocabulary and commitment that allowed for shortcut language, yet rich symbolism.

As Walt Whitman did before her, Muriel composed the "poems of democracy." Her subjects were highly visible. Her images, blurred at first, came clear when focused by one's own perception or experience. Muriel was the epitome of Alexis de Tocqueville's role of the poet of a democratic people. Such a poet, he wrote, would not feed "the legends or the memorials of old traditions" or deploy images "in whom his readers and his own fancy have ceased to believe; nor [would] he coldly personify virtues and vices which are better received under their own features." Rather, says the nineteenth-century French philosopher, the chief theme of poet for a democracy will be the "destinies of mankind, man himself taken aloof from his country and his age, standing in the presence of nature and God, with his passions, his doubts, his rare propensities, and inconceivable wretchedness."

I did not see Muriel after Fran and I were divorced in 1958, though I would hear occasionally about her from Lynne. Muriel died in 1979 after suffering a stroke. These days, her writing is published in new editions. An attractive excerpt of one of her poems appeared on posters in the New York subways and buses. This exposure to a broad public, I believe, would have pleased Muriel. A two-volume anthology of twentieth-century poetry, published in 2000, carried twenty pages of Muriel's poetry. An extensive biography of Muriel, a doctoral thesis, has been under way for many years. Her collected poems published in 1979 drew this comment from Thomas Lask in the *Times*: "We have taken her a little too much for granted, perhaps because she has appeared in so many public forums in other guises: on the side of the underdog, the unjustly condemned, the defenseless, those whom life outmaneuvered. We have forgotten that we have in our midst a considerable poet, one who has remained as loyal to her craft as to her social vision, a woman for whom the writing of the poem is the verbal equivalent of the political gesture."[3]

Over fifty years ago, in 1949, Muriel wrote in *The Life of Poetry* her testament to that art form, a projection for the future: "Our age is opening now.... [F]or the first time in history, among all the longings for communication which we can see everywhere: communication with the secret life of the individual, communication through machines, communication between peoples—we have the sense of the world . . . a sense of an age disclosing, undefined possibilities, new meanings for multiplicity, and new meanings for unity."[4]

Strangely, I treasure that nondescript metallic feline above our kitchen sink.

NOTES

1. Louise Kertesz, introduction to *A Muriel Rukeyser Reader*, ed. Jan Heller Levi (New York: W. W. Norton, 1994), p. xi.

2. Muriel Rukeyser, preface to *The Collected Poems* (New York: McGraw-Hill, 1978), p. v.

3. Thomas Lask, "Books: Muriel Rukeyser Revealed as Total Poet," *New York Times*, August 22, 1979.

4. Muriel Rukeyser, *The Life of Poetry* (New York: Current Books, 1949), p. 23.

4

"DR. BILL"
Restorer of Hands and Faith

B efore malpractice suits drove up the cost of medical insurance, my daughter Lynne was born.

The nature of her birth was traumatic for her mother and me, and it was a defining lifetime factor for Lynne. The nine-month preparation seemed normal, broken only by extended flights in a small airplane from New York to Puerto Rico for the governor's inauguration. We wondered whether those flights caused Lynne's abnormality, but we never discovered the reason for it.

Addressing Lynne's problem required thirteen years of heart-rending concern. Moments after her birth, one of Mt. Sinai Hospital's leading obstetricians called me aside and said, "Mr. Sussman, your daughter is not normal."

I shuddered. All manner of tragic possibilities rushed to mind.

"It's her hands," he said. "She has no fingers."

I asked, "What can be done about that?"

"I don't know. I've never seen anything like this," he replied.

"Do you want to see your wife?" he asked, adding, "You had better take this towel with you." Obviously, he expected her to burst into tears.

Together, we entered Fran's room; she was still recovering from the delivery. The doctor repeated the same harsh, cruel report. Lynne was "not normal," and he didn't know whether anything could be done about it. We asked to see Lynne. She looked normal in every way except for the long shirt that covered what should have been fingers. Each hand ended with rounded flesh surrounding the bones and musculature of what should have been her fingers, as though a closed fist marked the end of the forearm.

At this delicate moment, in the presence of this indelicate doctor, we vowed to search for a better answer. Our respective parents were appalled and did not hide their reactions. There had never been such a problem in either family; to this day, there is no adequate explanation. Digital deformities, we later found, are rare but not unknown. Rarer still was the complete nature of this case: both hands and all fingers were involved. Fran and I never discussed the special problems Lynne would have without fingers; we talked instead about how to fix the situation.

The calmest in our families was Aunt Gussie, perhaps because she worked in the administration at Mt. Sinai Hospital and knew most of the surgeons there. The next day, she told us that Dr. John Garlock, chief of surgeons, agreed to see Lynne. We were delighted that he would even greet us—he was the big man on staff. Several months later, we visited his office with Lynne. Garlock specialized in gall bladder removal and the like. He looked at Lynne very briefly, said he would separate the digits starting in her eleventh month, and told us curtly, "Bring her in then." Just as impersonally, he added, "You know, I was a plastic surgeon for many years." That should have been a warning signal, but we did not recognize it. The fact was, Garlock had never done hand surgery; not plastic surgery for many years. And the field had advanced dramatically, especially during World War II. We were grateful, however, for the great man's willingness to take his chances—Lynne's chances, as it turned out—some months hence.

While we waited, Fran and I nurtured Lynne and acted as though the hand problem did not exist; we considered it merely waiting time before corrections would be made. But the first operation, at eleven months, was deeply disturbing for us. Garlock operated under general anesthesia. Without alerting us in advance, he took a large skin graft from Lynne's small stomach, placing it around the exposed portion of the digit that should have been the right thumb. It was not a thumb, however, but a three-jointed digit that was not opposable to the rest of the mass, but was beside it, as fingers are positioned, side by side. Most startling to us, Lynne was bandaged on most of her body, covering the graft. Her entire right arm was in a large cast.

We were shocked by this first sight, even more so by Garlock's abrupt order to us: "Take her home tomorrow, change her dressings every day. Bring her back in six months and we'll do the other hand." At this rate it would be many years before Lynne would have ten fingers. Garlock would not even discuss the future with us. He disappeared, saying no more.

His order to change the bandages left us with searing experiences each day. The stomach scar simply did not heal well. Removing the gauze was a bloody and painful experience, for all three. This went on, night after night. We later discovered that the scar had developed uneven keloid tissue that would never heal properly.

But we also discovered amazing resilience in Lynne. From the day she came home after the first operation, she crawled around her playroom ignoring the fact that her entire right arm was laden with a huge dressing that prevented her from using it at all except as a rigid pole. With that, she could bat balls as other children could not. With the recently released finger (in place of a thumb) she could press a spoon against the bandaged "fist"—and feed herself—long before most other kids were taking any food by themselves. She could bang on a small piano with that single digit, and make noise. This was somehow satisfying to her and, strangely, to us.

Just when all this became routine it was time to return to Garlock for a second operation. The bandages were removed from her right arm and hand. But when she came out of the operating room, her stomach was once again entombed in a large, bloody bandage, and her left arm was fully mummified as her right had been before. And again, we went through the terrible process of changing the stomach bandages each night. Now, however, Lynne could become ambidextrous—kind of. Now she would use her new left digit, still mainly bandaged, as a second thrust to her unbandaged right digit. She not only managed but made an advantage of the newly encased arm as she played in the park with children who would marvel at her "advantage." Their parents, often, would stand back aghast. Sometimes they would ask gingerly what kind of accident had produced this problem.

Over the next eighteen months, Garlock would put Lynne through three more general-anesthesia operations and subsequent five-day hospital stays. He released five digits on each hand through the same process as the first year. By then, Lynne was doing all the normal little-girl things—only more so. She had made other advantages of adversity. The ten digits, however, were all three-jointed "fingers"—there were no thumbs. Furthermore, the digits were unbending, with the nail joint frozen down at a forty-five-degree angle.

After the fifth operation, I asked Garlock when we should return for further work. He looked at me sternly and said, "That's it. No more. I'm not God." Then in utter defiance he added, "You came to me for ten fingers, and I gave you ten fingers."

When I protested that the fingers could not bend, he said that was because there were no joints. Lynne, then, would never have more than 10 percent use of her hands—and always in awkward ways. We were crushed, but we could not take this for a final answer.

The next day, I took Lynne to Gunther Lomnitz, my family internist. Gunther had been a friend since he escaped from Nazi Germany just after his internship in Berlin, and he was also a patient and friend of my father. I asked Gunther to X-ray Lynne's hands and see what might still be done. The X rays, still before me as I write, are revealing: they show not only joints in every finger but *six* fingers on each hand, including a tiny second "small" finger at the end. Clearly, Garlock had never taken X rays before operating five times!

I asked Gunther for the name of the best hand surgeon. He sent us to the head of hand surgery at Columbia-Presbyterian Hospital, who in turn gave us the names of three hand surgeons and discussed each with us. Two were fully established, middle-aged specialists; the third, J. William Littler, was a young man just back from the war in the Pacific, where he had performed hundreds of hand restorations and created new procedures in the process. The negative aspect: Littler was still a resident in surgery, not yet formally approved for hand-surgery specialization in a civilian setting.

We chose Dr. Littler without hesitation.

Bill was to become Lynne's teenage "crush"—and our hero forevermore. He began a series of twenty-one operations, from Lynne's third year to her thirteenth; with each procedure a new world opened for Lynne. Remarkably, Bill never grafted skin, never required more than an overnight stay in the hospital, never made a bandage larger than her hand, and never asked us to remove a bandage. On the contrary, he treated Lynne as his little girl and didn't flinch when she ran her new fingers through his bushy eyebrows. He was never too busy to answer our questions or to describe precisely what he planned for each operation and for those to follow.

An unusual bond developed among the four of us. Bill, we learned, had not begun life as a doctor; he was a sculptor. That probably accounted for his special talent for fashioning hands. He switched to medical school just in time for war service and the challenges wrought by severe wounds to young air force personnel. Littler's civilian talents enabled him to improvise new procedures for operations that the military service had not yet discovered. Indeed, when he returned to New York it was clear that he was far ahead of the profession. He was reluctant to press his innovative work, lest he anger the medical "powers."

We discovered this reluctance after Bill had performed remarkably on Lynne's hands. He had quickly removed the sixth digits and separated fingers, two at a time, releasing the joints so that she could bend fingers for the first time. But his pièce de résistance was the creation of two thumbs. For everyone, thumbs are essential for most uses of the hands. The key function is opposition; it enables hands to perform many acts of strength and control otherwise impossible. For Lynne, Bill had created a procedure that he later described in the *Journal of Plastic and Reconstruction Surgery* and for which he won a certificate at the 1952 annual meeting of the American Society of Plastic and Reconstruction Surgery. Bill's reticence came to light when the *Saturday Evening Post*, then the foremost weekly magazine, assigned a feature writer to prepare a major article, with photographs, of Bill Littler's history and achievements.

The writer interviewed Lynne, Fran, and me. She had heard of Bill's remarkable reconstruction of Lynne's hands, not to mention his amputation of the finger that was to become the thumb. The digit was reduced by one joint and rotated to provide opposition, and the appropriate tendons were shortened and reassembled to enable thumb motion. In his journal paper, Bill describes this with great restraint for other surgeons to repeat. He concludes, "Having provided the necessary length to a thumb amputated through the metacarpal . . . the three elements achieved pertinent to useful function are *sensation, stability, and independence of movement*" (emphasis added). Bill gave Lynne all three, twice over.

When Bill was interviewed, he insisted that this lengthy article should not feature him but describe the field of hand surgery. He clearly did not want to irritate his elders by starring in a national magazine article. This was still the time when ethical doctors did not seek personal publicity. The published article carried photographs of Bill, Fran, and Lynne but spoke, too, about advances by other men in the field. Lynne's case, however, was described at length.

When the article appeared in 1955, I wrote to John Garlock. I said he may have seen the *Post*'s piece on hand surgery and its mention of Lynne, his former patient. I continued,

We were . . . pleased to have one of your stature agree to operate on Lynne for what, to us, as completely shocked and unknowledgeable laymen, was a unique and mystifying abnormality. . . . This feeling of gratitude persisted up to the moment of our final meeting with you. . . .

You had called us to your anteroom to view the single X-ray print of Lynne's two hands. The exposure had been made in the presence of my wife and me several days earlier [*after* the fifth operation]. . . . You examined the X ray and said that you had done all that could be done for Lynne. I asked whether you thought there was any possibility of further work. You said no, because she did not have working joints in any of the fingers. I asked how you could tell from that angle, since her *bent* fingers had been shot from the top, and the joints thereby telescoped. I had been a picture editor and knew that at that angle, with the fingers so bent, you had to face the telescoping of bones. That apparently made it appear that no joints were present. I asked a third time whether this could have happened.

You put your hand on my shoulder and said flatly, "No!"—that there was just so much that science could accomplish. "You came to me for ten fingers," you said, "and I've given you ten fingers." . . . It was quite providential that our intuition led us to ignore immediately your warning that day to "stay away from plastic surgeons." . . .

Then we discovered William Littler. . . . He seemed to have the human quality which we had found to be increasingly important in providing for the emotional adjustment of Lynne.

We soon also discovered that . . . creative surgery means not only the making of new anatomical parts, but the imaginative creativity of the surgeon who frets and ponders and discusses—because he's as human as the layman who bears the problem—and comes up with a *new* technique for that old problem.

For example, a technique to build a new thumb without using even a millimeter of body skin graft. Our great realization was that this man did it almost as much *because* of the emotional problems involved for Lynne as he did because of the physiological possibilities. I'm sure, Dr. Garlock, that in your most inspired moments in the field of abdominal surgery you accomplish just that kind of innovation to meet perplexing problems. You will understand, therefore, why we have deemed ourselves so very, very fortunate to have allowed no time to pass after our final meeting with you. For we have often felt that you spoke in utter frankness when you said at the end, "I can do no more."

Within two days I received this note from Dr. Garlock's secretary: "Dr. Garlock instructs me that he would like to see the condition of Lynne's hand [*sic*]. Please call this office for an appointment." I responded by acknowledging Dr. Garlock's "present interest in Lynne's development" but did not make an appointment. "As you can well understand," I said, "we have always tried to limit [Lynne's] medical and surgical visits to those absolutely essential for future work. It is this careful handling of such matters that has resulted in her fine attitude and outlook. Perhaps, later on, at a far less impressionable age, we can arrange a meeting." He died before a meeting with Lynne was even considered.

Bill Littler's work on Lynne's hands ended in 1959 when she was thirteen. They met several times thereafter for purely friendly reminiscence when Lynne returned to New York from college. She had played the piano and French horn at the High School of Music and Art, earned a doctorate from Harvard, and taught teachers there and at Cambridge College. She featured science in her early-education curricula designed for other teachers.

When he retired, Bill Littler was regarded as one of the nation's leading hand surgeons. The *W* in my son David's second name recalls the family's debt to those bushy eyebrows.

In 1999, I had the searing duty of informing Bill that Lynne was dying of breast cancer. She had had a mastectomy seven years earlier, followed by several years' remission. When cancer resurfaced, Lynne used her professional research talent to find a far-out protocol for further treatment: it was stem-cell transplantation. This required horrendous month-long complete isolation while all her blood was "cleansed" outside her body. She developed pneumonia but survived for a year of further emergencies. Still harsher therapies were tried. Yet Lynne's spirit remained optimistic. She never considered death. Her struggle was linked to overwhelming concern for her son Benjamin. At a memorial service, Lynne's oncologist said that the truest sign of a patient's courage is her reaction to a doctor's frank statement that he could not promise that a treatment would be successful. "Lynne," he said, "five times chose such revolutionary procedures after I said, 'I don't know.'" In total, she had had almost as many hospitalizations as her years. She was fifty-three.

In her last month, Lynne insisted on an all-night, seven-hour drive from her hospital bed to a *bat mizvoth* ceremony for her niece Jane in the Adirondacks. Soon after, as we scattered Lynne's ashes on a dune on Cape Cod, I said, "Lynne came down from the mountain to the everlasting sea."

Grandnephew of a poet, my grandson Benjamin, then eleven, wrote this poem:

Ashes
They are as gray as a bad day when nothing is going right
They are as soft as skin
But yet as hard as the cold air on a fall day by the beach.

You imagine her just popping up any second
But she doesn't, she stays in her dark, gloomy home underground.

They don't blow away
They are there like a rock that has been there for a hundred years.

Your throat turns dry from the salty air
That hits your face like a smack.
You start to cry one drop, two drops, then three; they keep coming
You never want to stop.

We start back to the cars, no one says a word for we are too sad to speak.
It had been a long day and it wasn't going to end . . .

I miss you Mom.

Monday, October 18, 1999

5

INGA ARVAD

Our Spy—and Jack Kennedy's

Throughout my first twenty-five years, I was often too young. I entered college at sixteen, playing grammar by ear and math by instinct. But the difference was most noticeable in "social development," difficult at sixteen when your peers are three years older.

This is not nostalgia for what might have been; just a report of my startling discovery—late—of what went unnoticed before my eyes. I will not say it was an opportunity missed; that would be presumptuous. Let's say I was too immature to notice a juicy story before my eyes. It unfolded every day for eight months, and I did nothing about it. That occurred in the city room of the Graduate School of Journalism of Columbia University. There, of all places, one should have recognized a good story; with more maturity, perhaps, a romantic opportunity.

It was the fall of 1940. The war in Europe was a year old and seemed to be stalemated. Sixty-five of us comprised that year's class. Several would die in war; one would serve most of his career in the CIA; another would become director of Senator Fulbright's Foreign Affairs Committee; another would be managing editor of *Fortune*; another, a forty-year CBS News broadcaster; one, PR chief of a Howard Hughes operation; and others, spread across the journalistic landscape.

But then there was that slinky young woman in the first seat of the first row. (We were seated alphabetically.) Her name was Inga Arvad. My desk was in the rear. I would see Inga each morning dressed mainly in black suits and dresses, smoking a cigarette from a long holder, occasionally visited by a man just as well turned out and looking just as tense as she. Both were obviously European in speech, dress, and mannerism.

Several of us had completely uninformed opinions about Inga. We assumed she was a spy. We had heard that as a journalist in Europe she had already interviewed Hitler and Goebbels. It was, after all, a short trip from Inga's native Denmark to Nazi Germany. But the political distance was great; how had she managed this? And why?

I got the answers fifty-five years later. I was reading Nigel Hamilton's biography *JFK: Reckless Youth* and turned to part 9, "Inga Binga."[1] It was preceded by a full-page head shot of "Danish-born journalist Inga Arvad" taken in 1941, the year I knew her. (This narrative is largely Hamilton's reconstruction of the Arvad-Kennedy letters.) In the photo she was devastatingly beautiful and seductive. Some fifty pages are devoted to the future president's romance with Inga. The torrid, complex relationship is liberally documented by their correspondence. It seemed that Inga was the only woman to whom Jack ever repeatedly offered marriage. Inga provided ample sexual gratification, but much more. She was highly sophisticated, and by the time she and Kennedy met, she was wise in the ways of men, family relationships, and power.

Inga was born in Copenhagen in 1913. Her father died of malaria in South Africa when she was four. At eleven she trained as a dancer at the Royal Theatre, studied piano, and at sixteen was crowned beauty queen of Denmark. She competed in the Miss Europe contest, turned down a job at the Folies Bergère in Paris, and eloped with an Egyptian diplomat. She was seventeen at the time and divorced him two years later. The next year she married a movie director almost twice her age. They quarreled on the set. He left for Africa and she became a journalist in Berlin. It was 1935.

Inga interviewed Hitler twice, and Goering and Goebbels once each. Someone photographed her with Hitler in his box at the Olympics. That photo was to haunt her—and Jack Kennedy—and nearly end her American career in journalism.

In 1940, she brought that colorful background to Columbia's journalism school. Without knowing the details, even we neophytes sensed this was a singular young woman. We did not know that, when the rest of us graduated, Inga moved up very quickly. On Broadway in New York, she literally stopped Arthur Krock, Washington bureau chief of the *New York Times*, and asked him for a job in Washington. He recommended her to Cissy Patterson, publisher of the *Washington Times-Herald*, who hired Inga to write a social column. Krock later said he was "stupefied by the beauty of this creature."

By chance, Inga was to share an apartment with another staff writer, Jack Kennedy's sister Kathleen. The eager, young ensign Kennedy turned up at a dinner party, and Inga and Jack were instantly attracted to one another. Inga was still Mrs. Paul Fejos, but her husband was out of the country frequently on what he said was an exploratory mission in Peru for the "Swedish Sphinx" Axel Wenner-Gren. The latter was suspected of running arms for the Nazis. The secrecy of Inga's relationship only added further to her woes when the FBI tried to analyze her probable spy connections.

She saw in Kennedy, the exciting young naval officer, a potential president. Not bad foresight. She could have married that young man—he asked her repeatedly—but she demurred. She had been divorced and was still married to a second man she planned to divorce, even as she spent weekends and many nights with Jack Kennedy.

The protracted affair involved (1) the angry response of Joe Kennedy, Jack's father, who used his political power to separate the couple; (2) J. Edgar Hoover, who deployed the forces of the FBI to harass her, tap her phones, burglarize her apartment, and in other ways try to prove that Inga was indeed a spy; and (3) President Roosevelt, who was called in to separate the lovers.

The FBI believed the worst about Inga and especially her connection with Jack Kennedy. Hoover went to Roosevelt with his suspicion, and FDR responded, "[I]n view of the connection of Inga Arvad, who writes for the *Washington Times-Herald* [a formerly isolationist paper], with the Wenner-Gren expedition's leader, and in view of certain circumstances which have been brought to my attention [including the affair with Ensign Jack Kennedy], I think it would be just as well to have her specially watched."

The word went public quickly. Walter Winchell, the creator of gossip columns in the tabloid press, picked up the story. His distinctive opening shrill cry on radio had attracted me as a child: "Good evening, Mr. and Mrs. America and all the ships at sea, let's go to press." And to press he went on January 12, 1942: "One of ex-ambassador Kennedy's eligible sons is the target of a Washington gal columnist's affections. So much so she has consulted her barrister about divorcing her exploring groom. Pa Kennedy no like."[2]

For months, the FBI listened to every word that passed between Inga and Jack over telephones. The conversations were almost entirely romantic, or else they were discussions of Jack's problems with his father or mother. Inga provided appropriate balm and "motherly" advice (she was twenty-eight and he twenty-four, but she seemed wiser). For months, FBI analysts could not discover who "Jack" was. When they found out, they were certain that Inga was after codes or other information. Jack was assigned to the Bureau of Naval Intelligence. But he had access only to low-level information, and he passed none. He was entirely concerned with his sex life, his career, family relationships, and the poor conduct of the war. The FBI agents, mystified, believed they were missing something crucial to national security. But the couple's letters were still in Hoover's file after he died. Apparently, in Hoover's style, they were retained to blackmail a future office holder.

Inga provided an almost melancholy prediction of what Jack Kennedy could become, with a sad reflection of her own distance from that future: "Plan your life as you want it. . . . Go up the steps of fame. But—pause now and then to make sure that you are accompanied by happiness. Stop and ask yourself, 'Does it sing inside me today.' . . . And wherever I may be, drop in. I think I shall always know the right thing for you to do. Not because of brains; not because of knowledge; but because there are things deeper and more genuine—love, my dear."

Later she wrote that if she could do what she wanted today she would go out west, "buy a small place, purchase a lot of the best books, settle down. . . . Before I left I would make sure I had your baby along with me. You say why mine? Well, not because I love you—I obviously must have a tiny weakness for you—but because you are the kind the world ought to swarm with. You have just sufficient meanness in you to get along and enough brains and goodness to give to the world and not only take."

All that was before Jack Kennedy went overseas to command PT 109, nearly die, and return a hero. All the while he corresponded with Inga and received regular reports about her from friends. In his absence she went her way. She was divorced and began and ended another relationship. She moved to California and became a prominent journalist. Jack went there as soon as he reached the United States, but the romance was over. Jack was disillusioned, and Inga was relating to the Hollywood set. In January 1943, the front page of the *Boston Globe* carried an exclusive interview with Jack Kennedy on the PT 109 incident. The byline: Inga Arvad.

Today, she is buried in the desert beside her Hollywood husband, one of the most respected Western film stars of his era.

NOTES

1. Nigel Hamilton, "Inga Binga," part 9 in *JFK: Reckless Youth* (New York: Random House, 1993). Hamilton's extensive reading and reporting of the Arvad-Kennedy correspondence is summarized in this chapter.

2. Neal Gable, *Winchell: Gossip, Power, and the Culture of Celebrity* (New York: Vintage, 1994), p. 306.

6

RELIGION, THE MIDDLE EAST, AND FREEDOM HOUSE

H arry D. Gideonse was a founder of Freedom House, its moving spirit, and president for several terms while also serving for twenty-six years as president of Brooklyn College. He was a distinguished economist and political scientist who gained national prominence appearing regularly on a national radio panel from the University of Chicago. In October 1948, shortly after the creation of the state of Israel, Dr. Gideonse addressed the American Council for Judaism (ACJ), an anti-Zionist organization that holds that religion and nationalism should be kept apart. Dr. Gideonse voiced support for that belief and rejected the growing demand that American Jews consider themselves in "exile" until they "return" to the land of Israel—a forceful Zionist and Israeli governmental objective. It was a position the *New York Times* strongly opposed, and so the paper featured Gideonse's remarks.[1] There was an immediate attack on Gideonse from prominent Zionists, coupled with a successful effort to remove Gideonse as president of Freedom House. The effort was sparked by a Freedom House board member who had a Zionist organization as a public relations client.[2] Gideonse was replaced by Robert J. Patterson, former U.S. secretary of war. Three months later, I became an executive of the American Council for Judaism; eighteen years later, executive director of Freedom House. By then, Dr. Gideonse had twice been returned as president of Freedom House. He interviewed me for the FH post after Leo Cherne, an FH leader, proposed me. Cherne and I had collaborated when I created the ACJ's Philanthropic Fund, which brought Jewish refugees to their new homeland in the United States.

Not until 1973 did I discover in the Freedom House files Dr. Gideonse's controversial speech and this story. Both served to underscore the following moral: the midway in politics is harder to traverse than the streets of midtown New

York. More difficult still is the middle way in religion, especially in Judaism, with its bitter clash between the politics of Israeli nationalism and the diverse theology of the Jewish religion. Where politics and religion meet, the victim can be not only the human spirit but the physical well-being, even the life of the believer or the dissenter. Holy wars, Inquisitions, and unspeakable brutality conducted in the name of religion or religious nationalism continue in the Middle East (a "middle" that is often at an extreme).

I grew up in the non-Zionist (non-nationalist) tradition of Reform Judaism. That middle way of Judaism blended religious practice with one's civil life in a democratic society. Various degrees of religious orthodoxy or religious conservatism retained many separatist practices developed in earlier times and more restrictive places. Jewish opposition to Zionism originated in Western Europe in the mid-nineteenth century and was widely converted into a politicoreligious code by Orthodox-born Jews who became Socialists or Bundists in Eastern Europe. In 1885, opposition to Zionism was formally adopted by the American Reform rabbinate as the Pittsburgh Platform. The organization of Reform rabbis declared two years later, "Zion was a precious possession of the past. . . . [A]s such it is a holy memory, but it is not our hope of the future. America is our Zion." The Reform tradition modernized some religious rituals and emphasized the prophetic books of the Old Testament, rather than the nationalistic aspects of Judaism. This was Judaism's middle way—integration of the religion into the new democracies rather than assimilation out of Judaism.

Other branches of Judaism as well as secular Jews, who considered themselves Jewish only by virtue of their family history or culture, broadly shared the view that America was their home and not *galut* (exile in a diaspora) and that they did not need to "return" to Palestine. That land was, indeed, a place to house refugees or those Jews whose practice of Judaism encouraged settlement in the Holy Land. This view of America was shared by an offshoot of the conservative wing of Judaism, the Reconstructionists, who strongly opposed Orthodoxy, the third major branch of Judaism. These non-Zionist or anti-Zionist Jews believed that Judaism was flourishing in America despite the fringe attacks of anti-Semites and even "Jewish quotas" in colleges, banking, and corporations.

I absorbed this form of Judaism when I attended the religious school of Congregation Emanu-El, New York, the "cathedral" of world Reform Judaism. At ten I conducted a service and at twelve delivered a sermon and thought of becoming a rabbi. Rabbi Samuel H. Goldenson, one of Reform's leading American rabbis, confirmed me and Fran, my first wife. Several years later, he was to help form the American Council for Judaism, the anti-Zionist organization I headed for many years. In 1934, my confirmation year, I played the role of "chairman" of an organization raising funds to help Jews threatened with death in Nazi Germany. Before six thousand people, I spoke from the stage of the Roxy Theatre, then New York's largest. Afterward, I drew a picture of my impression. In the blackness viewed from the spotlighted stage, I could see only diminishing channels of aisle lights stretching toward the distant exits. My stage appeal for German Jews was made at the very moment my wife-to-be Marianne and her family were fleeing Germany ahead of Hitler's fury. It would be fifteen years before I would face the dilemma of helping Jewish victims without supporting Jewish nationalism. It would be twenty-four years before I would meet Marianne and we would marry.

At Emanu-El I was president of several youth groups and after the war became adult programmer for them. As a youth, I helped write and produce plays to raise funds for charities. These plays attracted young Jews with theatrical aspirations. Betty Perske was there briefly—before changing her name to Lauren Bacall and marrying Humphrey Bogart. Alexander H. Cohen—later responsible for 101 Broadway and London productions by the most distinguished playwrights, including Arthur Miller—started with us at Emanu-El. He later created the Tony Awards for television. As teenagers, Alex and I wrote the book for *Ball and Chain*, a musical. That summer, Alex rented the Locust Valley playhouse on Long Island. Fran played some roles, and I managed publicity.

That fall of 1941, Alex bankrolled his first Broadway production. Several nights before opening, a mutual friend told me that Alex needed five hundred dollars to raise the curtain. I was leaving the next day for a newspaper job in Puerto Rico and couldn't spare the money, yet Alex found it anyway. On schedule, he opened *Angel Street*. It drew instant acclaim and is still one of the longest-run mystery plays (and, renamed *Gaslight*, is one of the longest-running films as well). The residual income from that $500 investment could probably have put my children through college. On Alex's death in 2000 the *New York Times* devoted a half-page obituary, with a six-column head, to "one of the last old-time independent theatrical producers."

At Emanu-El there was no support for the nationalistic campaigns of Zionism, though members practiced Judaism and contributed liberally to appeals for Jewish refugees. The congregation included influential leaders in business, politics, and journalism. On High Holy Days, I would see Herbert H. Lehman, then governor of New York, walk down the center aisle to the first row. He was joined by brother Arthur, an eminent jurist, along with the Sulzbergers of the *New York Times* and the Newbergers and Loebs of Wall Street.

I had an unpleasant memory of Newberger, then president of Emanu-El and head of the brokerage firm that bore his name. My parents regularly waited outside the religious school to drive me home for Sunday lunch. That day, my mother greeted Newberger saying, "I understand we are distantly related through families in Frankfurt, Germany." Newberger replied, "Oh, poor relatives!" It wasn't clear who he meant: the Frankfurters or the Sussmans.

Years later, Rabbi Elmer Berger asked me to run the New York chapter of the American Council for Judaism. The post was bound to be controversial; Israel had just been created. The "for Judaism" organization would oppose the rising tide of politically oriented "for Israel" groups among American Jews. The

ACJ had become an embattled organization even before its formal birth. Hitler's campaign to murder Jews as well as Judaism aroused emotions that silenced rational discussions of alternatives to Jewish nationalism. Council members were called "traitors," "self-haters," or "Jewish anti-Semites." Before he was murdered by a Jew, Israeli Prime Minister Yitzhak Rabin, managing an Arab-Israel peace process, saw automobile bumper stickers reading, *Rabin boged*—Hebrew for "Rabin is a traitor." His assassin was a product of the best religious-Zionist schools in Israel.

Lessing J. Rosenwald, then chairman of Sears Roebuck, was the first president and a contributor to the ACJ but never a great benefactor. He was modest but patriarchal and rejected those who flattered him or Edith, his wife. Quietly he provided philanthropic support for refugees while arguing publicly against the political implications of Jewish nationalism. His brother Edward was a mainstay of Zionist fundraising in the United States. Some Jews would regard them as the bad and the good brothers. Lessing was a significant collector of rare books and lithographs. At his home in Jenkintown, Pennsylvania, he showed me through his collection designated for the National Gallery in Washington, where it may now be seen.

At the ACJ, a staff of a dozen executives labored long hours against the growing emotional and political pressures generated by Zionist and increasingly "non-Zionist" groups; the latter, mainly the American Jewish Committee, which swerved toward the Zionist position under the great emotionalism of the day. The hottest place in Elmer Berger's hell was reserved for the American Jewish Committee, and I suppose they regarded the American Council for Judaism with the same disdain—particularly since we attracted to the ACJ some of their prominent members. Under such strains, Elmer directed the Council with a short rein and a fiery temper, mixed with quixotic humor. He wrote, spoke, and planned tactics after only brief clearance with Lessing Rosenwald and few others. He cajoled, even browbeat the staff into performing as effectively as a group twice its size. Elmer had no regard for personal amenities. He created humorous but denigrating nicknames for executives and then insisted they join him daily for lunch at Schrafft's. After looking at the same menu led by frail tea sandwiches he would begin with something like, "Well, what are you geniuses up to today?" Whatever the reply, it would not please him. After awhile, I made other lunchtime appointments. Elmer was suspicious of this, particularly when he knew I sensed among board members their growing opposition to his personnel practices. I tried with little success to serve as mediator.

Eventually, Elmer was asked to step down as executive director, and I was named in his place. That was based partly on my performance for several years as the creator of the Council's religious education program. I took seriously "for Judaism" in the organization's title. Indeed, we had often been criticized for being only "negative"—*anti*-Zionist. I recognized that many families wanted to enroll their children in religious schools that emphasized Reform Judaism, not

Jewish nationalism. Elmer gave me a free hand to develop this program. Indeed, despite his reputation of being involved only in Middle East issues and especially eager to advance Jewish-Arab contacts, he took special interest in the religious education program. He led me through many of Judaism's original sources and appropriate commentaries.

I developed a complete religious school curriculum for kindergarten through twelfth grade, with weekly classroom themes and supporting texts for each grade for the entire school year.[3] I traveled the country establishing schools in thirteen cities. Teachers in almost all cases were parents who wanted this kind of religious education for their own children. I provided preparatory sessions for parent-teachers. The schools grew into complete congregations in Denver and Highland Park, Illinois, housed now in their own temples. Historian Thomas A. Kolsky, recently describing the influence of the American Council for Judaism, said that this religious education program was the organization's most successful undertaking.[4] While gratifying, I do not accept this as a true evaluation of the ACJ and Elmer Berger's role in it. His analyses and prescience may be rediscovered long after the names of many Zionist heroes are forgotten. His life is a major clue to the changes, for better or worse, in American Judaism during his lifetime and perhaps beyond. Elmer died at the age of eighty-eight in 1996.

Elmer, then executive vice president, was very gracious when I retired from the ACJ. He listed requirements of the council director, but the description fit *him* far better than it fit me:

> To do the job, the patience and discipline of the scholar is needed. But there is afforded little if any of the freedom from pressure which most scholars today enjoy. The passion of the crusader is needed, but it must be constantly understated, restrained, curbed because in trying to effectuate the corrective, the council's hard documented facts appear as fantasy . . . to the innocents, the brainwashed, to those who prefer to evade or avoid the facts. There are dreams to be dreamed by those who work in the council's vineyard: essentially the dream of a new emancipation for American Jews who are not only accepted as individuals in America, but who are willing, as individuals, to accept America; or to labor for its evolution and change in the voluntary caste-free patterns which are the classics of our democracy.

I said of Elmer,

> I have seen [him] in all of his public and many of his private moods. I shall miss his pungency . . . and his perception. Like Judaism, which mingles harshness and love, Elmer is most stern in defense of that which moves him most—in response to threats to individual freedom or to the free spirit of Judaism; he is most impatient with those closest to him who do less than is possible; most harsh on those who compromise with truth or freedom—sometimes, all too many of our coreligionists fit both categories—and sometimes, in quiet ways

virtually unknown to anyone except [his wife,] Ruth, in the truest spirit of Judaism, Elmer reflects the deepest philanthropy and thereby the purest humanity. Outwardly, he is still the troubler of Judaism and, as we know best, Judaism needs one now no less than two thousand years ago. It is sometimes difficult to share the same office with a troubler—he and I would agree. But this country, its Jews, the council needs one. . . . I am sorry I cannot become the Boswell of this troubler.

I did, however, define my understanding of Judaism.

After the Holocaust, the defeat of Nazi Germany, and the creation of the state of Israel, my early religious instincts led me to interpret Judaism and the continuity of the Jewish experience as something far more than a struggle for survival in a largely unfriendly world. Indeed, I came to see the End of Judaism (to borrow a popular political science formula) as largely in the hands of Jews themselves. In democratic countries with viable civil societies, it was now up to each religious group to assure its own survival. For Jews, given their history of oppression, this was a relatively new opportunity; but I believe it is an opportunity being squandered out of fear and misunderstanding generated by Jews themselves.

Not only intermarriage reduces the number of practicing Jews. Too many others restrict their "Jewishness" solely to providing financial or political aid to the state of Israel and weighing their personal acceptances as Jews by the scale of America's momentary support for Israel's geopolitics. Clearly, the Holocaust happened. Millions of Jews (and others) died. Worldwide, more Jews survived than perished. That is hardly a satisfying observation; but neither is it utterly pessimistic, as the growing mythology suggests. Jews survived Egyptian slavery, Roman desecration, and Spanish autos-da-fé, as well as the German Holocaust. Jews did not survive in order to suffer again or even to survive without purpose. They survived as Jews because they carried with them a certain hope for a better future, not only for Jews but for everyone. That hope, generated and sustained by faith, is an ethic, a way of living, not of dying; doing so both as an individual and as part of a historic religious people. In different ages, in different places, the symbols and practices of Judaism have changed. No one is capable of practicing *all* forms of Judaism that are part of this tradition. It remains, then, for each Jew to respond to the religious imperative in what, for each individual, is an appropriate way within Judaism.

One cannot fulfill even the minimalist interpretation of Judaism, I believe, without a commitment to the obligations of ethical practice and social justice that are inherent in the religion. That obligation goes beyond the family and the fellowship of Jews; it commits Jews to the uplifting of oppressed human beings, whatever their religious belief. This commitment impelled Jews in the civil rights movement to march in Alabama for the liberation of blacks. It calls on Jews to understand the travail of Palestinians as well as Israelis.

Such a commitment is imperiled by the tribalistic worship of false gods: the equating of the future of Judaism with the success or failure of the state of Israel, as well as the emphasis on Jewish survivalism—for its own sake—as the common objective of modern Jews. If one must draw sustenance from tragedy, suggests Rabbi Michael Goldberg, turn to the Exodus rather than the Holocaust. Exodus, he says, is the "master story": God led the Israelites out of Egyptian slavery in order to fulfill an eternal covenant, a linchpin in God's redemption of the world—not survival for survival's sake.[5]

We who never faced the Holocaust are not morally justified to speak critically of its victims. But we can examine what Goldberg calls the cult of Jews who, from a distance, acquiesced thereafter in linking the religious experience of Jews and the objectives of Jewish institutions to the survivalism inherent in making the state of Israel central to the future of Judaism. That "civic Judaism" is quite different from a civil society—the democratization of governance and the participation of all citizens in that polity.

Once Hitler targeted Jews for extermination, Jews in America were traumatized. For sixty years there was no public discussion of how to serve religious and humanitarian imperatives of Judaism without mortgaging them to the nationalism of the state of Israel. Some American Jews in the 1990s were beginning to recognize the dilemma; rabbinical scholar Rabbi Jacob J. Petuchowski declared, "Jews who so recently have been the victims of nationalist emotionalism run wild in Europe should be the last to wallow in an aura of nationalist self-satisfaction which permits of no rational analysis of the true state of affairs." Ironically, the clearest advice to American and Israeli Jews for dissipating the dilemma came from an assistant secretary of state—after years of discussions with Elmer Berger.

The rabbi had already provided a detailed statement for John Foster Dulles's visit to the Middle East in May 1953, the first U.S. secretary of state to go there. Dulles adopted the Berger position and declared, "Israel should become part of the Near East community and cease to look upon itself, or be looked upon by others, as alien to this community." This, he added, "will require concessions on the part of both sides." A few years later, Assistant Secretary of State Henry A. Byroade told an ACJ meeting that "Israel should see her own future in the context of a Middle Eastern state and not as headquarters of worldwide groupings of peoples of a particular religious faith who must have special rights within and obligations to the Israeli state." He did acknowledge, though, "the natural feeling of affinity one feels for a brother of his own religious faith" and the desire to provide philanthropic support. On April 20, 1964, after extensive discussions among Rabbi Berger, Prof. W. T. Mallison of George Washington University, and the State Department, another assistant secretary, Phillips Talbot, issued this clarifying letter for publication in international journals: "[The Department of State] does not recognize a legal-political relationship based upon the religious identification of American citizens. It does not in any way discriminate among American citizens upon the basis of their religion. Accordingly, it should be clear that the Department of State does not regard 'the Jewish people' concept as a concept of international law."

This rejects the fundamental concept of Zionism, or Jewish nationalism, as operative in American or international law. Decades of pro-Zionist lobbying in Washington and fund-raising across the United States had been based on precisely the irrevocable linkage of Judaism and Israeli nationalism.

The State Department's message brought increased attacks on the Council, Rabbi Berger, and the so-called Arabists of the State Department. Indeed, Elmer was particularly attacked for meeting with moderate Arabs and suggesting that other Jews open such dialogues. It was easy to demonize Elmer for associating with Middle Easterners who were not Jewish. Israeli Prime Minister Yitzhak Rabin was bitterly denounced and then murdered for negotiating with Yasir Arafat. And Prime Minister Golda Meir probably would have been abused as Rabin was if it had been known that her associates met with Jordanians. She made it, however, onto an Israeli postage stamp.

Elmer's "crime," apparently, is that he was a premature negotiator in the complex Middle East power struggle in which the nature of Judaism—in America and elsewhere—was at stake. The rejection of Elmer Berger, the person, even as some of his ideas became acceptable in Jerusalem and Washington, and among Jews as well as others, was a source of bitter disappointment to him. His acerbic personality and his stringent ideas were certainly a factor in his wide rejection. After leaving the ACJ he hoped that he might find an advisory niche in Washington's Middle East structure—but that was not to be. He asked whether I had ever been approached. I had been asked at different times whether I would serve as deputy director of the United States Information Agency (USIA), assistant secretary of state for human rights, or ambassador to Zimbabwe. But I took my name off the lists.

Until the second *intifada* (uprising) in 2001–2002, both American and Israeli Jews were slowly, often painfully reexamining their relationship. Some Israeli texts for schoolchildren were revised to remove myths and explain the facts of Arab relations. Peter Novick argued that the Holocaust had been exploited to help communal leaders address their immediate problems.[6] Some American Jews face an "identity crisis," wrote Amy Dockser Marcus in the *Wall Street Journal* (Sept. 14, 1994): "For Jews in Israel, peace is dawning at long last. But for Jews in the U.S., the turmoil is just beginning." She quoted an Israeli Jew: "We are not a tiny version of America. We have more in common with the Druse [a sect of Islam living in Israel] than we do with American Jews." The latter, however, have concentrated on Israel's needs, she wrote. She quoted the head of Boston's Combined Jewish Philanthropies: "We now have to answer, what does it mean to be a Jew [in America] in the modern world?"

That is the question Elmer Berger addressed when no one else would.

I sought my answer when I went to the Middle East for the first time in 1996, thirty years after I left the ACJ. I visited Israel, the Palestine autonomous areas, and Jordan. I was overwhelmed by the historic and archaeological aura of those lands. With every step one seemed to walk with long-distant antecedents: these were not only Hebrews, Judeans, or Israelites but Hasmoneans, Moabites, Hittites, Greeks, Romans, Turks, and countless others whose names are lost to history. Indeed, there were antecedents of Arabs and Jews here long before there were Israelites and Judeans. This was not a new thought, but it deepened my awareness that this birthplace of three major religions has been burdened with ungodly atrocities, perpetual fear, and a deep sadness.

Conversations there reconfirmed my personal commitment to the separation of state and religion. The bitter fruit of the opposite policy has prevailed since Israel's creation in 1948. This was amply demonstrated at meetings of the International Press Institute (convener of my visit to Israel) in speeches by Prime Minister Shimon Peres, two supporters of his successor Benjamin Netanyahu, and Dr. Hanan Ashrawi, spokesperson for the Palestinians. They were forced to deal with the future of the "peace process" and the damage to it just weeks earlier by four Palestinian-terrorist bombings in Jerusalem and Tel Aviv.

My visit confirmed two beliefs: first, the Israeli settlers had indeed taken great strides to create a political entity, though they still struggled to build a homogeneous state composed of disparate racial, linguistic, and nationality groups as well as widely differing Jewish traditions—all this at great expense to the large number of Arabs they displaced and colonized.

Second, Elmer Berger's proposal in 1967 for the peaceful resolution of the Arab-Israel struggle, after Israel had won that war—the suggestion of which led to his firing from the ACJ—might have been no more difficult to pursue in 1967 than it is thirty-five years later. Countless more Arabs and Israelis might still be alive and physically whole, and a new generation of anti-Israel terrorists in the Israel-controlled West Bank and Gaza strip might not have emerged. Whether tested in 1967 or in 1996, the peace process would have incurred risks, as both prime ministers Rabin and Peres frankly stated.

The history of Israel-Arab relations is marked by recurring wars spurred by outrageous terrorism committed by Arab and Israeli extremists whenever peace seemed even faintly nearer. The preelection bombings in 1996 were sparked by Palestinian terrorists probably directed from Iran. Related enemy assaults triggered a major Israeli bombardment of Qana, Lebanon, that killed more than 170 women and children in a refugee camp. Some 300,000 Lebanese were driven from their homes. Ari Shavit, a columnist for *Haaretz*, a major Israeli Hebrew-language newspaper, said in the *New York Times*, "So now Qana is part of our biography. Precisely because we have tried to deny and ignore the outrage, it remains affixed to us. And just as the Baruch Goldstein massacre of praying Muslims in Hebron and the murder of Yitzhak Rabin were extreme manifestations of some rotten seed planted in the religious-nationalist culture, it now seems that the massacre at Qana was an extreme manifestation of rotten seeds dormant in our secular Israeli culture: Cynicism. Arrogance. Egocentricism of the strong."[7]

Still, Peres expressed to us his conviction that the peace process must go forward. At the same time, he closed off Gaza and the West Bank, forbidding entrance to Israel for Palestinians who work, get food, medicines, or hospital care in Israel. This caused physical and economic hardship and, in some cases, serious health problems for the Palestinians. Mixed signals probably cost Peres the election.

With this in mind, it was disturbing to walk through the streets of Old Jerusalem. At every turn are caverns, shrines, and markers that peel away the archaeological layers of competing traditions, repeated violence, and mindless destruction of structures that were legacies for all the world. Saddest of all, one realizes that mindlessness and destruction continue to this very moment—and for the same reasons that every preceding civilization not only tore down another's temples and desecrated its most sacred images but also murdered worshipers who responded to a different call. Old Jerusalem, encircled by a wall, symbolizes human divisiveness.

I entered Jerusalem through the Zion Gate and walked to the Wailing Wall. Armed security guards watch every visitor who descends the steps into the large open plaza before the wall. Orthodox Jews in black coats and prayer shawls walk to and from the wall, *dovening* aloud. There is unmistakable earnestness in these men, young and old. Women are fenced into a small area at the rightmost end of the wall. At the opposite end, providing the most holy aspect for prayer, is an alcove formed by an adjacent building that abuts the wall.

There several dozen men and boys with *pais* and *talit* chant in unison, facing the wall in that darkened tunnel-like place. This is presumed to be closest to the site where God would be most likely to hear prayers. Directly behind the wall is believed to have been the Holy of Holies in the First and Second Temples, the narrowly prescribed area where no human, only God Himself, is said to have trod. The First Temple was built in 963 B.C.E. by Solomon, destroyed by Nebuchadnezzar in 586, and rebuilt as the Second Temple in 536 on the same site, which was then destroyed by the Romans in 70 C.E. The precise location of the temples is not known, but it is presumed to be behind the Wailing Wall, probably on the very site of the Arabs' similarly historic and religiously important Dome of the Rock. The beautiful golden-domed structure covers the rock where Muhammad is said to have ascended to heaven, making this one of the holiest places in Islam. Indeed, the Western Wall—a holy site in Judaism—was supposedly constructed to keep religious Jews from touching, even accidentally, the Holy of Holies in the place of the ancient temples. So intertwined are the histories and theologies of these two peoples.

Even as a non-Christian walking through Jerusalem's Via Dolorosa, one senses the emotionality of the place where Jesus was crucified. A few steps away, remnants of the Cardo reveal the Greek streets and shops, followed by Roman revivals. In the same narrow stalls where Greeks and Romans hawked their wares, Palestinians and Israelis—before the *intifada* of 2001–2002—offered modern goods lighted by dim electric bulbs. The same narrow passageways were cluttered with sellers and buyers of fruits and scents.

My feeling of melancholy increased as I walked. So much had changed, yet so little in the minds of people. An occasional jeep of the Israel Defense Force (IDF) would move through the passageways, each vehicle with two armed soldiers observing every aspect of Old Jerusalem where, in a few days, another terror-bomber would blow himself up while delivering his deadly assignment.

Days later in Jordan, I stood on Mount Nebo and gazed at Jerusalem and Jericho. The Jordan River flowed narrowly in the foreground. Mt. Nebo was presumably the place where Moses died. He had completed the long trek across the desert from Mount Sinai but would fail to enter Jerusalem, the "promised land." Standing on that place one could see the present state of Israel and Jordan. The day before, I had been in the Golan Heights and observed Syrian troops across the no man's land occupied only by the UN force. From that place in the Golan, Israeli tanks in 1967 moved quickly to the very suburbs of Damascus, only forty-five miles away. Amman, the capital of Jordan, is about the same distance from Israel's border. At that moment, it was easier to go from Jerusalem to Amman than from Amman to Baghdad in Iraq! The Jordanians spoke freely to Israelis, whereas the road and the dialogue between Amman and Baghdad were restricted. Yet all are in a small neighborhood.

Such limited geography has nurtured turmoil and death for millennia. The river Jordan is an example of how nature's limitations, magnified by human conflict, perpetuate disaster for all who inhabit the region. The river is a great disappointment, whether viewed from the Golan or the valley of the Galilee. Despite its biblical importance and history, the river is just a narrow stream. Since Israel was established, mediators have tried to use the Jordan as leverage to induce peace between Arabs and Israelis. Arabs feared Israelis would increasingly divert the stream, thus depriving Jordan of this vital resource. In 2002, Israelis threatened reprisals after Lebanon set up a pumping station at Wazzani in the south. David Lilienthal, father of the Tennessee Valley Authority (TVA), tried in 1949 to develop a water resources plan for the Golan area. The plan was intended to advance the Arab-Israel peace process at that time; however, after several unproductive years, Lilienthal quit.

Going to Israel, I carried a plan produced over some years by Boaz Wachtel, an Israeli working at Freedom House on proposals for the international use of waterways serving the embattled region. Boaz's plan included maps of the 1973 conflict exactly as we were briefed by the IDF before seeing the Golan cross points. One map also showed the route of the national water carrier as it presently exists. I saw parts of this vital pipeline as it snakes down from the sources in the Golan to its southernmost points just east of the Gaza strip at the Egyptian border. The pipeline serves all of Israel as presently constituted. One funny point: a tourist knelt beside the Jordan River in the Golan to fill an empty bottle with authentic water from the fabled river. My guide said, however, the man might just as well turn on the tap in his hotel room; that, too, is Jordan river water, with some chlorine added. But as with so much in these lands, symbolism counts.

The Boaz plan calls for a diversion of 1,100 million cubic meters a year, or 3 million cubic meters a day, from the elevated Atatürk Baraji lake in southeast Turkey (or from the Seyhan and Ceyhan rivers 160 and 240 kilometers west of the lake) to be equally divided among Israel, Jordan, and the Palestinians. We heard at the IPI Congress from a Turkish representative that his country is ready to provide this assistance to the Middle East peace process.

Two subterranean pipelines would carry the water, mostly by gravity, through western Syria to a north-central point of the Syrian-Israel border on the Golan Heights near the city of Qunaytra. The plan includes the creation of an artificial boundary, a tank barrier structure, particularly positioned on the demilitarized zone of the Golan. Water would be diverted from there to fall through extensions in the upper Yarmuk River and from the western Golan slope to the Sea of Galilee. This water system could provide two stimulants for an Israeli military withdrawal from the Golan: (1) setting up a compensating security system and (2) providing substantial new water flows.

Boaz contemplates that a reduction of Israel's strategic need to maintain control of the Golan Heights is possible with the construction of the tank barrier/water control structure on the border, and a substantial reduction of Syria's ability to launch sudden, massive ground armored assaults into the Golan and northern Israel. This barrier could be dismantled after twenty years of peace, he notes. The structure could bridge the Israeli and Syrian positions and allow for gradual Israeli withdrawal from the heights under secured terms that may be acceptable to the Israeli public.

Boaz points out that there is built-in assurance that Syria would honor the arrangement of a water flow from Turkey through Syria to Israel. Syria, he notes, has a good reputation of keeping agreements that it signs. (There had been no Syrian incursion in the Golan since that agreement was signed more than twenty-five earlier.) If Syria interferes, it would only deny itself its share of water and power from the project and might also force military and economic action (regional and international) sanctioned under agreements relating to the project.

I believe, however, that if there is renewed fighting on the Golan it will be between the Jewish settlers of the Golan and the Israeli forces ordered to evict those settlers as part of a comprehensive peace treaty signed with the Arab states. Representatives of the "Golan residents committee" made it clear to me they would fight to retain land and buildings held by two generations of settlers, with a third generation already in the nursery school. "We will never give up the Golan," Marla van Meter, the residents' spokesperson, told me. I said that the looming crisis was inherent in David Ben-Gurion's policy fifty years earlier of placing settlers on an outer defense perimeter. It is by definition challengeable and vulnerable. Ms. van Meter disagreed. "No different," she said, "than you Americans populating the Mexican border, and calling it Texas and California."

During my few days in Jordan I was struck by the difference in the morale of the Israelis and Jordanians. Israelis—their soldiers and guns highly visible—

were fearful, suspicious, uncertain of their future (as well they may be, given the reality of terrorism and unsettled questions of borders, neighboring populations, and the status of their capital city). Jordanians, however, were convinced that peace had arrived nearly two years earlier. No military were visible. Construction of homes and hotels was booming, largely funded during the first Gulf War by Jordanian workers expelled from Kuwait, who brought home their oil money.

After the Israeli-Jordanian peace accord, tourism in Jordan tripled. Many Israelis for the first time could stand on Mt. Nebo one day and, as I did, travel the next day to Petra, capital of the Edomites, an Old Testament wonder. Leaving the village of Petra you follow a narrow dirt path through the Siq for a mile. The path darkens as rose-colored limestone cliffs rise on all sides; only a sliver of sky can be seen. With each movement forward, the rock takes on colorful new shapes hewn by wind and water through the centuries. Suddenly, out of the dimness appears a rose-red brightness. Tall carved stone images appear directly in your path, a temple of the Roman period. The Corinthian columns and statues were hewn out of the face of the rock. The monument is some 150 feet high. Past the temple is an eight-thousand-seat amphitheater built by the Romans in 106 C.E. out of sheer rock. Farther on, many major rock carvings reveal burial places and assemblies of the antecedents. They appear in a profusion of colors: rose, purple, crimson, and saffron.

With the *intifada* of 2001–2002, however, most tourism in Petra ceased.

Related to tourism, one little-noted development may be a hopeful sign for a more peaceful future in the region. At the southernmost tip of Jordan is the port city of Aqaba, literally a stone's throw from Eilat, at Israel's southern point. Over the years, both Jordan and Israel built small airports at Aqaba and Eilat to serve their respective countries. But as with the Jordan River bridges, for decades all direct movement between the two countries was barred. Now, quietly, an airport has been built to serve both Aqaba and Eilat; it was a joint venture based on the peace agreement. After disembarking, a passenger could walk out the airport's eastern door and enter Jordan or take the western door and be in Israel. That is indeed the peace process at work.

Such practical steps seemed impossible from 1948 to the day Anwar el-Sadat visited Jerusalem. Yet such steps were in our minds at the ACJ when we tried, with admittedly little success, to separate the modern practice of Judaism from Jewish nationalism. We were castigated as "self-haters" and worse. Elmer Berger bore the brunt of such attacks, but I felt them too.

After the assassination of her husband, Leah Rabin, widow of the slain prime minister, faced the dilemma "What does it mean to be a Jew?"—for Israel and for Reform Judaism. Significantly, she expressed solidarity with Reform Judaism in the face of the religious parties' effort to blot out Reform in Israel. Referring to those who sent the assassin to kill her husband, she said, "They do not sanctify our Torah; it is not holy to them. They have a value more holy to them, a political value: land. It is more important than a man's life." That man, her husband, had referred to Reform as "the other Judaism, that is ready to listen, to accept, that has different values and ways to respect our faith, so that man and his faith may live."[8]

Subsequently, an Israeli religious paper called Reform Jews *rodifim*, or pursuers. In Orthodoxy, a pursuer may be killed to prevent a crime. Prime Minister Rabin was called a *rodef* before he was assassinated. I believe that if Elmer Berger had not retired, he would have been a victim of assassination and the "logic" of religious extremism.

In 2002, Thomas Friedman of the *New York Times* heard this question asked in Israel: "Is Judaism a threat to Israel?" Too many schools, he said, "give more emphasis to the value of the land than to the value of life."[9] In 1880, Rabbi Emil G. Hirsch, a venerated leader of Reform Judaism, declared that "Judaism protests . . . against the dogma of materialism, it does not less raise its voice against the materialism of dogma."[10] Jerusalem is thus an *idea*, not an address, a metaphor for the time when the world may live in peace. That calls for an end to the dogma centered on a single Jewish nationalism.

In June 2002, during the suicide bombings in Israel, Henry Siegman—who had been a young refugee from Nazism, had studied for the rabbinate, and for sixteen years headed the pro-Zionist American Jewish Congress—called the Palestinian struggle for a state "the mirror image of the Zionist movement" that led to the creation of Israel in 1948. "This does not excuse suicide bombings," he said, "but the way Israel deals with these outrages is suspect as long as they are exploited to extend the occupation and enlarge Israeli settlements" on Palestinian land. He added, "Future Jewish historians who will be writing about our times will not be kind to us because of such political and moral blindness."[11]

In a letter to me shortly before he died, Elmer explained his original motivation for his anti-Zionist career: "I never veered from my enthusiasm for the transcendent and universal principles of the Judaism of the literary prophets of the Old Testament. Yet the widespread public debate over the political destiny of Palestine, the unwarranted and basically fallacious Zionist claim to represent something called 'the Jewish people' (a euphemism for all Jews), the deliberate omission of any political justice for the indigenous Arab inhabitants of Palestine—all led me to intensify my study and understanding of the conflict in Palestine at a time when increasing numbers throughout the Western world were becoming concerned with postwar plans for peace."

In 1990, as a requirement for his ordination as a rabbi in America, Mark Glickman completed a scholarly 181-page biography of Elmer Berger. He called it "One Voice against Many." Glickman concluded:

> I began my research very sympathetic to Zionism and actually quite hostile to Berger and his views. . . . I have come to believe that Berger's notion of a democratic, de-Zionized Israel is one which carries a great deal of merit. I have not come to this decision lightly. . . . An Israel which would cease seeing itself as a Jewish state, and which would instead be a Western-style island of democracy

in the Middle East, would ideally (and I am admittedly speaking in ideals here) be a much calmer place than it is today. All citizens of the country, regardless of their religion or original nationality, would have equal status in its national life. Legalized discrimination against Arabs would cease to exist.

The benefits would be external as well. A de-Zionized Israel would lead to a radical redefinition of Israel-Diaspora relationships. No longer would Israeli *sh'lichim* [agents] enter the Diaspora communities and rouse the ire of Jews there by urging that they all leave their "homes" and make *aliyah* [emigration to Israel]. The Law of the Return [automatic citizenship offered all Jews in Israel] would have to be repealed, and the very notion of *aliyah* eliminated. By the same token, Diaspora Jews would no longer have the right to play "armchair" politician and thus anger the Jews who live in Israel and have to deal with the consequences of their actions in a very real way. Diaspora Jews would also have no need to feel embarrassed when Israel behaves in a shameful way....

Although Israel as a Jewish nation would cease to exist, Jewish culture could continue to flourish.... This break would be mitigated by a certain affinity which Israeli and Diaspora Jews would feel for one another as members of "the *mishpocheh*" [the larger family].... There would be a separation of "church" and state within Israel ... American Jews can be shown that Judaism can be thrilling, exciting, and most importantly, can address their own needs in very deep and significant ways.... As a Jew I feel impelled to dream—to dream with perhaps the naive hope ... that someday we will be able to look each other in the eye—Jew to Jew, Jew to Arab—and that together we will be able to sit under our vine and fig trees, and be afraid no more.[12]

Ideas have consequences: in this case, a young rabbi's discovery of Elmer Berger's inflammatory ideas.

NOTES

1. "Policy on Israel Called Strategic: Gideonse Says Aim is U.S. Security," *New York Times*, October 28, 1948.

2. Harry D. Gideonse, telephone conversation with author, November 29, 1973, and letter to author, December 12, 1973.

3. See Leonard R. Sussman, "The Sacred and the Profane in Judaism," *Religious Education*, May–June 1960.

4. Thomas A. Kolsky, *Jews against Zionism: The American Council for Judaism, 1942–48* (Philadelphia: Temple University Press, 1990), p. 193.

5. Quoted in Allan C. Brownfield, review of *Why Should Jews Survive?* by Michael Goldberg (New York: Oxford University Press, 1995), *Issues* (American Council for Judaism), spring 1996, p. 1.

6. Quoted in Allan C. Brownfield, "It Is Time to End the Doomsday Rhetoric of a 'Second Holocaust,'" *Issues* (American Council for Judaism), summer 2002, 9–10.

7. Ari Shavit, "How Easily We Killed Them," *New York Times*, May 27, 1996. Adapted from an article by Shavit in *Haaretz*.

8. Quoted in "Leah Rabin Expresses Solidarity with Reform Jews," *Special Interest Report* (American Council for Judaism), May–June 1996, p. 2.

9. Thomas L. Friedman, "Land of Life," *New York Times*, November 19, 1995.

10. Quoted in Howard A. Berman, "The Faith of Classical Reform Judaism," in *Issues* (American Council of Judaism), summer 2001, p. 1.

11. Quoted in Chris Hedges, "Separating Spiritual and Political, He Pays a Price: Henry Siegman," *New York Times*, June 13, 2002, p. H33.

12. Mark Glickman, "One Voice against Many: A Biographical Study of Elmer Berger (1948–1968)" (thesis for ordination, Hebrew Union College–Jewish Institute of Religion, 1990), pp. 169–74.

7

THEODOR GASTER
Anthropologist-Matchmaker

N ew York has its own archaeological digs: eighteenth-century slave burial
plots and Revolutionary War meeting houses. The city also houses
anthropologists who can speak the languages of the Fertile Crescent and thus
decipher words written thousands of years earlier.

One such man was my friend Theodor Gaster, a scholar of the old school—
very old. He was one of the first translators of the Dead Sea Scrolls, which
changed the world's knowledge of the wellsprings of Judaism. He authored the
abridgment of Sir James Frazer's classic *The Golden Bough*, the pioneer study
that linked primitive concepts and modes of thought to the institutions and customs they inspired.[1] He traced the evolution of human behavior from the savage
to the civilized through his studies of magic, taboos, sexual practices, supersti-
tion, and wizardry, divining from these the roots of contemporary social, scientific, and religious ideas. Theodor, like Frazer, built a magnificent behavioral
bridge from the past to the present.

Theodor was more than an anthropologist; he mastered twenty-nine languages and dialects—and could be witty in all! I recall one evening at his apartment. Mostly Columbia University professors were present for an informal
supper. Off in one corner sat Theodor and a linguistic specialist exchanging jokes
in Aramaic. They roared at humor no one else in the room could understand.

That was the evening Theodor had invited me with the warning that he was
also expecting Marianne Gutmann, recently divorced, as I was. "But nothing is
intended here," he added quickly. I said I hoped so, because I didn't like marital
prearrangements. (Neither, it turned out, did Marianne.) To prove it, I spent most
of the evening avoiding conversation with, or even a gaze directed to, Ms. Gutmann. Around ten o'clock, as the crowd thinned, we began talking over cake and

coffee. Two hours later, we were still chatting, and only the Gasters remained. Some weeks later, we decided to announce our intention to marry soon afterward. That was forty-five years ago. We have been thankful to Theodor ever since.

That was not my first close encounter with Theodor (spelled without an *e*—he was named by his father, the chief rabbi of England, in honor of Theodor Herzl, founder of modern Zionism). It was a sign of Theodor's singularity, if you will, that he and I became friends while I ran the religious education department of the *anti-Zionist* American Council for Judaism. Theodor's unparalleled scholarship in comparative religions, especially of the Near East, attracted me; at the time, I was creating a young people's curriculum in religious education for schools of Judaism. My work stressed the relationship of Judaism, in all ages, to the civilizations in which it was practiced. In brief, I favored the universal aspects of Judaism, rather than the nationalistic. Theodor was the best authority anywhere on this approach to religion. He had been chief of the Hebraic section in the Library of Congress, curator of the department of Semitic and Egyptian Antiquities in the Wellcome Museum, London, and Fulbright Professor in History of Religions at the University of Rome. Theodor provided fresh views of the history and origins of practices of Judaism. I translated these ideas into stories, pictures, and games for young people of all ages, presented in a weekly magazine and in other texts.

Working with Theodor was at once a graduate-level education and a bout of humor drawn from the same context. He did not spare anyone, including anti-Zionist Jews, who sometimes welcomed his universal approach to Judaism for what he regarded as the wrong reason: an escape from the rigors of Judaism's orthodoxy. But then, he himself had not been a practicing religionist, probably to the discomfort of his father, the chief rabbi.

Theodor was highly skilled in many ways, but not in the art of abiding people he deemed fools—and they were legion. Not because he felt superior, but because he resented time wasted over ideas he regarded as patent folly. He provided lengthy discourse on such "ignorance" with matchless humor. Most of the time he would simply leap to the end of the argument, long before his conversationalist had arrived there, and pronounce the argument false and the issue closed. Most of the time he was absolutely correct, but that did not win friends or even admirers among academic colleagues.

Theodor was a great success on the lecture circuit. His appearances at the Ninety-second Street YMCA in New York attracted sold-out audiences. He brought to life the most abstruse artifacts of the distant past. His audience left feeling it had walked the paths of ancient Babylon or sloshed through the Reed Sea—not the Red Sea. The ancient Israelites, he would show, did not need God to separate the waters of the Red Sea for the escape from Egypt; rather, the geography of the time, as well as the literature, suggested that tall reeds, looking for all the world like a roiling sea, had been passed through by the fleeing horde. Theodor also cited the mistranslation of the ancient writing to restore the "reed" to the metaphoric "sea."

But, as was expected, such fresh insights angered the orthodox scholars and religionists of Christianity as well as Judaism, as well as the academic bureaucrats. I discovered this when Theodor told me he was tired of living the life of an academic outsider. He was writing distinguished books and gaining unanimous accolades for those works, but he could not find a permanent university post. Part of the reason—a small, yet real reason, I believed—was his acerbic personality. It was endlessly humorous and sophisticated in the living room or on the one-night-lecture circuit, but it was probably difficult to abide on a full-time faculty. The truth was, Theodor simply knew too much for most of his academic peers. But perhaps most important, he was regarded as a "Jewish" scholar. He was, of course, much more than that, as his abridgment of Frazer's *Golden Bough* demonstrated.

I recognized his dilemma and tried to help. I persuaded Hays Solis-Cohen to raise some funds to contribute to Columbia University, because Theodor had discovered there was an opening in the Department of Religion. Hays was the head of his family in Philadelphia, whose ancestors were among the first Jewish settlers in the American colonies. Hays, a Sephardic Jew, was a devout religionist who supported literary and philanthropic causes. He was also a partner in one of the leading law firms in his city. Hays provided funds, which I relayed to Columbia University to endow a chair in the Department of Religion, with the understanding that we could not name the scholar to occupy the chair. I accepted this bow to academic freedom; but there was informal understanding that Theodor would be considered for the post.

Ultimately, Theodor Gaster was in fact appointed to the chair in the religion department of Columbia. But Theodor was not happy there; there had never been, and was not then, a "Jewish" scholar in the department. Judaism had always been taught by mostly Protestant academics from their point of view. There was little opportunity in that department to employ Theodor's obvious skills in anthropology, comparative religion, or linguistics. I was disappointed that Theodor had not found a suitable niche at Columbia. Some years later, he left Columbia for a full-time professorship at Fairleigh Dickinson University in New Jersey. Although this was not the Ivy League, Theodor was able to profess with far greater freedom and approbation.

All his life, Theodor Gaster was differently regarded by different observers. Some found him just too difficult to engage. Yet he left behind priceless legacies: his anthropology gave the modern reader easy access to the richest works of human imagination; he restored long-forgotten ideas and relics; and he did this with humor and verve, as well as erudition. Despite his disclaimer, he was also a pretty good matchmaker.

NOTE

1. James George Frazer, *The New Golden Bough*, ed. and with a foreword by Theodor Gaster (New York: Criterion Books, 1959).

8

THE HUNTERS
A Sterling Family's Visit from the Feds

At 3 A.M. on June 7, 1995, federal drug enforcement officers banged on the door of a small frame house off a dirt road in Cavendish, Vermont. They showed a search warrant to William Hunter, aged forty-one, and carted off his five computers, leaving behind three crying children and his wife wakened out of deep sleep.

I have known Will since he was five, one of four children of magnificent parents Edith and Armstrong Hunter, both trained as Unitarian ministers. Will himself is a graduate of Exeter, Yale, and Harvard Law School, a Rhodes scholar at Cambridge, former Vermont state legislator (he was twenty-one when he won his first term), publisher of a weekly newspaper, and—perhaps the reason for that midnight call—lawyer to impoverished clients who paid him in maple syrup, cheese, a tie-dyed cummerbund, and occasional dollars, but not enough to make his annual income more than $20,000. Yet the Feds seemed to think he was laundering drug money.

Everyone in the mountain town of fifteen hundred inhabitants and the surrounding valley stood behind Will Hunter. They told visiting newspaper reporters and CBS network news that Will is chronically overcommitted and a passionate champion of the underdog, and they swore by his honesty and keen intelligence.

I called Edith, Will's mother, the day the lengthy story broke in the *New York Times*. Neither she nor Will knew then where the matter would lead. There was stress. No charge had been filed against Will, but the client the Feds sought had a criminal record. As a lawyer, Will had helped the man set up a real estate purchase. Involved, then, was the ethical and legal question of Will's client relationship with the man. On the humorous side, Edith told me, Will hoped the Feds would do him a favor. They took his computers presumably to examine correspondence with the suspect. But Will had been writing five novels simultaneously. Yes, he was always overcommitted. He was practicing law and publishing a newspaper and the state's law record while also writing novels. He had served as an elected legislator in the Vermont House while publishing his newspaper, had spent half the year in London on a Rhodes scholarship, and, incidentally, obtained a Harvard law degree—all at once!

What favor did he hope the Feds would provide? He had "lost" part of one novel on the hard drive of a computer. He hoped the Feds, searching for felonious correspondence, would find his novel and recover it for him. They did not—nor did they charge him with anything criminal.

Will's nightmare reveals as much about the criminal justice system in Vermont as it does about Will and his family. Drug enforcement people there have short-circuited the constitutional protection of citizens for some time. Too often, they knock on doors with flimsy or no evidence and fish for leads. The agent in charge of Will's raid tried to justify the expedition by saying it was very low-key. He said, "There was no brandishing of weapons, no kicking down of doors." But the heavy knock in the night is traumatic enough, especially for children, awakened to discover the Feds' flashlights shining in their eyes.

That was not the end of Will's nightmare. The Professional Conduct Board of the state bar association investigated Will's service to his clients. Some swore by him; others said he neglected them because of his overcommitment. Will voluntarily relinquished his license to practice law while the committee considered suspending him for three years. He offered an unusual defense: he claimed he had long suffered from attention deficit disorder (ADD). Some chemical anomaly could account for his assuming diverse jobs simultaneously and being constantly self-harassed. "It's been an eye-opening experience to find out why I have been constantly tardy all my life," he said. He was then placed on an antidepressant medication, which has since helped him keep appointments and normalize his life.

While he awaited a final determination by the ethics committee, Will Hunter was publishing two law journals in addition to his weekly newspaper. Indeed, the *Vermont Lawyer*, a monthly, and *Vermont Law Week*, a semimonthly, keep all Vermont lawyers informed about their profession. Even during his hiatus, Will was prominently quoted in a general publication on matters of law. The Feds never pressed charges against him, though two of his former clients are in prison. To resolve the matter and end the strain on his family, though, Will finally agreed to accept a misdemeanor charge.

When Will was six years old, he was familiar with the word *law*, but in a different context. "Do you know what I used to think?" he asked his mother one day then. "I used to think that *law* was a place," he said. "What do you mean, *law*?" Edith asked.

"Well, you know," Will responded. "Someone says he has a sister in Boston and a brother-in-*law*. I used to think *law* was where his brother was, like Boston was where his sister was."

Now Will knows better—about in-laws and about law. Not only what Harvard taught him about fine points of jurisprudence, but about the disparity between justice for rich and poor as well. When Will graduated from law school he had many offers from major law firms; he chose instead to place a wooden shingle on his lawn in the hamlet of Cavendish. The raid by the Feds had shaken Will's faith in the law and even in whether he should fight to continue his law practice. A paralegal who had once worked for Will said after the raid that Will's "big heart" led him to give people a second chance after a past mistake or conviction. Several of his clients had criminal records. "As you can see from what's going on," the former paralegal said, "that's maybe a bad thing for him to do, because some people you just shouldn't give chances to."

Edith Hunter, I believe, tends to share that caution, whether or not she has told Will. But, looking back, it would be difficult to separate that six-year-old Will, thinking through words and human relationships, from forty-one-year-old Will, still questioning all things—overextending, particularly, his compassion for people who need chances.

Will was blessed growing up in a remarkable family. I met Edith first when another extraordinary woman, Sophia Lyon Fahs, invited me to serve on the curriculum committee of the Council of Liberal Churches. The committee met twice a year at the offices of Beacon Press in Boston, which published the religious education series used in Sunday schools of the Unitarians, Congregationalists, Friends, and other liberal groups. I had just finished writing a full K–12 curriculum for Jewish Sunday schools associated with the American Council for Judaism and had also developed a series of books on Judaism that avoided the Jewish nationalism so prominently featured in books then prepared by the mainstream Jewish bureaucracy. Sophia Fahs had heard of my approach and asked whether I would join her group—I was the first Jewish participant.

Mrs. Fahs, nearing her ninetieth year, was widely known as one of the great liberal reformers of religious education in America. She was born in China, where her parents were missionaries. She grew up in a small Ohio town before the turn of the twentieth century and was deeply affected by John Dewey's philosophy of education, as was my longtime friend Sidney Hook (see chap. 20). Whereas Sidney enlarged Dewey's work in the political-action sphere, Sophia Fahs built on Dewey's approach in religious education. Both Sidney and Sophia Fahs took Dewey in new directions.

"John Dewey's philosophy of experiential, exploratory, and inwardly purposeful education," said Mrs. Fahs, "came alive for me, and I became absorbed in the problem of how to adapt this educational philosophy to education in religion." It was a "conversion experience," Edith Hunter would later write in her biography of Sophia Fahs.[1] In 1904 Dewey came to Columbia University to lecture at Teachers College. There Sophia Fahs directly absorbed Dewey's insights gleaned partly from the new science of psychology.

Dewey believed that the school should be an instrument for improving the society. Today, as in the past, schools are charged with being conveyors of a society's values and traditions, but in an increasingly multicultural America the traditions to be conveyed are unsettled and confusing. In this state of flux, with growing numbers of children virtually parentless, schools are also conceived as guard posts from the dangers of the cities. Dewey argued against dividing students into "poor" to be trained for utilitarian tasks and "rich" to be given a liberal education.

He fostered universal education in the matters of living together. That was the democratic spirit of education, Dewey argued. The basis for this education, said Dewey, was in the child's natural impulse to conversation. This presupposed, of course, the openness of the child to engage in something other than destructive "street" action, which employed weapons instead of words.

Edith Hunter followed in Sophia Fahs's tradition, not only in curriculum meetings but in the books Edith wrote in her own style as a writer and educator for children. It was perhaps no accident that among Edith's most successful books was *Conversations with Children*; in it she borrowed extensively from conversations with her own four children.[2]

"What a miracle it is to be able to convey our thoughts, our feelings, our wonderings to other persons in conversation," Edith wrote. "To be able to wonder together about aspects of human experience that have perplexed other thoughtful growing persons—all of these are miracles too easily taken for granted." And to converse with children is an added boon, she pointed out—to teach religion through the give-and-take of conversation has been used by Buddha, Socrates, and Jesus, among others. You never know where conversation may lead: sometimes to history and even politics—and law. Edith described to me this conversation with Will. Riding in a car, they

> had passed several statues relating to the Revolutionary War, and he had asked many questions. . . . I had made a not very successful—but, I felt, necessary—attempt to clarify the [political] power situation that existed about 1775. Nothing had been said for some time. Then with a big sigh it came out:
>
> "You know, even us, way down now," said Will, then barely six, "if it hadn't been for those men who didn't want to be for kings, we wouldn't have our freedom now."

Edith's book provided fifty themes for conversations with children that raise ethical, scientific, human-relationship, and other questions that are fundamental to liberal religious consideration.

From my first hour at the Beacon Press curricular meetings I gravitated toward Edith. We read and critiqued scores of manuscripts for publication by Beacon. Almost as a courtesy, my name appears in the acknowledgments of many of these authors, but my role was truly small; Edith's was central. Indeed, she was also a prolific writer for popular magazines as well as books.

Army and Edith were my friends for more than forty years. Their lives, together with their children and grandchildren and with their community, are the clearest model of an intensely ethical and unselfish daily experience. Soon after we met, they moved from Milford, New Hampshire, to a rambling farm house in Weathersfield, Vermont, that had been a family homestead for generations. The Hunters produced crops for their own year-round consumption and raised pigs to barter for milk and other basics they could not grow. The weather-beaten house was extended as the family grew, and the barn was converted for additional rooms, then to house the Hunter Press.

The press was not just a journeyman print shop, as so many others. But in the American colonial tradition, where printers such as Benjamin Franklin became journalists and indeed educators of the democratic polity, Army and Edith became the publishers of the *Weathersfield Weekly*—the political educator and soul of the town and surrounding community. In that same spirit, Will Hunter later created the *Black River Tribune*, a weekly in Ludlow, a few miles beyond Weathersfield.

Will and my son David shared time at the *Weathersfield Weekly*. David was seventeen, a year younger than Will. David described that summer of 1971 in a letter (or was it a contract?) he wrote to Army: "I would be very glad to work a half-day, each day, without salary for the purpose of learning the printing business, under Will's supervision. I also understand that I can work the rest of each day doing odd-jobs, and carpentry for a salary. . . . I am looking forward to this summer, and I hope all goes well in the printing business."

In visiting foreign countries and their journalists I always admire the courage and stamina it takes for small presses to pioneer in unlikely environments. Sometimes governments are hostile; often economics cannot sustain the drive to write and publish. The *Weathersfield Weekly*, in a relatively poor town of fifteen hundred, made its way for fifteen years because of the indomitable spirit of Edith and Army Hunter. I had read their more than 750 issues and was moved to recommend to the Pulitzer Prize board of Columbia University that it consider the weekly for some recognition. The paper was about to shut down. I had no greater success in this nomination than many years later when I formally nominated Barbara Crossette of the *New York Times* for a Pulitzer. (The *Times*'s foreign desk undermined Barbara's nomination then, but that's another story.)

Today, the *Weathersfield Weekly* could be considered a model for what is now projected as "civic" or "public" journalism. Debates over this model rage at press-association and editors' meetings. Critics ask, how does public journalism differ from old-style coverage of community events or civic concerns? One answer: "old-style" coverage was generally reactive; editors generally waited until local politicians or civic leaders placed an issue on the community's agenda. Not always—editorials sometimes raised questions that aroused broader interest. But the new public journalism would place the press in a more proactive mode. Newspapers and broadcasters would launch campaigns to educate the public to basic changes and new ways of examining old problems. A thin line would be drawn between factual, "objective" coverage and space or time given to arouse fresh concerns or solutions of community problems.

The *Weathersfield Weekly* successfully pursued this course. It displayed "meritorious public service," a characterization the Pulitzer committee should have applied but didn't.

The *Weekly* brought together people from across the ridge, and from the several schools and granges, from the six churches—and wove them into an understanding community. That had never existed in the three-hundred-year history of the region. Indeed, the *Weekly* regularly described the history and traditions of the local families and their landmarks. People came to know one another as more than neighbors, as integral parts of a distinct community—not one divided many ways by acts of postal employees and telephone linesmen.

The *Weekly* was neighborly conversation. It was as much a religious experience in the liberal interpretation of theology as Edith's conversing with children about ethical issues and human interaction. The *Weekly* was also good journalism, by any interpretation.

News in the *Weekly* was written mainly by Edith and an assistant who covered nearly all meetings. Army also found writing talent among readers. As a consequence, some received recognition and even stature among the citizenry.

In 1994, nearing the age of seventy-five, Edith decided to run for a seat in the Vermont House of Representatives. Will had already served six years in the House and four years in the Senate. This would be the state's first mother-son legislative tandem on record. She was then a justice of the peace and a school board member. Edith said she sought a seat in the legislature because "I don't want to be represented by someone [i.e., her opponent] who thinks Rush Limbaugh is a great fellow." Edith favored funding education through income rather than property taxes; called for tax-supported, universal public health insurance modeled on Medicare; and favored tax support for small businesses to aid the economy. She opposed plans to build a brewery in Weathersfield, saying the plant should be placed in Claremont "where things are already ruined."

Perhaps the cruelest cut made during the campaign was the published "charge" that Edith probably "does the majority of her shopping . . . where there are a plethora of shops, low prices, and no sales tax." The attack was answered by a supporter who wrote, "This woman doesn't shop! She has never set foot in a Wal-Mart or even Kmart. She grows all her own vegetables, buys milk and meat from a neighboring farmer, and trades with local business wherever possible. Her husband buys staple groceries in Windsor."

The morning of the election, Army later reported, "Edith and I woke up wishing to tell the other the same thing: that we felt she would spend the winter at home and not be going to Montpelier to represent our town and neighboring Cavendish in the Vermont House." Both got their wish. The national Republican landslide reached to Weathersfield. Army concluded, "The days are full and good."

Shortly before he stopped publishing the *Weekly*, Army wrote, "We've had a minimum of ads. Making money was not our goal; providing information about town affairs was. We've felt that the basis of our political system is an informed electorate. We have tried to strengthen that basis. We know that when we stop publishing it will be impossible—yes, impossible!—for Weathersfielders to know what they have come to want to know week after week about their town and their neighbors and their elected and appointed leaders."

One Weathersfielder commented on what would be missed when the *Weekly* stopped printing. "It's scary," he wrote. "If our town officials act the way they do under press scrutiny, how will they act when there's no press scrutiny?" That question may be applied to every level of American society, right up to Capitol Hill and the White House. Making money was not Will Hunter's goal either; making justice was.

And writing the history of one's own place in the world: that is a major avocation of Edith Hunter. At eighty-three, she appeared frequently as a historian-commentator on Vermont Public Radio. For a Vermont magazine, Edith described her skiing around the ten-acre field on which the Hunter farm and house stand. "At the far edge of the white expanse the woods begin," she writes, "and beyond the woods looms our great monadnock, Mount Ascutney. As always when I stand in that field I think of all those who have stood where I stand and have looked up at that mountain. Surely generations of Native Americans snow-shoed here. Surely they too marveled at the sight of this 'peaked mountain with steep sides,' a definition for the Algonquin word 'cas-cadnack,' from which some think the word 'Ascutney' is derived."

Others stood there, Edith recalls. Submit Hawks Grout with her three small children were taken captive on July 27, 1755, by French and Indians. They journeyed along the Black River into Weathersfield and on into Canada. Four years later, Submit was ransomed by her husband Hilkiah Gout. And in 1722 the family settled by the Black River in Weathersfield. Edith writes, "What thoughts must have gone through [Submit's] mind whenever she lifted her eyes to Mount Ascutney!"

When the Revolutionary War hero the Marquis de Lafayette made a grand tour of the United States in 1825 some local patriots started to build a road up the side of "Ash-Cutney Mountain" to provide Lafayette with a better view of the scenic wonder. Edith is not certain the road was ever completed. But she is sure that "Lafayette at least saw Mount Ascutney before being greeted by five thousand people in [nearby] Windsor."

She adds, "After skiing across the field to the stone wall, I turn and, traveling in my own tracks, start back in the direction of our house. It is a lovely sight—the large, white, south-facing Federal-style house with green shutters, huge barns east of it, and open fields to the south, east, and north."

The first house on the land was built between 1788 and 1800. Near the house are two thousand-year-old maples. Edith knows the long history of the people of Weathersfield, as well as its tree and the boulders deposited twenty thousand years ago. She has been president of the Weathersfield Historical Society and takes children on history walks.

Some years ago, Edith was introduced by a Brownie leader who said, "Mrs. Hunter is going to tell us about Weathersfield history." One little girl looked at Edith with awe and asked, "Was she there?" Edith paused a moment and then said, "Yes, and so are you."

And so is her husband, Armstrong, buried since 1999 under a tree facing an ample flowing field.

NOTES

1. Edith F. Hunter, *Sophia Lyons Fahs: A Biography* (Boston: Beacon Press, 1966), p. 62.

2. Edith F. Hunter, *Conversations with Children* (Boston: Beacon Press, 1961).

9

DANIEL PATRICK MOYNIHAN

The "Lone Ranger" and the "Tiger"

As I arrived at Freedom House in 1967, one board member was slated to remain one of the longest-lasting friends of the organization—on and off the board of trustees: Daniel Patrick Moynihan.

I had admired Pat since he was hired by Leo Cherne in the 1950s to serve on the International Rescue Committee (IRC). Leo had recommended me for the post at Freedom House. When he worked for Leo, Pat was still completing his PhD at Tufts's Fletcher School of Law and Diplomacy. Leo also employed William Casey. Pat was to become domestic advisor to presidents, Bill the controversial head of the Central Intelligence Agency (CIA), among other key posts. Their paths would cross many times; but Pat would go on to considerable achievement in the academic world, while keeping his hand in New York and national politics. He parlayed this combination into the ambassadorship to the United Nations and then to India before his repeated election to the U.S. Senate. Wherever he served, Pat was his own man, a lone ranger.

When I became director Pat had a bad attendance record, so I asked him to leave the board. He did, without rancor. When he went to Washington in 1969 as counselor to the president we invited him back on the board. By then, the Vietnam War had heated up—the Tet Offensive against Saigon and many other U.S.-"protected" areas in the south had shaken American support for the conflict. We sought a middle course for Freedom House. We did not take positions on the military aspect of the war but rather on the dangerous divisions within American society. Pat, I felt, was fashioning his own positions then on such a policy. He was welcomed back aboard.

But his less than complete support for a military expansion of the war disturbed many of his old-time friends—particularly Norman Podhoretz of *Com-*

mentary magazine and Irving Kristol, the father of neoconservatism, two who shared much of Pat's sociopolitical background in New York.

Pat's analysis of American society, particularly race relations and the problems of black citizens, also meshed well with Freedom House's view on that nettlesome subject. His sound academic analysis of the black family structure pointed out the deterioration of the two-parent standard, with the consequent lowering of educational and employment possibilities for children and dangers ahead for coming generations. He advised President Nixon that this deepening sociological problem could be ameliorated only in small part by government but had to be confronted by black society itself.

Pat used the phrase "benign neglect" to describe his recommendation for lesser rather than massive governmental action to address the black societal problem. Pat was immediately, viciously attacked by black organizational bureaucrats. The "benign" response—an understanding of and commiseration with a deep problem that mainly defied governmental solutions—was ignored. "Neglect" was the word that demonized Pat for years to come. The only black leader who supported Pat's analysis was Bayard Rustin (see chap. 18 and appendix C), who later joined the Freedom House board. Bayard would try unsuccessfully to persuade Martin Luther King, Jesse Jackson, and others to address the deteriorating family structure of their own people. Jackson did— thirty years later!

After these broad attacks, Pat left the Nixon cabinet and became ambassador to India. I visited Delhi in 1974 while Pat and his wife, Liz, occupied the U.S. embassy there, and I gave him an answer I still regret. I had just completed a week-long seminar in Saigon, South Vietnam. With north-south fighting intensifying, and Saigon passing laws further restricting the press, the U.S. State Department sent me to discuss with Vietnamese journalists the fundamentals of a free press (see chap. 33).

After I left Vietnam shortly before its collapse, I spent some time in Thailand and then went on to India for a short visit. I phoned Pat at the embassy. He seemed glad to know I was in Delhi, but he was about to leave on an official mission and wouldn't return before I left the country. Then he broke off and said, "Len, how about joining me? I'm going up to Bhutan to represent the United States at a formal installation. It will be a very colorful affair." Adding another week to the trip and the thought of recasting my itinerary overtook my good sense. I declined to accompany Pat—and have regretted it ever since.

Pat returned to the States soon after and became U.S. ambassador to the United Nations. Several times he asked me to sit in with him during heated debates. Leonard Garment, later to be Richard Nixon's legal counsel to the very last moment of his presidency (Leonard advised Nixon to resign), was at Pat's side at the UN. Pat made many stirring speeches advancing U.S. foreign policy, mostly defending it from onslaughts by the Soviets, who were bolstered by numerous third world delegates. These were the dark days of the Cold War. One of Pat's chief props was the Map of Freedom I had devised; it showed the numerous not-free countries in black, the as-numerous partially free countries in gray, and the one-third minority of free countries in white. Pat would point out that most countries attacking American policy were themselves in the not-free or partly free categories. They were, he would point out, hardly credible spokesmen for human rights or political freedom.

When asked for specifics at press conferences, he would say, "Call Leonard Sussman at Freedom House." Our phones would ring repeatedly. I tried to match our statistics with Pat's high rhetoric. Pat advanced our political-rights survey as well as his own policy objectives. He once called me "Tiger," but I never understood why.

Pat has been extensively reported and caricatured since he was a professor at MIT and Harvard—even earlier, when he coauthored *Beyond the Melting Pot* (1963). The book asserted that the Jewish and Irish immigrants and their descendents were not, as had been assumed, "melting" into an assimilated New York City but instead were retaining many of their ethnic loyalties and habits.[1] I had not accepted this conclusion as inevitable for all time, though the book—just as Pat's "benign neglect" later—focused realities seldom brought to public attention. I rather believed that *integration*—not immediate *assimilation*—of diverse groups was under way and that this process was producing a new social structure with its own new loyalties and habits. Bagels, which had been the traditional bread of Jews on the Lower East Side, had indeed been adopted by the non-Jewish upper crust uptown. From there, bagels criss-crossed the nation to become a national food (particularly on Sundays with cream cheese and lox— both no longer "ethnic"). More definitively, the rate of interreligious and interracial marriages was heading for new highs. Stand-pat conservatives in all religions would bemoan the statistics, but the trend proceeded. Integration was happening, melting pot or no. The endeavor to stem the integrationist tide by ethnically oriented *political* action did more than stress laudable religious, social, or musical traditions; such efforts tended to pit racial, religious, and nationality groups against one another. This was starkly visible in the growing antipathy between black and Jewish groups.

Black extremists targeted Jewish landlords and businessmen as the cause of economic decline in black "ghettos" (the very word was coined in older times to describe far more severe restrictions and ultimately physical attacks on Jews in many European cities). Jewish organizations, meanwhile, were publicly expending large resources and political action to support the military and political objectives of the state of Israel. The fact that many Jewish groups in the 1950s had strongly opposed black-segregation laws seemed to have been forgotten. In the 1970s and 1980s, black extremists exploited anger over continuing racial inequalities—economic and social—to turn the black underclass against the still-rising Jewish middle class.

The real culprit, as Pat Moynihan and Bayard Rustin would point out, was the breakdown of the black family and the prevalence of black children having babies, whose fathers were disappearing. As sober analysts would also point out, this was not a black problem alone. Similar trends were apparent among poor whites. It took the bitter debates in 1995 over changing the beleaguered welfare system to raise this fundamental problem to national attention—some thirty years after Pat spotted this dangerous undermining of America's social structure.

Lewis H. Lapham in *Harper's* once provided Pat's description of his own political prowess. Pat undervalued his own expertise while describing his Washington colleagues all too accurately. Lapham recalled a conversation with Pat while both waited to perform on a radio talk show:

> Moynihan observed that no politician could possibly know or understand everything that his audiences expect him to know or understand. He ran through a long list of subjects on which he was supposed to be fully and definitively informed—education, health care, foreign policy, highway construction, the multiplication of cancer cells—and then he laughed at the absurdity of the proposition. "The thing is impossible," he said, "but I'm not allowed to admit that it's impossible. If the people guessed how little their rulers know, they might become frightened."
>
> . . . Government becomes representative in the theatrical, not the constitutional, sense of the word. "It's like a fourth-grade Christmas play," Moynihan said. "The little boy comes onstage wearing a crown of paper stars and saying that he's the north wind. I do the same thing when I stand in front of a microphone and answer questions about the intelligence services or what happened in the Cold War."
>
> He laughed again, more merrily than before, and when he was called into the studio, he paused at the doorway to strike a theatrical pose. Looking over his shoulder, he said, "Enter the north wind."[2]

NOTES

1. See Daniel Patrick Moynihan and Nathan Glazer, *Beyond the Melting Pot* (Cambridge, MA: MIT Press, 1970).

2. Lewis H. Lapham, "Notebook: Washington Phrase Book," *Harper's*, October 1993, p. 11.

10

FULBRIGHT'S "ACCIDENTS"

A member of the U.S. Foreign Scholarship Board asked me to name three persons who might examine the Fulbright exchange program and write a book-length critique. I provided three names and added that the assignment interested me. "We were hoping you'd say that," came the reply. I got the year-long job myself, which required round-the-world travel, as well as some one hundred lengthy interviews in the United States and abroad. I met top officials, leading businessmen, and distinguished educators in many places.[1]

Mention the name Fulbright and you get widely mixed reactions. Cold Warriors of the Vietnam era regarded Senator Fulbright as an unconscionable turncoat. He had lent his prestige as chairman of the Senate Foreign Relations Committee to support the Tonkin Gulf resolution, which President Lyndon Johnson interpreted as enlarging his war powers. Fulbright later used that same Senate post to attack the American role in the war and especially the administration's conduct, which he termed "arrogant." Johnson severely cut the Fulbright scholarship-exchange program. The senator told me that Johnson probably said, "Oh, well, that's Fulbright's—no good anyway." Actually, Fulbright was probably too kind; the president more likely sputtered some unprintable order to his intellectual-in-residence Charles Frankel (see chap. 21). And much against his own judgment, Charles passed on the order.

But then there are some two hundred thousand scholars—more than half from 130 other countries—who say their lives were unalterably improved because they received Fulbright scholarships. Scores of scholarship recipients overseas and across the United States told me that their admiration for Bill Fulbright—at that time, 1991, still a living idol—was limitless. My book about the history of the Fulbright program, I said, was favorably biased but not pie-in-the-sky.

That was not the whole story about my relationship to Bill Fulbright, though my earlier contact did not influence the book. As I was about to leave the army in 1945 I took an exam for the Foreign Service; I was attracted by the opportunity to serve overseas in a cultural affairs role. Such assignments were beginning to appear in occupied Germany and, I assumed, eventually Japan. Such thoughts were ended, however, by the offer from Luis Muñoz Marin to open the Puerto Rico government's information office in New York. It was, after all, my hometown, and I would be taking to it the expertise I had acquired during four years in Puerto Rico. I never lost interest, however, in U.S. educational and cultural programs abroad.

Nor did I forget Senator Fulbright. As chairman of the Senate Foreign Relations Committee he held protracted inquiries into evasions of the Foreign Agents Registration Act. In the mid-1950s, I asked him to come to New York to address the American Council for Judaism (ACJ), for which I had devised a lecture program. Other speakers included Norman Thomas, the Socialist leader, and Dr. Bayard Dodge, president of the American University at Beirut. The ACJ was dedicated to separating Judaism from Jewish nationalism (Zionism; see chap. 6). The Zionist movement had lobbying arms in the United States that operated as religious or philanthropic entities but had outright military or political objectives and activities. In this regard, it seemed appropriate for Fulbright to discuss the parameters of the Foreign Agents Registration Act. He did this rather circumspectly and served a useful purpose.

The young congressman from Arkansas who was an ardent military interventionist in 1940 had intrigued me. He had been a strong supporter of William Allen White's Committee to Defend America by Aiding the Allies, a committee that evolved as Freedom House. With the war still on, this obscure congressman had secured passage of a resolution calling for the creation of, and U.S. membership in, a United Nations organization.

Bill Fulbright found that the use of legislative power came easily to him. He would try a new tack. In 1945, a freshman again, this time in the U.S. Senate, he would initiate an intellectual exchange program for the United States. Years later, Bill Fulbright would tell me how he created the Fulbright program. Here is how our interview went in his law office early in 1991:

What started you down the road to the "Fulbrights"?
Basically responsible for the Fulbrights was my own Rhodes scholarship in 1925. Without it, I never would have been here in Washington. I came from [Sumner, Missouri,] a little village in the Ozarks, to Fayetteville. At that time it was a town of five thousand, quite remote from the big world. The only way you could get out or in was on the railroad. It was lovely. I liked it, but I didn't know anything else—I hadn't been to places like New York or San Francisco. I played football at the University of Arkansas, and we would go to Texas. That's about all. I hadn't seen the world, but I never thought I was deprived. We first lived on

a farm and then my father moved into town, a little town. I had no history except Fayetteville.

But you put no emphasis on sports in the Fulbright scholarships, as did Rhodes.
I didn't attempt to lay down the details. Rhodes had set three qualifications. Leadership was one. Another was sports, and that's the reason I got it. There were several applicants in my year who had academic standing as good or better than mine. None of them had the combination and football! [Fulbright was a B student.]

What made you think of creating academic scholarships?
I was looking for potential political leaders. I was in politics, and the inspiration came from World War II and the nuclear bombings. The idea was how to avoid war in the future. No matter what the reason for war, you've got to settle it some other way. There's no way to survive nuclear bombs. I don't know what this government is thinking about, buying more arms. It's stupid: exhausting the country's money, the biggest debt in the world. It's disgraceful.

To give you an example, take Alexander Yakovlev, adviser to Mikhail Gorbachev in the Soviet Union. Yakovlev had a scholarship [to study the New Deal at Columbia University in 1959]. There's no doubt he has had an influence on Mr. Gorbachev. [Yakovlev is credited with having persuaded Gorbachev to release human rights activist and physicist Andrei Sakharov from internal exile.] Yakovlev understands that the United States, while it challenges and sounds pretty ominous, and even attacks little countries like Grenada . . . I'm sure Yakovlev tells Gorbachev, "Oh, yeah, they look big but they're not going to attack us. They may be stupid, but they're not that stupid; so you can afford to cut down [armaments] and change our approach." Which I think is a substantial reason why Gorbachev changed his approach in our relationship. I think that's a very concrete result of Mr. Yakovlev's influence. He's one of the few people who can say to Gorbachev, "Look, I've lived in that country. They're a peculiar people. They're very conceited and they talk big, but they're not going to attack you." We have done stupid things but we haven't been so stupid as to attack the Soviet Union. We got into both world wars late, we didn't really challenge anyone, we didn't initiate the wars.

My own experience in the Rhodes scholarship opened my eyes. The idea that people you meet abroad are somehow different, and enemies, is dissipated. You can't believe they're bad people. I had the same feeling about Russians. I went out of my way to get acquainted with Anatolyi P. Dubrynin, the Soviet ambassador. Isolationism may have been a fine idea for Americans until the invention of radio, the airplane, and nuclear weapons. We could isolate ourselves from the effects of wars. Young Americans and young Russians or Englishmen who come here will be leaders and will develop a negative attitude toward war. It doesn't mean you love each other, but you know war is no longer the right way to solve problems. I still think that has validity. I like to think that Mr. Yakovlev and the others have contributed to that idea.

Did being a college president generate the Fulbrights?

I was a professor and became college president briefly. I was fired by the governor because he wanted to get back at my mother, who ran the local newspaper; she had attacked the governor. I ran for Congress and then the Senate against the governor. So I got into politics purely by accident. Politics is one of the most interesting activities you can have; you're dealing with people.

How did you use politics to design the Fulbrights?

I introduced the first bill in September 1945, just a few weeks after we had dropped the bomb over Hiroshima. Going in with this bill was another opportunity to do something for peace. I had already responded in my resolution to create the United Nations. There was no opposition to my bill on the scholarships. They didn't have any idea what it was about, and they didn't provide any appropriation. The argument I made was, "Look, for World War I debts you got nothing. In 1933, you just wrote off those big debts. Now, we can at least get something. They could at least take our students and let them go to their schools." And that's all the bill provided, just authority to use credits. Appropriations came later, after the scheme proved itself and people could see it was a good thing.

You didn't mention your peace motive, or even "mutual understanding"?

I was very conscious of both. But Congress was very sensitive, and I was advised to get the bill through without getting it bogged down in a lot of controversy. The administration sent up a bill proposing ways to dispose of leftover U.S. wartime properties in Europe. I simply attached my amendment to it. President Truman's attention wasn't focused on my bill. I wouldn't know what was in his mind. I brought the bill out at five o'clock under the unanimous-consent procedure. Normally both parties have just a few members present. If nobody opposes a bill it passes without objection. If I had not been very careful the bill might have been destroyed in a controversy. In 1945 we were a very isolationist country. Six months later, in the hall one day, I saw old man [Kenneth] McKellar, senator from Tennessee, who was chairman of the Appropriations Committee. He looked upon me as an upstart. "Young man," he said, "that measure you had is a very dangerous bill. If I'd a-known about it I would have opposed that." He said, "Don't you know it's very dangerous to send our fine young boys and girls abroad and expose them to those foreign isms?"

Did the program proceed as you had envisioned?

It did, until 1965. Then Lyndon Johnson fell out with me over the Vietnam War and—I can't say whether he called attention—anyway, they cut back the Fulbright program severely, from about six thousand grants a year to about two thousand. And the appropriation then was still very small. I can't help but think he said, "Oh, well, that's Fulbright's—no good anyway." He wasn't particularly interested in the program.

If the program is nonpolitical, is it in the national interest?

Yes, it's in the long-term national interest, not in the immediate national interest to influence our policies today with the [former] Soviet Union or anybody else. That's why it's so difficult to explain to congressmen. They can't afford to be concerned about what it's going to be like ten, twenty years from now. You see the program is more than forty years old, and you're just beginning to see an effect; just now do I recognize people like Yakovlev. It takes so long— but I still regard the program as political. It has political influence. It will enable people to find a way to avoid war; that's its main purpose. When I was young I had a little car and used to drive some students who were in the ROTC (Reserve Officer Training Corps). That impressed me very much, the future of warfare—I didn't like it—friends could get killed, you know. In the long run there are political implications in educating bright, young people that war is not an alternative.

People speak of getting "a Fulbright." How do you feel about "Fulbright" becoming a common noun?

I've gotten used to it. In politics you are subjected to all kinds of criticism as well as praise. And after you've been in politics for thirty years these personal things don't affect you one way or the other. But, yes, I like to be associated with this sort of thing—that's true.

The interview ended when Senator Fulbright's new, much younger wife arrived with some bundles. He hopped to his feet to assist her, his eyes glowing. They exchanged a few pleasantries, and I left them.

Just months earlier, Harriet Mayer married Bill Fulbright, who was eighty-six at the time; his wife of many years had died several years before. The new Mrs. Fulbright was director of the Fulbright Association, the group of former holders of a "Fulbright." She resigned when she married Bill, saying, "I've got my Fulbright!"

NOTE

1. See Leonard R. Sussman, *The Culture of Freedom: The Small World of Fulbright Scholars* (Lanham, MD: Rowman and Littlefield, 1992).

11

KHAKI AND BLONDE

There is another kind of "passion for freedom"; the reader may decide whether this story belongs with the rest.

Prior to a visit to a Central American insurgency in 1984, I was standing at a pay phone near the boarding gate to the shuttle to Washington. The passenger assembly, late Friday evening, was small and almost silent. I was talking to Marianne about the trip south when she worried again about security. To change the subject, I said almost plaintively, "I really do *miss* those khaki slacks." (They had disappeared the month before when I needed them in Nigeria.)

As I said that, a tall, striking blonde at the phone beside me swung her head toward me and smiled most engagingly. In the quiet room my complaint had rung clear. So did *her* brief phone conversation:

"This is Cindy. I'm on the eight o'clock."

She hung up the phone, sat down, and took out half-finished needlepoint and began working the needle.

My phone conversation ended.

"Would you believe they wouldn't let me on a plane to L.A. last week until I sheathed my needle?"

I believed it and admired her needlepoint; it was an intricate Chinese dragon in four oranges and yellow.

"Too bad about your khaki slacks," she said, swinging her shoulder-length hair out of the way of the needle.

I assured her I was not as bereft as I may have sounded and was instead thankful to have avoided the Friday night traffic snarl the radio was reporting. We found we both had taxi owner-drivers who used good judgment in missing the tie-up.

That led to job categories. Hers was modeling and acting. She modeled swimsuits and ski clothes.

"When might I have seen you?" I asked.

"I recently completed two films that will appear this fall on Playboy cable. One is a mystery and the other is for the high school set."

Sometimes, she said, she does posters that sell for $25 each. "I did a charming one in a yellow bikini, down on one knee, with orange sky in a beautiful setting. It was a pretty picture," she said, "but some jerk said to the photographer, 'Why don't you get someone with larger breasts?'"

She made a falsely deprecating gesture with her lips and jaw, tossing her hair back out of the way of the needlepoint in her lap.

Our flight was called, and we took seats together in the half-empty plane.

"Tell me, Mr. Khaki Pants," she asked, "What shall I call you?" I told her, but I think she had already seen the answer on my American Express card, for she asked, "Why don't you get a gold card?"

I said that was the same question my wife had asked me the night before. "I see no value in it," I answered. "They charge you $25 more for privileges I don't need."

"But it impresses blonde models," she replied.

I said I didn't like to rely on a card—but I let the sentence drift off. It had begun to sound misleading. "My younger son is interested in the theater," I said.

She seemed interested: "Good, but what does his father think? Mine was disappointed," she added. "I was making twice as much at IBM as I do now with two agents. But I won't give it up. I came to New York from Georgetown, and Daddy gave me a week, then a month. That was two years ago. And now I won't quit until I get an Oscar—probably at age 42."

I said that was a long way off.

"No, only twenty years."

"You'll be married by then."

"I'm not in a hurry. And I won't live with anyone before I marry. Not me. Lenny wants me to. He's my old boyfriend in Bethesda. He asked me to marry him three times. But he won't leave Bethesda."

"Why?"

"His friends are there. His job is there. If we can't settle our first disagreement how can we marry?"

"Have you lived anywhere but Georgetown (where she went to college) and New York?"

"Yes, for several years I lived in the Seychelles, when Dad was the naval commander in charge of the U.S. satellite station. He's retired now, at Annapolis, but he has a dream house, still, in the Seychelles."

I said I always wanted to visit there. And after asking me about Freedom House it was natural for her to ask whether we rated political rights in the now-sovereign Seychelles. We do: "partly free."

The forty-minute trip was almost over.

"Well, goodbye, Mr. Khaki Pants," said Cindy, as we walked off—I to the baggage-collector, and she to the man who would meet her.

She was off—to Bethesda.

As she said, whirling her hair over her coat collar, "It's time for my fix. There's something to be said for regularity."

Now, about that gold card . . .

PART TWO

WALKS IN THE WORLD

12

THE NOT-SO-SMALL WORLD OF ITHIEL POOL

S everal mornings each week, as I walk from my home to my office, my trail leaves the Bowery, passes east of Chinatown, and heads down Water Street toward the foot of Manhattan. I pass Oliver Street, where New York State governor Alfred E. Smith was born—the man who projected Franklin D. Roosevelt into presidential politics after Smith lost the White House race, mainly because he was Catholic. A plaque over a church school tells the world that has forgotten Al Smith—and his distinctive brown derby hat—that the governor's only formal education was in this small elementary school run by nuns. Al Smith led the nation's most important state, created a national slogan for politicians of his day—"Let's look at the record!"—and gave Herbert Hoover a run for the presidency, just before the Great Depression wiped Hoover from office and made way for Roosevelt's New Deal and a social revolution that lasted until 1995. (In that year, under a Democratic president and a Republican Congress, the rollback of earlier social legislation gained momentum.)

As I walk through Al Smith's neighborhood, just twenty strides from St. James Place, there is an undistinguished break in the building line. It is a triangular plot enclosed by a high iron fence. Behind it are crumbling markers and headstones. Aged trees make grassy knolls impossible. There is a semblance of neatness amid the inevitable decay. A metal plaque declares this the first cemetery of Shearith Israel, the Spanish and Portuguese synagogue. The congregation for more than a century has been housed on Central Park West. The small cemetery, one of the oldest landmarks in Manhattan, was established in 1656 by some of the first settlers. Nearly all the city's population lived south along the waterfronts. The cemetery was then on the outskirts of town. The few Jews in the city were mainly Ashkenazic, from Western Europe, but there was a lively Sephardic

(Spanish-Portuguese) group, for whom the synagogue and the cemetery were as important as life and death. "These individuals," says Robert Marc Angel, "laid the foundation of Jewish life not only in their city, but in this country."[1]

As a young man, I visited Shearith Israel occasionally and met its distinguished rabbi, David de Sola Pool. He stood out from the Reform rabbinate by his Sephardic dress and more conservative theology. He converted that religious conservatism into a social credo that met the needs of perilous Depression days. Rabbi Pool was the national spokesman for Sephardic Judaism in America. His wife, Tamar, was a granddaughter of the early Jewish settlers in modern Palestine. She came to the United States in 1904, earned a degree from Hunter College, a traveling fellowship to the University of Paris, and married David ten years later. Meanwhile, he had earned degrees at the University of London and a PhD from the University of Heidelberg. By 1917 he was a member of Herbert Hoover's food conservation staff. Their first child was Ithiel, with whom I was to have an eminently satisfying relationship.

Ithiel de Sola Pool comes to mind, first sadly and then joyously, every time I pass that rundown triangular oasis of stone markers on an unlikely street in Chinatown. He died of cancer in 1984. For several years, knowing death was imminent, he intensified his work with students and colleagues at the Massachusetts Institute of Technology. He wrote speedily and incisively to summarize a lifetime of diverse interests. Ithiel was the consummate Renaissance scholar. During the fiery days of campus disorders, I would discuss with him the protection of the *idea* of the university and academic responsibility amid revolutionary change. Ithiel was among the scholars I organized as the International Council on the Future of the University. We took him to Venice as a major participant in one of several historic meetings.

Or we would discuss the role of the scholar functioning "in the national interest" during the Cold War. That meant supplying academic intelligence to national policy-makers. They needed to know how the latest scientific and technological developments could be employed to bolster national defense. It was a time of largely unknowable danger—impractical idealists and Communist apologists notwithstanding. Was engagement a proper role for scholars? Ithiel thought so; some colleagues did not. Given the vital challenges of the time, I shared Ithiel's view.

His political-intelligence interests began in World War II and continued for some time. But there was another side to Ithiel's remarkable career, one that came to be our point of contact in his last years. Vehement critics felt that Ithiel subordinated scholarship to national policy. On the contrary, he believed in the liberating potential of science and technology—particularly information-flow technology—and did not trust political leaders to deal wisely with such vital channels of a democratic society. This conviction led me back to Ithiel, as I related new communication technology to the enhancement of democratic systems.

At the time, I was writing *Power, the Press and the Technology of Freedom:*

The Coming Age of ISDN.[2] Ithiel had already written definitive articles on this theme and was working on his memoirs, which were published posthumously (under Eli M. Noam's editorial effort) as *Technologies without Boundaries: On Telecommunications in a Global Age.*[3] Though my book appeared first, I clearly owed a debt to Ithiel for the guidance he provided in earlier writings; for example, his small book on the history of the telephone.[4] I read this as a precursor of problems posed by the impact of government on communication technology in our revolutionary age of global telecommunication. Even in a free society, governments first control new technology such as the telephone; in the United States, requiring the phone company to serve distant, unprofitable customers in return for the right to become a government-approved monopoly. And, moreover, to serve as a common carrier, telephone companies must transmit every conversation without interfering with the content of messages. This precedent was set in the nineteenth century, when the United States gave subsidies to the building of privately owned railroads: they had to carry everyone's freight or passengers without interference. This policy was applied by Vice President Al Gore early in the Clinton administration, when he gave White House support to the "information superhighway." It would be privately built and managed, he said, but with a commitment to universal access—not just for the rich, or the information-rich.

I had urged such a commitment earlier, but I believed that some government regulation may become inevitable. Ithiel Pool had proposed landmark policies for the telecommunications revolution. He noted that American governmental control of such technologies eventually were relaxed, and diversity of the flows followed. This was Ithiel's philosophical conviction, and he had recent history on his side. For decades, the Federal Communication Commission demanded that broadcasters adhere to the "fairness doctrine." The FCC said that radio and television that were licensed to use the public's airspace must comply with government rules concerning fairness in programming. This dictum was seldom enforced, but it enabled special interest groups to argue their way onto radio and TV. Then, in the late 1980s, the FCC ended the fairness doctrine, saying that the greatly expanded number of broadcast outlets ended the "shortage" theory on which the fairness doctrine had been based. Ithiel was correct: regulation does pass.

He also recognized that pragmatic politics, flavored by market economics, was necessary to encourage diversity and freedom. Long before others, Ithiel foresaw the implication of the satellite: distance was no longer a barrier, but rather became an encouragement to long-distance communication. Ham radio buffs in the 1920s tuned crystal sets to distant transmitters, and then exchanged postcards by slow mail to verify a far-off radio signal was received. Today, tens of millions on the Internet tap into databases a continent away or down the street, all on the same small screen.

Such facile communication is possible, Ithiel realized early, because different communication technologies would merge—computers with telephone and television, sound with picture, telephone with satellite, entertainment with news (for better or, mostly, for worse). He also foresaw the revolutionary changes that communications would bring to economics: the magnification of international conglomerates, the globalization of finance (more money is moved in one business day over global networks than the total volume in all the world's treasuries), and the restructuring of major industries along channels of communication rather than primary reliance on resources in the ground: a new industrial age, with unexpected dislocation to formerly skilled employees and old-industry employers.

Perhaps most important, Ithiel realized that the new "comm tech" could empower the individual as never before; hence his emphasis on "technologies without boundaries" and my belief in "the technology of freedom." They were the same, with the same potential for freeing the human spirit, through the ability not only to communicate but to interact with other humans and, indeed, access the vast reservoir of human knowledge, past and present.

I believe, perhaps more than Ithiel, that the nature of the competitive market, tying one communication network to another, can have a double effect. On the one hand, this centralization of word power is necessary to provide maximum access to diverse information and interactive communication. Such networks do, indeed, enable us to "speak" instantly, in real time, to another person online, anywhere on the planet. Such networking also allows us to see a picture in the Louvre or a book in the Library of Congress one minute and a "live" dance in the Sahara the next moment. That astounding capability requires intricate switching of telecommunications networks. Switching, even done electronically, requires some central brain—a control point.

Who is to master such controls? Who in the private world of international electronic conglomerates? The answer is coming from the wild scamper for large-scale mergers. One week Disney's merger produces the biggest global communication system, topping Time Warner, for several years the world's biggest. Then, weeks later, Time Warner merges with Ted Turner's cable and broadcast systems to comprise a still larger global network. Still later, America Online and Time Warner became the biggest communications conglomerate ever. This leapfrogging increasingly centralizes control of the content of communication, not just the economics of shareholder profits. The government expressed some concern. Antitrust laws, in disuse for many years, could be dusted off to determine whether the expanded conglomerate leads toward a monopoly.

Such governmental inaction, perhaps, would have pleased Ithiel. He had every right to fear governments. We both examined other governments' actions worldwide and found ample reason to fear official regulation. Since the earliest days of the telegraph, European and third world governments have owned and controlled their countries' communication systems through their post, telegraph, and telephone (PTT) agencies. Today, some of these have been modernized by adding "telecommunications" to the governmental name. Privatization of many PTT systems is now proceeding; however, even the democracies of the European

Union discuss quotas to exclude American film imports and laboriously consider ways to assure "responsible journalism" through legislation aimed at independent news media. I am widely quoted declaring that only one-third of all countries have a free press. Certainly there is need to be fearful of governmental intervention in the information networks. But who will monitor the merger-prone communication conglomerates if not government, especially the U.S. government?

Many other countries, particularly 120 or so in the developing world, have for two decades complained about "cultural imperialism"—the domination of news, information, and entertainment flows from New York, Hollywood, London, and Paris. The U.S. government has strongly, repeatedly rejected such criticism. Now, in response, defenders of the status quo argue that the new comm tech will provide instant access for anyone, anywhere to vast information sources; and, indeed, to conversational responses in real time. That would be democratization of the information age.

Will this diversity and opportunity flow from market competition? Or is the opposite likely: will competition drive marketers to merge and reduce diversity of content, limiting it mainly to what will sell time or space to commercial buyers? If so, will government have to step in to protect diversity? Ithiel Pool believed that government policy inevitably reduces diversity and favors central controls. I do not agree—at some difficult-to-define point, regulators should insist that media moguls assure access and diversity of content—just as the United States did when the railroads and the telephone were start-up, innovative carriers.

It's tricky, but so are many other aspects of this democratic society. The First Amendment notwithstanding, the Supreme Court has held that a reporter may be forced to testify and even reveal sources and notes if a defendant's case requires such information. Journalists have been jailed for contempt when they refused. The courts insist on the ground that a reporter is a citizen first, a journalist second. That represents the inevitable tension in a clash of rights: the right to a free press vs. the right to a fair trial. Someone—the court—must decide. So it is the last resort needed for regulation of mergers that may either threaten the free flow of information or keep it robust.

In the 1950s, Ithiel Pool conceived a research idea with breathtaking potential. He observed that two strangers frequently meet and soon discover they have mutual acquaintances. "It's a small world," one will likely say. Ithiel noted that much political networking, job hunting, word-of-mouth business sales, and many other human contacts reveal intermediaries coming together.

Networking. Ithiel made a huge leap: *several intermediaries—friends of friends—may link most pairs of people in the world!* He estimated that seven intermediaries might be needed for such global transaction. Sound familiar? The successful Broadway play four decades later had the leading woman recall that "someone once said *six* degrees of separation link everyone in the world." She was making the point that we are a single human family, and should interact fairly with different races and peoples—a noble thought. John Guare called his play *Six Degrees of Separation* (six is more closely connective and crisp-sounding than seven). Neither the Broadway nor the Hollywood version credited Ithiel de Sola Pool or his colleagues with the basic concept.

Ithiel did not stop with the original idea. He spoke repeatedly about the small-world phenomenon. He believed it was scientifically provable; a tough assignment. He was convinced there was pragmatic value to such research for marketing, for social activism, and in government organization. Ithiel asked Karl W. Deutsch, his political science colleague at MIT, to recommend a mathematician who could collaborate on a small-world study, and Manfred Kochen was their man. They interested Stanley Milgram, a renowned social psychologist, who devised the "Small-World Method." This is a passport-like document that includes a target person shown by a picture, name, location, and occupation. The passport is passed from one acquaintance to another aimed at reaching someone who knows the target person. Meanwhile, everyone along the route taken by the passport is recorded. The chain of contacts is revealed.

As the project developed, intricate mathematical formulae were devised. There were never adequate funds, however, to test the hypothesis on a large scale. Three of the original investigators died, but the concept did not. My 1992 book *The Culture of Freedom* was subtitled *The Small World of Fulbright Scholars*. The book described my year-long study and evaluation of the Fulbright scholarship exchange program (see chap. 10). I wrote, "Social scientists estimate tantalizingly that a chain of *seven* such intermediaries can link most pairs of people now separated anywhere in the world. The Broadway hit *Six Degrees of Separation* evoked the same theme. By exchanging 180,000 students and scholars from 130 countries for nearly five decades the Fulbright program has created a putative network that is a small world growing ever larger and ever more useful to mankind."[5]

Soon after the book appeared, I elaborated the small-world concept of Ithiel de Sola Pool and his colleagues in an op-ed article in the *Los Angeles Times* and stressed the relationship to the Fulbright scholarship program then under political attack.[6] My article drew a warm response from Mrs. Pool, who thanked me for giving Ithiel credit for the concept that had now become common Broadway and Hollywood terminology. I also heard from another widow of the small-world consortium. Many months later, I received an astounding book-length manuscript from another researcher—a younger man who had taken up the small-world challenge. Through intricate mathematical and logical constructs he examined the network formation of Americans with AIDS. Clearly, Ithiel's concept is alive and moving slowly ahead. For example, in 2003, Duncan J. Watts published his long journey to engage several scientists of various disciplines in the search that Ithiel de Sola Pool began.[7] In an age of technological networking, it is essential to examine and ultimately define the mysteries of human networking.

Meanwhile, beware of exploiters. In the Broadway play that conveyed this theme, a liberal Jewish family on New York's Park Avenue is visited by a young black man who says he is a friend of their son and a fellow student at Harvard. The visitor engages in several antisocial acts, but the wife excuses them by reminding her husband that "it's a small world." She repeats "six degrees of separation" to evoke understanding and forgiveness.

The black visitor takes further outrageous advantage of his hosts. The fact is, this story was based on reality. A clever black con man had wormed his way into the home of a famous white writer and performed essentially as depicted. When the play became a hit, the same con man sued the author and others for "stealing" his story without paying him!

I found the play interesting, but I did not seem to have taken its immediate lesson. Some months later, as I walked from my office to teach at New York University I was stopped by a young black man who said, "You don't recognize me?" I paused, thought for a moment, and said I did not. He went on, "Well, I was younger when I visited your office. I am the son of your colleague." I showed no sign of recognition. "Who is the black man in your office?" he asked.

"Oh, David," I said.

"Yes. I'm David's son." And then he came to the point. He said he had bought a secondhand car that immediately died on the street and needed forty dollars for repairs. He would return the money to me that evening, after class, saying that he was a student at NYU. I offered to accompany him to the garage, but he quickly turned me away. I then handed him the money, and he asked whether I wanted him to bring me a sandwich at the end of class, along with the money. I thanked him and said no. Of course that was the last I ever saw of the forty dollars—but not the man.

Two years later, I was walking near City Hall after leaving my Wall Street office. A black man came up to me, wearing a heavy coat and a large hat. It was a cold day. He asked, "You don't remember me? I'm the brother of your receptionist in the office."

Instinctively, I asked, "Luz?"

"Yes," he replied, "I just left your office, but she was not there. I need ten dollars to buy gasoline. The garage won't take my credit card or a check. I'm a student at Pace Institute across the street." At that moment, I recognized the man. He saw that, turned on his heel and disappeared. Of course, Luz had no brother. I had been slow in matching the slim man two years earlier with the bulkier man in a heavy winter coat. And that was still not the end.

No more than two weeks later, Marianne and I were walking north on Madison Avenue on a sunny afternoon. We were talking animatedly. Suddenly, I looked up and saw a familiar black man coming south just inches away. I told Marianne who he was. She tugged at my arm, saying, "Don't stop!" I wanted to ask for my forty dollars back. As the man passed, he smiled and said, "You don't remember me. I'm your milkman's son."

It's a small world.

NOTES

1. Robert Marc Angel, quoted in Frank Bruni, "Cemetery Tells of Jewish Settlers of Seventeenth Century," *New York Times*, May 25, 1997.

2. Leonard R. Sussman, *Power, the Press, and the Technology of Freedom: The Coming Age of ISDN* (New York: Freedom House, 1989).

3. Ithiel de Sola Pool, *Technologies without Boundaries: On Telecommunications in a Global Age*, ed. Eli M. Noam (Cambridge, MA: Harvard University Press, 1990).

4. Ithiel de Sola Pool, *Forecasting the Telephone: A Retrospective Technology Assessment of the Telephone* (Norwood, NJ: Ablex, 1983).

5. Leonard R. Sussman, *The Culture of Freedom: The Small World of Fulbright Scholars* (Lanham, MD: Rowman and Littlefield, 1992), pp. 1–2.

6. Leonard R. Sussman, "The World Is Smaller Than We Think," *Los Angeles Times*, January 4, 1994.

7. Duncan J. Watts, *Six Degrees: The Science of a Connected Age* (New York: W. W. Norton, 2003).

13

ANGEL RAMOS
Cablese at War

A s I walk daily now to the river bank at Wall Street, I recall an overcast December 4, 1941, when I mounted pier 15 at that very street. A Ward Line ship docked there would take me to Puerto Rico for a job I was offered only three days earlier. I had been a copy editor on Moses Annenberg's *Morning Telegraph* and *Daily Racing Form*. Briefly, I was "Mr. Consensus," perhaps prophetic for a life at the political center. I wrote a daily column averaging all the selections of veteran handicappers at seven tracks with nine daily races. I was regularly surprised by the Friday afternoon routine of the horserace-wise editorial and press staffs. They lined up at the rear door of the plant to pay off the bookies for failed bets each week.

Then a telegram came from San Juan offering me the post of cable editor on the *World-Journal*, the English-language daily owned by *El Mundo*, one of the finest newspapers in Latin America. I was recommended by classmates David Safer and Russell Jandoli, who had been reporting for the *World-Journal* for several months. This was to be my first travel overseas. I welcomed the opportunity remembering my prediction in June 1940 that the United States would be at war in eighteen months. I wanted to go where there might be some newsworthy action.

I was not completely alone. On board was Jules Kaplan, a patient of my father who owned a unique business selling merchandise to American military post exchanges overseas. San Juan was one of his regular ports of call. By sheer coincidence, we sailed together. The ship was the main link between the island and New York but on this wintry sailing had few passengers and much cargo. Neither the ship nor the Ward Line survived World War II.

Our departure itself was ominous. We proceeded no farther than the Statue of Liberty when a thick fog bank settled in. We anchored there for the night, with the Staten Island ferries scuttling by. Next morning, a parade of twenty-three New York-bound ships moved slowly past. We sailed at a snail's pace down the New Jersey coast. For a time it seemed the ship might not complete this voyage: just hours out of the harbor we ran into a severe winter storm. Huge waves swept across the bow. I ventured on deck while there was still daylight, holding rails with both hands. Jules and I were among only 12 of 209 passengers at dinner. We were given a table at the most forward end of the dining room, where the rising angle of the narrowing superstructure negated some pitching of the ship. It rose at a steep angle, hovered shaking, then settled down at a reverse angle. To the despair of the struggling waiter, I ate ravenously each mealtime. Years of teenage sailing on small fishing boats were good preparation.

After two days of stormy weather, we entered the calmer Gulf Stream. We had just a day of that balmier passage when the most ominous moment came. The ship's public address system announced that Pearl Harbor, Hawaii, had just been bombed. The United States was at war with Japan. My June 1940 prediction that the United States would soon be at war was off by twelve days.

Jules Kaplan was particularly shocked. Many friends and customers were at Pearl Harbor. And he did not then know the status of his civilian business in the new wartime era. The ship's PA later told us that we were now under orders from the U.S. Navy. Clearly, there was concern that the next target might be in the Caribbean—the Panama Canal or the great U.S. naval installations at Roosevelt Roads in Puerto Rico. These protected the Canal and the South Atlantic lifeline to Europe, providing Lend-Lease arms and supplies to Britain and the Allies. We noticed almost immediately that our ship had ended its direct course and was zigzagging forward. This slowed our progress and brought us to the vicinity of San Juan at dusk. However, the Navy refused to allow us to enter the harbor. Metal submarine nets had already been put in place, and the Navy feared that if we were allowed through, a German submarine—many were in the seas around us—could follow and enter the protected harbor and its naval and air base. We spent the night of December 9 offshore. There were no lights in Puerto Rico. The island had gone into a blackout that would last for nearly a year. This despite the highly visible southern moon that cast brilliant light over the land. I slept restlessly because I did not know what to anticipate next morning.

At 6:00 A.M. we disembarked. I was met at the pier in the heart of San Juan by Dave Safer. He was to be my apartmentmate and, still after more than sixty years, my friend. Dave put my luggage in a cab, and we wound up the narrow, bustling streets to the tallest building at the time, *Mundo*'s six-story plant atop a hilly rise in the Old City.

I was introduced to Angel Ramos, publisher of *El Mundo* and the *World-Journal*. Angel was the model Western self-made man, quite different from Latin men of substantial wealth and power at the time. His quick smile and limited English suggested a certain hesitation at this first meeting. But I was wrong. He had been born in poverty and had a meager education but persisted as a shrewd, some would say ruthless, businessman. He bought *El Mundo* when it was just another struggling daily, pouring profits into new printing equipment in order to have a fine modern plant. He purchased many news services from the states and made *Mundo* the most reliable publication in the Caribbean. In the years before the war, when the United States was building major military installations across the island, he saw that the large influence of English-speaking troops would support an English-language daily. He created the *World-Journal*, an afternoon paper given considerable independence from *El Mundo*. Indeed, the much smaller staff of the *W-J*—bolstered by three newly minted Columbia journalism graduates—operated differently than the slower-paced morning paper. On the local scene we often beat our giant parent paper to significant stories. We covered U.S. national and world news in far greater depth than *Mundo*, though we had many fewer pages.

Moments after I was introduced to Angel Ramos he led me into the large, modern city room. I was given a desk near the radio receiver that linked the *W-J* to the United Press in New York. This was to be my job: cable editor—a unique assignment then and now. I replaced Carl Hartman, who had been hired by the Associated Press. Fifty years later, Hartman covered my press conference in Washington announcing my report for Freedom House of press-freedom violations worldwide.

In our first meeting, Ramos told me that every few moments I would be handed a sheaf of paragraphs, each on a separate waxed blue sheet. The takes had been radioed, one letter at a time, from New York, and were transmitted to me exactly as they were being received at the foreign desk of the UP in New York from correspondents around the world. Separate paragraphs often intermingled bits of unrelated stories. The short takes had to be carefully reassembled and rewritten because everything was received in cablese. This was the international wire services' means of limiting communication costs. Radiotelegraph charges were exorbitant. The carriers, however, would accept as single words the most telescoped creations of words the mind of correspondents and their home desks could devise. For example, if I were to tell the UP, "I am going to New York," the cost would be figured at the rate of six words transmitted. But if I sent "Newyorkward," the UP would be charged for only one word. Cablese produced many strange locutions. It was my job as cable editor to decipher the words, reassemble the paragraphs as the correspondents sent them, and then rewrite the story filling in background where needed. Much was usually left out of original dispatches to save space and money.

I would start at 2:30 in the morning and work with increasing speed to the 11:00 A.M. deadline. Once the press bells clanged and the building shook with the day's papers rolling off, I could wash up and prepare some feature material for the next day. By noon, Russ Jandoli, Dave, and I would leave the building for a restaurant on the main avenue. As we sipped Cuba libres, newsboys would run in a pack from our building and then fan out across the city hawking our morning's work: "*Worl-Yurnal! Worl-Yurnal!*"

In that popular restaurant, well-heeled businessmen would take the paper even as they poured a half-cup of sugar into their coffee—"It's good for business." These were sugar growers, *central* operators, bankers, and other industrialists who liked the conservative editorials and news coverage of *El Mundo* but were suspicious of that upstart daily run by Continentals (the euphemism for non–Puerto Ricans). Angel Ramos, to his credit, took pride in the *World-Journal* as his contribution to improved overseas journalism.

The paper gave him some stature in the States, with United Press, and in the national news media. He was one of the UP's most profitable customers anywhere. Indeed, many of the stories I rewrote from the UP wire were tagged "PROPRENSA," stories destined for *La Prensa* in Buenas Aires, another profitable client of the UP. *Prensa* had helped open the continent to the UP and make that service for a time the leader over the Associated Press. Ramos had placed himself in a strategic position vis-à-vis the newspaper business in Latin America and the U.S. mainland. He was in line for a Cabot Award from Columbia University and, I thought, a Pulitzer Prize some day. After I had left Puerto Rico for New York I offered to help Ramos get a Pulitzer Prize nomination for *El Mundo,* but he did not rise to my offer. He probably still resented my having left the *World-Journal* to become the hated Gov. Rexford G. Tugwell's press secretary. Ramos had asked me then, "Why are you doing this? Is it money?" He knew I had been recently married. He added, "We can give you a $5- or $10-a-week raise." I was earning $25 a week at the time.

Ramos ran *Mundo* with an iron fist but allowed William J. Dorvillier, my boss, more freedom running the *World-Journal*. And, ironically, years later, after the *World-Journal* had closed, Bill became the first editor of the *San Juan Star*, a second English-language paper owned for a time by Scripps-Howard. Under Bill's editorship, the *Star* won a Pulitzer for its local editorial campaign.

After my first day of work at the *World-Journal* I finally unpacked my luggage at 21 Cruz Street, a four-room apartment about five blocks from the office across the Plaza of San Juan. I entered the building through a wrought-iron gate, walked across an open interior courtyard, and climbed the marble steps to the apartment. It housed, in addition to Dave and Russ, Henry W., son of a prominent Southern publisher, and John Hoag, an anthropologist from Harvard, the son of an army base commander stationed in Puerto Rico. An unlikely quintet.

Dave had become the appointed cook, I served as food carrier on shopping missions. Arriving home, Dave and I would quickly strip and grab yesterday's newspaper—and swat giant, flying, hard-shell roaches. The apartment had no windows or screens, only shutters that remained open most of the time. Dave had a charming Puerto Rican friend, Carmen, who called me "Leng." That code word, six decades later, still signals for Dave and me an instant reference to our San Juan days. Dave left Carmen and Puerto Rico to enter the army. We met again unexpectedly when the troopship on which he served as army lieutenant put in briefly at San Juan. After the war, Dave worked with the CIO supporting free labor development in Europe. He later handled public relations for CBS Laboratories, was involved with Howard Hughes' technical development, and served as professor in the California university system.

Russ spent much time curled on his bed moaning about Peggy, left behind in the States. When I next met Russ, many years later, he headed the journalism department that he founded at St. Bonaventure College (now University). I was about to ask about Peggy when I was introduced to Mrs. Jandoli (not named Peggy), Russ's first and long-term wife. I never met Peggy. When Russ died, the journalism school was named after him.

Henry had a full double life. He worked on the *World-Journal* but freelanced, both as a business and an avocation. He lived part of the time with a prostitute he befriended. He assured us that no money passed between them. One night we heard fast-running footsteps on the cobblestone street and then Henry's urgent plea to open the gate. We dashed down and let him in, just ahead of his knife-bearing girlfriend. Henry assured us this was how he learned Spanish quickly.

Henry told us that after the war anyone wanting to get ahead would be asked, "What did you do in the war?" Henry responded by joining the merchant marines and sailing off. When last seen, after the war, Henry appeared across four pages of *Life* magazine. One full-page photo showed him in a hammock strung between palm trees in Havana, a beautiful young lady fanning his brow—the model expatriate journalist in Cuba's pre-Castro days.

My Spanish came slower than Henry's, though I had a passing acquaintance with two prostitutes. Every morning at 2:15, as I walked through the darkened streets to the newspaper, I would pass two young women soliciting at the corner of the main plaza. We would exchange "Buenas dias." They must have had a hard time in the nightly blackouts. By day, that street corner was crowded with young men-about-town watching skirts of young women blow high in the wind.

Only the radio operator and I would occupy the large city room for five hours until the *W-J* staff arrived at about 7:30. By that time I had written most of the day's war news. I bolstered the latest eyewitness accounts from the Russian winter front with extrapolations from Napoleon's experience a half-century earlier. News from the States was also my beat, but that was severely censored. I was out of the States for the entire war, so it was years before I caught up with what had happened at home from 1941 through 1945. The postwar book *While You Were Gone* helped.

I covered some local stories and wrote a business column for a short time. But I was free after 11:00 every morning. I asked Angel Ramos whether he minded if I took on a daily fifteen-minute news program for the CBS affiliate. Ramos gave approval as long as I didn't use my name! That, I presume, he regarded as his property. After all, he had paid my boat fare to San Juan. So I produced, wrote, and delivered a daily news broadcast under the name of Leonard Richards. I competed quite successfully with the Armed Forces Radio Service news program, mainly because I had no restrictions on coverage or style.

I gained—and gave up—a commercial sponsor for the news show. The vice president of Carioca Rum lived in the house adjoining ours in Hato Rey. He was married to his boss's sister. The two men had been big-time liquor dealers in Brooklyn (whether this was during or after Prohibition was not clear). Our neighbor had "gone native" more than linguistically. He played the guitar like a professional, but too often he chose strange times to demonstrate this. He would arrive home at three in the morning, find the entry barred by his wife, and then play burning love songs on the guitar to gain entrance. The sound, of course, radiated through *our* bedroom as well.

Perhaps partly to sustain my goodwill, our neighbor asked whether Carioca Rum could buy commercial time on my radio program. The FCC then had no restrictions on liquor commercials, so I agreed. In fact, I also wrote the commercials. I visited the plant to get some new ideas for the rum ads, at my neighbor's suggestion, and I was shown through the entire process, from blackstrop to bottled rum. However, I was appalled at the odors and the sheer pollution of the liquids as well as the air, so I dropped Carioca Rum from my broadcasts and soon afterward moved away from the guitar-playing neighbor.

Even with the *World-Journal* stint and the daily broadcast I was still free in the afternoons. In the heat of the day it was impossible to sleep, so I took a third job writing most of the copy for a monthly magazine published by one Kenneth Tugwell (a colonial-era Briton, no relative of the governor). The magazine was a holdover from the scant tourist days before the war, carrying mainly social notes about the elite families and the foreign business and diplomatic corps. As Leonard Richards, I provided the longer articles that filled space between the social reports.

There was still spare time. I filled it writing occasional freelance articles for *Business Week* and the Overseas News Agency (ONA). My favorite piece for *Business Week* was an enthusiastic prediction that after the war the Caribbean would be awash in large-scale commercial fishing industries. Unfortunately, it never happened. The most widely published article I produced for the ONA appeared under large headlines in many newspapers, including the lead paper, the *New York Post*. I wrote that piece on my last weekend before entering the army. I had taken a sailboat to St. Thomas; during an early-morning walk along the waterfront I observed a whaleboat with a small kicker unloading crates at the wharf. Two men hurriedly moving the crates were speaking French. The men and the marking on the boxes interested me: they were unloading cases of wine labeled "Martinique."

Normally, that would be of little interest to all but wine merchants or connoisseurs. I asked the boatmen where they had come from. "Fort-de-France, Martinique." I had a news story. This was early April 1943: France, the colonial occupier of Martinique, had fallen to the Nazi Germans. Two first-line French warships, which had been at sea when France fell, made it to Martinique and came under the command of Hitler's forces. The U.S. Navy, hard-pressed by

Nazi submarines in the South Atlantic and Caribbean, feared that the two major French warships would attempt to leave Martinique and harass U.S. and Allied shipping and sea routes for thousands of miles. The U.S. policy consequently sought to deny all ship movement into and out of Martinique and neighboring French Guadeloupe. This policy would presumably also ignite an island revolt against Nazi occupation run from Berlin.

The secretive delivery of cases of wine to the U.S. island of St. Thomas meant that the American blockade of Martinique had been pierced. So my report for the ONA stated. It was widely published under large headlines. I hadn't used my byline for this, but the pseudonym suggested by my wife, Fran. The report evoked immediate consternation at the Sixth Naval District, headquarters in San Juan for the entire Caribbean leading to the strategic Panama Canal. The name of the writer was not known to navy censors who controlled the mails as well as press credentials for the theater. I heard quickly from army friends that the writer was being sought. But a day later I was inducted into the army and heard nothing further about the matter—at least not directly.

But there was an odd twist, because Puerto Rico, where I entered the army, was considered an overseas combat area. Consequently, there was no basic training except for Puerto Rican inductees. I was therefore dumped in a regular-army outfit, the Seventy-eighth Combat Engineer Battalion. I was given a rifle, a duffle bag filled with gear, and half a pup tent. I arrived at the unit in an ice truck, which dropped me on a beach where the battalion was preparing for the next day's joint maneuvers with the navy. I slept that night without cover because I did not have a partner for the necessary second half of the tent. Well before dawn, I was awakened by something moving on my stomach. I raised my head and saw a foot-long, black land crab making its way slowly across my body. I swatted it off with a boot and gave up sleeping that night. Not much later, we were aroused for a daybreak exercise for which others had been prepped but about which I was completely ignorant.

We were led onto a small craft and moved into the Caribbean. Anchored at sea was a large naval vessel down whose sides were rope ladders. The point of the exercise was for the Seventy-eighth to climb those ladders with full equipment on our backs. Suddenly, it all became clear to me. The navy was training the army (and I suppose the marines and others) to board those two French warships at Martinique. This would have been exquisite retribution for my pronouncing the blockade broken and thereby making it a domestic political issue. Fortunately (for all of us concerned) the navy decided to play a waiting game. By July 1943, Martinique's high commissioner radioed Washington that he was ready to accept changes in French control "to avoid shedding blood." Mine, perhaps? The French ships sat out the war in Martinique and were later returned to Paris's control. Today, when I teach press ethics at the university I mention my reporting the blockade story under wartime conditions and solicit student reactions. Most students judge my article censorable; I agree.

My entering the army had an interesting background. I had registered with my draft board in New York. With the war on, ships were being sunk daily. Many of these carried mail to and from Puerto Rico. It was almost a year before word got to me from the draft board. I answered their queries and waited. But I knew that neither my job at the governor's office nor at the *World-Journal* was close enough to wartime action. I took a post then as editor in the Foreign Broadcast Intelligence Service of the Federal Communications Commission. (The FBIS later was transferred to the CIA.) My function was to prepare for instant transmission to Washington the shortwave broadcasts from enemy transmitters in Germany, Italy, the occupied countries, and some points in South America believed to be assisting the enemy. I edited the work of some five translators working in about ten languages around the clock.

We monitored innocuous-sounding reports that might reveal troop movements, officer transfers, social or political unrest, or even emergency calls from sinking ships at sea. We had the right to cut into other transmissions to Washington and go into the White House or the Defense Department, skipping the FCC, for messages regarded as urgent. We were able to locate several ships in distress.

During this service I learned that the FBIS was planning to open a similar monitoring station in Africa as soon as General Eisenhower had secured a landing area on the continent. That station would bring in enemy broadcasts from Europe far more clearly. I obtained the FCC's permission for a transfer to Africa and then asked my draft board in New York for its permission to go. I received this extraordinary cable: "This draft board must refuse your request. We have no power to send you into a war zone." Odd—as far as the army was concerned, I was already in one. And as for the war effort, I would perform more direct service in FBIS-Africa.

I still read FBIS reports almost daily and occasionally recall those days in the sweltering henhouse-like structure in Hato Rey, Puerto Rico, when the FBIS was a new adventure in American intelligence-gathering.

After skipping basic training I left the combat engineers under a cloud. I had been told by the department headquarters public relations captain—while I was still a civilian—that I could work with him after I entered the army. But I was assigned to the engineers, a regular army outfit averaging three hundred pounds per man that carried heavy parts of pontoon bridges as though they were matchsticks. The average vocabulary was five hundred words, mostly words with four letters. I remembered the promise to serve at headquarters.

On my first overnight pass I headed to San Juan and announced my availability to the captain. He said he would arrange my transfer. The truth was, he needed me. He had landed his captaincy on a fluke. Before the war, he had been a lowly reserve officer with a civilian-job classification that suggested newspapering. Actually, he was a paper deliverer.

I returned to my outlying post and was almost immediately called in by the company commander. He threatened me with a court-martial for going outside proper channels to secure a transfer. Several weeks later, on another pass, I told this to the headquarters captain. He persuaded the commanding general to issue the transfer. When I returned to my post the battalion adjutant-general called me in. This time I seemed headed for serious trouble. He spoke harshly, reminded me I had broken rules again, and said, "Get the hell out of here by 0600 hours tomorrow."

I did, but only with some sense of guilt. For I had been told the Seventy-eighth Engineers were alerted for duty in CBI—the China-Burma-India theater. One of my first assignments was to take a Signal Corps photographer to the San Juan dock and cover the departure of the troopship. On deck were my old buddies. They saw me—I felt like a deserter. Even more so months later, when rumors came that the Seventy-eighth was in bloody action in the CBI and lost most of its young officers. That report and my sense of guilt stayed with me for a long time.

Finally, fifty years after the war ended I sent the Department of Defense five dollars and asked for the wartime record of the Seventy-eighth Engineer Battalion. I then received the formal military record, which stated that the Seventy-eighth Engineers had become a screwed-up battalion. On the day I had covered its departure, thinking my former buddies were off to bitter fighting in the CBI, the battalion was shipped off to New Orleans and its entire personnel either separated from service or reassigned. My five decades of guilt ended.

After leaving the engineers I was assigned to military intelligence. My work was mainly drafting the commanding general's speeches and reports, including his message upon the death of our commander in chief, Franklin D. Roosevelt. One day, however, I was sent by the chief of staff on an extraordinary mission in the Dutch islands. The U.S. Army's venereal disease rate was rising disastrously there, and the Dutch disclaimed any responsibility. *Their* women could not be the cause, they said. A nasty international incident was brewing.

I took a Signal Corps camera and proceeded to Curaçao under the guise of a morale booster. Barely minutes after I left the small reconnaissance plane (having been seated warily in the bomb bay), I hailed a local taxi outside the airport. My assignment quickly fell into place.

"Want a girl?" I was asked by the driver.

"Suppose I do?" I responded.

"I'll take you to the hotel and we'll pick up the girl," said the driver. "I have a mat in the back of the cab."

It seems the "girls" were transient visitors from Venezuela who took the morning ferry to Curaçao or Aruba and turned a few tricks on the garbage dump outside of town, returning home that evening. Indeed, Dutch women were not involved.

So I took some photographs of the cactus and the monument to Peter Stuyvesant's leg buried there, and then I returned to Puerto Rico to write my report. Before long the army supervised a hygienic "Happy Camp" for the troops, and the VD rate returned to normal.

Though he provided a major turning point in my life, I didn't see Angel Ramos again. Many years later, upon his death, he left a sizable fortune to the Angel

Ramos Foundation. His widow, Argentina Ramos, then the publisher of *El Mundo*, married Lee Hills, publisher of the *Miami Herald* and head of its parent, the Knight-Ridder chain of newspapers. Several times, Argentina Hills made grants from the Ramos Foundation for my books on press freedom. My association with Angel Ramos thus extended beyond fifty years, far longer, I am sure, than he would have suspected. And with one who had once defected to the enemy in the Fortaleza.

14

LUIS MUÑOZ MARIN
Social Revolutionary

In January 1946, I collected army discharge papers, took off my uniform, and the next day opened the Puerto Rican government's Office of Information in New York. One of the first assignments from Gov. Rexford G. Tugwell in San Juan was to manage press arrangements for the inauguration of Jesus T. Piñero, the first Puerto Rican to become governor of the island. Though he was appointed by President Harry S Truman and not elected by Puerto Ricans, this was nevertheless a step toward greater home rule for Puerto Rico. I was a small player in the movement to raise the economic potential of the people and enlarge their political capabilities as well. Under Spanish and U.S. rule, they had never escaped poverty or been permitted to solve their problems in democratic fashion.

For the inauguration, I was assigned a DC-3 airplane—chartered by a Puerto Rican industrialist—and asked to fill it with prominent mainland journalists. It was not an easy task. The newsworthy emigration of Puerto Ricans to New York had not yet begun. Even as a junket for journalists, the subtropical island in midsummer was hardly alluring. The tourism plant was not yet under construction. Wartime hardships still seared every city street and village. The social revolution under Tugwell's guidance had little resonance on the mainland. If known at all, it was regarded with some skepticism as another socialist experiment. And anyway, where was Puerto Rico? Many Americans then could not place it on the map. In the immediate postwar news world, Puerto Rico was a nonstory.

I managed to round up a respectable press group representing wire services, photographers from several agencies, major New York and Washington papers, Spanish-language correspondents, and several syndicated columnists. At the last moment, I still had five empty seats. I asked my parents and my wife Fran (then five months pregnant) to come along.

We took off from LaGuardia under a heavy overcast, and the weather got worse as we flew south. The pilot told me in the air he would not try to make San Juan nonstop. We landed in North Carolina to refuel and take on fried chicken for an extra meal. It was going to be a long flight. Over Cuba and Hispaniola we ran into torrential rains. The DC-3, then the workhorse of the airlines, was to be severely tested. The plane was no larger than commuter planes today. In the roaring rainstorm the pilot took us under the worst clouds, too close to sea level for comfort. It was a black night. The sound of twin propellers provided some reassurance, offset by gusts of wind that seemed to stall the plane in midair. Gusts blasted sheets of water against the windows. During the worst buckling of the plane, my father made his way haltingly from the front to the rear, where I was seated with Lee Mortimer, a particularly nasty Washington columnist who was later punched in public by Frank Sinatra. Mortimer had fallen asleep after consuming quantities of Puerto Rican rum and hearing my story of imminent economic development in Puerto Rico.

"Do you like this sort of thing, this flying?" my father asked. It was his first—and last—flight. I told him the plane would hold up. If I was right, I was deemed knowledgeable. If not, well. . . .

We taxied onto the Isla Verde airport, were driven by official cars to our hotel, and by mid-afternoon, my only free time, I persuaded my family to visit Luquillo Beach. This was the magnificent broad shore about twenty miles from San Juan; the beach is now a favorite tourist attraction; then, it was desolate, except for an occasional pig-broiling party or collectors of coconuts under the majestic palm trees that shaded the beach. The surf rolled in for miles along the curving shore. Luquillo was utterly peaceful. Paradisiacal.

The four of us strolled among the palms. Two sturdy trees had a hammock strung between them. A pair of legs with especially large toes hung listlessly over the side. Nothing more. As we approached, talking, a head appeared from the hammock.

"Hello, Sussman," it said.

"Don Luis," I replied, "these are my parents and my wife."

He stopped the swaying hammock, rose briefly to shake hands, and then settled back, swaying.

"That's Luis Muñoz Marin," I told my parents. "He's the son of the Father of Puerto Rico, and one day will be the first governor elected by Puerto Ricans." I added that he was then president of the Senate, the island's most popular politician, and the power behind Jesus Piñero, who would be inaugurated governor the next day.

My father seemed little impressed by his first meeting with Muñoz, but he was still recovering from that miserable flight. I have regarded Muñoz as one of the great men of the century. If he had been born in a larger country, say, in South America or the United States, he may well have risen to significant power. Muñoz was nevertheless destined for international stature as the intellectual and political leader of Puerto Rico, and cocreator (with Teodoro Moscoso, my boss) of "Operation Bootstrap," a model for the development of poor countries. I was "selling" Bootstrap in New York.

One of the early cornerstones of Bootstrap was the building of a first-class tourist hotel, the beginning of a major industry. I accompanied Moscoso, director of Bootstrap, to the Plaza Hotel in New York, where Conrad Hilton and Ted were to sign the agreement to build the San Juan Hilton. This would be a dramatic deal. Bootstrap would build the structure, and Hilton would train hundreds of Puerto Rican employees and manage the facility in first-class style. Hilton would later own the hotel and make a profit free of taxes. This was the model for many other industrial developments in Puerto Rico. It was Hilton's first offshore venture.

I had known Don Luis as a confirmed bohemian before I first went to Puerto Rico in 1941. He had lived in Greenwich Village as a young man, writing poetry and articles for *The Nation* and avant garde magazines, and holding forth on the New Deal, Roosevelt's limitations, and the intricacies of independence for Puerto Rico. I had spent four years as an undergraduate at the campus of New York University in Greenwich Village. After working late on the college newspaper I used free chits at local bistros that advertised in our paper. Occasionally, I would see this oversized, intense man discussing Puerto Rico and its future in colorful colloquial English. He could discuss *independencia* with the ardor that suggested the Hollywood model of a Latin firebrand, but he could also shift gears and address the realities of American geopolitics and Caribbean economics. Then, independence for his island became a far more complex objective.

Muriel Rukeyser, another struggling poet (later my sister-in-law; see chap. 3) met Muñoz in those days when they both strolled the Village streets and debated in the bistros.

These early, brief memories would be filed with Don Luis's still more complex personal history. His father, Luis Muñoz Rivera, was the actual negotiator in 1898 of the transition of Puerto Rico from a possession of Spain to the United States. He acted with great dignity and acumen. He did not regard himself as a Spaniard in the West Indies, or later as a "Continental" on the island—but as a Puerto Rican. In Spain, he took advantage of the divisions there to negotiate an autonomous charter before the United States invaded. In the United States, as resident commissioner, he cleverly manipulated the complex forces in Congress. Young Luis learned much of this from his father and was to make a larger record of social and political change.

Muñoz Marin grew up believing that his destiny was to carry on his father's work. Just before the American invasion, Muñoz Rivera had negotiated an organic law with Spain that would have given the island a preferred market for her products and the right to buy food anywhere in the world where it was cheapest. This economic boon was essential for the poverty-stricken island, dependent on a single commercial crop—sugar—for money to buy food (which it did not grow lest sugar lands be reduced).

That economic burden increased as the population grew and the United States assumed responsibility for the three million inhabitants. Muñoz Marin was regarded by most of his countrymen as the anointed savior. He toyed with socialism as a young man but left that and poetry behind in Greenwich Village. In the mid-1930s, with Washington appointees controlling La Fortaleza, the governor's house, Muñoz Marin could only prepare himself for eventual leadership. One day he, like his father, would negotiate in Washington for an unique relationship with the United States.

I watched the younger Muñoz's campaign for the Senate presidency, the highest elective post for a Puerto Rican. In 1940, he had formed the Popular Democratic Party, the *Populares*. It would oppose the *Independistas* and the Republicans, the conservatives led by the sugar and banking families, and small entrepreneurs. The *Populares* had a small but vocal faction favoring independence for the island. They appealed mainly to the masses of agrarian workers, the *jibaros*, and urban slum dwellers. These made up the majority of the population by far.

As I walked to work in San Juan I would pass El Fanguito, the horrid mass of tin-roofed huts that hugged the rocky shoreline. They were crowded beneath the ancient seawall that the Spaniards had built to ward off marauding pirates and Britons. The stench from open drainage sewers was overwhelming. Infected dogs roamed among the huts, and cries of babies and young children signaled another generation born to physical and mental deprivation.

The fate of the *jibaros* in the mountains was no less horrific in this stricken land. They labored ten hours a day swinging machetes in the sugarcane fields and at dusk returned to tin-and-board huts on the *patron*'s land. They ate imported rice and beans and an occasional dried cod brought from New England—despite an ocean of fish nearby. Mainly oranges, grapefruit, and avocados were locally grown—a small boon for the inadequate Puerto Rican diet. Planting of cash crops, not food, had always been the principal economic commitment. It left the land in control of a few sugar industrialists, and food too expensive to be consumed in adequate variety or quantity.

Watching Muñoz translate such bitter realities into programs for change was a model of masterful political sophistication—political action worthy of any forum for pure democracy. He used radio as a mass soapbox. The *Populares* placed small receivers in the plazas of large and small towns—even in mountain villages far removed from regular travel. Such use of radio and television *today* is standard political procedure. But not in 1940, outside San Juan.

Radio was only the beginning. Muñoz rode into town on the back of a horse or donkey, his great legs dangling almost to the ground. The pathetic, undernourished animal could barely support the man's oversized body. White *Populares* flags with the red symbol of the *jibaro*'s straw hat fluttered from every available door post. Muñoz was greeted by affectionate shouts: "Don Luis! Don Luis!" Older men shook his hand. Children circled in wonderment. Muñoz found a central place, mounted a box, and began his speech. He had no prepared text—something more dramatic.

He pulled from his pocket the draft of legislation he vowed to pass once elected. Newt Gingrich and the 1994 Republican "Contract with America" seemed like an innovation. More than a half-century later, it was not nearly as detailed a political instrument as Muñoz's reading of an actual draft law. Muñoz not only read such texts—redistribution of land, building water and drainage systems, constructing a cement plant for mass home-building, diversified industrial development—he also answered questions about these proposals. This village meeting, if you will, was the ultimate form of grassroots democracy. Muñoz asked not only for a vote for himself and the *Populares*, but for the new laws. They all became intertwined. Muñoz was elected overwhelmingly, repeatedly—twice as Senate president, three times as governor.

Once elected to the Senate presidency, Muñoz had a difficult, almost impossible task. He did indeed pass much of the legislation he promised. Land ownership was restricted, and plots were distributed to farm workers. Rural water and sewage systems were improved, a cement plant supported construction, and small industrial plants were started, but the main conversion of the economy was a major, long-term undertaking, and not one to be started during wartime. Restrictions rather than expansions began the moment after bombs hit Pearl Harbor.

I arrived in San Juan two days later, December 9, 1941. The island was blacked out every night, limiting travel. German submarines sank many ships in every convoy passing through the Caribbean to Africa and Europe. In those convoys were ships assigned to deliver food, oil, and transportation equipment to Puerto Rico. For weeks, not a single ship got through to the island. Some were sunk, others were taken off the Puerto Rican run and assigned to other war fronts. Shelves in the island's food shops were emptying. For several months, Fran and I subsisted mainly on canned tuna fish—prepared in a dozen varieties.

No less fearful was the rapid stalling of public transportation. Most urban workers took the *guagua* every day. These noisy, evil-smelling, overcrowded buses were the mainstay of the island's commercial life. With gas rationing, even people with cars took the bus. Overloading quickly wore out the tires of the vehicles. One by one, the *guaguas* died at the roadside. The *World-Journal* carried daily reports of the *guaguas*, cited by number, dead en route.

To stem the mounting crisis, Governor Tugwell cabled Washington frantically for food and tires. He got little assurance. Finally, he flew to Washington and persuaded officials to assign a ship to Puerto Rico with food and tires. It was a highly secret commitment. Tugwell knew the arrival time. I was by then his press secretary and aware of the crisis. On the appointed day, Tugwell mounted the parapet of the Fortaleza with binoculars in hand. After a long wait, he viewed a disastrous sight. Off on the horizon, a cloud of black smoke rose steadily against the tropical sky. For days afterward, salt-soaked tires drifted ashore, utterly useless for the island's *guaguas*.

There were recriminations. The conservative press and the opposition parties blamed Tugwell for these and other problems. They blamed him again when he tried to deal with the island's inequities. As press secretary, I became an indirect target. I wrote a daily report of government activities broadcast in Spanish over a local radio station. My immediate superior was John Lear, former Associated Press correspondent in Latin America, who served as Tugwell's coordinator of information. One item in my report became an instant cause célèbre.

The government had bought a building near the Fortaleza to house official agencies. My report said that the Farmers' Association, housed in that building, refused to move out or pay rent. The association regarded this statement as libelous. A municipal judge, soon to retire, found Governor Tugwell and John Lear guilty of criminal libel and fined them two hundred dollars apiece. Tugwell, of course, had known nothing about the whole affair. But this was another effort to generate anti-Tugwell news in the United States and ultimately bring a congressional investigating committee to the island. The original story made headlines in the States—but the conclusion was not published: a San Juan federal appeals court ruled in February 1943 that the testimony against my broadcast was "illogical, absurd, and capricious." The judge warned that if such interpretation of broadcasts were to stand, "would we not have lost freedom of the press, of thought, and of speech?"

Muñoz did not support Tugwell publicly, though the island's popular leader understood that Roosevelt had appointed Tugwell to oversee the transition to greater insular self-rule, as well as the amelioration of its major economic and political difficulties. Tugwell had one constituency—the White House and Harold Ickes, to whom Tugwell reported in the Department of the Interior. Muñoz had quite a different immediate constituency—Puerto Rican intellectuals educated in U.S. universities who had complex plans for economic development.

One of the principal young, highly intellectual, pragmatic leaders in Muñoz's camp was Teodoro Moscoso, educated in the United States and energized by a burning commitment to industrial development as the prime key to Puerto Rico's future well-being. He created and managed Operation Bootstrap and was my direct boss, though he remained in San Juan.

I helped set up meetings with the press and others when Ted came to the States. I also did this once for Governor Piñero. He wanted a private visit with Cardinal Spellman, whose diocese included Puerto Rico. I made the arrangement, and at the appointed moment the governor and I marched up the steps of the cardinal's residence on Madison Avenue. As we entered, the cardinal came down the red-carpeted stair and met us halfway. The governor promptly knelt and kissed the cardinal's ring. The cardinal turned to me. I took his hand with the ring—and shook it.

Other principals in Muñoz's camp were old-line political leaders who accepted enough of the *independista* tradition to make them wary of "Continental" advisers, including Tugwell and the band of skilled specialists in land reform, economics, and agronomy he imported. Muñoz liked these Continentals, myself among them, and leaned heavily on their expertise—but not publicly. That was understandable: Muñoz was a consummate politician.

While governor, Tugwell did not seem to acknowledge Muñoz's need to maintain a certain distance, the need not to be perceived as a puppet or even a student of the former Columbia professor. Later Tugwell recalled his thoughts about Muñoz as the governor was leaving the Fortaleza:

[I]n his eagerness to reward political loyalty, [Muñoz] was falling into the old Puerto Rican fault of putting a technical label on an incompetent individual and expecting him to do a satisfactory job. That had been one curse of the island.[1]

His insistence on political appeasement was defeating every hope he had and alienating his best talent.[2]

What it took to gain office was what made it difficult to administer it efficiently. Muñoz could hardly be regarded as an exception when he was in fact an outstanding example of the rule.[3]

That is at once harsh criticism of Muñoz's political tactics, yet fulsome praise of his personal character. Of how many political leaders can it be said that they forgive even betrayal, and continue to work with the culprit? Tugwell displays in this criticism personal pique over Muñoz's failure to heed all the governor's advice. He accepted a good deal, if not all, as any intelligent leader would. Tugwell also failed to understand the demands of practical politics. Tugwell never ran for public office or had to satisfy a market demand. Yet, several years after he left Puerto Rico, Tugwell reassessed Muñoz and called him one of the three most effective democratic politicians he had known. The others were Fiorello H. LaGuardia, Fusion mayor of New York City, and Franklin D. Roosevelt. Not bad company. Said Tugwell, "Muñoz Marin led a movement and created a party which consolidated the latent power of the stricken Puerto Rican masses and used it to force into being a disciplined program for rejuvenation. This effort had a significance beyond itself. It soon became the wonder of a world looking for the means to lift backward peoples from the stew of poverty and demagoguery which had become so characteristic of the old colonial areas. He was the creator, as much as one man could be, of a new status for a whole people and a new relationship among political entities. The Commonwealth of Puerto Rico was a brilliant invention and its bringing into being a remarkable achievement."[4]

Tugwell's earlier criticism could be applied to most successful politicians in democratic societies. They must be sensitive to many interests and pockets of political power. They should not compromise fundamental principles though they must sometimes alter tactics or even extend objectives under the rule of the politically possible.

Tugwell was under unrelenting opposition throughout his five years as governor. He was opposed by the conservative elite (the sugar companies, other industrialists, and the major newspaper), the *Independistas* of course, but others in all parties who regarded any Continental as a carpetbagger. This, despite the fact that Tugwell was sent by Roosevelt precisely to end minute Washington domination over the island, and not incidentally to set in motion social changes that would relieve the island of its perpetual poverty and despair. This very commitment was seen as threatening by those who liked the status quo.

I fully shared these objectives and regarded them, as did Tugwell, as an extension of the New Deal. The complicating factor was the need to devise programs that fit the political and economic imperatives without harming the cultural traditions of the people. That latter requirement is what split Muñoz and Tugwell. Tugwell underrated the sensitivities of opponents who were not driven to defend unjust economic advantages but who resisted Fortaleza-imposed formulas. Industrialization and modernization—everywhere—would be accompanied by some changes, desired or not, in cultural traditions.

I faced the hatred of Tugwell before I joined the Fortaleza staff. Muñoz's social revolution appealed to me. When the governor needed a press secretary, I left my job at the *World-Journal* and moved to the Fortaleza. I was angrily asked by the newspaper publisher, "How could you do this? Was it money? Why didn't you ask me for a raise?" (see chap. 13 for more on this). Money was not the reason for my leaving. The newspaper was owned by *El Mundo*, the largest daily in Puerto Rico and the chief spokesman for the conservative opponents of Tugwell and Muñoz. They would criticize Muñoz in reasonable terms but demonize Tugwell. In the publisher's view, I had gone over to the enemy. I was especially attacked in the press for the daily fifteen-minute radio program I wrote and produced. The conservative opposition regarded this program as detractors today oppose *All Things Considered* on National Public Radio.

Three years later, after service in the army, I left Puerto Rico and established the island's information office in New York. I ran a documentary picture service distributing magnificent stills by former Farm Security Administration photographers Jack Delano and Ed Rosskam under the direction of Clarence Senior, a Columbia University sociologist. Delano and Rosskam had been in Puerto Rico filming dramatic, moving scenes of the island and its people. Delano continued to photograph and write on the island until he died at the age of eighty-three in 1997. These men were brought together in the 1930s by Roy Stryker for the FSA's historic documentation of the Dust Bowl and the dramatic western movement of the Okies. Later, employing these and other FSA photographers, Roy created for Standard Oil of New Jersey the model of corporate picture documentation. Roy helped my operation make our pictures available to news media, museums, and schools.

One photographer whose pictures were featured in my collection was Charles Rotkin. He had served in the Army Signal Corps in Puerto Rico, and published a book on the Air Force's mission in the Caribbean. He decided to seek a career in photography. Right after the war, he heard that the army was auctioning off some photographic equipment. But he arrived late—all that was left was a huge aerial camera. Charlie bought it; then he needed an airplane. Roy Stryker gave him an aerial assignment to shoot Standard Oil facilities, as well as surrounding cultural, ecological, and geographic formations. Charlie became an aerial documentary photographer overnight—and a popular one, appearing frequently in corporate publications, *Fortune,* and other class magazines.

Suddenly late in 1946, the picture file and my full operation was in demand. With the reopening of travel between Puerto Rico and New York, a major influx of citizens began. They came by the planeload, hundreds and then thousands a week. By the end of the first year, nearly one hundred thousand Puerto Ricans entered New York; most remained.

Housing, hospital, and school facilities were overwhelmed. The influx became a heated political issue. The press wanted to know why the migration began, enabling me to explain the key objectives of Operation Bootstrap: industrial development within a context of greater political autonomy—short of independence from the United States.

But the question often came: who is sponsoring or funding this migration? Mainland political conservatives said that Vito Marcantonio, the Labor Party (some said pro-Communist) congressman from the Bronx, was paying for the trips to enlarge his constituency. This was patently impossible. No one person or group could bankroll that sizable a migration. The simple answer: with the end of the war, air travel became available; tickets were inexpensive; families in New York helped provide support and some housing; and the pent-up demand for economic gain lured Puerto Ricans as it had attracted similar migrations for a hundred years.

I was asked by the New York Board of Education to help it deal with the sudden arrival of non–English-speaking children, and train non–Puerto Rican teachers to understand their new students. I proposed establishing special classes to provide Puerto Rican students with intensified English instruction. This idea was immediately vetoed by liberals such as the American Jewish Committee as discriminatory. Spanish speakers continued to pour into the schools and slow the teaching of all subjects for all students.

I made some headway with the press. Our complex story was getting reported and discussed. One day, as a particularly sensitive matter was being concluded between Washington and San Juan, I was asked to urge the *New York Times* to comment editorially on the proposal. I took the matter to the editorial board and the next day a *Times* editorial made a favorable recommendation. I received a humorous cable from Governor Piñero thanking me, saying he assumed I could therefore produce a *Times* editorial at will.

Working briefly for me in New York was Munita, the comely daughter of Muñoz and his first wife, Muna Lee, the marriage of Muñoz's New York period. Muna Lee, a poet and writer, worked in Washington for Abe Fortas, director of the division of territories and island possessions in the Interior Department. I reported frequently to Fortas. He was one of the shrewdest young lawyers in the Roosevelt administration, playing a major role in constructing the legal foundation for Puerto Rico's commonwealth status. Fortas later became a confidant of President Lyndon Johnson, who appointed him to the Supreme Court. But when his continuing relationship with the president was uncovered, he was forced to resign his appointment.

The editorial in the *Times* and the reaction it stirred among *Populares'* opponents in San Juan generated a disturbing attack on me personally. The attack was vicious in the Puerto Rican setting. In a formal presentation to the governor the matter was titled "Investigation of Charges against Leonard R. Sussman." I was warned by the Fortaleza that some highly placed Puerto Rican citizens, former U.S. Army officers, believed that during my service in military intelligence I had written a scathing denunciation of the fighting qualities of the Puerto Rican soldier. This was being portrayed as an assault on Puerto Rican manhood, reason enough to end my service in the Puerto Rican government. It was, in fact, character assassination, possibly for the purpose of replacing me with a Puerto Rican. In any event, the Fortaleza suggested I return to the island immediately and face the accusation. A colonel who had carried the matter to the governor talked the other officers out of going to the press and then "picketing the plane to prevent Sussman's getting off." There was, it turned out, a confidential report on me.

It was difficult to begin. No one would tell me who my accusers were. I suspected it was a group of high-ranking regular army officers who long resented the second-class attention they believe they received at the hands of the mainland officer class. They probably further resented my presence, a mere technical sergeant, in military intelligence and especially in the role of spokesman in the Antilles Department. In the army, I had also created and written a daily news service especially for Puerto Rican troops in Europe, Asia, and the Caribbean, intended to keep them in touch with Puerto Rico just as mainland troops were given news of their hometowns. After I left the army I was awarded the Legion of Merit for such work (relatively rare for an enlisted man).

I mentioned this in my defense memo, but suddenly I realized the basis for the charge against me. Sometime around mid-1944 I was called in by Brig. Gen. Thomas R. Phillips, chief of staff, and asked to write a paper on the history of military action and armed defenses in Puerto Rico from the time of the Spaniards until the present. I did some research and produced a respectably academic paper that was classified secret. That was the last I heard of it. More than a year later, as I was about to leave the army, I heard that there had been a serious flap at the generals' level. The War Department in Washington had asked for a precise estimate of the combat capability of Puerto Rican troops. The query was made apparently to determine whether Gen. Douglas MacArthur should accept a Puerto Rican battalion in the Pacific theater. General Phillips, asked to make the judgment, had a personal history of resentment. By virtue of some earlier controversy over the matter of air power, he had been forced to sit out the war in the

Caribbean. He apparently prepared a negative assessment of the battle capabilities of Puerto Rican troops. I assume that my history paper was attached to his
judgment. My name was probably still on my paper. Someone who saw the
whole report, perhaps all too briefly, may have believed I wrote the entire report.
Obviously, this was impossible; I was totally unqualified to write such an assessment and could not possibly have been asked to do so. But those who wanted to
remove me from the New York post must have been aware of this.

In any event, I was forced to clear my name. I spoke to a Puerto Rican friend
who had been a major in intelligence when I served, and he gave me unqualified
support. His superior, Col. Francisco Parra, who probably associated in the past
with the officers who had made the charge, stated that I was "very impartial and
had no prejudice against the Puerto Ricans." Parra suggested the inquiry talk to
Manuel Navas.

I had known Mano, a journalism graduate of Louisiana State University,
from my first day on the newspaper in Puerto Rico. In the days before the war,
he was a leading young socialite, the king to several beauty queens of Puerto
Rico. We served together on the *World-Journal* and in the public relations office
of army headquarters. Even in the army, Mano sustained an ample social life.
Sometimes he forgot to return to barracks overnight and stopped by just in time
for a 6 A.M. roll call.

Once he managed the impossible. He dated an attractive young reporter on
the newspaper who decided to return to her home in the States. But she had also
dated General Phillips. She went to his office to say farewell, and he arranged to
have his car and driver take her to the airport. Mano, ever alert, entered the car
after it left the general's office. With the general's star flying, the car passed
through the post's gate, and Mano, seated in the general's place—recently
demoted to private for an escapade—returned the salute of the military guards.

As my oldest civilian and military associate, Mano wrote a memo for the
interrogating group. Mano came quickly to the basic concern. He wrote,
"Sussman's attitude is practically that of a Puerto Rican." Praise indeed for a
carpetbagger, one who gratefully walked the San Juan midway, the very blue-
tiled cobblestones carried as ballast in Columbus's ships.

The investigation collapsed when the two high-level "informants" refused to
testify or allow me to confront them. I returned to New York and left the government when my function was moved back to the island. I was asked to transfer,
but I declined. By then, my daughter Lynne needed a series of operations that
could only be performed in New York.

In 1956, before I joined Freedom House, Luis Muñoz Marin was given the
organization's annual Freedom Award, along with Ramon Magsaysay, president
of the Philippines. Muñoz had been elected and reelected governor and was successfully straddling the searing question of the island's political status. The word
"status" had become a daily term in the Spanish press. Muñoz carefully worked
out commonwealth status as Puerto Rico's unique U.S. model. This was some-

thing between statehood and independence. It provided federal and state tax immunity for Puerto Ricans on the island while also assuring mainland investors in the island freedom from taxes. In return, the United States maintained military bases but provided only a nonvoting resident commissioner in the Congress. No votes for Puerto Ricans on the island except at Republican and Democratic national conventions—an interesting anomaly.

Muñoz is a hero to me because he is an achiever of the middle way. He gave up his satisfying theoretical (bohemian) life and chose to enter the turbulent social and political scene at home. He knew the political alternatives. As a young man, he had joined the Socialist party of Santiago Iglesias. As the son of a famous father, he also had entrée to the conservative elite. He was on good terms as well with the *Independistas*, who hoped that one day he would favor their cause. Muñoz not only walked among them all but also devised a course that borrowed from each but added a new, unduplicated consensual program: the commonwealth. It would take major grants from the U.S. treasury, return almost none; yield control of federal service programs on the island but populate them with Puerto Ricans; permanently resolve neither statehood nor independence, but create greater self-rule, including insularly elected top officials; foreswear a Puerto Rican military establishment, but secure equity for Puerto Ricans serving in U.S. forces, including their educational and pension guarantees.

Muñoz served as governor during difficult times. The *Populares* just barely retained the governorship immediately after he retired, but lost it to the Republicans in the next election. The *Populares* have since returned and lost again—so evenly divided is the electorate over the question of "status"—the *Populares* defend the commonwealth, and the Republicans call for statehood, unlikely to be acceptable even to a Republican-dominated U.S. Congress.

Several years after becoming executive director of Freedom House I received an invitation to attend the inauguration of Raphael Hernandez Colon, the next governor of Puerto Rico. I did not know this young leader but, as I suspected, Muñoz had asked that I be invited. The other official guests: Mayor John Lindsay of New York; Representative Herman Badillo, the only Puerto Rican in Congress; and the ambassador of Brazil to the United States.

We were given a tour of new developments on the island and were presented repeatedly as honored guests. The inauguration was quite different than Governor Piñero's. The Fortaleza and *Populares* bureaucracies were running state functions in their own style. I was pleased to be present, to see my old office, but especially to realize—as Muñoz may have proposed—that I was *persona grata* after all.

The finest history and analysis of Puerto Rico's reformation is Alexander W. Maldonado's *Teodoro Moscoso and Puerto Rico's Operation Bootstrap*.[5] The author credits Muñoz for carrying out a "democratic revolution," Tugwell for importing his part of the Roosevelt "brain trust" to Puerto Rico, and Moscoso, whose relentless drive created the most successful government development corporation in the Western Hemisphere.

In 2001, I was asked by the Press Freedom Center at the University of the Sacred Heart in San Juan to describe my new book *Press Freedom in Our Genes.*[6] Suddenly, the host discovered that I had had a history in Puerto Rico! A panel of historians was arranged to interview me on television. I was asked about my relationships with three governors, Tugwell, Piñero, and Muñoz, as well as the social revolution they began. Newspaper and radio interviews followed. Once again, I felt warmly at home.

NOTES

1. Rexford G. Tugwell, *The Stricken Land: The Story of Puerto Rico* (New York: Doubleday, 1946), p. 253.

2. Ibid., p. 357.

3. Ibid., p. 551.

4. Rexford G. Tugwell, *The Art of Politics as Practiced by Three Great Americans: Franklin Delano Roosevelt, Luis Muñoz Marin, and Fiorello H. LaGuardia* (New York: Doubleday, 1998), p. x.

5. Alexander W. Maldonado, *Teodoro Moscoso and Puerto Rico's Operation Bootstrap* (Gainesville: University of Florida Press, 1976).

6. Leonard R. Sussman, *Press Freedom in Our Genes: A Human Need* (Reston, VA: World Press Freedom Committee, 2001).

15

WENDELL WILLKIE
One World, One Life

I was suspicious of Wendell L. Willkie when he first appeared on the national scene in 1939 to oppose Franklin D. Roosevelt for the presidency. I had been an ardent supporter of FDR since he first ran for the presidency in 1932. I was twelve at the time but wrote letters extolling Roosevelt that were published in New York newspapers. Clearly, editors in the *Sun, Post, World-Telegram, News,* and *Times* were not aware of my age. I liked Roosevelt's New Deal (my father called it socialist at dinner table debates). But in 1940 (at age twenty) I also suspected that Willkie held dangerous views.

I had absorbed some of the political attacks on Willkie. He headed an electric-power holding company that was fighting the Tennessee Valley Authority, FDR's creation to bring low-cost government-operated electricity to poor rural areas. He was a presumably conservative Republican (though I didn't know then he had been a Democrat all his life until he decided to run for the presidency), and I had heard rumors (patently untrue, I later found) that he held anti-Semitic views.

I could not have known how my life would be touched by Willkie.

It is nearly sixty years since Willkie took a forty-nine-day, 31,000-mile tour of a world at war. Returning, he said, "Today, because of military and other censorships, America is like a beleaguered city that lives within high walls through which there passes only an occasional courier to tell us what is happening outside. I have been outside those walls. And I have found that nothing outside is exactly what it seems to those within."[1]

Clearly, Willkie was expressing his own wonderment at what he found abroad. He was starting a miraculous process of conveying his new-found ideas and conceptions and casting off some misperceptions. I had barely met Willkie at that moment, but I came to value him—more and more—as time passed.

Wendell Willkie never won an election, though in 1940 he gained worldwide attention in challenging twice-elected Franklin D. Roosevelt for the presidency. After a historic campaign that changed the nature of American politics, Roosevelt declared on election night, "I'm happy I won, but I'm sorry Wendell lost."

Willkie had transformed his personal image and in the process made it possible for Roosevelt to support Britain, beleaguered by Nazi Germany; prepare the United States to defend itself in World War II; and replace American isolationism with a clear commitment to defeat fascism and create a postwar organization for peace. Indeed, those commitments led to Willkie's role at Freedom House, where I later became responsible for the organization's programs and the operation of its Willkie Memorial Building.

As the 1940 election campaign closed, I was a student at Columbia University's Graduate School of Journalism. I was assigned on election night to cover the Willkie headquarters in New York. I met Willkie briefly late that night when it was obvious he had lost the race to Roosevelt, although he refused to concede even after his vice presidential running mate Charles McNary did. Willkie chain-smoked Camels, commenting that Democrats always lead in the early returns because they control the big cities. Then, cities began to introduce voting machines, whereas rural areas had harder-to-count paper ballots. Moreover, Democratic political leaders dominated the electorate in major cities.

Willkie sat quiet, watching the Roosevelt lead build up in states Willkie needed to win. "I've no hope now," Mrs. Willkie remarked. "I wish Wendell would get ready to go home." It sounded as though they had attended a social event and it was over. Edith Willkie was very much a sedate, apolitical homebody, unlike Willkie's sophisticated friend Irita Van Doren, the leading book editor of the day.

After midnight on election night, Willkie entered the grand ballroom of the hotel. The large crowd had dwindled to hardcore supporters and family. I was suddenly saddened by this scene. The large imposing figure who had risen to world prominence so quickly, who had spoken with increasing vigor and clarity of a new world outlook, now seemed almost alone in defeat. If the vote had been different, this room would have been filled to overflowing, as it was just six hours earlier. Although I had not been a Willkie fan I was nevertheless moved as the small crowd took up the chant that had projected the candidate surprisingly to the party's nomination just months earlier: "We want Willkie! We want Willkie!"

A few shouted, "We'll elect you in '44." Willkie smiled and assured the faithful he never felt better in his life. "Never quit," he added, and he didn't that night. Not until morning did Willkie send a congratulatory message to Franklin Roosevelt. He said, "I know we are both gratified that so many American citizens participated in the election"—the largest number ever up to that time. Willkie wished the president "all personal health and happiness."

Seventeen years later, in 1957, poet Muriel Rukeyser, my sister-in-law, published a moving, book-length prose-poem biography of Wendell Willkie titled

One Life after his world-circling report *One World*. Muriel described election night at the Commodore:

> The ballroom thins out, and the suite upstairs, until [Willkie] sits there almost alone. The boy from Columbia [I was twenty at the time], putting his notes away, looks up at Willkie. Numbers still streaming in past his eyes, easily, gently, filling in the almost empty room. Over the old streams, other millions, hardly any without its opposition. Never enough. None without its opposition. The boy from Columbia meets Willkie's eyes, exhausted blue; sits down again and pretends to write. Suppose I were president of Columbia? Willkie thinks, in the elevator. What is it like for [Roosevelt], up in Hyde Park? . . . or for McNary, so quick to concede, so early out there to bed?
>
> Now he has spoken his last to his final guests; spoken his last to the campaign people downstairs; to the newspapermen and their knowing foreheads. All of them walking well. As if on dry land. 2:15 in the morning. Cold 42nd Street outside, unbroken dark. Box of the radio silent filling without a sound in waves of numbers, little hundreds pouring.[2]

Wendell Willkie lost the 1940 election but made it possible for Roosevelt to arm for a war that was inevitable—and to try to win a peace that was less assured after the fighting stopped. The peace became the Cold War, and Willkie's contribution to winning that was no less vital, if far less apparent. That latter contribution to postwar challenges was made through Freedom House, an organization largely based on the ideas Willkie advanced in 1939–40 while supporting Roosevelt's bid to arm America against strong isolationist opposition. Willkie provided the decisive votes that enabled Roosevelt to pass the military draft by one vote in the House of Representatives. One supporting vote came from Rep. Margaret Chase Smith, who as Senator Smith became chair of Freedom House several decades later (see chap. 48).

Most Americans regarded the overrunning of Austria, Poland, Czechoslovakia, France, and the north countries as deplorable but not their business. That is, not until the Japanese navy attacked Pearl Harbor, December 7, 1941, sinking most of America's Pacific fleet and killing thousands of U.S. sailors and marines.

Muriel Rukeyser recalled of Willkie, "He is real; he is a myth; we can see our lifetime through him, with just that moment of distance already."[3] Willkie died in 1944 after fourteen heart seizures as he was considering the 1944 Republican presidential nomination.

Why, then, the myth? And why do I see at least part of my lifetime through him? As Muriel put it, "He knew the wish for powers he would never reach; defeat, and the recoil; the imaginative leap . . . in a movement which he was to perform many times and which we all recognize. And we knew, on his voyages, or flashing through his weaknesses at home, the other movement—toward the world, around the world, into the world."[4]

Translation: The "powers" and "defeat" were the presidency. The "recoil" was Willkie's postdefeat alliance with Roosevelt to support America at war, and a vision of a future peace. "Weaknesses at home" meant his failure to build a political constituency. But "the other movement" was Willkie's unparalleled flights to the war fronts in Europe and Asia, and his book *One World*. This marked the phenomenal conversion of an American provincial to an evangelistic one-worlder. Willkie's report to Roosevelt and the nation followed the geopolitical and philosophical basis upon which Freedom House had been founded in October 1941 by many of the same people who rallied around Willkie in his presidential campaign, and later in his One World tours and exposition of a postwar American doctrine.

Willkie touched me in ways I never expected.

Only decades later did I learn that Willkie had witnessed a scene in Puerto Rico in 1915 that, he said, impelled him "to work for a better balance with a social conscience." He had gone to the island to make money to become a lawyer. He worked as a sugar-lab chemist at a refinery in the east-coast town of Fajardo. While riding with a wealthy plantation owner, an emaciated canecutter crawled out of the cane where he had been hiding for several days after a workers' revolt. The *patron* hacked the man with a machete, almost severing his arm. The owner rode on, ignoring Willkie's plea that they "help the poor devil." Willkie remembered this all his life. Willkie told Gardner Cowles many years later that if he ever got in a position of influence he wanted to make a difference. I lived four years in Puerto Rico and served three years in the reform government's social revolution (see chaps. 13 and 14). I came away with similar convictions. (I also remember Fajardo for one day in 1942, when Fran and I nearly drowned in a small boat caught in a sudden storm off the coast.)

Willkie became a lawyer. He also had strong, almost "religious conviction," he wrote, that America should enter the League of Nations. Willkie, from the isolationist Midwest, made countless evangelistic speeches—including one on the floor of the Democratic National Convention in 1924—on behalf of the League. This emotional but losing battle was the first major confrontation between isolationism and internationalism as a doctrine of American foreign policy. Willkie's struggle for the League forecast his main political vision for the next two decades, a conviction that led him to join the board of Freedom House shortly after it was formed.

The men and women who invited him to join the Freedom House board were the same who had urged him to run for the presidency, then used their significant newspaper, magazine, and book connections to publicize his dramatic campaign that began with no political-party support and acquired little as the campaign developed.

Foremost was Irita Van Doren, a major book reviewer for the *New York Herald Tribune*, recently divorced after twenty-three years and, like Willkie, a southern-history buff. Willkie, at forty-one, had become the youngest president of a major utility system: Commonwealth and Southern. (Willkie became head of

C & S the same week in 1933 when Adolf Hitler became chancellor of Germany and Roosevelt was about to take his second oath as president.) The thirty-six-year-old wife of an executive at a C & S affiliate had written a large romantic novel of the Civil War. She called it *Gone with the Wind.* Willkie sent it to Van Doren, who saw its potential. No one, however, predicted it would become an all-time best-seller and movie classic. Few know that Wendell Willkie was the book's godfather. And probably neither Willkie nor Van Doren would have supposed that their relationship would grow into a full-time romantic link, or that Van Doren's New York salon would serve as the initiation of Willkie's political future. Franklin Roosevelt learned of the Willkie-Van Doren relationship but could not make political capital of it because of his own extramarital dalliance at the time.

Among the people Van Doren introduced to Willkie were Whitelaw Reid, publisher of the *Herald Tribune,* the primary Republican newspaper; Herbert Bayard Swope, editor of the fabled *New York World*; Russell Davenport of *Fortune* magazine and through him Henry Luce, publisher of *Fortune* and the still more influential *Time.* Davenport agreed to work strenuously for Willkie's nomination in 1940. His interest in Willkie—as with others having substantial publicity outlets—was Willkie's strong internationalism voiced in evangelistic terms.

Willkie was among future Freedom House leaders who supported Roosevelt's effort in July 1939 to revise the Neutrality Act so that the United States could help arm Britain against the Nazis. Republicans in Congress defeated that effort. But when Hitler signed a nonaggression pact with the Soviet Union and the Nazis invaded Poland, effectively starting World War II, Willkie stepped up his speechmaking to assist Roosevelt. The Neutrality Act was finally amended to aid those ready to resist Germany.

Willkie's commitment to an antifascist alliance-in-the-making—this in the face of strong Republican opposition—attracted a new set of prominent admirers, many of whom became Freedom House leaders. These included Francis Miller (see next chapter), a prominent North Carolina political-policy specialist who helped found Fight for Freedom at the Century Club in New York. The group became known as the Warhawks of World War II. They wanted America to end neutrality and fight beside Britain; their immediate goal was to help Roosevelt sell Congress on the Lend-Lease arrangement. That would provide England with fifty old U.S. destroyers in exchange for ninety-year U.S. leases on British military bases in the Caribbean. When I served in the Army during the war I visited many of these stations. Also attracted to Willkie for his stand on defense was William Allen White, editor-publisher of the *Emporia Gazette.* This small-town newspaper had earned a national reputation by the sheer integrity of White's editorials and the quality of the journalism he practiced. White created a grassroots organization to support Roosevelt in preparing the national defense. Significantly, White spoke from Kansas, the Republican heartland, through the group he brought together under the name, Defend America by Aiding the Allies. Of the two organizations, Fight for Freedom was clearly the more militant.

By October 1940, the two groups—Fight for Freedom and Defend America by Aiding the Allies—merged to form Freedom House. A quarter-century later, when I became executive director of Freedom House, Francis Miller was still active and a strong supporter of its programs. He also helped me gain membership in the Century Association, located at the partial birthplace of Freedom House.

William Allen White's son and widow were both active in my early days at Freedom House. As a distinguished journalist in his own right, William L. White moved far beyond Kansas. He shared with me his father's acerbic editorial-obituary of a newspaper-chain owner the senior White disliked:

Frank Munsey, the great publisher, is dead.

Frank Munsey contributed to the journalism of his day the talent of a meat-packer, the morals of a money changer, and the manners of an undertaker. He and his kind have about succeeded in transforming a once-noble profession into an eight percent security.

May he rest in trust.

Whitelaw Reid's son, "Whitey," was editor of the *New York Herald Tribune* when I arrived at Freedom House. He presided over the distinguished paper's final days. On the board, too, was Herbert Swope, son of Herbert Bayard Swope, the most prominent journalist of his day.

Willkie had a mixed persona for one seeking the Republican nomination. He had made a reputation as a college socialist. As early as 1925, he organized the Akron Citizens' Committee to oust Ku Klux Klan control of the school system (hardly the move of a bigot, nor was his 1944 urging of Roosevelt to end segregation in the armed forces—not accomplished until Harry Truman's presidency). Later, he had been a member of the executive committee of Tammany Hall, the New York City machine of the Democratic Party. He contributed to Roosevelt's first campaign. But what the public best remembered was that Willkie was a Wall Street lawyer and utility tycoon. That same public may have been further confused by Willkie's stance on foreign policies.

The men and women who rallied around Willkie for the presidential nomination in mid-1940 believed his internationalism could overcome his latter-day conservatism. In any event, they wanted to promote a bipartisan policy that recognized the crucial challenges to Western civilization. No Republican politician offered that prospect; indeed, most attacked Roosevelt for involving the United States in what they regarded as a "European war." That was hardly Hitler's pledge in *Mein Kampf*, the bible of Nazism. He promised a "thousand-year Reich" in which the "decadent democracies" would perish. And he had equally dictatorial allies—the Axis—in militarist Japan and fascist Italy.

With the 1940 election passed, Willkie wanted to see for himself the nature of the war Germany was waging against Britain, and the needs of the British to sustain their defense. Roosevelt gave Willkie a letter of introduction to Prime Minister Winston Churchill.

In February 1941, nearly a year before America was bombed into war at Pearl Harbor, Willkie spent time in bomb shelters as Londoners suffered murderous attacks by waves of German bombers. "I'm a tough old egg, I think," Willkie wrote, "but this moves me very deeply. I am almost spilling over."[5] Churchill heard that Willkie was walking the streets without protection during a Nazi air attack. He sent Willkie six white helmets and three gas masks. While bombs rained down, Willkie listened to a Labor member of Parliament denouncing the Churchill government for banning the Communist *Daily Worker*. Willkie later called this "the most dramatic example of democracy at work anyone could wish to see."[6]

Willkie returned home to a Republican party split by his exploit. Some leaders wanted to expel him from the party. But Willkie prevailed: the Republican National Committee approved a declaration that "after this war, the responsibility of this nation will not be circumscribed within the territorial limits of the United States; that our nation has an obligation to assist in bringing about understanding, comity, and cooperation among the nations of the world in order that our liberty may be preserved and that the blighting and destructive processes of war may not again be forced upon us."

Again in August 1942, with Roosevelt's blessing, Willkie set out on a second tour of the war fronts. This would be wider-ranging, still more dangerous and dramatic. Willkie had a converted Consolidated bomber and an army crew assigned to him. He took with him several close aides, including Joseph Barnes of the *Herald Tribune*, who would help write the book *One World*, an immediate best-selling report of this trip. Mainly, the book projected Willkie's philosophy of wartime action and peacetime planning for "one world."

The flight touched down first in Puerto Rico, where Willkie's son Philip was serving in the navy. I knew of their meeting; I was not yet in the army but was press secretary to Puerto Rico's governor Rexford G. Tugwell, a former Columbia University professor in Roosevelt's "brain trust." Despite the secrecy surrounding the Willkie flight, Governor Tugwell was told of the brief stopover. Phillip Willkie visited me many years later at the Willkie Memorial Building in New York. From 1945 to 1985 it served as the headquarters of Freedom House.

The Willkie plane, named *Gulliver*, flew to Brazil and stopped briefly at a secret U.S. base on the tiny island of Ascension, midway across the South Atlantic. After I entered the army and was assigned to military intelligence at department headquarters in the Caribbean, Ascension would play a major role in planning for the reassignment of thousands of troops and European-based aircraft. They would speed to Ascension and then on to the Asian war theater, after the collapse of Nazi Germany.

Willkie went on to Cairo, barely one hundred miles from where German general Erwin Rommel was fighting the battle of Egypt. Rumors abounded that the British were about to retreat and give up Egypt. To see for himself, Willkie drove in a jeep across the desert. He inspected the front at El Alamein with British general Bernard L. Montgomery. Willkie watched the exchange of fire; the general predicted the Germans in the desert would soon be routed. He urged Willkie to tell the press in Cairo. Montgomery said they would not believe good news coming from a British general. Willkie issued this simple statement: "Egypt is saved. Rommel is stopped and a beginning has been made on the task of throwing the Nazis out of Africa." The British Eighth Army held.

In Beirut, Willkie met General Charles de Gaulle, flamboyant leader of the fighting French and later president of France. The same day Willkie had tea with Bayard Dodge, president of the American University of Beirut. Dodge had long headed that prestigious school open to everyone. Said Willkie, "It is no exaggeration to say that Dr. Dodge gave me more hope and confidence for the future . . . than all the others combined." I met Dr. Dodge ten years later and still recall this soft-spoken scholar whose life was devoted to intercultural, interreligious education and who practiced his calling in a difficult environment.

While Willkie was in Turkey, then neutral in the war, the German radio complained of Willkie's presence in the country. Willkie, recently defeated in his run for the presidency, responded, "Invite Hitler to send to Turkey, as a representative of Germany, *his* opposition candidate."

In Moscow under siege, Willkie met dictator Joseph Stalin, still furious because Britain and America had not yet opened a second front in Europe to relieve the Soviet Union, which was suffering enormous casualties. At a formal dinner, Stalin upbraided the Allies. Willkie responded that Britain had stood alone before the USSR was attacked. He might have recalled that Stalin signed a nonaggression pact with Hitler that left the Nazis free to attack England, but he didn't. Instead, Willkie toasted Britain, the Soviet Union, China, and the United States—"united now and who, for the peace and economic security of the world, must remain united after the war." It was clear to everyone present, said Joe Barnes later, that Willkie "was rebuking Stalin."[7] He drank the toast.

Willkie was worried about Stalin and his postwar objectives. He had learned more about the Soviet Union than most observers, official or journalistic. He urged pressing the USSR *then* for postwar concessions on Eastern Europe, rather than waiting until Stalin's hand was stronger. Willkie detected in the Soviet leadership "a rebirth of the brutality and imperialism of the old Czarist governments." This was to be the reality of the Cold War and the challenge to Freedom House at war's end.

During the long flight to China, Willkie repeatedly discussed with Gardner Cowles (of the Cowles newspapers and *Look* magazine, later a supporter of Freedom House) how the Soviet Union could be bound during the war to participate after the war in a real league of nations strong enough to preserve peace, and promote a more equitable relationship between have and have-not nations. In China, Willkie said flatly that "the colonial days are past." He angered

Churchill, who said that the Atlantic Charter did not refer to the Pacific (and presumably India). Willkie said it is the "world's job to find some system for helping colonial peoples who join the United Nations' cause to become free and independent nations." He believed these questions should not be "hushed" until the war was over. Willkie's speech aroused Churchill to declare these famous words: "I have not become the King's first minister in order to preside over the liquidation of the British Empire."[8]

William Allen White editorialized from Emporia: "For the first time in human history, a major leader of a great republic spoke out specifically, naming names of nations and races, and demanding in terms definite and certain, freedom for all mankind. Mr. Roosevelt and the Atlantic Charter and Mr. Churchill have spoken of freedom but apparently with crossed fingers for Asia and Africa."[9]

On his return, Willkie spoke of America's "reservoir of goodwill" he found abroad. "All around the world," he said, "there are some ideas which millions and millions of men hold in common, almost as much as if they lived in the same town." One such idea, he added, was "the mixture of respect and hope with which the world looks to this country." He credited this not least to the hospitals, schools, and colleges that Americans—missionaries, teachers, and doctors—have founded in the far corners of the world. Perhaps he had Bayard Dodge in mind. I thought of this many times in writing my book on the Fulbright scholarships and the immense value of international educational and cultural exchanges. (At the time of writing, these are under threat of sharp reduction by a short-sighted Congress.)

Willkie particularly warned that it was no less important to know what the war was being fought for than to win the war itself. "We did not fight the Revolution because we hated Englishmen and wanted to kill them," he said, "but because we loved freedom and wanted to establish it."[10] Willkie reluctantly concluded that there was, indeed, no grand postwar vision encompassing everyone, friend and foe, in a bold plan for peace and development. He saw a lack of continuity in our foreign policy. Neither party, he added, can claim to have pursued a stable or consistent program of international cooperation. How much more frustrated would Willkie be today, several hundred wars later and no real vision for universal rapport on the horizon?

At home, Willkie saw no small postwar challenge. He made a startling charge for his day. After chastising the colonial powers abroad, he declared, "We have practiced within our own boundaries something that amounts to race imperialism."[11] He said, "The attitude of the white citizens of this country toward the Negroes has undeniably had some of the unlovely characteristics of an alien imperialism—a smug racial superiority, a willingness to exploit an unprotected people."

One World, published in April 1943, was an instant bestseller. It earned almost unanimous praise from reviewers. One million copies were sold the first seven weeks. *Foreign Affairs* said Willkie had struck "one of the hardest blows ever" against the "intellectual and moral isolationism of the American people."

Back home, Willkie supported unpopular civil rights causes—attacking Roosevelt for prosecuting Governor Huey Long, the Louisiana "Kingfish," and Earl Browder, leader of the Communist Party. Willkie was planning to write a book with Walter White, head of the National Association for the Advancement of Colored People (NAACP).

However, Willkie suddenly fell ill. He called to his hospital room Roscoe Drummond, syndicated columnist and Washington bureau chief for the *Christian Science Monitor,* one of the best newspapers of the day. Roscoe was an officer of Freedom House for many years. Willkie wanted to discuss whether he should endorse Franklin Roosevelt or the Republican Governor Thomas Dewey for the next election. He never made the decision. He died of multiple ailments on October 8, 1944.

By then, Willkie had indeed become a Republican who reflected a bipartisan international policy. As an unsuccessful candidate, however, he would take on greater stature than either he or the president might have imagined. Willkie briefly considered a total realignment of U.S. political parties: there would be a liberal and a conservative party, without naysayers splitting both parties. (Shades of the 1990s!) Roosevelt, too, was thinking about such possibilities. He told an associate, "Willkie and I together can form a new, really liberal party in America." Willkie responded, "You tell the president that I'm ready to devote almost full time to this."

Robert E. Sherwood, Franklin Roosevelt's speech writer and confidant, later wrote he believed in 1943 and early 1944 that if Willkie were to win the Republican nomination in 1944 Roosevelt would not have run for a fourth term. Sherwood later recalled: "Once I heard [Harry] Hopkins [FDR's closest adviser] make some slurring remark about Willkie, and Roosevelt slapped him down with as sharp a reproof as I ever heard him utter. He said, 'Don't you ever say anything like that around here again. Don't even think of it. You of all people ought to know that we might not have had Lend-Lease or Selective Service [military draft] or a lot of other things if it hadn't been for Wendell Willkie. He was a godsend to this country when we needed him most.'"[12]

Willkie's joining the Freedom House board with co-chair Eleanor Roosevelt, the first lady, was a demonstration both of the Willkie-Roosevelt relationship and the role played by Freedom House in creating a broad centrist program, particularly in international affairs.

I had known little about Willkie while he was active on the world scene. From December 4, 1941, until January 1946, I had been out of the United States and learned only what wartime censorship allowed the world beyond American shores to know. Certainly that did not include critical journalism of Willkie's role vis-à-vis Franklin Roosevelt, the wartime leader.

On January 1, 1967, I became executive director of Freedom House and thus a latter-day custodian of the Willkie heritage. This was to be a double role. First,

I would devise and sustain public programs in the spirit of Willkie and his early Freedom House associates. This I had been prepared for. I had a keen sense of employing politics to pursue social equity through the democratic process. The tools were fresh political ideas, sustained activism, negotiation, and compromising of competing interests and objectives.

I was not prepared, however, for the role of actual custodian of a nine-story building. That was the Willkie Memorial Building. It was an imposing late-nineteenth-century structure situated across from the New York Public Library on Fortieth Street, just west of Fifth Avenue. Freedom House acquired the building as its headquarters shortly after Willkie died, and in his name. The building was conceived, in Willkie's spirit, to house not only Freedom House but like-minded nonprofit organizations advancing the public weal. Tenants included the NAACP, the Anti-Defamation League of B'nai B'rith, a public housing group, public school volunteers, the U.S. refugee coordinator, and the group pressing for democracy in Latin America.

As executive director of Freedom House and the Willkie Memorial of Freedom House, Inc., a separate corporate entity, I became custodian of the bricks and mortar as well as the political heritage of Wendell Willkie. That was no small undertaking. The ornate building had a certain magnificence: intriguing three-dimensional gargoyles across the structure's front face, dark wood paneling in many rooms, extraordinarily high ceilings, a massive metal chandelier beneath a top-floor skylight, fireplaces throughout the building, and handsome red-brick outer facing. The subbasements housed intriguing examples of nineteenth-century boilers and elevator machinery, badly equipped for thirteen agencies doing business in late-twentieth-century style. I was expected to keep the stodgy elevators running, heat the large drafty building, and keep water flowing in its aged pipes.

More than that, I was expected to retain the impossible pricing of space. It began at $1.50 a square foot in 1945 and had risen to $7.00 when I took over in 1967—while the rest of the block was charging $20 to $40 a square foot for that desirable neighborhood. I raised rates slowly through the years but never enough to meet costs. When the city demanded major renovations to meet new fire and brick safety laws, it was clear I had to make a bitter choice: force Freedom House into bankruptcy to sustain the Willkie Memorial by using program funds for building operations, or sell the building and use the funds for Freedom House programs thereafter. The choice, once coldly faced, was simple: it was bricks versus ideas. In 1987, I sought a buyer for the bricks.

The logical customer was down the street: the Republic National Bank, which already owned much of Thirty-ninth and Fortieth streets, and all of west Fifth Avenue between Thirty-ninth and Fortieth. A $6 million purchase price was agreed. But that only began a torturous year, the worst in my life. The thirteen tenants banded together to resist the sale and demanded 75 percent of the proceeds! They claimed the building was community property. The original incorporator of the Willkie Memorial, then the attorney general of the state, and after

retirement still an officer of Freedom House, had warned me I might have difficulty selling the building—but he didn't say why. Bitter year-long litigation followed. It cost Freedom House $1.5 million in lawyer's fees and grants to the ten-
ants. But the worst was still to come.

The bank had told us it would use the building for its back-office staff. Late
on the night after the sale contract was signed, however, the bank sent workmen
up the face of the structure with sledgehammers to destroy the gargoyles that had
given the building a distinctive appearance. This destruction was clearly intended
to avoid having the building declared a landmark, presumably reducing its value
to the new owner.

The press immediately deplored the defacement. The Landmark Commission insisted it had not had time to consider designating the building for preservation. Yet the same Landmark Commission had long inhabited the Willkie
Building as an associate of our tenant, the American Institute of Architects. That
was not all, however. Some months later the bank's demolition crew began the
total destruction of the Willkie Building. As I write nearly a decade later, that
space on Fortieth Street is just a parking lot, though the *New York Times* had long
since reported, with extensive graphics, that a new structure would soon rise on
the plot—an annex to the Republic National Bank, whose principal owner died
in 1999 when an arsonist set fire set to the banker's Monaco home.

Now, decades after Willkie's death, America has commemorated the end of the
war in Europe, the dropping of atomic bombs on Japan, the end of the war in the
Pacific, and the creation of the United Nations. In all of this, there was no mention of Wendell Willkie. But then at the Republican National Convention in mid-
1944, not a word was said about Willkie either, though he had been that party's
presidential candidate just four years earlier!

Perhaps it is best left to poets not only to remember but to evoke the meaning
of one life. Muriel Rukeyser summed up Wendell Willkie's extraordinary life: by
seeking "many shinings of truth" Willkie lit a "flare" against "corruption and for-
getting." Rukeyser reminds us to "let us give us ourselves / Linked."[13]

One life, one world.

Archibald MacLeish, Librarian of Congress, called Willkie's death "the
stopped voice—the uncompleted sentence." Then, said Joe Barnes, "began the
great silence." The peace that Willkie had feared for was "fumbled and lost."[14]

The Cold War followed.

NOTES

1. Wendell L. Willkie, introduction to *One World* (New York: Simon and Schuster, 1943).

2. Muriel Rukeyser, *One Life* (New York: Simon and Schuster, 1957), p. 145.

3. Ibid., p. xiii.

4. Ibid., p. xiv.

5. Quoted in Joseph Barnes, *Willkie: The Events He Was Part of, the Ideas He Fought For* (New York: Simon and Schuster, 1952), p. 248.

6. Ibid., p. 308.

7. Ibid., p. 302.

8. Ibid., p. 308.

9. Quoted in Steve Neal, *Dark Horse: A Biography of Wendell Willkie* (New York: Doubleday, 1984), p. 261.

10. Willkie, *One World*, p. 68.

11. Ibid., p. 79.

12. Quoted in Neal, *Dark Horse*, p. 314.

13. Rukeyser, *One Life*, p. 330.

14. Archibald MacLeish, quoted in Barnes, *Willkie*, p. 388.

16

FRANCIS MILLER
Warhawk of World War II

Today, when I enter the quiet precincts of the Century Club, just off Fifth Avenue in New York, I recall Francis Miller's mellifluous Southern tones describing the origin of Freedom House, which he helped create. He introduced me as a member of the Century Club, where many of Freedom House's founders planned an organization that would influence America's course in World War II. Indeed, Franklin D. Roosevelt and Wendell L. Willkie (see previous chapter) were both members of the Century when they competed for the presidency of the United States in 1940. Eight Centurians have been president of the country.

The Century, the sanctum for New York's intellectuals, remains much the same today. The club's purpose is good conversation and the members' advancement of their cultural interests. No business papers may be carried in; no deal-making is allowed. Good talk is encouraged in the overstuffed chairs, the display of newspapers and magazines from abroad, and the floor-to-ceiling mahogany-paneled library, with its old-fashioned circular stair and volumes written largely by members of the Century. Large, ornately framed paintings by American masters abound throughout the house. One was recently sold for a high price to help pay to remodel the ancient structure. It resembles traditional London clubs to which Century members have reciprocal access.

The long table in the third-floor dining room accommodates only members who seek good mealtime conversation with other members. The larger dining room is set amid stacks of books, the food served by aging waiters who know many members before they sign chits. In the quiet, paneled alcoves members still discuss all manner of historic and current matters—just as did those men invited by Francis Miller before World War II who came to be known as the Century Group, or the Warhawks.

After Hitler invaded Poland in October 1939, I began publishing in the *Washington Square Bulletin,* the newspaper at New York University of which I was editor in chief, a series of articles on college-campus activities during the *First* World War. Many other university papers had been carrying strong antiwar articles accompanying campus demonstrations against war. Many of these demos were inspired or organized by Communist-led groups. That persisted until the moment Stalin and Hitler signed a nonaggression pact. Suddenly, the morning after the signing, the NYU student cafeteria was silent. Groups of the Young Communist League and their allies in the American Student Union were literally dumbfounded. I walked among them and heard utter disbelief. The day before, to the Marxists, the war was an imperialist conflict to be resisted. Now . . . well, now, what was the line to be? It was too early to say. Later, it would be defined: Uncle Joe Stalin and we were good friends, in this war together—but only after Hitler turned on his Soviet partner and attacked the Red Army.

The same debates were under way uptown at City College, where Irving Kristol, Irving Bell, David Bell, and Nathan Glazer were "arguing the world," in the words of Joseph Dorman's TV documentary. The young intellectuals' heady dreams of Marxism, he says, died a painful death with Stalin's purges.

I shared the latter-day view of the liberal Washington officeholder Elliot Richardson: the attributes of moderation are "empathy, understanding, rationality, skepticism, balance, and objectivity." Moderates, he adds, "try to see the world clearly and see it whole. They are realistic."[1]

In May 1940, as I prepared to graduate from the university, I sealed a short message in an envelope for my eyes only. The single sentence: "The United States will be in the war within eighteen months." Several weeks later—June 10, 1940—there appeared in the *New York Times* and many other newspapers a full-page advertisement signed by thirty prominent Americans calling for the United States to declare war on Germany. Later, it would be said, they "spoke the unspeakable." Most Americans favored Britain fighting defensively against the Nazis, but few supported American participation in that conflict three thousand miles away. There were pockets of vocal support for Britain among liberal Protestant groups, Jews, and citizens with Polish or Czech backgrounds (their European counterparts were under cruel Nazi domination). But mainly isolationist views predominated, fed by organizations such as America First, several profascist groups, and the defeatist reports of Charles A. Lindbergh, aviator-hero, and Joseph Kennedy, future president John Kennedy's father and President Roosevelt's ambassador to Great Britain.

A Gallup poll in June 1940 recorded 65 percent of Americans believing that if England and France collapsed, Germany would then attack the United States. Indeed, five of eight thought the United States would eventually fight. The same percentage thought the United States was not helping the Allies adequately. But only one American in fourteen favored declaring war on Germany.[2]

The private citizens who placed the war-now ad in newspapers were known as the Century Group, later to be organized as Fight for Freedom—and still later, after a 1941 merger, Freedom House. These were the Warhawks of World War II. Their organizer, Francis P. Miller, was to become a good friend, as was his wife, Helen. Their sophisticated activity directed at both Franklin Roosevelt and Wendell Willkie enabled leaders of both parties to push through Congress by a small margin the historic Lend-Lease Act, providing fifty over-age U.S. destroyers for Britain and helping defend the Atlantic ocean bridge vital for transporting other supplies to the embattled British.

I did not meet Francis and Helen until 1967, after their wartime papers, along with the documents of similar activists, could be opened and discussed. Francis would appear as a board member of Freedom House. It was always a pleasure to chat with him. He had been an executive of the Council on Foreign Relations and knew the intricacies of organizational operations. He had joined Axel Rosin in nominating me for membership in the Century Club—eminently appropriate since the club was the forum for the conception of ideas for Freedom House, the organization I would direct for twenty-one years.

It was fascinating to hear Francis's personal story. His soft, modulated speech unmistakably originated in the Valley of Virginia, farmland between the Blue Ridge and the Allegheny Mountains. As a young man, he was in Geneva for the World Student Christian Association and in 1917 fought with the field artillery in France. After the war, he attended Oxford. His Calvinism gave Francis Miller no choice but to support good over evil. "There are," however, he said, "no black and white . . . in human affairs; the gray predominates usually." But, he added, in Hitler "the black wells up." He saw in Nazism not just evil men but "demonic forces." You see them, he said, in a "lynching mob in the South." He could not understand what makes men go "utterly bestial," but he knew they had to be stopped.[3]

To start, Francis and Helen Miller invited some friends to their country house in Fairfax, Virginia. Helen enhanced Francis's organizational expertise in foreign affairs. She was Washington correspondent for *The Economist* of London and director of a policy analysis group. The Miller meeting decided that a call to war demanded wide public discussion; hence their newspaper ads raising the "unspeakable" question.

The text said Americans recognized that "Nazi Germany [was] the mortal enemy of our ideals, our institutions, and our way of life." If Britain and France were defeated, said the declaration, the United States would have to fight alone. The United States should therefore "immediately give official recognition to the fact and logic of the situation—by declaring that a state of war exists between this country and Germany," and send all possible military aid to our Allies.

There was wide press coverage and support, as well as attacks from the isolationist camp. I remember the acrimonious debates that summer of 1940. Francis reassembled his enlarged circle of supporters at the Century Club. The building itself was eminently designed for the purpose of the meetings: it is an oasis amid midtown noise and bustle. Yet it is not a rich man's (or, today, a rich woman's as well) hideaway. Members are selected for personal achievement in the arts, the law, journalism, public affairs, and related fields. Particular stress is placed on members providing interesting conversation. Those who met with Francis Miller those days in 1940 were known as the Century Group. Their conversations were intensely interesting; indeed, of national importance.

One who spoke "brilliantly" and in the tones of "an Old Testament Prophet"—Francis's words—was Herbert Agar. He had been an ordinary seaman during World War I and later London correspondent for the *Louisville Courier-Journal*. He became the paper's editor and won a Pulitzer Prize for a book on the history of the presidencies. Miller described Agar as "our conscience." Herbert Agar was to become the first president of Freedom House before he went off to World War II. At those conversations at the Century, when Herbert Agar talked, "you felt that Mount Sinai itself had spoken," Francis Miller recalled.

He and others decided to engage their prominent friends in agreeing to take on the Hitler war machine. Friends who joined them at the Century included Dean Acheson (later secretary of state under Truman), Allen W. Dulles (later Eisenhower's intelligence chief), James B. Conant (president of Harvard University), and Robert E. Sherwood (three-time Pulitzer Prize winner). The conversation was illuminating, even for the Century.

Their first major decision, which some later regretted, was sidetracking the war-now theme for the immediate purpose of supporting Roosevelt's effort to achieve the destroyer-base deal. In retrospect, that decision seems wise, even without the knowledge that Japan would soon attack Pearl Harbor and make war-now a moot issue. The group assumed responsibility for liaison between Roosevelt and his Republican opponent in the 1940 presidential race, Wendell L. Willkie. The group moved between the British Embassy in Washington and the U.S. press and between FDR and Willkie. The mission, as Francis Miller recalled to me, was to gain assurance from the British that they would indeed accept U.S. destroyers in exchange for leasing Caribbean bases to the Americans. There was some hesitancy, but in the end the British agreed. Then it was necessary to gain Willkie's assurance that if Roosevelt announced the deal he (Willkie) would not attack FDR for it. There were, after all, significant isolationist votes that could probably be added to the Republican column if Willkie chose the politically opportunistic course. After much soul-searching, Willkie did not attack the Lend-Lease deal; he gave it somewhat ambiguous support.

One of Francis Miller's major coups—he told the story as modestly as possible—was persuading General John J. Pershing, commander of American forces in the First World War, to make a national radio address supporting Lend-Lease at a crucial moment in the Congressional debate over the destroyer-bases act. Pershing was aging and ill, but a mutual friend of Francis and the general appealed to Pershing to perform this final national service. Herbert Agar persuaded the Mutual Broadcasting System to carry the speech. Agar and Walter Lippmann, the prominent *Herald Tribune* columnist, drafted the speech.

Pershing said it was his duty to warn the nation that "the British navy needs destroyers and small craft to convoy merchant ships . . . and repel invasion." The United States, he said, has an "immense reservoir of destroyers," and he urged the United States to make fifty of these available to safeguard as well America's "freedom and security." This was the first major public discussion of the destroyer deal. Secretary of State Cordell Hull was photographed congratulating the general after his speech.

The Century Group continued its public argument with other prominent speakers. By mid-March 1941, the Century Group organized itself into Fight for Freedom. Dorothy Thompson, the widely syndicated columnist, lent support (she was to become cochairman of Freedom House). Among the sponsors were the presidents of Harvard University, the College of William and Mary, the University of North Carolina, Mount Holyoke College, Smith College, Bowdoin College, Brooklyn College, and St. John's University. There were seven international trade union executives, including A. Philip Randolph, head of the Brotherhood of Sleeping Car Porters. Randolph's associate, the civil rights leader Bayard Rustin, and I were to have a special working relationship over many years and in many countries (see chap. 18 and appendix C). Other sponsors included many prominent personalities: Maxwell Anderson, Edna Ferber, George S. Kaufman, Moss Hart, Dorothy Parker, Edna St. Vincent Millay, Ethel Barrymore, Melvyn Douglas, Douglas Fairbanks, Lowell Thomas, and Lloyd Paul Stryker.

Fight for Freedom had a simple structure composed mainly of the executive committee that did the work and sponsors and others who lent their names to the public statements or made quiet visits to officials and the news media. One stalwart supporter was restaurateur Mac Kriendler, an owner of the 21 Club in New York. In 1967, Mac provided my first introduction to the board of Freedom House. He personally hosted the luncheon at which I was introduced to the board, and was presumably approved for the directorship. Actually, the executive committee had already decided on my candidacy. Mac displayed that day the strong pro-American spirit he still felt twenty-five years after the wartime struggle. He continued to host meetings for causes he deeply believed in.

Fight for Freedom remained embattled throughout its life. Sometimes it was chided for attacking opponents too strenuously. One example, Francis Miller recalled, was the organization's bitter tussle with Generoso Pope, the multimillionaire my late father-in-law Lawrence Rukeyser had helped to gain control of the cement business in New York (see chap. 3). In the 1940s, Pope was a Democratic Party leader and publisher of *Il Progresso Italo-Americano,* the Italian language daily. Pope had strong ties to Italy and had been photographed giving the Fascist salute beside Dictator Benito Mussolini. When President Roosevelt termed Italy's invasion of France a "stab in the back of a neighbor," Pope interpreted this as an assault on all Americans of Italian descent. In the presidential election, Pope supported Wendell Willkie but kept his Democratic Party position in Tammany Hall. Similarly, Pope made a bet-balancing contribution to Fight for Freedom. But the organization termed him a profascist and returned the money. The organization took the unusual (and unsuccessful) step of urging the attorney general to revoke Pope's citizenship, saying he had not renounced all allegiance to a foreign power.

By this time, my father-in-law and former partner of Pope was at City Island, New York, building barges for the U.S. Navy. These simple craft may one day have landed on enemy (Italian) soil.

What did Fight for Freedom accomplish? Francis Miller, at the time, had mixed feelings. He felt the central idea—declare war now!—had been sublimated to the immediate need to pass Lend-Lease. But this was a considerable achievement. Lend-Lease was a historic centerpiece of America's belated preparation for eventual belligerency to defeat an evil empire-in-the-making.

After the nation was fully at war in 1942, FDR congratulated the Warhawks for "the fine work you have done during the past year and a half." He wired, "Yours was not an easy task; but the vision and discretion which you brought to the work achieved very constructive results . . . a contribution to the national security and national defense which is incalculable."

Years later, after I had long since settled in as director of Freedom House, Francis invited Marianne and me to visit his summer home on a barrier reef near Kitty Hawk, North Carolina. Francis's gentility glowed in every word, every motion. Before lunch he offered a prayer spoken to acknowledge our presence. When he concluded, the Millers' aged dog slowly entered the dining room from the kitchen.

"He knows not to enter," said Francis, "until he hears 'Amen.'"

NOTES

1. Elliot Richardson, preface to *Reflections of a Radical Moderate* (New York: Pantheon, 1996).

2. See Mark Lincoln Chadwin, *The Hawks of World War II* (Chapel Hill: University of North Carolina Press, 1968), p. 30.

3. Quoted in Chadwin, *The Hawks of World War II*, p. 45.

17

ALEXANDER BICKEL
The "Middle Distance"

Alexander M. Bickel gave me a new term for the middle road in law, politics, and life itself. He called it the "middle distance." I had walked that path all my life. A master of the philosophy of law, Alex Bickel gave me a new rationale for my instinctive commitments. George Will called him "the keenest public philosopher of our time." Sadly, his time was too short. Bickel died of cancer at forty-nine.

Robert H. Bork, then solicitor general of the United States, regarded Bickel as "the only commentator who fully understood the meaning of Watergate for our legal order." Alex Bickel and I sat before a television set in my hotel room while the Senate investigation of Watergate was telecast live. We watched as John Dean, the president's youthful legal counsel, was interrogated. After receiving immunity, Dean admitted outrageous efforts by him, on order of the president, to persuade the director of the FBI and others to lie and engage in other illegal activity.

Professor Bickel turned to me and said, "Imagine *that* man, legal counsel to the president of the United States. What are we coming to?" "That man" was an inexperienced appointee who had no significant legal training, no apprenticeship of consequence in private law practice, no record of public service in the law. He was putty in the hands of a president who wanted a legal mouthpiece exactly like John Dean. This, said Alexander Bickel, was a sad moment in both the law and the presidency.

He paused, and then added, almost by explanation, "We may have brought that on ourselves. We never allowed Richard Nixon to become a part of the establishment, never permitted him to be treated as more than an outsider—even as president of the United States." To be sure, Nixon had been thunderously

154 A PASSION FOR FREEDOM

attacked since he first ran for Congress in California against liberal Helen
Gahagan Douglas. He had attacked her as a Communist fellow-traveler. Even
after serving in the House and Senate, when he was defeated for the California
governorship (before running for the presidency), he blurted out to the press after
midnight on election night, "You won't have Nixon to kick around anymore!"
But they did. Nixon won two terms as president, and—he believed—the press
continued to kick him around. That belief, paranoid or not, led to the Watergate
break-in and the White House's dirty tricks that brought down the Nixon presidency. "We never allowed Richard Nixon to become a part of the establishment,"
Alex Bickel had said.

We were seated before that TV set because I had brought Bickel together for
a weekend conference with his former adversary Whitney North Seymour Jr., the
U.S. attorney who was directed by Nixon's attorney general to prosecute the *New
York Times* for publishing the Pentagon Papers. A former Vietnam War analyst
had given the *Times* thousands of pages of secret policy documents of the origins
of the Vietnam War. The papers had been commissioned by Secretary of Defense
Robert S. McNamara. The bundle was called the Pentagon Papers. When the
Times published the first of the critical material, President Nixon ordered the Jus-
tice Department to secure a federal court order preventing any further publication of the papers. This initiated a landmark court case leading to the U.S.
Supreme Court.

Alexander Bickel was retained by the *Times* to argue the First Amendment
right of the newspaper to publish—without prior restraint—information in the
public interest it had been given. Mike Seymour argued for the government that
publishing the papers would threaten the safety of troops in Vietnam, undermine
the relationship of the United States with friendly countries mentioned sometimes negatively in the documents, destroy the confidentiality of the government's policy formulation process, and justify the stealing of government property (the papers themselves).

After a fifteen-day hiatus, the Supreme Court ruled that the government had
not met the "heavy burden of presumption against [the] constitutionality [of prior
restraint]." Thus, in this first effort in American history to use national security
as the reason to block news articles prior to publication, the court ruled in favor
of the newspapers by a vote of 6–3. The *Times, Washington Post,* and others then
carried additional excerpts from the Pentagon Papers.

The press had won the fight, but there remained a bitter aftertaste. The Nixon
administration felt more justified than ever in regarding the press as the enemy,
not just an antagonistic force. Indeed, Nixon prepared an "enemy's list" of print
and broadcast journalists—some of the most prominent—with whom the White
House was to have little contact. Conservative writers deepened the gap with
their more liberal colleagues.

When the scandals of Watergate erupted two years later, the conservative press
and like-minded politicians assumed that "the liberal establishment" was

exploiting a "third-rate break-in"—the burglary at the Democratic National Committee offices in the Watergate complex—to hinder the Nixon reelection campaign.

The gap widened. The mainline press was regarded by the administration as worse than adversarial. I believed that the country was coming to a dangerous pass. The credibility of the news media and of the government was challenged in increasingly bitter and derogatory terms by two large proponents: citizens defending the administration and attacking the press as untruthful and harmful, and other citizens denigrating the government as untruthful and dangerous. This, I believed, posed a crisis for a society whose freedom was based upon compromising adversarial tensions before they became solidified as the nearly traitorous work of enemies.

On that assumption I invited Mike Seymour, whose father Whit I had known for ten years, to come to Maryland University over a weekend to help set down some press-government guidelines on how this impasse might be resolved. He accepted; so, too, did his former adversary Alexander Bickel.

I also brought to the meeting the publishers of the *New York Post* and *Newsday*, the editor in chief of the *Christian Science Monitor*, the deputy secretary of defense (formerly a *New York Times* correspondent), the head of CBS Radio News, a university president, an executive producer of NBC News, the Washington bureau chief of the *Washington Sun-Times,* and a syndicated Washington correspondent. This represented a broad spectrum of political and professional views of government and the news media.

The participants were asked to define the real areas of press-government conflict, to set forth the operative constitutional rules, and to recommend specific common-sense procedures by which to maximize the flow of information to the public without destructive confrontation. We produced guidelines for government officials and guides for journalists covering government.

Bickel and Seymour came to agreement, not surprisingly, on the basic press-government relationship. Each yielded a bit more than either would have done in court. Seymour said that the main reason the case had come before a court was that "the decisional process had not gone on—the editors of the *Times* had not consulted with those who could tell them whether there were sensitive documents that would injure the public interest; and, therefore, the court was asked to intervene." He added, "The Supreme Court still thinks that is a valid issue. There are situations in which such a test will provide a basis for enjoining publication. Yet we should never have to come to that point where the courts are called upon to perform that function." If the government cannot be trusted to make such a judgment, Seymour said, then the editor has to make that determination. Doing so, said Seymour, the editor must then take responsibility for that action, and not simply run with the story because it is sensational. "A free press," he added, "carries with it an obligation that those who control the free press go through a rational process of decision as to whether or not to publish a particular story that may have adverse consequences."

Bickel responded, "I entirely agree." The Pentagon Papers case, he said, represented "a breakdown in what a decade before, or less, would have been the normal process. It was an attempt to cure the breakdown by bringing the judicial process in [prior restraint by court injunction], and I think very properly it failed, because that would not have been a proper cure."

He continued, "I tell no lies out of school. One very prominent journalist said when the case broke that this would never have happened ten years before. The story would have been checked out. There would have been a relationship of confidence such that he would have gone to someone, as the *Times* did with the Bay of Pigs story [the Cuban missile crisis], and said, 'Look, we have this stuff. What do you think should be done? What parts of it are good?' The assumption would be that nobody would try to stop him from publishing. The assumption would equally have been that no one was making his decision for him. There would have been an advisory session on the basis of mutual confidence, and the thing would have been straightened out."

Such an arrangement, Bickel continued, is "an untidy accommodation, highly unsatisfactory; like democracy, in Churchill's aphorism, the worst possible solution, except for all the other ones." Then, in a masterful summation, Bickel concluded:

> [The present system] leaves too much power in government, and too much in the institutionalized press, too much power insufficiently diffused, indeed all too concentrated, both in government and in too few national press institutions, print and electronic. The accommodation works well only when there is forbearance on both sides, albeit in context of an adversary relationship. It threatens to break down when the adversaries turn into enemies, as they have of late, when they break diplomatic relations with each other and gird for and actually wage war. Such conditions threaten graver breakdowns yet, as warlike clashes erode the popular trust and confidence in both government and press on which effective exercise of the functions of both depend.[1]

This last statement was prophetic. The enemies in the press and government fought ever more bitterly. Public opinion polls placed the credibility of both press and government at steadily falling levels. Years later, the Vietnam War's "lessons" drove President George Bush to seek congressional support for the Persian Gulf War—and then masterfully control every aspect of press coverage by both hard and soft censorship.

The press-control lessons of Vietnam had already been practiced when U.S. troops entered Grenada without a single reporter present, advanced years later into Panama without the press pool, and then planned for the Persian Gulf War.

In the 1995 clash over budget cutting, both Congress and the White House attacked the news media for confusing their message. This reflected the public's disgust over extremist politics and the failure of compromise, the *sine qua non* of democratic systems.

Alexander Bickel addressed this problem twenty years earlier. He noted that revolutions are born of hope, not despair. The budget-balancing exercise was indeed a domestic revolution: it would drastically reduce immediately all manner of public support systems for the poor and the elderly. Every revolution, however, Bickel noted, required the floating of messages of despair before hope could be trumpeted. The despair, in the case of budget cutting, was the projected bankrupting of America after the year 2000. The accompanying hope, in Bickel's premise, was the assumption that severe budget cutting now would liberate the next generation of Americans from impoverishment through vast payments on the national debt. Bickel was not alive to see this drama play out, but his words were prophetic.

He worried that "our recent revolutionists [in the 1960s and 1970s] have offered us hatred. They despise and dehumanize the person, and they condemn the concerns and aspirations of the vast majority of their countrymen." To reflect his disdain for extremist rhetoric, he quoted a Yippie pamphlet of 1970, following the Yippie riot outside the Democratic National Convention in Chicago in 1968. The pamphlet urged, "Burn your money. You know life is a dream and all our institutions are man-made illusions, effective only because you take the dream for reality. Break down the family, church, nation, city, economy, turn life into an art form and theatre of the soul. What is needed is a generation of people who are freaky, crazy, irrational, sexy, angry, irreligious, childish and mad . . . who lure the youth with music, pot and acid . . . who redefine the normal. . . . Burn your houses down and you will be free."[2]

There is not only the obvious irrationality of such "hopes." Their anarchism could destroy the very material benefits the revolutionists would share. Or, worse, as Bickel points out, "there is a name for the means that must be employed to create that system and maintain it. That name is tyranny."

Increasingly, as the third millennium approached, politicians drew dangerous inferences from the clear breakdown of family and the values that for more than two hundred years had held America's variegated society together. My fear was not principally that some demagogue would rise to power and lead the country into tyranny; rather, it was that some moralistic leader or group would equate "moral authority" with the choice of policies and the right to govern. This intrusion of moral authority into politics was apparent on the right and the left, whether among religious conservatives, religious fundamentalists, or social managers.

The bitter debates over specific abortion practices (even when all sides agree that abortion is undesirable as a policy), the clamor for school prayer of increasingly theological specificity, and the insistence that bedroom activities of citizens are subjects for political action—all these and similar issues transcend what should be normal political activity. Bickel recognized that "when bushels of desires and objectives"—such as the above—"are conceived as moral imperatives, it is natural to seek their achievement by any means. There is no need to fear that the same means will be open to others, because the objectives of those others will be understood to be bad and unacceptable whatever the means used to attain them."

Instead, Bickel argued, "One has to believe that no amount of opinion can be eternally certain of the moral rightness of its preferences, and that whoever is in power in government is entitled to give effect to his preferences. Then, but only then, it is crucial that everyone adhere to certain procedures, and that some means be forbidden to all."

Bickel returns—as he did in his conversation with me before the TV watching the Nixon investigation—to the matter of process. The democratic fabric, he says, "is held together by agreement on means, which are equally available or foreclosed to all, and by allegiance to a limited number of broad first principles concerning the ends of government. They change over time and develop, and become entrenched as they gather common assent. Beyond them lies policy, and there lie our differences."

But not differences based on fundamental means. And then this warning: "If most of the things that politics is about are not seen as existing well this side of moral imperatives, in a middle distance, if they are not seen as subject on both sides of a division of opinion to fallible human choice, then the only thing left to a society is to succumb to or be seized by a dictatorship of the self-righteous." This is the end to which "disenchanted and embittered simplifiers and moralizers must come," Bickel warns. He concludes, "But if we do resist the seductive temptations of moral imperatives and fix our eye on that middle distance where values are provisionally held, are tested, and evolve within the legal order— derived from the morality of process, which is the morality of consent—our moral authority will carry more weight. The computing principle [eighteenth-century British statesman Edmund] Burke urged upon us can lead us then to an imperfect justice, for there is no other kind."[3]

I have striven for that middle distance in many ways, over many issues. It is the synonym for compromise or, better still, consensus. Burke says it well: "The restraints on men, as well as their liberties, are to be reckoned among their rights."

NOTES

1. Alexander M. Bickel, "Press and Government: Aspects of the Constitutional Position," *Freedom at Issue*, September–October 1973, p. 10.

2. Quoted in Jason Epstein, *The Great Conspiracy Trial* (New York: Random House, 1970), p. 310.

3. Alexander M. Bickel, *The Morality of Consent* (New Haven, CT: Yale University Press, 1975), p. 142.

18

BAYARD RUSTIN
Builder of the King Legend

O f all the men and women I have worked with and often ghostwritten for—
senators, governors, journalists, businessmen—the most charismatic was
Bayard Rustin. The tall, handsome civil rights leader was most responsible for
building Martin Luther King Jr. into an American legend and then for saving King
from a scandal that might have sullied that legend. Bayard fared badly at the hands
of King and his associates, yet he never accepted defeat for his increasingly centrist political beliefs or for his lifestyle. His incomparable humor seldom faltered.
The humorous anecdotes which Bayard attributed to "grandma," who raised him,
were repeated with sharp ethical or moral points. Bayard made himself the butt of
his own humor, as few civil rights personalities did.

For example, he met me when he returned from a particularly difficult
protest visit at the border of Cambodia. As an officer of the International Rescue
Committee, he was examining camps sustaining thousands of refugees who had
escaped the murderous assaults of Pol Pot. Facilities there even for Western visitors were primitive. Bayard told me, with a twinkle in his eye, "I had to sleep
with Liv Ullmann," the beautiful Norwegian film star. His humor reflected
Bayard's glance inward: he was gay.

That reality limited Bayard's professional career at every crucial stage. He
was imprisoned for it as a young man. That record would be dredged up whenever Bayard approached a new level of success. He was hounded by J. Edgar
Hoover, longtime director of the Federal Bureau of Investigation. Hoover's FBI
monitored civil rights activists on the suspicion that they were subversive.
Weren't they organizing hundreds of thousands of citizens, white and black, to
protest laws on the books? Segregationist legislation was still "lawful" though
challenged as unconstitutional, but these laws would soon be killed by Supreme

Court action. The irony of Hoover's double slandering of Bayard—for being gay as well as a rights activist—was Hoover's secret kept until long after his death: Hoover, too, was gay.

Another Bayard "secret": his mentor, who headed the sleepingcar porters' union, A. Philip Randolph, accused Sumner Welles, deputy assistant secretary of state, of making advances to male black porters on a railway train. Much later, after he left public office, Welles become chairman of Freedom House, succeeded to the board eventually by Bayard Rustin, then head of the A. Philip Randolph Institute.

Bayard's sexual preference did not enhance his celebrity; rather, it limited his performance and his stature, simply because lesser men feared that association with him would somehow diminish their own effectiveness.

Martin Luther King Jr. owed his fame largely to Bayard, because the latter converted King to belief in nonviolence as a form of active protest. Bayard had sat with Gandhians in India and learned about that master's use of nonviolence against the British. In the 1950s, he was the main organizer of the Southern Christian Leadership Conference, which sparked King's rise to prominence. In 1957, Bayard set up the first national meeting in Washington, at which King spoke, by bringing King together with the grand old man of the black trade union movement, A. Philip Randolph. This meeting persuaded the Eisenhower White House to negotiate with civil rights leaders. Bayard was involved in most of King's strategies at this time, though he was never given public recognition. (See appendix C for Rustin's appraisal of King.)

A despicable exploitation of Bayard's sexuality was engineered by Adam Clayton Powell, the congressman from Harlem who regarded himself as the black leader of the Democratic Party. Bayard had proposed a massive demonstration outside the 1960 Democratic National Convention in Los Angeles. Powell mentioned Bayard while stating publicly that civil rights leaders were captive to some dark conspiracy. Powell privately threatened King: Unless he fired Bayard and did not demonstrate at the convention, he, Powell, would publicly charge that King and Bayard had a homosexual relationship. King crumbled. Bayard was turned loose.

Three years later, Bayard and Randolph conceived the now-historic March on Washington. Bayard was the logical choice to organize the massive event. He was vetoed for the top role for the old reason, but Randolph was named director—and Bayard would be his assistant. Of course, Bayard organized the March on Washington—then the largest such gathering in history, at which King made his majestic "I Have a Dream" speech. The event epitomized the usefulness of massive nonviolent protest. The March—mainly Bayard's brainchild—won support from the Kennedy Administration, for the first time, for significant civil rights actions.

When King was awarded the Nobel Peace Prize in 1964, he asked Bayard to accompany him to the ceremony in Oslo. Bayard told me the sequel: the night before the full-dress speechmaking, Bayard saw white prostitutes running naked through the rooms occupied by King, his brother, and others in the group. Bayard told me he managed to keep this "happening" out of the press. How word of this might have catapulted J. Edgar Hoover to action, and perplexed Adam Clayton Powell! I did not ask Bayard for his personal reaction, though I suppose he was by then somewhat inured, though certainly not oblivious, to the harmful influence of sexuality on politics.

I traveled many places with Bayard. I took him and four others to monitor the first election ever held in Southern Rhodesia (now Zimbabwe). This was also the first time an independent American group went abroad to assess whether an election was free and fair. Scores of such missions have been made since then, including many by Freedom House observers and groups sent by ex-president Jimmy Carter's human rights center at Emory University in Atlanta.

The 1979 election in southern Africa was complicated by the violent opposition of two guerrilla groups fighting inside Zimbabwe and on its several borders. Election booths would be set up near the fighting areas. Guerrilla radios announced that voters and voting booths would be attacked on election day. Bayard and I were flown from the capital to a distant village in the bush. The plane was an old British warplane with bucket seats in two long rows and no soundproofing. It was built for airlifting troops to parachute jumps over enemy territory. Bayard and I sat facing one another in the cold. Softly at first, he began to hum. His voice broke out over the discordant whirr of the propellers. Then he sang, full voice, rich and melodious, with the voice that I would hear in many different settings. He sang, of course, a freedom hymn.

We landed in a grassy clearing, and the plane immediately took off to avoid attack. Three or four rifle-bearers accompanied us to the temporary voting area outside a small village. After Bayard had heard enough electoral briefing, he summoned me to join him in a walk into the village. We were in the bush for about a half-hour before coming upon the huts of the village. We were a strange sight. This tall, bushy-gray-haired black man in a dark morning coat and felt hat, holding an impressive pearl-handled cane, accompanied by a white man with camera equipment, recording devices, and other suspicious paraphernalia. We used none of that here—just Bayard's friendly approach to young children. They came running from all directions, and formed a ring about us. Bayard spoke softly, held several children close, and with little or no verbal exchange conveyed friendship. It seemed strange that Robert Mugabe's guerrillas were barely twenty miles away across the border, threatening physical retaliation for the simple act of dropping a marked piece of paper in a voting box.

We returned to the balloting area. Hundreds of women were in line to vote at a single booth. Men were separated in another line. Each woman wore a different brightly colored headdress. Some held suckling babies at their breasts as they waited to vote. Clearly, this occasion was regarded as notable. Men and women wore their best clothing. Some walked ten miles to a voting booth and trudged home—this despite the intimidation of two rebel forces.

Bayard and I agreed that all parties, including the incumbent, a black minister, had used intimidation. Yet we felt the people had shown determination to change their system by coming to the voting booths. That counted.

But not for long. The next year, Prime Minister Margaret Thatcher made a deal in London with the insurgents that called for new elections that would virtually eliminate the existing power structure. It would put in place immediately the first dominant black political force. By that agreement, there would be a multiparty system including (for at least ten years) the white party.

Bayard and I were back in Zimbabwe in 1980 for that definitive election. The spirit of the country had changed dramatically. The two insurgent groups had pledged to avoid violence. With great flare, they campaigned with several other parties, including the weakened incumbent: mass meetings, parades, musical troupes, banners and buttons, and sound trucks. The voting would closely follow tribal lines, which meant that Mugabe was an almost certain winner.

While votes were still being counted a day later, Bayard and I went to Mugabe's headquarters to interview him. He was conferring with three representatives ("journalists") from the Soviet bloc. We sat at the distant end of a large room in which Mugabe was speaking to the others.

They remonstrated, "How could you promise a multiparty state?" He responded, "Don't worry. Give me time."

The day after he was elected, Mugabe delivered a conciliatory radio speech in which he said, "The wrongs of the past must now stand forgiven and forgotten."

Bayard and I read the future differently on that day in 1980. We published a lengthy analysis in the *Wall Street Journal* concluding that "black rule can be as authoritarian as any colonial system." We saw one-man rule coming to Zimbabwe.

Mugabe was true to his word given to the Soviet critics. By 1982 he sent a special army division into Matabeleland, the territory of Joshua Nkomo, the exiled grand old man of local politics and the leader of a smaller tribal group. The unit, trained and equipped by North Korea, would take "extralegal" measures, Mugabe told his parliament. "An eye for an eye and an ear for an ear may not be adequate in our circumstances," he said, "we might very well demand two ears for one and two eyes for one." Mugabe's so-called Gukurahundi terror campaign did far more mayhem than that. So did Mugabe's "veterans," who murdered and pillaged white farmers in the 1990s.

President Mugabe now rules a one-party state. He controls all daily news media, and has turned a prosperous, hopeful country into an impoverished, fearful one. Blacks, ironically, are his most numerous enemy, as Philip Gourevitch reported for the *New Yorker* magazine in May 2002.

By running the A. Philip Randolph Institute after his mentor's death, Bayard Rustin moved years ahead of the increasingly ineffectual civil rights movement. He recognized that the legal fight for black equality had been won. The next objectives were jobs and economic security. Ten years after Bayard's death, Jesse Jackson, the perennial campaigner, began to sound this note as his latter-day discovery.

Unquestionably, Bayard moved me most one evening in Madrid. I had taken him and a dozen dissidents from Communist countries to the first week of what became a three-year meeting of the Conference on Security and Cooperation in Europe (CSCE). We would direct the pleas of these victims of Soviet oppression to the Communist delegates from Eastern Europe as well as the USSR.

It had been difficult to organize the movement of these well-known but mainly impoverished refugees from Eastern Europe and the Soviet Union. Once they arrived in Madrid we brought them together, many for the first time. Some had been incarcerated in the Soviet gulag but had never met, though they were imprisoned for protesting the same oppression. They represented different backgrounds, different approaches; some had come from countries that fought one another or had been invaded by Soviet elements. All were united in demanding freedom for all. It was overpowering to see their first recognition of each another.

How tragic this became, then, when I received word about Andrei Amalrik, one of the brightest young Soviet dissidents (see chap. 24). His book *Will the Soviet Union Survive until 1984?* had just been published in the West, drawing wide attention. Non-Communists greeted it; fellow dissidents were not as approving. Some felt the book held out too much hope that the Soviet Union would somehow fall of its own weight. This was deemed a bad tactic by the dissident hardliners, because they felt that it might cause the West to relax its pressure on Moscow.

Late on the first evening of our alternative conference in Madrid, I received word that Amalrik had been driving through Spain en route to our meeting. It was late: the roads were slippery, and Amalrik was tired. He had just phoned my colleague Lucia Thorne (see chap. 52 for more on Thorne) to say he was on his way. He returned to his car and was passing through a narrow road in a small town when a large truck coming from the other direction grazed Amalrik's small car and killed him.

The next evening, the dissidents, Bayard, and others met for a scheduled quiet time together. Without planning it, Bayard sat cross-legged on the floor and began a soft melody that expanded into the most moving spiritual I have ever heard. This was Bayard's repertoire. The rich tones, expressing oppression and freedom, held that special group in thrall. Most did not know a word of English. Some could not converse in the language of others. Yet they responded as one to Bayard's voice and demeanor. They felt his anguish, and somehow his hope. Tears flowed. There was meaning beyond words.

For me, there will always be sadness, too. For what Bayard, as well as Amalrik, might have become. If only . . .

19

FRANCES GRANT
AND THE GUERRILLAS

Two New York neighbors, both civil and political rights leaders, accompanied me to El Salvador to observe the 1982 elections scarred by a bloody insurgency.

I didn't know it at the time, but Frances Grant was then eighty-three years old. I might have guessed she was in her late sixties. She was short, rotund, and high-spirited. Her age never was an issue—except for a brief time near guerrilla territory on the outskirts of San Salvador.

Bayard Rustin, the fabled civil rights leader, seemed younger than Frances—say, in his early sixties. He carried himself ramrod-straight, took long loping strides, helped by a sturdy hand-carved cane he secured on an African walk (see chap. 18).

One day we visited an impoverished "ghetto." The hapless were held in an unfenced area on the high plateau near San Salvador, the capital. It was deemed wise to remove these people from easy access by the guerrillas. But the high birthrate in the camp suggested the plan was not foolproof. The social theory, however, was interesting. The people were, in political science terms, the "underclass." They had almost no possessions and little hope for the future. They had to decide whether to join the guerrillas who promised food, loot, and some status. Instead, the army paid them a pittance but provided no status. Some therefore went in one direction; others in another. It is not unheard of in the United States for the poor to move into the military for employment and training. In El Salvador, the guerrillas were looked upon by some as an economic provider. That did not mean there was necessarily an ideological—a Marxist—attraction for all; for some, it was. The political rationale of the American administration labeled all guerrillas as driven by Marxist doctrine. Washington's support for this election rested on the assumption that the electoral process could produce a government that would solve the deepest problems of poverty and corruption.

There was a significant human aspect to the guerrillas. They were called *los muchachos*—"the boys"—by their followers. That was a holdover from the days before they were guerrillas, when the lower class was called *los muchachos* in a derogatory sense by the upper-middle and even some of the small middle class—just as in the U.S. South in days not long past the word *boy* for blacks was often used. And as I heard frequently in Rhodesia (now Zimbabwe), the guerrillas there were called *los muchachos*. The word that started as a pejorative became a symbol of guerrillas, the power of "the people." And so "the boys" became the defenders of the lower class, not without a degree of pride and status.

We decided to visit the ghetto, the home of the poor who did not choose the life of a guerrilla. We left our armored car at the foot of the steep incline. It was terribly hot, with no shade ahead, and our bulletproof vests were an added discomfort. Bayard refused to wear one. I insisted, however, that Frances don hers. It was the largest size available and must have been especially irritating. On the way to the camp, one shot came in our direction but wasn't even a near-miss.

Our car stopped at the camp, facetiously called Libertad ("freedom"). The area was engulfed in dust; bulldozers were building a road. Across from the camp was a cemetery. The camp itself was situated on a sharp rise of chalky soil forming a cliff at almost a ninety-degree angle. One reached the camp by mounting steps only a foot and a half wide hewn out of the soil and rock. The steps rose sharply with a sheer drop on the left and a slightly less precipitate fall on the right. There were no bars to hold. The climb wound directly up, with no level pauses. Looking up from the base, I insisted that Frances remain on the ground. She remonstrated and resented this but reluctantly agreed.

Bayard and I made our way to the pitiable scene at the top. In an area of about twenty by sixty yards lived two hundred people in huts made of paperboard and bamboo risers, with some blankets thrown over to make a roof. There was a clutter of little alleyways so that each hut was about two and a half feet from another, on all sides. On the bare ground inside the huts was simple wooden matting used as beds. No running water, just one central pipe at the top, from which everyone drew water for drinking or washing.

We climbed the chalky earth where children were playing baseball. Seeing us, they stopped and scampered away, but one or two older people greeted us. As we talked, all the huts emptied and nearly everyone gathered round. We attracted about 150 people in a circle. Our gun crew, suddenly appearing, watched at the perimeter. The naked children lost their shyness, ran about, and threw rocks off the cliff.

I said we had come to observe the elections but that we wanted to talk to them about their lives—*and* the elections. Their faces were grim, very intense. Their bodies bore signs of malnutrition. Clothing was worse than hand-me-downs. These people were simply in rags, held in place by a bit of sewing here and there. I said I wondered what they thought about voting. The interpreter, a bright young college student, said he wouldn't ask them that question. I asked why, and he said they weren't intelligent enough to understand. I didn't believe he thought this, but wanted to spare them some embarrassment. They had worries enough.

I reworked the question. I said we noticed the bulldozers making a new road beneath the camp, but I wondered what would happen when the rains came. They would probably wash away much of this encampment. These people had no place to go. They were kept there by social pressure: by being caught in the middle between the rebels and the suspicious military. And so I asked, in view of the impending problem of the rains, would it make any difference who won the election, and do elections really count?

A wave of thoughtfulness came over the group. One man raised his hand and said he had some hope that elections would make a difference. Another man shook his head negatively. I asked the interpreter to call on him next, but the interpreter refused. Another man favored the elections. Then I got to the naysayer with my limited Spanish. He said elections would make no difference. They hadn't in the past. Several young women up front smiled agreement. But most of the others remained passive. They looked straight at us, and I believed wanted to say something that would help. When I asked whether they would vote they shouted yes, yes, yes. That chorus included three-year-olds as well as older people. In El Salvador, as in many other countries, voting is mandatory at eighteen.

I chatted a while longer with one man about twenty-five years old. I asked him why he lives here. He said, "My father and mother are dead; I'm an orphan." No one works. There was nothing to do, and the land could not be tilled. Everything they ate or wore was given to them by the government or by these young, highly motivated interpreters. They were high school or college students who contributed time each week to help these people, in association with *La Cruz Verde* (an equivalent of the Red Cross).

Slowly, we made our way down the precarious incline. At the foot, from where we had started, we could see Frances Grant surrounded by about fifty women and young girls. She was holding an impromptu seminar on young women and their future. I might have known that Frances would not simply await our return. She lectured her audience sharply, without condescension. They must do more, she was urging, and not leave it to the men. And when she got back home, she said, she would get her women to do something to help—to send parcels, or lobby for more help. And, of course, Frances did just that.

But that might have been expected. Frances Grant was long the best-known activist in the United States and Latin America on behalf of human rights and democracy in this hemisphere. Her Spanish heritage began at birth: she was born in the remote pueblo of Abiquiq, the daughter of a pioneer of statehood for New Mexico. There, in the foothills of the Valle Grande mountains, she absorbed the atmosphere of Hispanic-American culture.

She graduated first from Barnard College and in 1918 from the Graduate School of Journalism of Columbia University. When Frances nominated me for its lifetime alumni award, I responded by joking that we had been classmates—she liked to hear that. But Frances had wider interests; she was a founder of the Roerich Museum, which sent her to Asia to write about the philosophies and culture of India and Tibet. The Roerich Museum had attracted Henry Wallace before he became vice president of the United States; in fact, during his campaign he was chided for associating with what was said to be a left-of-center activity.

From 1929, Frances devoted her time to Latin America. She lectured at nearly every university on the southern continent and started many intercultural exchanges. These included musical programs and public forums. She was responsible for the Roerich Pact, an inter-American agreement for the preservation of cultural ties. In 1935, it was signed at the White House by twenty-one republics. She founded the Pan American Woman's Association and the Inter-American Association for Freedom and Democracy. She led both for thirty years, into the late 1980s.

Through Frances's efforts, these groups spotlighted human rights abuses. José Figueres Ferrer, when president of Costa Rica, called Frances "the greatest fighter for democracy and human rights in the hemisphere." I watched Frances and Don Jose together, years later. He had left the presidency and was riding unashamedly about San Salvador in a small jeep. Frances was on a human rights mission. But they always had time for one another and for good-humored banter. Indeed, they resembled each other in many ways. Frances never married. Some slyly suggested there had been more to their relationship than as colleagues in good causes.

One of Frances's most courageous acts was her defiance of the Dominican Republic dictator Rafael Trujillo. She had joined Columbia University professor Jesus de Galindez in denouncing the bloodthirsty Trujillo regime. For his appointment with her, Galindez entered the subway at Fifty-seventh Street and Eighth Avenue and was never seen again. It became clear he had been abducted. Trujillo was obviously behind the kidnapping on the streets of Manhattan. Frances mounted a campaign to search for the missing professor and charged Trujillo with the deed. Despite the long arm of Trujillo's murderous forces, Frances continued battering the dictator and calling for justice. The body of the professor was never found. Frances lived to see Trujillo assassinated and a free country develop.

Frances never let threats of retaliation stop or even slow her human rights activity. In El Salvador, we had heard some shooting at about four o'clock one morning. At first there were single bursts of rifle fire and then rapid-fire automatic weapons in response; some pauses and then more single or double bursts followed by more pauses. This went on for about forty-five minutes. By morning, it was unclear what the outcome had been, but obviously the guerrillas were driven off. We decided to visit a cooperative farm about twenty miles out of San Salvador near a guerrilla area. The electoral commission that ran the transports refused at first to provide a car and driver, saying it was dangerous, but we felt they also didn't want us to move too freely about the countryside to interview at will.

This was a purely random interview with men who were on the executive board of the cooperative. They had been born on the property when the *patrona*, a woman, owned and ran it, and they grew up under that system. She was bought out by the Land Reform Act several years earlier. She was still in the country, but no one in this co-op saw her any longer. Now, two thousand people lived there, and all voted for board members and committees to decide on education for their children, welfare, productivity, which crops to plant, the rate of production, etc. They had been operating successfully for more than a year and had already produced some profit. The land, beside a lake, was in a beautiful setting. Most interesting, we were told they never had visitations from guerrillas. They had no protection, and they were never attacked.

This visit was especially interesting, I felt, because it highlighted a factor that was rarely discussed in Washington or by supporters of U.S. aid to the government of El Salvador. In the increasingly polarized debate of U.S. policy on Salvador, no attention was paid to the middle ground. One heard either support for the guerrillas (as a near-automatic response of American liberals to reports of death squads taking out innocent civilians who favored reform) or support for the government (intent on wiping out a Marxist threat that had the backing of the Soviet Union). In fact, the land reform program had moved ahead in El Salvador; the guerrillas were making little progress, though they could count on generous publicity; and the reformist government of José Duarte was marginally effective in creating a permanent democratic structure. It would take many more years of bloodshed before the guerrillas and a conservative government would agree to a cease-fire and eventually a peace, with some democratic institutions.

Through that long period, I had to decide repeatedly whether Freedom House should support continuation of U.S. aid to several Salvadoran governments. It was always a difficult call. I testified several times before congressional committees, acknowledging the brutality on both sides of the fratricidal struggle. Death squads loosely linked to the military were indeed engaged in frightful atrocities. In El Salvador, I met with AFL-CIO representatives who ceaselessly worked to bring to justice the murderers of several American trade unionists working with Salvadoran centrists. The guilty were well known yet roamed free. There was ample guilt all around. And there were some American journalists who had long since ended balanced reporting of the situation. I went on the *MacNeil-Lehrer News Hour* to discuss this. Marlene Hunter-Gault tried by her questions to have me accuse Ray Bonner of the *New York Times* of distortion, but I refused to name names. In the melee over press coverage of El Salvador, Abe Rosenthal, then executive editor of the *Times*, recalled Bonner. He later quit the paper but has since returned.

The Salvadoran people suffered the ill fortune of having their generation-long struggle for economic and political democracy subsumed by the Cold War played out in Central America. The participation of Cuba and the Soviet Union, countered by U.S. arms and political power, turned the small Salvadoran land into a battlefield. The feudal land policy controlled by a few wealthy families was slowly being replaced—too slowly. The country was ripe for alternatives: the ever-ready Marxist approach attracted some Salvadorans; the social democratic style attracted others. The guerrillas, wrapping themselves in the Marxist mantle, went for the quick fix. It did not work; instead, a generation of Salvadorans and the land itself were decimated.

Frances and I saw firsthand the cruel paradox of the country. We drove along a rutty country road in an armored van to a farm where some 250 people lived. They raised coffee, sugar, a kind of bean, and a pitifully small amount of food for themselves. We spoke to several *compesinos* (farm workers). They were poor but intelligent men. One had seven children; the other, two. They worked hard, lived close to the soil. We went into the house of a woman living alone. It was made of some mortar, very sparse, no electric lights. No running water, not even an outside toilet, just rags on a mat, dingy charcoal in an old burner, and three or four pieces of baked starch that looked inedible. It was impossible to justify this almost starvation-level standard of living, with the rich soil and the crops growing all around.

We returned to one of the main roads. Suddenly, up in the hill to our left, just about fifty yards above us, there was a crack of a rifle, followed by a second one. Two or three women standing at the side of the road simply pointed toward the hills, and smiled. Neither we nor the car with guns behind us stopped. It seemed quite normal. That was the horror, and the sadness.

One special memory of Frances remains with me. We decided to make an election-day visit to San Miguel, a major city distant from the capital but surrounded by guerrilla strongholds. Access was best by helicopter from San Salvador, and one was flown just for our visit. It was a small military helicopter that had obviously been donated from the scrap heap of the U.S. Air Force. The helicopter could take three passengers, a gunman, and an interpreter; Bruce McColm, years later my successor at Freedom House, joined us. We wore helmets and prepared for a windy, rather cool flight, because the helicopter was open to the air. We took off, rose to about five or six hundred feet—the maximum for safety over guerrilla territory—and flew at seventy miles an hour. Picture Frances, in her eighties, her grey hair squeezed into a military helmet, her eyes darting from side to side so as not to miss a view or an emotional sensation, examining the terrain and commenting simultaneously on the politics and the humanity of this extraordinary moment. The view was magnificent, but we saw houses still burning.

We flew east over the great Lake Ilipengo. We were convinced that in these mountains it was impossible to rout the guerrillas. We landed at a military base and were driven to the election headquarters. There were no signs of troops—life seemed normal. The streets were filled, the markets crowded, and people were going to and from church. And yet San Miguel, the third largest city in the country, was an enclave just south of the Morizon Department, which was almost completely controlled by guerrillas. There would be no voting in that department, which went all the way north to Honduras.

In San Miguel, there would be other problems. A few days earlier, the guerrillas cut three of the city's oil pipelines that led from the oil terminal. And so, although there were 240 trucks and buses ready to transport voters to the polls, there was not an ounce of gasoline. We held some interviews and hurried back to San Salvador to meet with President Duarte and the general who ran the junta's military.

Next day, Frances and I went south along the Pacific. We took a coastal road that wound into the mountains. That gave us a magnificent view of the ocean and the beach, the Pacific rolling in. It was incongruous to see this beauty and this openness in a country clearly at war. We came to a small town called La Perla and spoke to some women. They were hesitant, but Frances got through to them. She chatted with a pregnant young woman and her rather elderly mother. Frances asked the young woman whether she intended to vote. She said it was eighteen kilometers from this place to the polling box. The woman would have to walk that distance. Frances was indignant. She asked why someone wouldn't drive her. At that moment, a new Ford pickup truck drove up. It had special sides and people were standing in it. Frances talked to the driver and asked him to take the pregnant woman the next day. He said he had already been warned that his truck would be blown up if he moved a single voter to the polls. He couldn't risk his life's savings, he said. Oh, he added, there might be troops there tomorrow to guard that small crossroad, but what about next week when everyone else leaves? He knew he would be unprotected and the new truck would simply be burned off. It seemed doubtful that that woman would vote the next day.

As we chatted, one of the civil guards told us there had been indications of some guerrillas about thirty miles up the road, where we would have to make the turn to San Salvador. We decided not to go that way but to backtrack. But first, we did go a few miles ahead to a small fishing village. There were thatched huts and some fishermen walking about. In his net, one man had just caught a tuna about a foot and a half long, a huge mackerel, and about fifty sardines, all of this in a short time. This was a strange place. It was not only a fishing village but also had squatters—people who simply built huts and, in some cases, brick houses on land they didn't own. There were *haciendas* nearby, rather sizable ones that probably belonged to the landowners, who, I supposed, permitted the squatters to build. The fishermen were reluctant to talk to us, but one finally said he would vote because he felt "obligated." That was an interesting word: would he vote because someone had urged him to? Or did his conscience oblige him to do so? Was he doing it from some other pressure?

Near our drive that day, a civil guard was killed, and three voters injured. Father Theodore Hesburgh, then president of the University of Notre Dame, was an election observer near the shooting. When he discovered that the soldier had been killed he rushed over and performed last rites. The man's face had been blown away. Father Hesburgh carried with him the religious articles for last rites. He spent some time comforting the mother of the slain soldier and then left with her a small piece of his own garment.

It was a touching scene, though a bloody one. You came to know the sounds of different automatic and other rifles—even a distinction among the bombs. But you never got used to the fact that one of every three persons you walked past in the street carried some form of weapon. It was obviously a violent country, but it was amazing that the violence could be kept sufficiently in bounds so that the guerrilla threat was readily contained when it appeared. There was every indication that the guerrillas were losing support of the people. Yet most families must have had some guerrillas out there, either in close or distant relationship. It may have been the reason one woman told me, "Oh, the boys don't hurt you if you're a good person."

When we returned to San Salvador, several newsmen stopped us. They said there was a rumor that Frances and I had met with guerrillas. We denied it, but shortly afterward, we were summoned to the U.S. Embassy and were warned not to "fraternize" with guerrillas. We were indignant—we had not met guerrillas, at least not to our knowledge, and we were not employed by the U.S. government and weren't members of the American military. The truth was, it would have been dangerous to meet guerrillas. The death squads didn't like such behavior. They were known to arrange death in a "crossfire" incident, a plausible explanation for the perpetrator.

This incident demonstrated how complex the society and the insurgency was, a fact never properly reported in the press or adequately described by the Washington politicians. They oversimplified the Cold War aspects of the controversy, which, to be sure, were fully operative. There were indeed U.S. geopolitical interests involved. But underlying all this, were the age-old inequalities and inhumanities of the power structure in El Salvador. These were changing—all too slowly, but changing.

The election that year? More than eight hundred thousand votes were cast out of a possible million. Duarte's Christian Democrats lost, and the other five parties formed a coalition. But the war continued. Our Freedom House observer team concluded, however, that the election was a referendum on itself, a test of political party strength, and a mandate for peace. There was no evidence that the election had been marred by gross fraud or that intimidation or violence—though present—dictated the result. The government could start with a broader base than had existed since the early 1970s. Yet serious problems of human rights, security, lawlessness, and economic decline had to be addressed, our report added.

Two years later, I was back in El Salvador as a member of the official U.S. delegation to monitor the 1984 elections. I flew in Air Force Two with a half-dozen senators and thirteen members of the House of Representatives, including

Jim Wright as cochairman. (Later, Wright would be forced to resign as Speaker of the House by newcomer Rep. Newt Gingrich.) I was listed among a dozen "distinguished citizens." We reported immediately to ambassador Thomas R. Pickering, later ambassador to the United Nations and then to Russia.

The guerrillas were less prevalent this time. Clearly they had lost some following among the war-weary public. They did knock out electric power in San Salvador the night before the election, but that did not affect the election computers or the electorate. The death squads seemed no longer to be linked to the government, though it was likely that former army officers were still engaged in the bloody enterprise. On election day in the small towns we visited, people were dressed in their best clothes (as they had been in Zimbabwe years earlier). They waited patiently. Vendors did a thriving business. There was no electioneering, but poll watchers ("vigilantes") of every party wore partisan hats and colors!

I flew in a helicopter to El Paraiso, a tiny town near guerrilla-dominated territory. The town itself had been taken twice by guerrillas in recent months. The night before, a village just north had been raided. They burned the voting urns and the voting lists, yet we saw some of the people from that attacked town who had walked a long distance to vote in El Paraiso. That town was far from paradise—it was a hot, dusty place without a single paved street. The roadways were broad, and the houses mostly attached with wooden overhangs that shaded the walkways. Dogs, goats, cows, and children ran about the large town plaza. When our helicopter landed in a field a quarter-mile from the center, we kicked up a great cloud of dust. Children came running from town to watch us alight. They walked with us—one hundred or more—as we made our way to the main street and the *municipio* (town hall), where voting took place. The children were outgoing and friendly. Adults were more restrained than I had seen them in less threatened areas. Their eyes occasionally darted from us to the distance, as though to avoid committing themselves to friendly gestures to us.

The election was won by Duarte, the Social Democrat. It was the third election in El Salvador in twenty-six months. A civilian president had been chosen despite a pervasive guerrilla insurgency. The country had a chance to become a viable democratic nation, but it was not there yet. It was moving along that path but still needed further help. Clearly our official observer group would recommend U.S. aid. Jim Wright said he would support it, though it was a Republican administration's initiative and opposed by many liberal Democrats. When I mentioned this the next day to Jeane Kirkpatrick, U.S. ambassador to the United Nations, she doubted Wright would, in the end, support further aid to El Salvador; he did, however.

Air Force Two flew us back to Andrews Air Force Base. Cars with sirens wailing rushed us to the White House, and a meeting with President Reagan, Secretary of State George Shultz, and Secretary of Defense Cap Weinberger. The president thanked us for making the trip and for our report, which had already been given to the press. We found the election credible and hopeful. Reagan said he had been watching reports on television and reading headlines in the papers, and he found a different account. With eyes twinkling, he said he was an old hand at film-cutting techniques. He mentioned the voice-over on one network that day, which described voters being turned away at the polls because of administrative inadequacies, while showing a long line of voters waiting to cast ballots. "The implication," said the president, "was that hundreds of people would never vote." That was not true. These orderly lines did vote; it was the scattered voters who did not know where to join lines who had trouble.

Then Vice President Bush urged unofficial observers to speak. I said, "Mr. President, it is important to keep in mind—as the press seldom does—that the real test of an election or any democratic process is not what takes place in a single day. Too often the press just examines a moment in time and says, 'It was a bad show.' That tends to denigrate the process. Instead, the appraisal should be made over a long time span, showing where the society has come from and where it expects to go. On such an assessment—and compared to the 1982 election, which I also witnessed—this is a further step along a long road to democratization."

So it was—a long road. And it did produce a pacific, relatively free society. In 1990 the government and the guerrillas agreed to a UN-mediated negotiation, which led to a complicated peace accord signed in January 1992. The guerrillas agreed to disarm, and the military cut its force by half and eliminated the counterinsurgency units. The 1994 election was the first in which all political parties from right to left were able to participate, a significant step toward consolidating the peace process.

We only had a glimmer of this possibility, however, as Jim Wright and I left the White House together ten years earlier. He had been given a small White House jet to take to New York in order to speak on behalf of a black politician, and I hitched a ride with him. As we left the White House meeting still in session, President Reagan said to me, "Tell your story to the pen-and-pencil boys out there." The press waited for us in front of the portico. Wright changed clothes hurriedly as we flew north. Despite the long travel that day, he was ready for a dinner speech in New York, a returned favor like many that would apparently help him win the House Speakership soon afterward.

But when I recall visits to El Salvador, I think first of Frances Grant in her eighties, vibrant, inquisitive, reaching out—and, of course, in that windblown helmet flying a battered helicopter to speak with men and women who deserved a better life.

20

SIDNEY HOOK
Philosopher with Rolled-up Sleeves

A s an undergraduate at New York University I really majored in campus journalism. Much of my waking time was spent editing the daily newspaper. I had converted it from a tabloid to a six-column paper and featured what now would be called op-ed articles on national and international subjects. But to complete course requirements I majored in—of all things—philosophy. That may seem esoteric, even eccentric, but not when you understand that Sidney Hook, chairman of the department, became my intellectual mainstay—as a student and for fifty years afterward as friend. Sidney was a hands-on philosopher. No earthly concern, no ethical dilemma was beyond his ken. Sidney supported revolutionary politics during the Great Depression, and abandoned it along with the Soviet Union and Communism when he learned the truth about both. Says Alan Ryan, "Hook saw the process as a matter of growing out of a youthful infatuation and arriving at a sensible middle age."[1]

Saul Bellow wrote of Sidney Hook, "Activists like Hook made a difference. Their victory in the Cold War can't be measured but must be acknowledged. . . . What we need to consider is their combining of theorizing with effectiveness. I give Hook full marks for the wars he fought and admire him despite his evident lack of sympathy with my way of looking at things. He was the active, not the contemplative sort."[2]

At eighty-four, Sidney settled down long enough to complete his memoirs. On those pages he would describe his life of fighting for his beliefs with precision and persuasion. He had already survived several critical illnesses and, as he said, stopped *re*writing the book so that it would not be published posthumously. I was delighted to receive his book *Out of Step: An Unquiet Life in the Twentieth Century*, with this handwritten note from Sidney: "To Leonard and Marianne with affectionate regards from Sidney Hook, April 1987. I have this inscription for your own copy. I deliberately avoided any reference to anything political because Ann and I both feel our relationship to you and Marianne is primarily personal, transcending politics. Best, Sidney Hook."

This note and book was, for me, an unsuspectingly warm and personal gesture, one to be particularly treasured because outside of his family Sidney seldom displayed emotion. And rarely did he "transcend politics." He was the embodiment of logic, rationality, and the rule of reason. To sum up his six-hundred-page memoir, Sidney wrote, "Some philosophers belittle man by asking him to look at the immensities without; others belittle him by asking him to look at the perversities and selfishness within. Humanism denies nothing about the world or human beings which one truly finds in them, but it sees in us humans something which is at once more wonderful and more terrible than anything else in the universe: the power to make ourselves and the world around us better or worse."[3]

Sidney's long life of intellectual and political engagement demonstrated his unrelenting commitment to change the world for the better, only rarely acknowledging that some things cannot be improved. He therefore seldom found serenity—but we are all better for it.

Sidney challenged my intellectual serenity as a college student. Whether I always recognize it or not, his influence persists. One of my most gratifying moments came several years ago: as I taught a final session at New York University that semester, a graduate student told me, "You're following the Socratic method of Sidney Hook." I had no illusion that I was approaching Sidney's erudition or teaching style, but it was a compliment I cherish nevertheless.

Sidney's teaching method did influence me at an early age. The course that impressed me most was his philosophy of history. Each week during the semester he would assign reading in another philosophy of the development of civilization. We would search, presumably, for that single analysis of history that would describe the full span of human existence and thus serve as a guide to human affairs. Most exciting was Sidney's own acting out of each philosophy of history. He presented each as though a committed exponent was trying to persuade you of its merit. He offered analysis, analogy, and response to critiques. He built up each as though this was his personal philosophy of history. So it went for two sessions each week. At the third meeting, however, Sidney utterly destroyed each week's philosophy as an acceptable single analysis for all seasons and all time.

We started with biblical sources of the nature of man and the interplay among competing tribes, religions, and nations. We went on to the Greeks' concept of the love of wisdom as a guiding force, the emphasis on reality, causes and principles underlying being and thinking. Then on to Christian theology, the Renaissance, the empiricists, the pragmatists, and the scientific influence of Whitehead and Bertrand Russell. We knew of Sidney's own relationship to the pragmatists and John Dewey. Dewey, probably the greatest American philosopher, owed some of his prominence to Sidney's professional and personal relationship. But Sidney did not spare Dewey.

We waited eagerly, however, for the turn of Karl Marx and dialectical materialism. We knew of Sidney's personal history: he had been a chief scholar of Karl Marx's writing. He wrote a definitive book on Marx, in which Sidney stressed the continuity between Marx's contributions and the intellectual tradition of the West. He tried to bring to a higher level the challenge of a "democratic collectivist" society to the capitalist order. He would write, "It did not seem to me in principle impossible to develop a kind of Americanized Marxism."

Sidney believed in a "communism without dogmas." He dissociated himself from the theory and practice of the Communist International controlled by the Soviet Union; that in itself was remarkable for the time. Sidney was regarded as a "Marxist," yet he resisted political entanglements with the Communist movement. Knowing this, we waited eagerly for Sidney's three-session exposition of Marx in the course on the philosophy of history. Certainly we would find that he had found his ideal system for historic analysis. The first two sessions corroborated that judgment. Sidney gave a virtuoso performance. Marxism had its finest two days. But on the third day, just as with the other philosophies, Sidney destroyed Marxism as a definitive, sole analysis of history.

This demonstrated Sidney's great ability to employ the Socratic method to draw out students' own responses. He helped develop intellectual skepticism based on the fullest understanding of the facts.

Later, I realized that Sidney himself was undergoing a major transformation at that moment. Earlier in his writing he had refrained from criticizing certain unhealthy developments in the Soviet Union, partly because he did not know what was really going on there in the 1920s, and partly because he was trying to influence Marxists and did not want to be labeled pro or con by any of the warring groups. In the classroom, however, Sidney did not withhold criticism of Marxism, leading to spirited debate among students, particularly engaging the campus Communists and fellow-travelers. By my time, the late 1930s, Sidney was a marked man among the radical students. The course in the philosophy of history became a battleground.

Another student, Morris Janowitz, and I were the main critics of the Marxist position. We opposed the party-line atmosphere introduced into the classroom. I was editor of the campus newspaper, and Morris, a year behind me, was an assistant editor. We conducted on the pages of the paper some of the debate in that class. Morris later became a principal opinion poller in the army, wrote several definitive books on military culture, and for years was chairman of the sociology department of the University of Chicago. He served there with another good friend, Edward Shils, who earned the highest global award for sociology. For many years, Ed taught six months each year at both Cambridge University in England and the University of Chicago (see chap. 22).

Ed and Sidney were friends, and they were similar in some ways. Both had come from poor Jewish backgrounds and rose to the intellectual heights. Both were engaged all their lives in protecting the freedom of academic inquiry. Both entered the public arena as an extension of their research and teaching. Both had strong liberal tendencies yet in later life were regarded—perhaps erroneously—as neoconservative. For, in truth, each was fearlessly, almost furiously idiosyncratic.

Sidney Hook displayed independence at one crucial turning point in his life. Shortly after the 1932 election of Franklin Roosevelt, Sidney was asked to meet with Earl Browder, leader of the U.S. Communist Party. The Depression was at its nadir, Sidney believed, and neither the Republicans nor the Democrats had campaigned for real social reform. Indeed, Roosevelt had promised a balanced budget, as did Herbert Hoover. FDR, of course, almost immediately began to set in place the high-spending social programs of the New Deal. But Sidney had publicly endorsed the Communist candidate as a protest vote.

Earl Browder apparently read more into this endorsement than Sidney intended. Browder said he wanted to hear why Sidney had criticized orthodox Marxism with its emphasis on social evolutionary determinism—the inevitability that a socialist society would follow the collapse of capitalism. Browder, moreover, wanted to hear what was to come in Sidney's latest book at the printer, *Towards the Understanding of Karl Marx.*

Sidney discovered several reasons for the interview. Browder wanted Sidney to induce John Dewey to write and speak favorably about Marxism. Dewey was regarded by Communists as an "honest liberal"—one who did not support Communism but did not attack the Soviet Union. Aides of Browder present at the interview challenged parts of Sidney's summary of his forthcoming book. Sidney held his ground: he dismissed as nonsense the idea that Marx's (or Hegel's) dialectic was a "higher logic," transcending the laws of ordinary logic and mathematics, and thus superior to the scientific method. To believe in inevitable Communist ascendancy, one would have to sustain that "nonsensical" position, Sidney held. He mentioned elaborating this position in his course at NYU on the philosophy of history. I would later hear him go through these paces in that unforgettable course. Browder and the others regarded this as an outright attack on Stalin as well as Marx and Lenin. The meeting with Browder broke up.

One year later, Browder called Sidney again. This time the ground had been prepared for an extraordinary meeting of the two men. Shortly before, the party's official organ, *The Communist*, had republished the full text of Sidney's attack on Marxism under the title "The Revisionism of Sidney Hook." *The Communist* carried a point-by-point refutation of Sidney's thesis. It was unprecedented, however, for the party to print the attack of one declared to be "an enemy of the party, of the Revolution, and of the international working class." This move was apparently part of a larger game.

Browder put it clearly to Sidney. The debate over Marx and Engels was relatively insignificant now, Browder said. What was primarily important was the

defense and survival of the Soviet Union. He stressed the importance of influ-
encing American opinion, mentioning the damage done to the party by the so-
called Lovestone faction—the American Communists who had finally rebelled at
the dictatorial policies of Stalin and his effort to control the American party. And
that is where Sidney could help. (Soon after I came to Freedom House, I included
Jay Lovestone, then in his eighties, in a thirty-session seminar for New York City
teachers. This history by an ardent Communist leader turned virulently anti-
Communist was revealing.)

Browder asked Sidney to visit chief metropolitan centers from Boston to San
Francisco and build circles of sympathizers, individuals not known to be politically active but who could be persuaded to be friendly to the Soviet Union and
the U.S. Communist Party. When crucial issues arose, Sidney would be expected
to signal a trusted local correspondent and urge him to write letters to the press,
national and local, stating positions that "we believe" would further peace and
social justice. Browder also asked Sidney to organize workers in government
bureaus in Washington. This dual organization of workers was intended to undermine the established unions, particularly among sensitive employees of the fast-
expanding federal government. Finally, Sidney was asked—because of his academic standing—to travel to campuses across the country and find scholars sympathetic to the Soviet Union who were working on scientific and industrial
projects. Sidney would report on new work being done in military and industrial
fields. "The reports of your informants would be channeled through you to us,"
Browder stated.

Sidney later said, "I was in a state of panic." He added, "Stripped of its
euphemism, this was a request that I set up a spy apparatus."

Sidney sought a way out of the conversation. He told Browder he could not
give up his academic career. Anyway, he said, he was not applying for membership in the Communist Party. Browder responded, "Sometimes it is an advantage
to be able to say that one is not a member. You would be surprised to learn the
names of some persons whose applications for membership we have declined."
Finally, Sidney declared that his differences with the party were not only theoretical but political. "I have never accepted the doctrine of social-fascism or the
Comintern line." Social fascism, of course, was the equivalent in far-leftist doctrine of the collectivist control of all citizens by far-right dictatorships. Apparently, Browder—the ultimate pragmatist—said not even this mattered, as long as
Sidney did not attack the Soviet Union publicly. But Sidney concluded that he
was not about to give up his "professional life as a philosopher" to become "a
professional revolutionary."[4]

Sidney Hook was his own man throughout his long life. He was primarily a
teacher, whether in the classroom, as an analytical writer, or as a political activist
and commentator. As a teacher, he was chosen professor of the year at NYU. As
a wider commentator, he delivered the thirteenth National Jefferson Lecture in
Washington. As an activist, he received the Presidential Medal of Freedom. He

was relentlessly dedicated to the search for truth, wherever it led, and the power of intellect to advance human freedom, especially the freedom of the academy.

Sidney tackled the most intricate issues concerning the limits of dissent in a free society. He was often misunderstood or his views willfully distorted. No issue was more fraught with controversy and bitter denunciation than efforts by some legislative committees to trace Communist Party membership of teachers and fire them from their posts. I would discuss these questions with Sidney in the 1960s, when campus disorders, sparked by anti–Vietnam War demonstrations, exploded across the country. Sidney handed me a copy of his article *Heresy, Yes—Conspiracy, No,* written in 1953. He defended the right of teachers and scholars to hold any views at all, including Communism and fascism. He opposed federal or state investigations of teachers, arguing that faculties themselves must uphold the standards of professional ethics and rule against violators under rules of due process. If a teacher served clandestinely as a member of a cell to promote the undermining of free society itself and reflected that commitment in his teaching—then, said Sidney, no, heresy was not acceptable in a teacher.[5]

In 1970, when campus disorder spread not only across the United States but similarly in Italy, France, Germany, and England as well, I organized an international council of top scholars to examine how the academy could defend itself. Paul Seabury, political scientist at the University of California, was my initial colleague; Charles Frankel, philosopher at Columbia University (see next chapter), joined us next. Both men wanted to hold off inviting Sidney Hook until the group was better formed. I was dismayed at this but was assured Sidney would soon be invited to join. Sidney (understandably, I believe) was hurt. Before long, he decided to act on his own.

Although my council would remain small—some said elitist—by design, it would concentrate on the international aspect of revolutionary changes under way in the academy. Sidney would concentrate on the American scene. He organized University Centers for Rational Alternatives (UCRA). This group soon attracted several hundred academics, including some of the most distinguished, on scores of campuses across the country. Sidney was the prime mover in UCRA for the rest of his life. It published a newsletter that carried case histories of current horrendous attacks on scholarship and the principles of academic freedom. After Sidney's death and in his spirit UCRA continued to defend individual academics and university standards on such issues as affirmative action, "politically correct" curricular development, and related questions.

Sidney was a member of the Freedom House board during most of my tenure as executive director. This enabled us to focus our mutual beliefs on fresh concerns. Sidney rarely spoke at board meetings, but his incisive pen helped clarify many board statements on domestic and international issues. His view generally carried the day on that politically disparate board.

In 1978, I asked Sidney to write for *Freedom at Issue* his first public discussion of the complexity of affirmative action. The Supreme Court had just ruled in the

Bakke case that in order to go beyond racism it was necessary to use race as a criterion for selection for education or employment. Sidney said it was "demonstrably foolish to hold that, in order to go beyond racism, we must begin by practicing it."[6] I had also asked Nathanial R. Jones, another board member, a leader of the NAACP and soon-to-be federal judge, to address *Bakke*. He held that "race is a permissible factor in shaping remedies." I asked both to respond to the other. Sidney concluded, "If it is morally wrong to discriminate *against* a person because of race . . . then it is also morally wrong to discriminate *in favor of* a person because of race, unless he or she has been previously victimized by discrimination in that specific situation."

Sidney's philosophy of freedom in a free society meshed with Freedom House's fundamental beliefs. Early in 1949, he was invited to the Sorbonne in Paris to report on the Freedom House demonstration earlier that countered the Cultural and Scientific Conference for World Peace, a creation of the Soviet Union held at the Waldorf-Astoria in New York. Sidney declared, "I have more in common with a democrat who differs with me on economic questions, but who firmly believes in civil rights and a peaceful method of resolving our economic differences than with any professional Socialist who would seize power by a minority coup, keep it by terror, and take orders from a foreign tyrant. Hitler and Stalin (both of whom invoke the term Socialism) have written in letters of fire over the skies of Europe this message: Socialism without political democracy is not Socialism but slavery."

Such explicit descriptions of his personal creed nevertheless confused some of Sidney Hook's observers. They heard him support a democratic socialism in theory while denouncing the socialisms he knew. He was known to favor New Deal reforms yet break with the Democratic party of Jimmy Carter. He was a strong supporter of civil rights in America and civil liberties worldwide yet early on saw problems of reverse discrimination in affirmative action programs designed to assist blacks and women. Even when others labeled him a neoconservative, he held to the ideal of democratic socialism. He was, in brief, a profound critic of the passing scene from whichever vantage point one observed it.

Just a year before he died, I called Sidney to refresh my memory about a point he had made in class fifty-five years earlier. For a book I was writing on press freedom I wanted to include a chapter I would call "Don't Fear the Slippery Slope." Sidney had held forth decades earlier on the logical fallacy of the slippery slope. Now, he gave me a complete replay of that lecture, and I made it the centerpiece of my chapter. I have since used it often in my own classes. The point is simple: it is erroneous to assume that because you take an initial position it must follow that your entire subsequent course irrevocably follows from that first decision. You may halt and reverse at some point; outside interruptions may alter your course; time may change the flow of events; or you may simply stop dead and choose another way. I use the analogy of the skier. Just because you are poised at the top of the mountain does not mean that you cannot alter your course, stop your movement, or even fall willingly or unwillingly. The slippery slope is only as unalterable as you care to make it.

Sidney was troubled the last few years of his life by severe illnesses. Once, he awoke from an operation and thought he had already died. Sidney never believed in God, certainly not in an afterlife. He was perplexed. He pulled through but then worried that another illness might leave him incapacitated. He told me he worried mainly about his wife, Ann. She had been diagnosed with another serious illness. Both seemed to care for the other without great concern for themselves.

Sidney addressed his death with the same logic and reason that dominated his whole life. In an op-ed article in the *New York Times*, March 1, 1981, he gave cogent reasons for ending his life. "I would cheerfully accept the chance to be reborn," he wrote, "but not to be reborn again as an infirm octogenarian." He added, "Long ago, Seneca observed that 'the wise man will live as long as he ought, not as long as he can.'"

Sidney received many letters opposing his view that "the responsibility for [voluntary euthanasia] . . . must be with the chooser." I wrote to him that the very clarity of his op-ed piece, its appealing style and finely hewn logic attest to the great error that would have been made if doctors had heeded his plea to end his life then. What a loss even a few years more would be for many of us. In fact, his sizable memoirs were concluded after that *Times* article appeared; so did the prestigious Jefferson Lecture and a presidential award—not to mention many public statements on diverse issues.

One expected Sidney to speak in clear, logical terms and most of the time on social and political issues of the day. What less would you expect from a man who had tussled with John Dewey, Albert Einstein, Bertrand Russell, Norman Thomas, Bertolt Brecht, Arthur Koestler, and others? But at his old country house in South Wardsboro, Vermont, Sidney was relaxed and ever the inquirer. He would want to hear about life elsewhere—not just the life of the mind or of politics. How were Lynne and David and Mark? How was each progressing? Sidney particularly asked about David, for whom he had written a strong letter of support for his entrance to the University of Pennsylvania. And wasn't I fortunate that all three were seriously pursuing careers? It seemed that Sidney regarded this as exceptional then; it also indicated that Sidney was still very much concerned about the generation coming along, and what they took from their teachers.

Wasn't that what he meant when he wrote that "a great teacher is a sculptor in snow"? He said, "We remember teachers rather than courses—we remember their manner and method, their enthusiasm and intellectual excitement, and their capacity to arouse our delight in, or curiosity about, the subject taught."[7]

Sidney Hook was a great teacher.

NOTES

1. Alan Ryan, "From Left to Right," review of *Young Sidney Hook*, by Christopher Phelps, *New York Times Sunday Book Review*, December 14, 1997, p. 27.

2. Saul Bellow, "Writers, Intellectuals, Politics: Mainly Reminiscence," *The National Interest*, spring 1993, p. 131.

3. Sidney Hook, *Out of Step: An Unquiet Life in the Twentieth Century* (New York: Harper and Row, 1987), dedication page.

4. The full version of the story of Hook's meeting with Browder is in Hook, *Out of Step*, pp. 166–73.

5. These ideas can also be found in Sidney Hook, "Heresy, Yes—Conspiracy, No," in a pamphlet titled "The Nature of Liberal Civilization" (1953).

6. Sidney Hook, "*Bakke*—Where Does It Lead? The Triumph of Racism?" *Freedom at Issue*, September–October 1978, p. 6.

7. Hook, *Out of Step*, p. 53.

21

CHARLES FRANKEL
Intellect in Politics

Another hardworking philosopher helped shape my view of the university and its role in public affairs. My second campus in New York (after NYU), where I received a graduate degree, was Columbia. More important, at Columbia I engaged Charles Frankel, the philosopher-turned-intellectual in the White House of Lyndon Johnson.

Charles Frankel and his wife, Helen, were murdered as they slept in their home in Bedford Village, New York. Two burglars were convicted many months later. But no penalties for this vile deed could replace the loss to American scholarship and the application of high intellect to the political scene.

I had talked to Charles shortly before he was killed. I had asked whether he would spend that night in his Manhattan pied-à-terre just off Fifth Avenue. He said he wanted to go home and get some rest. The newspapers carried the awful story the next day.

Charles was still active in a small organization I had created in England in 1970. I had assembled the machinery, but Charles was the prime mover in attracting participants. He was, however, the second on board. Paul Seabury, political scientist at the University of California at Berkeley, and I had initially discussed the need for a small group of distinguished scholars to address the serious campus disorders in their respective countries. We saw this as a challenge not only to academic freedom but to the maintenance of a civil society vital to human freedom.

The wave of demonstrations against the Vietnam War had divided several major American universities; Berkeley was only the first to bear the brunt of great disruption. Attacked were not only the war policies of the Johnson administration but the entire academic system, especially the curricula, reflecting

185

diverse traditions of intellectual achievement. Paul and I persuaded Charles Frankel to take the lead in forming an international consultation.

We met in Norwich, England, on a bleak weekend in September 1970. The call from Charles and Paul was limited to sixteen scholars from five countries—England, France, Germany, Italy, and the United States—to examine the state of universities in democratic societies. Clearly, the visible manifestations of campus turbulence obscured from the public and civil authorities certain fundamental inner alterations already discernible in the faculties. The purpose of the consultation was to examine this transformation of the university already under way and the preservation or renewal of serious academic activity.

The consultation exchanged information, country by country, on the perceived dangers to scholarship and the university, and adopted a general program to counter threats in the several countries directly affected. The group organized itself as the International Committee on the University Emergency. Later, the name was changed to the International Council on the Future of the University, the word "emergency" being deemed too temporary.

Participants at Norwich included François Bourricaud, University of Paris; Nikcos Devletoglou and David Martin, London School of Economics; Wolfram Fischer and Richard Löwenthal, Free University of Berlin; Seymour Martin Lipset, Harvard University; Ernst Nolte, University of Marburg; Giovanni Sartori, University of Florence; Edward Shils, University of Chicago (see next chapter); and Fritz Stern, Columbia University.

Charles Frankel opened the discussion. The outlook for the Western university was dim in the short run, he said, but he was more optimistic about the longer term. He anticipated that academics opposed to politicization might have to "take their lumps for the next five years or so." Later, perhaps, people would look back and say, "Yes, they were right on the basic principles. We need to get back to the neutral university."

He said it is an odd commentary upon the intelligence of nonradical university professors that, unlike student radicals, they are blissfully unaware of the contagious effect of their actions upon other universities. He said, "I find it difficult to excuse what happened at Columbia after what happened at Berkeley. I find it even more difficult to excuse what happened at Harvard after what happened at Columbia." In each case there were violent takeovers of university facilities.

Marty Lipset reported that about 10 percent of the American student body sees itself as radical. These students, he added, are "gravely alienated from the larger society." Their percentage may seem small, he said, but among eight million students the disaffected number was about eight hundred thousand. Among elite schools, the percentage was higher. The percentage calling themselves conservative was 15 percent, larger than the radical group. He foresaw a student shift to the right, which came dramatically in the 1990s.

He noted that three hundred thousand university teachers were in their twenties and probably shared the discontent of disaffected students. Years later, many bright radical students as well went into the academy and generated curricular changes or calls for changes. In the 1990s, this generated attacks on the professoriat as dominated by "politically incorrect" standards, and radicals set "multicultural" objectives that would replace the traditional books and authors. Charles Frankel, however, did not resist intercultural teaching. On the contrary, his career had been based on an internationalist, intercultural approach to education.

In Norwich he heard reports from the other countries of horrendous physical as well as professional assaults on professors.

Giovanni Sartori said the politicization of the university was an international, not just an American, phenomenon. He emphasized the role of the news media in producing a "contagion of unrest." The youth culture, moreover, had adopted as a "vogue" the political attitudes about which they know little, but are persuaded to follow the fad of disruption.

Richard Löwenthal said the anti-Vietnam demonstrations were not just an American phenomenon but were also felt by European students, who live with the armament race and the H-bomb and believe the West is wrong in the Cold War.

Ernst Nolte said the "lack of democratization" had been the sin of the German university. The professoriat was very conservative; students therefore organized to politicize the university, he said, so that it would not again become "brown," that is, fascist. Laws now made it possible for students and teaching assistants to participate in all university bodies. University rooms could be used for political lectures. There was a general revolt against full professors. They did have great power, but now that was being reduced, and students were given 15 percent of the vote in the faculty senate. Students revolted again, and the number was changed to 20 percent for student participation. This led to student domination: as meetings dragged on, the faculty would leave and students remained to vote their changes.

François Bourricaud said French professors would tell you that everything was a mess at their institution, "but my classes are fine." Reformers in the government asked all academic departments to decide which other departments they wanted to "marry." Not only professors but students had to express preferences for the kind of university they wanted. Interdisciplinary arrangements had to be made. If a sociologist made an arrangement with a historian, that was considered bad because they both belonged to the same faculty under the old system. But if a sociologist made an arrangement with a dentist that was good. This law "will feed the anarchic potentialities of the French university to a greater extent than the activities of student radicals," Bourricaud said.

Giovanni Sartori noted that the centralized state system of education in Italy produces administrators who are politicians. Those professors who would resist, he said, have no access to the central government. Students and teaching assistants do have access, however. When professors did protest, their views were simply set aside as "corporate interests." Formerly, professors' chairs were distributed by party affiliation, one for the Communists, one for the Catholics. Now they are distributed by student attitudes. The government gave in to the teaching assistants' lobby, the strongest of all in the universities. Fifty percent of Italian faculties are simply not functioning, Sartori said. Professors do not teach; grades are given gratis. Professors are generally ashamed to say what is really going on. Students receive a salary from the state, so they must pass. No examinations are given. By one law, anyone could gain admission to any faculty, and anyone could make his own curriculum. The faculty at the University of Rome had five thousand applications for separate curricula. All of them were approved in ten minutes.

Students drew up plans for study for themselves that omitted all examinations. Even in the medical faculty. Sartori said that once that law was signed he decided never to go to a doctor credentialed after that year, or consult a lawyer approved then, or walk into a building constructed by an architect whose diploma was dated after that year. A short time afterward, Sartori immigrated to the United States to occupy a major chair at Columbia University.

Over the next ten years, the Council raised numerous issues to public attention and produced a series of studies of university problems in many Western European countries and the United States, holding major conferences in both areas. Several hundred scholars in twenty countries became members.

Charles Frankel's potential for still greater contributions to American scholarship—and politics—can be seen from his distinguished record. He was primarily a professor of philosophy—in the traditional (Greek) sense. A philosopher was a master of all intellectual pursuits, first among equals. Charles occasionally moved beyond the academy but never left far behind its high standards and inspired commitments to sharing truths.

It was not surprising that the International Council quickly named Charles its first chairman. He had studied the French universities at their request and went abroad to study American educational and cultural policy. When he returned, he was made assistant secretary of state for educational and cultural affairs. He was known as the intellectual-in-residence at the White House. President Lyndon Johnson had observed John F. Kennedy relying on Harvard professors (as had Franklin Roosevelt and his Columbia University–dominated brain trust). Now Johnson had his Columbia man.

Charles had a difficult time. The Vietnam War dominated the president's thinking. He would call in advisers, Charles told me, and unleash the most colorful, most profane language Charles had ever heard. Many curse words were composites of others or newly minted Johnsonisms.

Charles's mission was to improve American educational and cultural policy abroad. The existing policies, he felt, were wrong and their mode of operations outlandish. He believed that not enough attention was paid to the role of scientific and intellectual groups. They do not have special rights in public affairs, he said, but they had become a power to recognize. This power should be applied to foreign policy. "The lines going out from the arts, sciences, and education have become the life lines for most societies," Charles said. How depressed he might be today to discover the vast retraction of this idea in the United States. The endowments for the arts and humanities are being critically curtailed. The Fulbright scholars exchange program, which Charles fought to free from State Department political control, faces severe reductions.

The foresight Charles demonstrated was both idealistic and practical. He cited Voltaire, saying that intellectuals, whatever their nationality, share the same principles and constitute "a single republic." However, Charles, the practical man, said that "Voltaire exaggerated the facts in his own day. *Les honnêtes gens qui pensent* are not always honest, they do not always think, and national and ideological divisions among them are severe." And yet there are common problems and standards. Foreign policy, he said, should "try to facilitate and encourage the further development of the network of intellectual and cultural partnerships across the borders . . . making for the gradual evolution of an international political community."

Charles found three prevailing official attitudes about educational and cultural exchanges: (1) as an arm of propaganda, (2) as an exchange of technicians for economic development, and (3) as seeking "mutual understanding" between nations—the term used in the Fulbright program.

Charles thought the last "a civilized view, and a realistic one." As he spelled it out, he provided a roadmap for several efforts I would make through the years at UNESCO and in pressing for wider use of electronic communication. We did this long before e-mail and the Internet had become household words. Said Charles:

> Educational and cultural diplomacy is not simply an exercise in the spreading of good will. It has, or should have, quite specific purposes. A first purpose should be to develop arrangements, technical and human, that will lead to a more equitable distribution in the world of ideas and information. There ought to be facilities for the regularized, efficient dissemination of knowledge that would ensure that the necessary kind of knowledge goes to the people who need it, and would allow them to tap into the immense reserves of knowledge that have been built up in the United States. What was needed . . . is what might be called an international knowledge-bank. And to this the United States could make a major contribution.

As a matter of style, he recommended "quiet diplomacy." Our culture has its "charms," he said, "but tranquility and self-effacement are not among them." He saw the need for less bureaucracy and less hustle, a less conspicuous government presence and a less conspicuous American presence.

Charles was appalled at the bureaucratic decision that then took the educational and cultural affairs program out of the State Department and put it in the new U.S. Information Agency he regarded as an obvious propaganda arm of the government. To confuse matters further, the cultural affairs officers overseas were to be paid by the State Department while working for the USIA. At their posts abroad, cultural affairs people would work under the political affairs officer. Hardly quiet or unobtrusive diplomacy. When I went around the world, years later, to examine the Fulbright scholar exchange program, the relationship between cultural affairs and political affairs officers was still a live issue. In the late 1990s, the USIA and the Fulbright program were returned to the State Department.

American overseas educational and cultural programs supported by non-governmental universities and foundations have long provided international exchanges. And U.S. commercial products in the cultural field—films, television, cassettes, newsweeklies, religious radio broadcasts—have long dominated their respective fields. They draw the ire of developing countries who accuse America of "cultural imperialism" and of undermining indigenous cultures in Africa and Asia. Even the European Union in the 1990s threatened to apply small quotas to the number of American films that could henceforth be imported into the European nations. Canada has laws restricting the volume of U.S. news and entertainment that can cross the border.

But foreign restrictions did not limit an important aspect of American cultural exchanges: avant garde films and writings, "small" books and poetry, and literature and music that the marketplace deems only limitedly profitable. These are distinctly American creations.

Charles Frankel termed American educational and cultural policy abroad "the neglected aspect of foreign affairs." That is as true today as when he said it nearly forty years ago.

Charles put these words in the mouth of President Johnson in September 1965: "We know today [that] ideas, not armaments, will shape our lasting prospects for peace; that the conduct of our foreign policy will advance no faster than the curriculum of our classrooms; that the knowledge of our citizens is one treasure which grows only when it is shared."[1]

NOTE

1. Spoken by President Johnson at the Smithsonian Institution's bicentennial celebration, September 1965; quoted in Leonard R. Sussman, *The Culture of Freedom: The Small World of Fulbright Scholars* (Lanham, MD: Rowman and Littlefield, 1992), p. 27.

22

EDWARD SHILS
The Personal "Soul,"
Privacy, and the CIA

Minutes after my son David was handed his master's degree at the University of Pennsylvania commencement, Edward Shils, the honorary doctoral recipient that year, congratulated David and asked about his future. Ed held several doctorates. He was the recipient of the world's highest honor for sociologists—a European award that carried a $100,000 stipend. He had been for many years chair of the Department of Sociology of the University of Chicago. It was the most prestigious department in the field. Ed's deputy, later also chair of the department, was Morris Janowitz, my undergraduate classmate at New York University, whom I appointed editor in chief of the daily newspaper when I graduated.

Ed Shils spent forty-five years on the University of Chicago's elite Committee on Social Thought. He was perhaps the most respected scholar on a campus at which most everyone had a doctorate. He was a distinctive personality in careful conservative dress that hid a crisp, seemingly brusque manner. Ed's colleague Saul Bellow, the Nobel- and Pulitzer-winning novelist, considered Ed not only a mentor but a role model and editor. Ed was defiantly clear in writing and speaking and insisted on proper use of language. Ed Shils figured in Bellow's novel *Mr. Sammler's Planet* and edited the manuscript. Ed appeared again in Bellow's *Humboldt's Gift*, where the Shils character was described by the novelist as the man "whom I admired and even adored . . . the only man with whom I exchanged ideas."[1] Bellow, however, in his later novel, *Ravelstein*, ravaged Shils.

But that day in Philadelphia, Ed chatted briefly about David's going on to Columbia Law School. Ed had helped David get into Penn and may have been disappointed that he was not choosing an academic career. Serving first as general counsel, David then became executive vice president of the New York Yankees and later general counsel of the MTV networks.

Ed rose to academic prominence from a poor Jewish family that stressed excellence. He pursued that all his life, especially as founder and editor of *Minerva*, the international journal devoted to advancing scholarship and academic excellence. Jason Epstein wrote that Edward Shils "was death on intellectual fraudulence."[2] *Minerva* could be found in university libraries in many countries and was read by the world's most serious scholars. Ed edited *Minerva* from a small room adjacent to *Encounter* magazine, edited by Mel Lasky, in London's theater district. Ed shared space, too, with *Survey* magazine, the product of Leo Labedz (see chap. 25).

All three publications were edited by extraordinary men committed to sustaining democratic freedoms, particularly in the intellectual and political fields, during the coldest days of the Cold War. I was closely associated with all three during the last twenty years of the magazines' existence. *Encounter* had been created by the Congress of Cultural Freedom when it was funded by the CIA at the end of World War II. By then, the Soviet Union was wooing Western intellectuals to support promises of a socialist utopia.

Before creating the German magazine *Monat*, the first to be financed secretly by the CIA, Mel Lasky described the new publication's rationale which would apply to *Encounter* and the other CIA-funded periodicals. Despite victory in war, he said, "we have not succeeded in combating the variety of factors—political, psychological, cultural—which work against U.S. foreign policy, and in particular the success of the Marshall Plan [the extraordinary U.S. reconstruction aid] in Europe." The cultural war with the Communist bloc, Lasky stated, was basic to sustaining America's presence. This reflected a "serious void" that he called "real and grave." The void was the failure to win "the educated and cultural classes" in Germany—and, he might have added, failure among the intelligentsia in the United States as well. In the long run, Lasky added, these classes "provide moral and political leadership."[3]

When the CIA's cover was blown in 1967, the secret funding of these magazines and related programs was widely termed deceitful and scandalous. Little attention was paid to the vast program of disinformation sent worldwide by the Soviet Union and its puppets, abetted by intellectual fellow-travelers in America and Europe, who saw no evil in the Soviet gulag-state; instead they directed their anger at the democratic country providing outlets for writers and artists to express their own views, even critical of American policies. Indeed, it was never publicly revealed that a large number of CIA operatives in Washington were long-time political and intellectual liberals. And, in retrospect, it is clear—as it must have been to the CIA at the time—that the anti-Communist hysteria of the McCarthy period would not have permitted *liberal* anti-Communist writers and artists, such as those who frequented the CIA-funded publications, to gain a hearing in the United States and Europe.

Jack Sussman, the author's father, near his dental office opposite Gramercy Park, New York, in 1942. (*Photo from collection of Leonard R. Sussman*)

The author, who was executive director of Freedom House for twenty-one years, where he designed global surveys of press freedom as well as related political rights programs. He had previously been a journalist and press secretary to the governor of Puerto Rico. (*Photo courtesy of Freedom House*)

Lynne Sussman, the author's daughter, earned a doctorate from Harvard and taught there and at Cambridge College. After twenty-six operations to correct congenital hand deformities, she learned to play the piano and French horn. She died of breast cancer at the age of fifty-three. *(Photo by Leonard R. Sussman)*

Muriel Rukeyser, a leading American poet and author of a biography of Wendell L. Willkie, the popularizer of *One World*. *(Photo © Rollie McKenna)*

Wendell L. Willkie, whose best-selling book *One World* presented a report of his wartime worldwide tour, undertaken at the request of President Roosevelt. *(Photo by Bachrach)*

Alexander Bickel (right) was defense attorney for the *New York Times* in the Pentagon Papers case in 1971. When the *Times* began publishing these massive secret documents of the Vietnam War, federal attorney Whitney North Seymour Jr. (left) secured an injunction that the Supreme Court later overturned, 6–3. Bickel and Seymour appear here at a Freedom House conference to develop press-government guidelines for the future. *(Photo by David A. Sussman)*

American civil rights leader Bayard Rustin (center) banters with campaigners from several parties while monitoring the first election ever held in Rhodesia (now Zimbabwe), in 1979. The author is standing at left. *(Photo from collection of Leonard R. Sussman)*

Frances Grant, the foremost Latin American human rights activist, in her eighties, rides a helicopter to monitor elections in war-torn El Salvador. *(Photo by Leonard R. Sussman)*

Harry D. Gideonse, long-time leader of Freedom House and for twenty-six years president of Brooklyn College, presents the Freedom Award to fifteen dissidents from the Soviet Union in absentia. *(Photo courtesy of Freedom House)*

Nomavenda Mathiane, the leading black woman journalist in South Africa during the apartheid period. *(Photo by Leonard R. Sussman)*

Aristedes Katoppo, a leading editor in Indonesia during the oppressive period, was exiled and then banned, yet still consulted by other editors—a "ghost" in the city room. *(Photo by Leonard R. Sussman)*

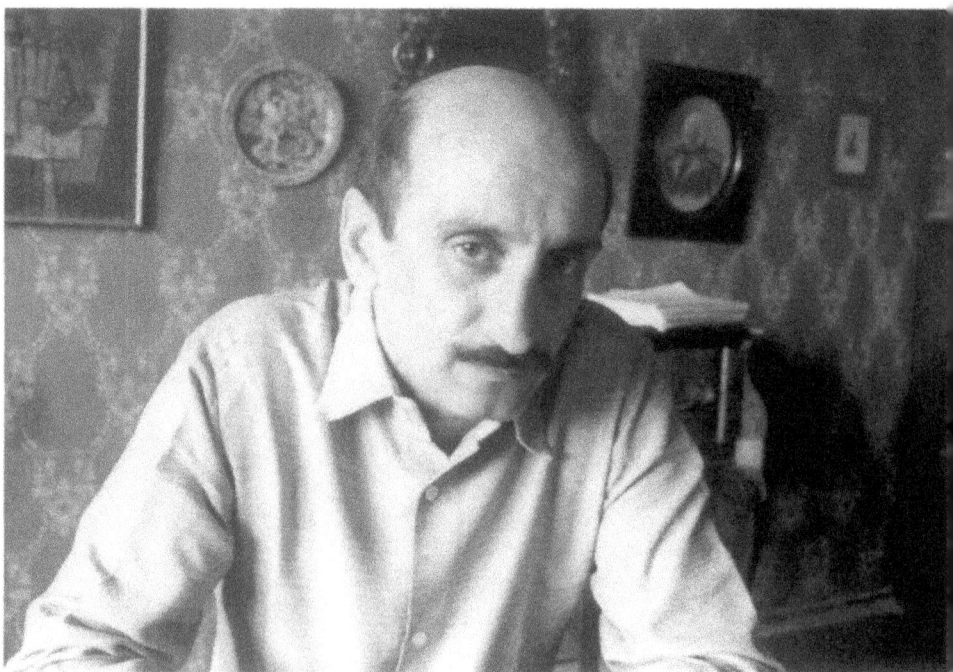

Sergei Grigoryants, shown here after ten years in Soviet prisons, tested Gorbachev's "new freedom" by publishing a hand-typed newspaper, *Glasnost. (Photo by Leonard R. Sussman)*

Gloria and Humberto Rubin in their Paraguayan radio station, which was physically attacked and shut down by the Stroessner dictatorship. *(Photo by Leonard R. Sussman)*

Margaret Chase Smith, United States senator from Maine (1949–73). Her Declaration of Conscience was the first challenge to McCarthyism on the Senate floor. She was also the first woman to head a congressional committee on military affairs. *(Photo courtesy of the Margaret Chase Smith Library, Skowhegan, Maine)*

Jonas Savimbi (center), leader of the Angolan rebel force UNITA, on his first visit to the United States. At left is Carl Gershman, president of the National Endowment for Democracy; the author is standing at right. *(Photo courtesy of Freedom House)*

The Dalai Lama (right), the Tibetan Buddhist leader in exile, speaks with Whitney North Seymour, chairman of Freedom House, which arranged the Dalai Lama's first visit to the United States. *(Photo by Leonard R. Sussman)*

After the CIA withdrew support, I secured much of the corporate and foundation funding for *Encounter* and *Survey*, as well as a substantial association for *Minerva* when Ed needed assistance. This latter arrangement stemmed from my earlier creation of the International Council on the Future of the University. Ed shared with Charles Frankel and Paul Seabury the initial impetus for establishing ICFU (see previous chapter). When Charles was murdered we prevailed upon Ed to assume direction of the organization. He agreed with the understanding that *Minerva* would be taken under ICFU's wing to provide some administrative support for the magazine. *Minerva* would still be run from London, where Ed lived half of each year. He had long taught at both Cambridge and Chicago.

Ed was soft-spoken, almost self-effacing. He refused all his life to be called Doctor or Professor—just Mister—and his biography does not appear in *Who's Who in America*, though it is certainly merited. His students regarded him as only a fair lecturer, but as a seminar leader he was superb. He demanded that graduate students read as much as he—a tall order.

He inspired a taste for the classics, one he celebrated in *The Calling of Sociology*: "A classic is not a monument," Shils wrote. "It is a continuous opportunity for contact with an enduring problem, with a permanently important aspect of existence as disclosed through the greatness of a mind. It never becomes archaic, even if its stylistic idiom is out of fashion. It remains a classic as long as the problem with which it deals remains problematic, relevant, and insoluble in any definitive way."[4] This allusion to the continuing relevance of the classics implies their universal values. The classics would become a fighting issue in the 1980s, when academic campaigns for multiculturalism threatened to replace classics with cultural elements drawn from the ethnic, racial, and geographic histories of present-day students. Ed's classics included Aristotle, Thucydides, Machiavelli, Adam Smith, Alexis de Tocqueville, Max Weber, Émile Durkheim, and the history of Polish peasants in Europe and America. Ed Shils knew the outer limits of student capabilities. As a young graduate student at the University of Chicago in the 1930s, Ed had translated Karl Mannheim's difficult *Ideology and Utopia* from the German.

During World War II, Ed Shils served in the Office of Strategic Services (OSS), forerunner of the Central Intelligence Agency (CIA). He analyzed overt and covert reports on the morale of the Wehrmacht (the Nazi ground forces) following their collapse on the Eastern front. He examined the huge losses in the ranks of German noncommissioned officers. He discovered that those losses undermined morale among the troops being mobilized to defend the coast of Europe against the Allies' D-day invasion. With the loss of the platoon leader there was no primary group "in-feeling" necessary to forge a new fighting unit. Ed Shils applied the "primary group" criterion to many other forms of civilian as well as military situations.

His cherubic face could hardly mask his sharp wit directed at pseudo-scholars. He would probably dub them one level below fools. His professional life was dedicated to raising ever higher the standards for higher education and resisting the political compromises that eroded scholarship. Shils ceaselessly attacked intellectuals on several continents who participated in what he regarded as the great intellectual crimes of this century: their support, knowing or unknowing, for the tyrannies of the political left or the right. He held that Jean-Paul Sartre, Herbert Marcuse, and other "ambassadors of student radicalism of the sixties" are responsible for the international intellectual crisis of the late twentieth century.[5]

We had a warm relationship despite my journalistic, rather than academic, background. I believe Ed sensed my long-time ambivalence: I admired the academy and tried to bring some of its better attributes to the practice of journalism. I also applied journalism's tools to examine the shortcomings of academics. Ed liked that, too.

He had sublimated his Jewish background but took opportunities to recall it with some sensitivity and even humor. Unlike Mel Lasky and Leo Labedz, Ed Shils was an iconoclast. He was most at home in the library or classroom, yet always in touch with the world outside; else he could not have been the premier sociologist. He was able to see the "big picture," which he described in his classic work *Center and Periphery: Essays in Macrosociology.*

Every society, he wrote, may be considered as a center and a periphery. "The center," he said, "consists of those institutions and roles which exercise authority—whether it be economic, governmental, political, or military—and of those which create and diffuse cultural symbols—religious, literary, etc.—through churches, schools, publishing houses, etc. The periphery consists of . . . the recipients of commands and beliefs, . . . and of those who are lower in the distribution and allocation of rewards, dignities, facilities, etc."[6]

Yet Shils believed that in a civil society, unlike a thoroughly dictatorial one, center and periphery had some needs in common. "A civil society," he wrote, "is not a society of complete mutual transparency or visibility." He added, "Everyone needs to be allowed to live somewhat in the shade—both rulers and ruled—in order to 'keep' what 'belongs' to them."[7]

This is an appeal for privacy. It acknowledges that news media, for example, are instruments of the "center" but cautions nevertheless that both center and periphery need "space." This is an issue that was first projected by a young lawyer destined to be a distinguished Supreme Court Justice: Louis D. Brandeis, writing with Samuel Warren in the *Harvard Law Review* in 1890, castigated the newspapers of his day for sensational violations of privacy. He called for a law to establish a right to privacy. (The word *privacy* is not mentioned in the Constitution.) Public opinion polls throughout the latter half of the twentieth century, however, reflect strong criticism of the American news media for invading the privacy of individual citizens, even those with some official or celebrity status.

Ed Shils, nevertheless, regarded the late nineteenth century as a golden age of privacy. The press was mainly serious-minded, despite the sensationalism of crime coverage and the deserved muckraking investigations of political corruption. The technology of surveillance had not yet developed. The turn of the century, however, marked new intrusions into privacy. Though age-old intrusions such as slavery and the limited rights of women received some attention as the century ended, the question of privacy was mainly unaddressed. Shils wrote:

> Intrusions on privacy are baneful because they interfere with an individual in his control of what belongs to him. The "social space" around an individual, the recollection of his past, his conversation, his body and its image all belong to him. He does not acquire them through purchase or inheritance. He possesses them and is entitled to possess them by virtue of the charisma which is inherent in his existence as an individual soul—as we say nowadays, in his individuality—and which is inherent in his membership in the civil community. They belong to him by virtue of his humanity and civility—his membership in the human species and his membership in his own society. A society which claims to be both humane and civil is committed to their respect. When its practice departs from that respect for what belongs to the private sphere it also departs to that degree from humanity and civility.[8]

Published in 1975, this remark implies a strong condemnation of many practices now common in American television, in the tabloid press and, sadly, even in the frequent lapses of the self-proclaimed "serious" press.

Inroads on privacy began in the mid-twentieth century and have snowballed as technology has expanded exponentially in the last two decades. In *The Naked Society* Vance Packard noted the undermining of privacy by 1964: centralized, urbanized living restricted privacy and encouraged crime, which in turn expanded police action; corporate competition inspired secrecy and tight security, producing a garrison-state mentality; market surveys increasingly "tested" consumer habits; surveillance tools and investigation became a private industry; and electronic equipment and the expansion of credit systems provided access to growing sources of private information.[9]

Shils noted that privacy had become a growing problem because it had been overcome "in the expansion of the powers and ambitions of elites and in their difficulties that they encounter in attempting to govern and protect and please vast collectivities."[10] Deckle McLean describes four kinds of privacy questions:

1. Privacy as access control: controlling one's personal boundaries and the release of one's secrets; not having one's mask stripped away.
2. Room to grow: cultivating interior processes for understanding, enrichment, and integration of character and personality.
3. Privacy as a safety valve: resting and recuperating from the public arena.
4. Privacy as respect for the individual: insisting that one is more than a cipher and respecting others for being more than ciphers.[11]

One can read into each of these privacy boundaries the common invasions by the news media of the "private space" of both public and private individuals.

In my course on press ethics I try to be specific. I point out the distinction between what is lawful and what is ethical. It is possible to be lawful and unethical, and ethical, yet run afoul of some law. An ethical journalist works within the law, even taking the penalty when he knowingly evades it, such as refusing to respond to a court subpoena for information about a defendant. Within the law, though, restraint is needed to avoid an invasion of privacy that cannot be rationalized as fulfilling a higher social value.

Such restraints are often difficult. The mere massness of mass media today converts almost any public activity into a public spectacle. If a situation is deemed unusual or "newsworthy," a court case involving the most private person can suddenly appear on Court TV or the feature page of a daily newspaper. Identifying sexual assault victims—and alleged perpetrators—is an obvious invasion of privacy. It is symptomatic of many other concerns. Witnesses, not only those suspected of criminal activity, may be forced to provide intimate details of their lives. Even when covering the courtroom testimony of such witnesses, despite their press-freedom privilege, reporters should be expected to use some discretion in withholding sensitive information.

Reporters often display insensitivity in disaster coverage. Holding a live microphone in the face of a grieving widow or asking a kidnapping victim's wife how she feels at that moment is easily recognized now by audiences as insensitive—despite a common urge to hear the answer. Yet insensitive the question remains, and an invasion of privacy at a heartbreaking moment. Victims of economic fraud may be loath to have their case revealed publicly, though it may well be a public service to report the incident without personal identification. Information about a person's credit rating, sexual preference, long-dead minor police record, divorce details, and many other intimate facts may surface in disaster reporting. Such facts should be carefully weighed for direct relevance to the present report, and restraint used. There is an easy tool for displaying restraint: ask the subject, "Do you want to share your story with us [meaning the vast audience]?" Some may welcome as cathartic the chance to speak publicly; others may demur. The response should govern.

Threats to personal privacy today are far more extensive than journalists provide by their insensitivity. The vast bank-credit and credit card system provides instant data about everyone's material worth, tax returns, promptness of debt repayment, indebtedness, and voluminous details of expenditures for goods and licit and illicit recreation. When this data is linked to social security information there is easy access to health records, employment, and "the keys to the kingdom"—access through social security numbers to a wide variety of other governmental databanks in which a citizen's past and present are stored. Not least, maybe surveillance or other files of the Federal Bureau of Investigation or even the Central Intelligence Agency. These files may be secured through the Freedom of Information Act and revealed by journalists.

The struggle for the personal "soul"—as Ed Shils somewhat self-consciously noted before alluding instead to "individuality"—is the paramount human tension in the new millennium.[12] Whether defined in theological or sociological terms—Ed provides the choice—the struggle is clear. The plea for privacy symbolizes what is wrong with mass society. Big government, big news media, and corporate conglomerates have been seen as the inevitable wave of the future. The individual is subsumed in the mass. Yet the mass, particularly mass communication, enables individuals at the farthest reaches of the planet to be connected to each other. That linkage consumes some privacy but enables the individual to expand his personal choices. In recent years, publics have begun to rebel against bigness of all kinds. There is a growing cry for individualism—or, by ignoring it, to encourage citizens to opt out of the body politic. As in most dilemmas in a democratic system, there is perpetual tension, a call for tradeoffs. Thus the times call for civility. Its leaders must be skeptical, cautious, prudent. As Peter Coleman observed about Shils, his men of civility "live from day to day, or year to year, improving or reforming our arrangements when necessary or possible, but always determined to keep the ship afloat and on an even keel."[13] Shils did not believe the age of ideology had ended, only that it had subsided. Millenarianism and romanticism are in our bones. The problem, Coleman adds, is to keep them under control: to strengthen the middle road.

The test ahead, then, will be to expand communication linkages at the discretion of the individual, with proper restraint against invasions of personal privacy and the obliteration of cultural differences. It is essential to examine the right of privacy as Louis Brandeis initiated the discussion, and as Ed Shils addressed the question in more contemporary, academic terms.

"A society which claims to be humane," Ed Shils points out, "is committed to respect" the privacy of the individual and advance along the Midway with civility."[14]

NOTES

1. Quoted in Brent Staples, "Mr. Bellow Writes On, Wrestling with the Ghost of Edward Shils," *New York Times*, April 22, 2000.
2. Quoted in Staples, "Mr. Bellow Writes On."
3. Quoted in Frances Stonor Saunders, *The Cultural Cold War: The CIA and the World of Arts and Letters* (New York: New Press, 1999), p. 29.
4. Quoted in Jerzy Zubrzycki, "Edward Shils: A Personal Memoir," *Quadrant* (Australia), January–February 1996, p. 61.
5. Ibid., p. 63.
6. Edward Shils, *Center and Periphery: Essays in Macrosociology* (Chicago: University of Chicago Press, 1975), p. 39.
7. Ibid., p. 344.
8. Ibid., p. 347.

9. Vance Packard, *The Naked Society* (New York: D. McKay, 1964).

10. Shils, *Center and Periphery*, p. 339.

11. Deckle McLean, *Privacy and Its Invasion* (Westport, CT: Praeger, 1995), pp. 51–57.

12. Shils, *Center and Periphery*, p. 344.

13. Peter Coleman, "Books: Civility, Edward Shils," *Quadrant* (Australia), March 2002, p. 81.

14. Shils, *Center and Periphery*, p. 344.

23

NEEDED: *INTELLIGENT* INTELLIGENCE

I t was a great boon to toss a problem with political and moral overtones to philosopher Sidney Hook (see chap. 20), Sen. Margaret Chase Smith (chap. 48), and presidential adviser Leo Cherne. Their sound advice long outlasted their official tenure.

Indeed, as recently as 1996 journalists were startled at the renewed eruption of a twenty-year struggle against the CIA's use of reporters as intelligence operatives. The practice was reluctantly revealed in 1975–76 by the Senate's Church Committee. Some fifty American journalists had secretly worked for the CIA abroad. Moreover, some agency people posed as reporters overseas. As a result of these findings, George Bush, then director of the CIA, issued a directive limiting such activity. His successor, Adm. Stansfield Turner, stated that the special role of the U.S. press afforded by the Constitution requires the CIA to pursue "a careful policy of self-restraint . . . in regard to relations with U.S. news media organizations and personnel." But Stansfield also stipulated that exceptions can be made with the "specific approval" of the CIA director. The press objected twenty years ago, but nothing was done about it.

Astoundingly, I believe, the *New York Times* that same year, in the case of Freedom House, acted like the CIA itself. The *Times*'s report on Leo Cherne's appointment to the President's Foreign Intelligence Advisory Board (PFIAB) mentioned that Cherne was an officer of Freedom House and also of the International Rescue Committee. The *Times* noted published reports that the IRC had received some CIA funds in the past and also stated that Freedom House had received money from the J. M. Kaplan Fund, recipient of CIA money. The basic facts were erroneous. The Kaplan Fund had made a small grant to Freedom House years *before* the Kaplan Fund received a dollar from the CIA. There was, moreover, no policy or funding link between the IRC and Freedom House. I wrote to the *Times*,

> Linking CIA funding and Freedom House was not only arbitrary; it was downright mischievous. An interesting parallel was provided by recent reports that some newspaper correspondents had been sharing information with the CIA. *Times* men may have been involved. The propriety of this aside—there may be disagreement whether a journalist should share some information with his government—the attitude of the *Times* has been clear: it sought to clear its name of even the suggestion that any *Times* reporter may have collaborated with the CIA. Presumably, the *Times* believes it would be onerous to have it known that a staff member collaborated with, or received funds from, the CIA. Yet the *Times* linked Freedom House with the CIA even after your reporter ascertained from his own sources that there was no factual basis. Why the double standard?[1]

Then, after I wrote to George Bush for public clarification the *Times* ran this box: "In response to a request . . . Freedom House, an organization that monitors the degree of freedom enjoyed by the citizens of various countries, has received from the Central Intelligence Agency an assurance that the CIA has never passed funds to the organization."[2] The *Times* then repeated the earlier charge.

In 1996, John Deutsch, then CIA director, said he would activate the "exception" if necessary and use American journalists for CIA purposes. Apparently, only an act of Congress can persuade the CIA to drop the press tool from its action kit.

Apart from the troubled history of this practice there are good reasons to stop it: (1) The U.S. intelligence community has a $28 billion budget and forty thousand employees—certainly enough for other, less harmful paths to information; (2) by exploiting journalists the CIA actually undermines the ability and credibility of the press as an open source for intelligence as well as the public—and a check against the CIA's own information flow; and (3) the procedure threatens serious harm to U.S. journalists working abroad.

These revelations, which first surfaced during the Cold War, were seized then by operatives in the Soviet Union and Eastern Europe to smear all American journalists abroad as CIA agents. The Soviets' "news" reports, of course, followed a strict line dictated by the Communist Party. Soviet propaganda thus projected U.S. journalists as a mirror image of KGB operatives. Worse still, this charge against particular American journalists served to bar them from some countries or from access to information inside the Communist bloc. In some cases, American journalists went to foreign prisons as spies. The most notorious abuse of this Soviet ploy was the month-long incarceration in 1986 in Moscow of Nicholas Daniloff, reporter for *U.S. News & World Report*, who was finally exchanged for a leading Soviet spy held in the United States. The following year, Gerald Seib of the *Wall Street Journal* was arrested in Iran and accused of being a spy.

In March 1996, an editorial in the Iranian press stated that the American government had "admitted" that "American journalists pursue covert operations for the CIA." That citation was CIA Director Deutsch's latest statement that he might use the press as an "exception." The Iranian editorial took the next step: it said that the "CIA pawn," Christiane Amanpour, one of the most reliable, independent CNN correspondents, should be expelled from the country or "put on trial for her false claims." Meanwhile, CNN's Iraqi driver in Baghdad had been tortured for several weeks by the secret police, who wanted him to identify CIA agents posing as journalists.

The issue arose again in 2002. A report leaked from the Department of Defense stated that its new Office of Strategic Influence would include "black" or false news as part of its effort to influence foreign governments. Days before Defense Secretary Donald H. Rumsfeld (a former Freedom House board member) killed the office, I published in the *Los Angeles Times* an op-ed article attacking this resort to disinformation. The Soviet Union had first established "Department D" in the KGB security services—D stood for *dezinformatsia*. Half the Soviet "journalists" were actually KGB operatives. Soviet disinformation published for years in African and Asian newspapers reported that AIDS had been created in a Maryland laboratory to depopulate developing countries. Indeed, disinformation as a battlefield tactic to mislead an enemy is acceptable. Even the rare use of black news has led adversaries of the United States to charge falsely that American reporters overseas were in the pay of the government.

I addressed such issues in April 1986 when I asked Sidney Hook; Margaret Chase Smith, who served on the U.S. Senate's CIA subcommittee; and Leo Cherne, a member of the PFIAB, to ponder the role of intelligence with regard to geopolitics, national security, and—no less—morality.[3]

Senator Smith said that a senatorial investigation of the CIA was long overdue. "I have not the slightest doubt that Congress has been derelict in its responsibility on the CIA," she said. In the Senate she was "constantly frustrated," for example, by the CIA's reluctance to provide information she requested on the comparative strengths of the United States and the Soviet Union. Such information was withheld, she said, because the CIA claimed it feared public leaks of intelligence data by members of Congress. She agreed this occurs but added that administration officials also use such information for their political purposes.

In response to my query, Senator Smith proposed the *abolition* of congressional oversight committees on the CIA. Instead, she suggested creation of a permanent—not ad hoc—five-member joint commission composed of the Speaker of the House, the president pro tempore of the Senate, the most junior associate justice of the Supreme Court (freshest from ranks outside the Court), the vice president, and a representative of the public appointed by the president and confirmed by both houses of Congress. She urged that the public representative and chairman come from a party other than the president's to assure some element of political independence.

"The first function I would assign to such a commission," said Senator Smith, "would be to write the charter for the CIA defining not only its proper areas of activities but, as well, the proper relationship between it and the president, the Congress, and other agencies of government"—certainly, too, the clear restriction of the CIA from exploitation of journalists and the news media.

Leo Cherne noted that there was a crisis of belief not only in the U.S. government but in all forms of authority—this was the 1970s, leading to far greater public skepticism in the 1990s. He acknowledged there had been serious mistakes made by intelligence agencies, particularly in surveillance of Americans at home. But, he concluded, "The world's troubles are great and our problems in dealing with them manifest." However, he said, "Intelligence cannot help a nation find its soul. It is indispensable, however, to help preserve that nation's safety while it continues the search."

It was Sidney Hook who placed this "search" in the context of a clash between pragmatism and principle, between geopolitics and morality. His starting premise: "We must maintain *intelligent* intelligence operations." He addressed three basic issues: "The *first* is whether the normal political process can cope effectively with the problems and perennial crises of foreign policy, or whether there is a domain in which ultimate decisions must be entrusted to a dedicated corps of trained specialists responsible to the executive power. The *second* is whether principles of morality can and should operate in guiding the conduct of foreign policy, and to what extent the national interest should be subordinated to such principle. . . . The *third* is what moral choices are open to a democratic nation . . . which is threatened by aggressive totalitarian powers and ideologies."

In foreign policy, he said, "Critical judgment usually follows only after the experience of bitter fruits of disaster." The democratic process is usually too slow and unwieldy. "There are good pragmatic grounds therefore for sharing with the citizenry the determination of foreign policy," Hook added. Yet "popular influence on foreign policy is [often said to be] undesirable because it tends to be naive and moralistic. It assumes that what is good or bad, right or wrong, honorable or dishonorable, in private ordinary life is no less so in the life of nations at peace or at war." He recalled the words of Camillo Cavour, the Italian statesman: "If we did for ourselves what we did for our country, what scoundrels we would be!"

This may seem plausible, Hook quickly stated, but it rests on a confusion between basic moral values. "No moral principle by itself determines what action should be taken because, when we are in an agony of doubt about what we should do, more than one principle applies." This is true in personal relations as well as in public policy. "Because we should tell the truth," Hook declared, "it does not follow that we should tell the truth if someone is intent upon killing or maiming or robbing others." Said Hook, "Every situation of moral choice is one in which the choice is not between good and bad, right or wrong, but between good and good, right and right, the good and the right. One good may be overridden by a greater good; one obligation by a more pressing one. Ordinary human life would be impossible if we did not recognize and act on these considerations."

This, said Hook, does not justify "some current degenerate forms of existentialism according to which individuals are free to decide for themselves what is right or wrong without any appeal to moral principles or ideals, but merely on the basis of what they desire." Morality should be actively engaged as a standard for action.

Morality also has a role to play in determining the national interest. Hook termed "untenable" the doctrine that the pursuit of "national security justifies the use of any means to ensure it." Such means, he said, "may adversely and unacceptably affect the constellation of other ends—our institutionalized rights, freedoms, and services—whose security we are defending." Nonetheless, there may be a conflict between the ends and values whose presence defines a free and open society.

Freedom of the press can severely prejudice a person's right to a fair trial. Speech may be used to incite a lynch mob to deprive a person of life and limb. "At any definite time," said Hook, "the conflict of freedoms should be resolved by the action whose consequences are more likely than those of any other action to further the total structure of freedoms in a community." Hook supported the suspension of freedom of the press for a few days with respect to certain features of a court case, with unlimited freedom to comment subsequently. That, he said, is "less undesirable than the miscarriage of justice that may result if such freedom remains unabridged." Most journalists, however, would not agree, and would probably take the banning to a higher court. Hook commented sardonically: "Some of those who protest in the interest of a free press that there is an absolute right to know in such cases do not extend it to the right to know the sources that the press relies on in its investigative reports." Journalists do, indeed, argue their right to maintain the secrecy of sources. Otherwise, they say, informants will go silent. But by the mid-1990s there was a strong public backlash against statements in the news media attributed to undisclosed sources.

Hook acknowledged that national security may be invoked just as a pretext for arbitrary and illegal personal or factional interest. In the Watergate scandals opponents *within* the democratic process were treated as if they were *enemies* of the democratic process.

What moral choices, then, are open to a democratic society faced by enemies abroad? Some measures of secrecy are needed. For example, agreement on nonproliferation of nuclear weapons requires some quiet method for monitoring compliance, or its absence. Making such knowledge public would invite counteraction and defeat the detection of noncompliance. Also needed, said Hook, is intelligence information concerning an adversary's (or even an ally's) penetration of America's vital secrets—political and economic, as well as military.

Most complex of all, Hook implies, is our system's assumption that "officials and journalists alike will demonstrate a high sense of responsibility." Each, he says, "must be aware of the inevitable and necessary tension between governmental secrecy and the need for the public to know; yet each must recognize, in the absence of an absolute demarcation of their repetitive territories, that *some* secrecy is essential to survival of freedom, and each has a duty to discover where the invisible line rests in each situation."

Sidney Hook concluded a peroration in 1976 that is no less appropriate today:

> Those who on a priori grounds condemn an action without regard for its consequences in preserving the structure of democratic freedoms are guilty at the very least of blatant hypocrisy. This does not give carte blanche to any fool to undertake any project because it seems to him advantageous at the moment. Here as elsewhere there is no substitute for intelligence—for intelligence ultimately responsible to the authorized representatives, legislative or judicial, of the democratic community. It is sometimes necessary to burn a house, or to permit it to burn, in order to save the village. This does not bestow a license for arson. We must recognize the evil we do even when it is the lesser evil. But if it is truly the lesser evil then those who condemn it or would have us do nothing at all are morally responsible for the greater evil that may ensue.

Hereafter, the CIA's covert use of U.S. journalists, even in an extraordinarily "exceptional" case, would be a heavy burden for the intelligence community to bear.

Intelligence, I learned as an editor in the Foreign Broadcast Intelligence Service during World War II, comes in many forms, not least important, in the humor going round even in tightly censored societies. An example from the Cold War era:

> Two Eastern European washroom attendants were going before a committee to have their jobs upgraded. The first questioned is shown a circle and asked what it represents. "A women's washroom," she replies.
> "Correct."
> Shown a square, she is asked what this represents. "A men's washroom."
> "Correct."
> And now a third question: a square painted red. "A Communist Party washroom."
> "Absolutely correct. You pass!"
> As the first woman left the room the second was about to enter. She asked the first how it went. The first replied: "Easy. There were only three questions: two technical and one political."

This spoofing of Party bureaucracy and its linguistics is matched by the following, one of several variations of Cold War humor:

> Three dogs discuss their problems—American, Polish, and Soviet. The American dog says he's often misunderstood and when he barks, he complains, he is given meat.

The Polish dog says, "What's meat?"
The Soviet dog says, "What's bark?"

The following specifically Soviet humor was told to me by Nicholas Daniloff, imprisoned for a month in a Moscow prison of the KGB:

A KGB interrogator asks a Moscow citizen what he believes about foreign affairs.

He answers, "What I read in *Pravda* [the official Communist Party newspaper]."

He's asked, "What do you believe about domestic affairs?"

"What I read in *Izvestia* [another official daily]."

"What do you believe about *glasnost* [the latter-day Communist 'opening']?"

"What I see in Tass reports [the Soviet wire service]."

Getting irritated, the KGB interrogator asks, "But what do you yourself believe?"

"I believe what I read in all of the above, but what I *think* I don't believe."

(For a joke along the same lines once told by President Reagan, see appendix B.)

The twentieth century has had a diverse crew of censor-propagandists. Vladimir Ilyich Lenin set down the Soviet credo in 1902. A newspaper, he said, should "become a part of an enormous bellows that would blow every spark of class struggle and popular indignation into a general conflagration." Italian dictator Benito Mussolini took up the cry in 1912, saying, "Journalism is not a profession but a mission. Our newspaper is our party, our ideal, our soul, and our banner which will lead us to victory." Joseph Goebbels, who ran Nazi Germany's Ministry of Propaganda, declared that "not every item of news should be published: rather must those who control news policies endeavor to make every item of news serve a certain purpose." And so he did. All three censor-propagandists clearly rejected Benjamin Disraeli's warning to the British House of Commons in 1855: "News is that which comes from the north, east, west, and south, and if it comes from only one point of the compass, then it is a class publication, and not news."

One can generalize Disraeli's admonition: to be credible, news reporting must be diverse in subject and balanced in presentation, and it must reflect differing points of view. Or one can take Disraeli literally (as would developing-country critics of Western journalism): news coverage should include people and events from all points on the compass, not mainly the like-minded and the power centers.

Indeed—*North*, *East*, *West*, and *South* produce the acronym *NEWS*.

NOTES

1. Leonard R. Sussman, letter to the editor, *New York Times*, March 5, 1976.

2. *New York Times*, March 11, 1976.

3. Results of this discussion were published as "Intelligence Agencies in a Free Society," *Freedom at Issue*, March–April 1976.

24

ANDREI AMALRIK
Death of a Prophet

*The prophet and the martyr do not see the hooting throng. Their eyes are
fixed on the eternities.*
> —Benjamin Cardozo, Justice of the U.S. Supreme Court

Andrei Amalrik's tragic dash to death in Spain in 1980 was only partly
the result of my inviting him to participate in our alternate conference
of dissidents linked to the formal Commission on Security and Cooperation in
Europe (CSCE). Once our demonstration had been planned, Amalrik could not
stay away.

He asked how one man—Joseph Stalin—could maim, starve, and murder tens
of millions of fellow countrymen. Why did so many do so little to stop the carnage?

A few tried. I met some of them through the years. They were, it turned out,
ordinary men and women who did extraordinary deeds. Some survived the carnage; all were transformed. Andrei Amalrik was one of these, although—ironically—even in freedom he could not escape a tragic fate.

In 1970, at the age of thirty-two, Andrei Amalrik published *Will the Soviet
Union Survive until 1984?*[1] Five years earlier, in 1965, he had been exiled for a
year in Siberia for critical writing. The book was banned in his homeland but created a sensation in the West—so great, indeed, that I placed him among the fifteen major dissidents we honored with the 1973 Freedom Award. Among fellow
dissidents listed on the metal plaque were Maj. Gen. Pyotr G. Grigorenko, the
military hero later sent to a psychiatric warehouse because of his dissidence;
Andrei Sakharov, the atomic physicist and Nobel-winning human rights leader;
Alexander Solzhenitsyn, exiled for his anti-Communist Nobel-winning writings;
and Vladimir K. Bukovsky, one of the earliest human rights activists interned in

a mental institution. All had become world renowned for courageous opposition—inside the Soviet Union.

For his book and other acts of his own, Amalrik was expelled from the Soviet Union in 1976 and then made his way to Paris. In November 1979, as his "deadline" of 1984 neared, we interviewed him in Washington; some of his thoughts appear below. We were intrigued by this young dissident and his clear perception of where the Soviet Union was heading. Less than a year later, I organized a "parallel" nongovernmental conference in Madrid at the outset of the official thirty-five-nation meeting of the CSCE. The conference would reveal human rights abuses in the Soviet bloc—it would "name names." I asked many dissidents to participate in our unofficial conference and address appeals of conscience to the formal CSCE.

I invited Andrei Amalrik, but we were soon devastated by his tragic auto accident. His car was hit by a truck; a metal part slashed through Amalrik's window, hit his head, and killed him instantly. I received word late that evening. With the help of Lucia Thorne, my Freedom House colleague (see chap. 52 for more on her), we had the body brought to Madrid. The next morning was ghastly: while Lucia comforted Amalrik's young widow, I faced the grim details of funeral arrangements. A frightful scene ensued. The hearse driver would not relinquish the body unless he received one thousand dollars. The individual who should have paid refused to do so. The expense, he said, had not been budgeted. I finally took the money from my wallet, and the funeral service proceeded. It was a harrowing experience for everyone. Amalrik's widow remained with us as a fresh symbol of the evils and dangers the dissidents had all experienced.

Looking back at those fateful fifteen awardees of 1973, the death toll has risen in the ensuing twenty-two years.

- *Vyacheslav M. Chiornovil,* imprisoned for twelve years for his 1965 book on twenty Ukrainian dissidents—the volume published in the West—and for his legal brief asking the UN to aid human rights activists, became part of the mainstream political movement in Ukraine known as "Rukh." He was assassinated in 2000.
- *Major General Grigorenko* died in New York in 1986 after a long illness. To the end, he fought for the rights of the surviving Tatars to return from Central Asian exile to their homeland in the Crimea.
- *Anatoly Levitin,* the Russian Orthodox layman who spent ten years in concentration camps for defending religious believers and freedom of conscience, died later in Switzerland.
- *Anatoly Marchenko,* a worker twice imprisoned for nine years for describing the labor camps, died in prison in 1986—even as the Soviet Union itself was dying.
- *Andrei Sakharov,* released from internal exile, died in 1989 in Moscow after a stirring speech in the Russian Congress.

- *Yuri T. Galanskov,* poet, pacifist, and editor of a dissident collection, was sentenced to seven years in forced labor camps, where he then wrote petitions for other prisoners. His health deteriorated, and he died in a camp at the age of thirty-three, in 1972.

Some survive:

- *Larissa Bogoraz,* an activist who defended her first husband, Yuli Daniel, after his arrest in 1965, helped lead the human rights movement, for which she served four years in exile in Siberia. In fragile health, she now lives in Moscow and is still active in human rights affairs.
- *Vladimir Bukovsky* not only survived internment in a psychiatric asylum but, after exile, wrote extensively on the subject and became a prominent activist in the West. He and I differed over the value of the CSCE and the expectations of change it held out to the oppressed. He felt that the Helsinki Process was merely rhetoric, as harmful as the policy of détente—avowed nonbelligerence in the Soviet-American relationship. I believed that the CSCE's publicizing of human rights abuses, forcing responses from the Soviet bloc, even though studded with falsification, was bound to undermine the Communist bureaucracy eventually. Bukovsky earned graduate degrees at Cambridge, where he lives and writes.
- *Natalya E. Gorbanevskaya,* a poet, demonstrated in Red Square against the Soviet invasion of Czechoslovakia and was forcibly interned for three years in a prison psychiatric hospital. After she was released, I met her in Paris, when she began recording the biographies of dozens of other dissidents. She writes now for *Russkaya Myhsl* (Russian Thought), a distinguished journal.
- *Rollan Kadiyev,* a theoretical physicist, was sentenced to three years of forced labor for defending the rights of his people, the Crimean Tatars. He is still active in Tatar affairs in the Crimea.
- *Veniamin G. Levich,* an eminent scientist and supporter of humanitarian appeals, was removed from his posts when he applied to emigrate to Israel. After six years of hardship, he emigrated in 1978.
- *Leonid I. Plyushch,* a mathematician specializing in psychocybernetics, was dismissed from his institute for participating in human rights activities, declared insane, and was forcibly administered drugs. He now lives and writes in Paris.
- *Yury A. Shikhanovich,* a mathematician at Moscow University, was dismissed and sent to a mental hospital for contributing to the *Chronicle of Current Events,* the record of Soviet dissidents sent secretly to the West. He has returned to teaching at the University of Moscow, assists the Sakharov archives, and served on President Yeltsin's human rights commission.
- *Alexander Solzhenitsyn,* Nobel Prize–winning novelist, who wrote contin-

uously during his long exile in the United States, returned to Russia in May 1994. He conducted a television program for some months before it was discontinued in 1995.

This was the courageous band I selected in 1973, with the help of Edward Kline, an extraordinary private American who was the father-protector of many Soviet dissidents. I would not change the list today, except perhaps to add names not known to me then. This group included men and women of diverse religious, national, occupational, and even political backgrounds. All, however, were dedicated nonviolent opponents of a harshly violent system. Some were young, some older, but all put their lives and their families at risk for that eternal commitment to human rights: that concern for the other in us all.

This band of otherwise ordinary people faced martyrdom in an utterly antireligious society. Andrei Amalrik symbolized by his words, deeds, and death the ironies of a system gone mad. He foresaw its doom, if not his own. When he wrote *Will the Soviet Union Survive until 1984?* he gave the year of George Orwell's classic novel an optimistic possibility. To Orwell, this time was the epitome of Big Brother's domination by every means possible; Amalrik's 1984 would be the ending of his government's oppression and its collapse.

He wrote in 1970. Nearly ten years later, Amalrik was in Washington testifying before the congressional committee that oversees the CSCE—the very organization that would meet in Madrid two years later, and for which Amalrik would race to his death. Fate seemed to pose endless ironies for this otherwise ordinary life.

In Washington, we interviewed Amalrik about his prescient book.[2] We asked whether the Soviet Union would, indeed, survive after 1984. He replied, "I can give you the precise answer only five years from now. The date is more or less fiction, but the trend of Soviet policy is still as I wrote it ten years ago. The problems I described then are now the real problems in the Soviet Union: nationalism, lagging industrial and agricultural productivity, and the [oppressive] relationship between authority and the people."

Had there been changes which he hadn't foreseen? "No. . . . Developments have been in the direction which I predicted. But when I wrote I was a young man—a young man thinks events will go very fast. Events really move much more slowly."

Did he think that liberalization was possible from the inside? "The type of society that exists in the United States [is] impossible in Russia—yet a higher degree of human rights and more involvement of the people in the development of the country are possible. But first we need three things: (1) part of the ruling group must begin to reform from above; (2) an active sector of public opinion must be able to lend independent support to the movement; and (3) there must be international support for that movement. So if in the future there are these reforms, then liberalization of the Soviet Union will become possible. The other possibility, of course, is a war against everyone inside the Soviet Union!"

*Did the Helsinki Accords and the CSCE, which provided the continuing rev-
elation of human rights abuses in the Soviet bloc—did they have an impact inside
the Soviet Union?* "Yes. The impact on the regime may not have been very great,
but there was an impact on public opinion in the Soviet Union. . . . [M]any
people, not from the intelligentsia but from the working class, tried to use the
Helsinki Accords to their own interest. They tried to invoke the protection of the
Helsinki Agreement. It is interesting that, in all its history, the Soviet government
signed many international agreements. Most were only for decoration and not
taken seriously. For the first time, part of the Soviet population tried to use the
Helsinki Accords in their own interests. That has been a big change, if not yet
'liberalization.'"

Sensing *that* change as others he foretold, Andrei Amalrik would race off to
Madrid and the CSCE.

After seventy-five years, the Soviet Union died in 1991, just seven years
later than Amalrik's literary question suggested. Then began the tumbling toward
Amalrik's instantly relevant analysis of three aspects of "liberalization"—or
"internal war."

Young Amalrik left a clear legacy. He said, "For some, ideology becomes a
religion; for others, religion becomes an ideology. I do not know which is
worse." Everyone who values freedom, he said, "is confronted by the problem of
creating a new ideology which will transcend both liberalism and Communism
and make its central issue the indivisible rights of man." He added,

Some people say that in order to achieve social and economic rights it is necessary to sacrifice civil rights. A less extreme view holds that it is first necessary
to feed people and only then worry about freedom. This view is, first, immoral,
and second, historically mistaken. It is immoral because man has not only a
stomach but also a head and a heart. To be fed is no great thing—a peasant feeds
his horses so that they can work. A slave who has eaten his fill retains the psychology of a slave if he has never thought about freedom while he was hungry.
If you respect hungry human beings, you should not only feed them but also
convey to them a sense of their human dignity. Unless these two processes
progress hand in hand, we shall live in a monstrous world.[3]

NOTES

1. *Will the Soviet Union Survive until 1984?* (New York: Harper and Row, 1970).
2. The following quotes are taken from an interview with Andrei Amalrik, published
as "Amalrik: Changing the USSR," *Freedom at Issue*, November–December 1979, pp.
19–21.
3. Andrei Amalrik, "A Well-fed Slave Is a Well-fed Slave," *New York Times*, February 3, 1977.

25

LEOPOLD LABEDZ
Cold Warrior Supreme

O f the three magazine editors Freedom House assisted during the Cold War, the most colorful was Leopold Labedz. On a bright June day in 1993, a covey of Cold Warriors met at Freedom House to pay tribute to that fallen comrade.

The character of the assembly testified to the quality of the man memorialized. On the program, which I moderated, were Zbigniew Brzezinski, son of a Polish diplomat who defected when Communists took over his country—Zbig became national security adviser to President Carter and my long-time associate at Freedom House; Robert Conquest, the singular author of volumes that first estimated the tens of millions of Soviet citizens murdered under Stalinism; Leszek Kolakowski, the distinguished Polish scholar; Irving Kristol, early editor of *Encounter* magazine, still coeditor of the *Public Interest*, and godfather of many neoconservative publications; Walter Laqueur, author of many anti-Communist volumes, and historian of the Cold War; Richard Perle, speechwriter and assistant to Sen. Henry "Scoop" Jackson, a leading congressional liberal anti-Communist (Perle became President Reagan's assistant secretary of defense); Richard Pipes, Harvard professor and sometime government consultant, who analyzed Soviet doctrine and tactics extensively; Norman Podhoretz, editor of *Commentary* magazine, who turned from youthful leftist to hard-line Cold Warrior; and Edward Shils (see chap. 22), the leading American and British sociologist and editor of *Minerva*, the international journal for scholars and scholarship, published in a London room next to that occupied by the subject of this day's memorial.

It must be remembered that the Cold War was two-sided: Lenin took power in 1917, destroyed the Russian economy, precipitated a famine that claimed five million lives, and began a massive campaign of terror. Stalin, Lenin's successor, did even worse. He created a privileged class, the *nomenklatura*, ran purges whose killing rate was the greatest in history, enslaved the peasants, and further impoverished the vast population—all in the name of high idealism. The other side of the Cold War: widespread U.S. anti-Communist policies informed by a small band of intellectuals and politicians in the West who understood the horrors of Communism and its expansionist potential worldwide and persuaded America to deploy military and public-diplomacy deterrents.

The Labedz ceremony was, in reality, a testament to the Cold Warriors in public diplomacy. Labedz's career spanned the Cold War, the decisive struggle of his era. This memorial marked the era's end, as well as his death. For three decades he edited *Survey* magazine, the distinguished journal of East and West studies. Leo and *Survey* played a central role in the struggle. Indeed, the struggle consumed Leo. He witnessed the worst horrors of the twentieth century. Born in 1920 in Symbirsk and educated in Warsaw, he saw the rise of fascism and Communism, the Holocaust, and the Stalinist purges, resulting in the death of many in his family. He fought in World War II in Asia and Europe. He came to political maturity with a personal understanding of totalitarianism and devoted his life to opposing it: documenting its crimes, exposing its lies, defending its victims.

Leo was a supreme editor and author. He tussled over every word in every issue, sometimes delaying publication for months to rewrite and recheck facts. He was at heart a scholar as well as a fierce polemicist. He dissected an opponent's distortions with steely strength and absolute accuracy. He was an unusual combination of activist and scholar. He had other mixed qualities: he spoke to friends with tremendous force but also with a fundamental kindness and geniality that were the heart of his personality. He was jovial, yet in the end Job-like.

Several years before he died, Leo was hit by several cruel fates at once. During a lifetime of concentration on research and writing he completely ignored the responsibilities that accompanied the financing of *Survey*, a problem he left to others. A friend at *Encounter* raised much of the money to publish *Survey*; I handled the American end of the fund-raising, which accounted for three-quarters of the magazine's income in later years. But no one, especially Leo, bothered to maintain income and expenditure records that would satisfy the British tax agency. Indeed, Leo simply placed incoming foundation funds, which I forwarded, into his own bank account. He paid magazine bills out of that account, and kept a pittance for himself. He had almost no private life, certainly few costs except for food and housing. He was completely indifferent to his own welfare. He lived on a diet of chips and Polish sausage. He never touched green vegetables and would remove them from his plate with great disdain. He lived in a tiny room cluttered from ceiling to floor with publications and manuscripts. Some were forty-year-old issues of *Pravda*, the key Soviet daily created by Lenin, and obscure copies of Indonesian Communist sheets. He consulted these infrequently, but when necessary could pull a particular document from a cluttered corner. A friend said his flat was so cluttered, "he needed to take a running long jump to get into bed." Leo's phenomenal memory, however, reduced his need for document-checking.

His primitive financial record-keeping caught up with him at a tragic moment. The tax authorities, assuming his accounts reflected actual personal income, sued Leo for hundreds of thousands of pounds in back taxes. At that moment, he was virtually bankrupt. He had not published an issue for many months. He had been stricken with diabetes and had one leg amputated at the hip. Months later, a second leg was taken. While in the hospital, a fire broke out in his apartment. Most of his historic files and piles of publications were consumed. Mel Lasky and other friends put together an issue of *Survey* featuring Leo's best work.

Slowly, Leo emerged from seclusion. He managed a wheelchair, appeared at pubs, and resumed his verbal combativeness. I resigned, finally, as chair of the Survey Charitable Fund. Leo lived to see the collapse of the Soviet Union and to receive a hero's welcome upon returning to a free Poland. Many of his intellectual friends among the underground now served as ministers in the new democratic government.

He was an unlikely hero, a brilliant, relentless, often lonely but always powerful voice of freedom. Leo's father was a Polish army doctor, and Leo studied medicine in Paris. He returned home in 1939 when the Nazis invaded and saw the Russo-German partition of his homeland under the Hitler-Stalin pact. His father was employed in a sanatorium for the Soviet elite, and Leo served as a young father-confessor for survivors of Stalin's purges. When the Germans attacked the Soviet Union, Leo was taken east. He joined General Anders's Polish army, harried through Central Asia. There, Leo nearly died from typhoid. Later he fought with Polish forces against the Italian fascists at Monte Cassino, Italy. Corporal Labedz, ever the scholar, angered his tank comrades by replacing ammunition caches with books.

Walter Laqueur (who much later published my first book) hired Leo Labedz in 1955 as an assistant at *Survey*. Under Leo, the journal attracted considerable attention, even in the Soviet Union. It was translated for members of the Soviet Politburo. Leo found a publisher for Alexander Solzhenitsyn's classic *One Day in the Life of Ivan Denisovich*. Leo also edited Solzhenitsyn's *A Documentary Record* (1970) and brought to the West Andrei Amalrik's writing in "comparative totalitarianism."

Communism was no less a menace to human freedom than Nazism, but Communism was more dangerous because of what Norman Podhoretz called "the intellectual intolerance and determination to suppress free discussion displayed by [Communism's] camp followers in Europe and elsewhere."[1]

Anti–anti-Communism, the popular cry of the liberal left, was a threat to Freedom House. It was a direct challenge to cultural freedom, and ultimately to democratic societies.

Leo Labedz took on not only the acknowledged Communists—they were an easy mark for him—but he also attacked "the barbarism of the New Left" in democratic countries. He was outraged by the student revolts of the 1960s and no less critical in the early 1970s of the détente policies of the Nixon administration. He regarded this as akin to the appeasement of Hitler in prewar Europe. This led Sen. Henry Jackson and his aide, Richard Perle, both liberal Democrats, to invite Leo to testify before congressional committees on his "unfashionable analysis."

Interestingly, the leadership of China invited Leo to Beijing to discuss Soviet policies. Years earlier, he had been the first to publicize the split between Soviet and Chinese Communists. When Leo returned from China, he told me he had been treated like a foreign dignitary. He was shown generally secret areas, including the vast bomb shelters beneath Beijing constructed to withstand air raids. Several years later, when I was brought to China to discuss the creation of think tanks, I was also shown the air raid network. It included extensive hospital, dining, and other facilities. I assume the Chinese wanted word to get out that they were prepared for an assault.

If Leo was sometimes hard on Perle, the eminent hardliner, for not pursuing sufficiently robust policies toward the Communist bloc, he was occasionally displeased with me for similar reasons. I recall one extraordinary phone call to me from Leo in London. We had just completed drafting the latest findings in Freedom House's Comparative Survey of Freedom. For a decade, the survey had been conducted by Raymond D. Gastil. One year he raised Poland's rating from "not free" to the low end of the "partly free," even though Polish military still controlled the Communist government under a broad diktat from Moscow. Leo lectured me for more than an hour about the error of our analysis and the negative impact it would have in Poland itself. Leo, I believe, had heard that I had faced a similar reaction on the Freedom House board: some members wanted us to retain the "not free" designation for Poland.

Gastil, however, had created criteria for determining the relative freedom of a country. On that basis, he detected sufficient movement inside the country to warrant the new judgment. The Catholic Church, a powerful force in the country, increasingly resisted Communist practices. The Solidarity labor movement under Lech Walesa, with strong underground support from American labor unions, was uniting workers and staging demonstrations. Pirate radio broadcasts and even some underground television was moving into Poland almost at will. The Polish military, consequently, was showing signs of easing restrictions, even negotiating with the opposition. In light of all this, Gastil felt justified in moving Poland barely out of the "not free" category. I supported him at the board meeting, mainly with these arguments but also on the ground that he deserved to have academic freedom for the survey, a largely scholarly and not a polemical enterprise. There are occasional board-staff disagreements, though the survey and its dozen creators generally dissect nearly two hundred countries with professional skill.

So it went with Leo Labedz that year. Poland remained partly free in our survey. Soon afterward, the Berlin Wall fell, and Poland's Solidarity movement became the Polish government. Leo returned home briefly, as hero. Perhaps our survey was a bit premature, but we did read the straw in the wind. For Leo, however, a country—by *his* definition—could never be partly free. It was free, or it was not. And even then, when free, it was always in danger of having freedom eroded by complacency or by "useful idiots," Lenin's term for softhearted democrats who could be manipulated for totalitarian objectives.

Richard Perle said, "No one more than Leo so richly deserved the pleasure derived from the withering of the totalitarian menace."[2]

Leo suffered greatly during the last five years of his life, but he never complained. Diabetes led to confinement in a wheelchair and loss of a last chance to resume publication of *Survey*. Ed Shils (see chap. 22) best described Leo Labedz:

> [He] was about five feet eight inches in height. He was as bald as a monk. His cheeks were pink without being florid; his broad brow was equally pink. He had bright blue eyes. His torso had the shape of a rugby football. His wrists and ankles were slender and trim. His shirt was always white and freshly laundered, his suit well pressed; his shoes perfectly shined. Wherever he went, he carried a heavy, inevitably overstuffed black briefcase, not at all shabby but a little the worse for always being jammed full of cuttings, books, papers, and manuscripts. He walked rapidly in rather short steps. He had a marvelously sweet grin, slightly mischievous, slightly embarrassed; as he grew older, the smile saddened.[3]

Not present in Washington that day was Mel Lasky, editor of *Encounter* magazine for most of its existence. In their distinct ways, Mel and Leo aggressively defended Western democratic culture from those—especially in the West—who fell prey to Communist blandishments. Several months earlier, Leo had attended *Encounter*'s final ceremony in the shadow of Berlin's Brandenburg Gate. The magazine ran out of funds just as the Cold War ended. Mel called to Berlin the remaining stalwarts for "A Last Encounter with the Cold War."

Bernard Levin wrote of the meeting in the *Times* of London that those in the conference "were the motley army which, without a shot fired, fought for the truth against lies, for reality against mirages, for steadfastness against capitulation, for civilization against barbarism, for the peaceful word against the brutal blow, for applauding courage against excusing cowardice, for—put most simply—democracy against tyranny. And we were right, entirely, completely, provably, joyfully, patiently, and truthfully right."[4]

Gone before Soviet Communism's end were Sidney Hook (see chap. 20), Arthur Koestler, and Raymond Aron; but present that day in Berlin were other warriors: Robert Conquest, Edward Shils, Peter Coleman, Irving Kristol, Norman Podhoretz, Gertrude Himmelfarb, Elena Bonner (wife of Andrei Sakharov), Vladimir Bukovsky, and Leopold Labedz.

And now Leo was gone; soon after, Ed Shils.

Anthony McAdam, who described the event as "a civilized funeral in Berlin," concluded, "We are all in their debt."

NOTES

1. Norman Podhoretz, speech given at the memorial for Leopold Labedz at Freedom House, June 15, 1993.

2. Quoted in the obituary for Leopold Labedz, *The Daily Independent* (London), March 30, 1993.

3. Edward Shils, "Leopold Labedz," *Quadrant* (Australia), January–February 1996, p. 51.

4. Bernard Levin, "Encountering Ghosts in Berlin," *The Times* (London), October 15, 1992.

26

NOMAVENDA MATHIANE

Black Woman Journalist
in Apartheid South Africa

All but one of my walks on New York's midway were solo. The exception: my tour-guide role for Nomavenda Mathiane, the diminutive journalist from South Africa. She was in town to publicize her first book, which I published after spending time with Noma in Soweto, the vast black "township" outside Johannesburg. During the fiercely oppressive apartheid years, when I visited three times, Noma became her country's leading black journalist published in white-run magazines and newspapers. Noma earned her reputation the hard way: by being honest about cruel race relations, and no less honest about corruption among some black leaders, particularly the wife of Nelson Mandela. It took courage for Nomavenda to take this middle course and infuriate large portions of both races.

We discussed her book *Diary of Troubled Times* during a long walk and a drive through Soweto at the peak of the bloody disturbances there. Our later walk down Manhattan's midway was a return favor; far less exciting, though Noma insisted that surviving New York's crowded thoroughfares took no less courage than she had exhibited in Soweto. (I rejected that comparison.) Walking in New York, she recalled the following fictitious tale about the complexity of communication in what was still an apartheid state, the races separated by law and practice: A white man was driving a Mercedes at some speed down the center of a South Africa highway near a turn in the road. Along came a black woman driving a Toyota. She had to bear sharply to the side to avoid a collision. As she came screeching to a stop she screamed at the white man: "Pig!" He ignored her, kept driving down the center of the road—and killed the pig!

The story reflects stereotypes: white male affluence and power, black female pragmatism and humanness, movement in opposite directions across a narrow passage, black precision, white ineptness, and most of all the inability to converse across the racial divide.

The apartheid government itself reflected these stereotypes. Many of us were in Johannesburg at the invitation of the *Daily Star* for a conference on press freedom. Some of our visas had been held up for several weeks until the paper broke the logjam. It told the government, "It would be folly to bar any visitors of prominence." Doing so, said Harvey Tyson, the editor, "would prevent a free debate and create merely a protest meeting elsewhere." He said that "if they barred even one, none would come, and the meeting would be held in another African country." The government deliberated, he said, and "finally took the risk of facing any criticism." It might even listen when someone shouted "Pig!"

But not for long, as we soon discovered. Tyson told me that no real newspaper could publish a normal edition without facing prosecution. There is a "mare's nest" of regulations. But, he added, "You do what you have to do." The crux of the problem, as he saw it, was that "one side believes in orderly reform toward democracy; the other side believes in immediate transfer of power to all the people. Both sides believe the other is trying to achieve its objective through violence." There is, he said, "no middle ground left in our society." There is instead a "deep hole between two cliffs." The choices he set forth:

- You must choose security, or take up violence in the name of freedom.
- You must side with oppression in the name of law and order, or you must side with revolution.
- You must choose cooperative democracy, or "people's democracy," when both in historical experience are as far from democracy as you can imagine.

I spoke to Tyson later. The personal dilemma for an editor with integrity, he told me, is to know when to leave the job for another line of work—when one can no longer struggle in good conscience but has become merely a puppet of the establishment. Tyson left the paper some time later, but I could never reach him for an explanation.

Several who did not leave the struggle were Denis Beckett, nephew of British playwright Samuel Beckett, and Nomavenda Mathiane. Denis and Nomavenda were the mainstays of *Frontline*, the nonracial magazine that Freedom House briefly helped fund. Noma was a vivacious, almost perpetually sparkling, bristling personality and a perceptive writer. She was a walking (sometimes leaping) library of information about South Africa and its people. I later published as a book a collection of her writings in *Frontline*. In her essay on South Africa's future, Noma described the widely differing definitions of freedom by interviewees. "Freedom is more costly than oppression. Freedom has small print which people ought to read," said one. "Freedom, what is freedom? I don't know," another replied. "The right for us to move into white areas and for poor whites to move into black areas," said a third. "But," another responded, "have you ever heard of whites moving *down*?" The ghettos will always be for poor blacks, and not for whites, it was said. Noma concluded her essay, "But the more people I spoke to the more I realized how abstract a noun freedom is. If we had more understanding about what was at stake, perhaps there would be less fear, and less dreams."[1]

Noma sat in front of a computer writing her weekly article. The walls of *Frontline* were covered with satirical cartoons published in the magazine. Somehow, Beckett and his small flock could get away with biting humor that would never appear in the daily press. Perhaps he was safer because he was an Afrikaner with heritage as far back as any of the government censors. The difference: the Becketts, man and wife, in their Afrikaner church and in their personal relationships, worked hard to demonstrate racial integration; featuring Noma regularly was just one example. Their children attended mixed-race schools and had mixed-race playmates. Denis frequently used socially conscious humor in conversation with apartheidists. His magazine raised hard questions about the pragmatics and costs of racial separation. His readers knew these were real issues that could not be wished away by purely emotional or chauvinist litany.

It was time for Noma to drive me through "her" country. We spent the next seven hours on the move without stopping for breakfast or lunch. Before leaving Johannesburg Noma drove me unannounced to a building in the heart of town. She introduced me to Black Sash women (all white) counseling blacks, young and old, who needed assistance for food, legal aid, employment, and other forms of emergency help. The blacks sat patiently on rows of wooden benches waiting to be called. Some Black Sash ladies were matrons, some rather young women serving coffee or generally helping. These women also went on picket lines and engaged in other demonstrations. Their clients looked much the same as welfare recipients elsewhere, though perhaps more silent and outwardly emotionless.

Next we went to a nearby office where black women in heavy, colorful blankets with large baskets on their heads entered a room with posters decrying hunger and sick children. This was the place where Zulu women came from great distances to bring the articles they created for sale in local shops. The women seemed confused by the city and the building elevator. Eight tried to crowd in one lift with baskets still on their heads. Noma motioned several to wait with us for another lift. Only then did they smile at her a bit—and look suspiciously at me.

From there we walked to another building that had to remain nameless because of its role as a black activist headquarters, though it was within a few blocks of the thirty-six-story Sun Hotel and other residential towers in the center of the city. We walked up a few winding stairs when the lift didn't work. At the end of a narrow corridor we entered a small waiting room where two very weary-looking men were seated, obviously waiting to be admitted to another room. The walls were covered with liberation slogans, signs remembering Stephen Biko, slain in police custody, and others urging, "Free our children!" Through another door we met a stocky man who had immediately separated himself from a conversation with a second man. He came to us as both men were looking suspiciously at me. The one greeted us warmly when I was introduced by Noma as "OK."

There was some personal chatting about when he had gotten out of Robben Island, the severe detention place where future president Nelson Mandela had spent much of his prison time. This man had been there eight years. He seemed calm, self-contained, almost affable. He spoke of a meeting that night and of a convoy to go to it, and he urged Noma to attend. We were then led through another door, this one unlocked to let us through, where five or six men sat waiting on a raw wood plank. More signs and symbols. And then through another door, to a room where two women stood. They looked particularly strangely at me until I was introduced by Noma. Behind them, from floor to ceiling, were sheets of paper pasted to the full wall. The sheets contained the names, printed three inches high, and phone numbers of lawyers available in emergencies. There were some marks beside some names indicating preferences. There were no names of black lawyers, I was told. They generally go into more lucrative practices or do not serve the purpose of this room. This was the operations room for securing legal aid quickly for persons who were detained or who had "disappeared."

Probably much more originated in these rooms. As we left, I was told, "You have just been to the headquarters of the ANC/UDF"; the top headquarters was in Lusaka, Zambia. It was the long-banned liberation group proclaimed to feature the use of violence, though Oliver Tambo, head of the African National Congress (ANC), that week in Lusaka urged his followers in South Africa not to use necklacing and other violence against other blacks. Necklacing was the placing of an automobile tire around the neck of a victim and then setting it afire, a gruesome death by flame.

The United Democratic Front (UDF), supposedly independent of the ANC, was purportedly nonviolent and democratically ruled "inside" the country. The UDF avowed separation from the ANC which had some Marxist leadership. There were, of course, factions within each. It was said there were as many as fifteen thousand to twenty thousand black detainees at that moment—the mid-level organizers of any opposition or potential opposition. The top leaders had long since been taken off and, if returned and active, were immediately swooped off again. Thus there was little opportunity for any but defensive action such as tracing detainees and, when found, defending them in court. The courts still maintained a semblance of lawful activity, but they could not declare legislative actions illegal (unconstitutional); if they did try to release prisoners, the legislature quickly toughened the law. The repeated laws and regulations concerning censorship were examples of mounting controls.

After a short stop at the national trade union headquarters we drove to Soweto. It was one vast, open plain of one-room houses and some shacks. They stretched as far as the eye could see, perhaps ten miles off until the stream of houses disappeared over the hills—and still on and on. The official figures said

1.2 million people lived in Soweto; unofficial numbers were 1.5 million, but the best estimates I got from knowledgeable sources in Soweto and the government showed 2 million and growing. But what after saturation? Hundreds of people already lived in shacks, like the shantytowns of the American Depression; yet here they could afford better housing but couldn't find it.

We visited the Funda Center headed by Stan Kahn, who previously was a professor of sociology and anthropology at Cape Town. Here, he taught young blacks remedial reading and other subjects. He described the history of black education. In the 1950s, the government's plan was to *ill*-prepare blacks for their future. Black teachers were accredited by low standards, not just as paternalism but to assure the low level of instruction. Only a small proportion of government funds for education went to black students. Indigenous languages were kept the vehicle of instruction, and English was introduced only at the level beyond which nearly 85 percent of students dropped out. Illiteracy was assured, and job possibilities severely limited.

Although state expenditures improved somewhat in the 1970s, most of the funds went into buildings and maintenance. Whereas funds for whites kept classes at twenty-five students, there were still fifty blacks to a class. Their books and materials were second-rate at best. From 1983 to 1986, violence against the state began in these schools—right there in Soweto. Kahn showed me the bridge across which a gang of black teenagers—hopped up on adrenaline, their mouths caked with white discharge—marched chanting into his office. They wanted Gobby, a UDF youth who was in Kahn's private office at the moment. Kahn got him quickly out the back door and gave him money to leave town. The young man escaped but the gang occupied the library and demanded that Kahn hand over Gobby for burning (necklacing). Kahn had already phoned blacks who had strong ties to both the warring factions. They arrived and literally negotiated for the life of Gobby. He was saved, but the gang went on to find another, less fortunate, victim.

No education was possible in those years, and a generation of blacks lost a chance to prepare themselves. I saw clusters of them—comrades—in my long visit to Soweto. They stood at corners looking sullen. Some wore provocative caps and T-shirts often with American symbols, probably from the U.S. embassy, which, I was told, imported such clothing. They looked grim not only at a white but at a black in company with a white. Noma was distinctly uncomfortable when we stopped for gas, and a gang of eight approached. They were about fourteen to eighteen years old, looking threatening and moving about the car. One with an earring in one ear, said Noma, was a burning comrade last year. We passed a high-flame smoky fire set in a garbage container. Before we could see the source Noma grew visibly concerned. She was relieved but added, "Last year at the sign of smoke I'd turn around and go straight home and cry." Another necklacing.

There was some sign of hope. We went to the Careers Center, where Sebolelo Mohajane asked me to speak to a group of fifteen early teenagers. They had been denied formal schooling during the years of militancy but were now studying on their own. They had dropped the slogan of years past—"Liberation now, education later"—and reversed the priority. These were well-dressed, attractive youths, obviously self-assured and highly competent in English. They were preparing to "write"—to pass the state A-level exams that would qualify them as the equivalent of high school graduates in the United States. Most would go on to university. I said that they were on the right track now and had opportunities ahead. Later, one asked me whether I thought Syracuse University was a good place to go; I assured him it was. This was the most encouraging memory of that day.

We went from there to the heart of Soweto. It became immediately apparent that the vast area was divided by *ethnicity* (the state originally tried to keep all the Vendas together, all the Zulus, and other formerly tribal groupings; that persisted, but not entirely), *political orientation* (whole areas were UDF, others Azanian People's Organization, etc.—a distinction involving the potential use of violence, or the commitment to socialism, or to a democratic non-Socialist objective, or to a solidly capitalist government), and actual economic *class distinctions* nearly as sharp as the differences in the white population both in the city and suburbs of Johannesburg.

The mostly separate houses (some were attached, but all were one level) were almost all protected by barbed wire, iron grating, and, in wealthier areas of Soweto, walls and central alarm systems. We first visited the lowliest of the houses, if one could call these shacks "houses." They were about twenty by twenty-five feet for a family of two to four or more. The state built them of wooden frames enclosed by tin and small windows. There were plots of hard-caked, clay-like soil for five or ten feet around each house. I went inside one with a young woman who seemed much older than her actual age. Her five-year-old boy followed. There was an oil stove and a sink but no running water. Nor was there electricity. The large outhouse was in foul condition and regularly generated fighting among the women over who should clean it. There was no communal or government supervision. There were people here the government had evicted from other lands deemed "white," but no provision was made for their sustenance here. On the contrary, the state charged each shack dweller about forty dollars a month. These were mainly people who could afford to move to better housing, as one explained to me, but could not find a place in Soweto or elsewhere. The hope, of course, was that more blacks would be allowed to move into Johannesburg. Many commuted daily to jobs in Johannesburg and were far removed by time and place from tribal backgrounds. But the sheer numbers alone seemed to make remote such transitions into existing city housing. Yet years later, this would be the biggest challenge for the administration of President Nelson Mandela, former resident of Soweto.

I visited a low-income house built by the state. Some eighty dollars a month was paid in rent—this took much of the income of the family. The twenty-by-forty-foot house had several rooms and many beds. Now, after many years, there was electricity and running water, but little hope for further change. The middle-class houses seemed most active in several ways. They were a bit larger, with some small gardens in front or back. Noma's house, as her sister's, were examples; so, too, was that of Percy Qoboza, the editor of a black newspaper (see chap. 28). They were neatly maintained, had pleasant touches of art and comfort. They had a separate kitchen and bath, a lounge room, and two bedrooms. In almost all cases, this was insufficient for growing families, and Soweto families are large. Noma had two daughters and a son. One daughter lived most of the time with Noma's divorced husband in another township. Her younger daughter, obviously very bright, went to a private elementary school. Her son, somewhat older, seemed just as willing, just as ready for broader education but went to a far less encouraging public school. He seemed less self-assured than his sister, and Noma treated him that way. She was thankful that they both came through the violence that had beset teenagers the past several years. They were neither victims nor participants—despite the fact that her son was taunted by his peers for living on the "wrong" side of the Soweto tracks—in the middle-class housing area.

In the same area we drove down broad streets that separated the UDF (ANC) houses from those of the socialist Azanian People's Organization (AZAPO). We came to two burned-out houses. The UDF had set them afire when a gang from one side of the street crossed over. Along another street, a burned-out house told this story: a UDF man was being harassed by the small children of the AZAPO. He went to their families to complain. Next day, the AZAPO gang went across the street and burned the man's house to the ground. Later, he took a gun and went into the AZAPO area and shot dead an AZAPO child. Soon after, the AZAPOs went to another area, where the man's father lived, and shot him dead.

Finally, we visited an obviously upper-income neighborhood of Soweto. The houses were all different, with one- or two-car garages. They were built of stone or cement rather than wood or tin, and many had barred windows, walls, and other security measures. We entered one house, again unannounced. This was the home of a significant black artist. I chatted briefly with him about his work and the shows he had put on in SoHo, New York (the Solomon Gallery), and one coming in Johannesburg. Clearly, he was talented in watercolor, pencil, and bronze sculpture. His walls were covered with his own paintings and the work of contemporaries. Several imposing bronzes stood in his sizable living room and halls, serving as an informal display of his work.

As we prepared to leave Soweto, Noma wanted to show me Winnie Mandela's two houses: the one she lived in, and the "palace" that "the Mother of the Nation" had just built, while her husband still languished in prison after twenty-three years. Winnie had become a celebrity, but so much negative reaction followed the construction of the palatial home—reaction mainly from blacks—that she delayed moving in. Part of the opposition came after a long and critical article by Noma in *Frontline*. Noma had written that some in Soweto said that

Winnie Mandela was "taking her role as a 'First Lady' too heavily." She was said to act as a spokesperson for groups from which she was carrying no mandate and had built that huge house, which was not reported in the newspapers. Wrote Noma, "They ask whether this is to be a State House, or in whose name it is owned, and where the money is coming from."

We approached the house in which Winnie then lived, but Noma could see five yellow-clad bodyguards in the street—members of her Mandela United Football Club. Noma stopped the car a block away, backed up and said, "I can't do it. They'll get me." We took another street, and I saw the rear of Winnie Mandela's mansion. It was a stone dwelling covering about half a block, set on one of the high points of Soweto. There were fortress-like elements and a full brick wall surrounding the estate, with an inner wall providing added protection. Though it was difficult to see them from that distance, the two walls gave the impression of a moat separating the manse from the outside world. One wondered against whom the dweller was to be protected.

Or what, in fact, Winnie Mandela was prepared to do to pursue her agenda, quite apart from that of her husband. After his release and rise to political power, Winnie was formally charged with complicity in the murder on her Soweto property of one of her "boys." Several other young guardians were tried with her for the crime. She received a light sentence and before long was cavorting again. Nelson Mandela divorced her, but she continued to exploit his name and threatened to mount a political campaign of her own. As she aligned herself with the most violent faction in Mandela's party, the ANC, she was a growing embarrassment for the president.

The question of violence was very much with Noma and me as we prepared to leave Soweto that day in 1987. Coming toward us were four teenagers, two on either side of a bloodied young man. He was barely able to move as they propped him up. We could not tell whether they were helping him leave a fight scene or were indeed taking him somewhere for further drubbing. The year before, Noma would have had no doubt; even that day, she accelerated as we passed.

I returned to South Africa in 1994 for that remarkable event in the country's history: the first free election for all its people, black and white. The deep scars carried by black citizens surfaced unexpectedly as I watched a children's television program. A buxom, fiftyish Danish woman was interviewing seven-year-olds in Soweto, with a young black woman serving as interpreter. The Dane asked many kids the usual question, "What do you want to be when you grow up?" Now, with a new day dawning, some could say "lawyer," "doctor," or "teacher." But one round-faced girl replied, looking directly at the camera, "White." The Danish interviewer was obviously stunned. All she could say was, "But I'm old, ugly." And then the camera pulled away, as she went on.

Hours before the election, a group of mixed-race teenage students seated on the lawn of a school answered questions about their future. A white student said that whites regard the future, particularly social relationships, out of *fear*, whereas blacks come to them mainly out of *anger*. Another white woman in a colored skirt with flowing blonde hair said the two races have different cultural backgrounds, making it difficult to meet except in sports. Another said, "black guys and gals have different ways, have been brought up differently." She wondered whether a new government can deal with that. An equally attractive black woman, asked whether she agreed, replied yes. A black man said, "The only people dying are blacks. I want the government to sort out the violence. That's my first priority." Another black man said, "Wherever you go, the white man runs the government and the business. I want to have my own choice to make my own rules for blacks."

Within days, that last man had one wish fulfilled: Nelson Mandela won the presidency. But it was soon clear that the child who wanted to be white reflected a deep-seated scar that would not disappear through electoral processes. And the black teenager who worried about violence would have no end to his concern, even with a black president in office.

I met briefly with Archbishop Desmond Tutu at a barbecue at the University of the Western Cape, stronghold of opposition to apartheid, which won for him a Nobel Prize. He danced unabashedly to a fast local number, and just as unreservedly praised the journalists present for their role in bringing down apartheid. In masterful theatrics, Tutu asked the press to stand and applaud themselves. "You helped tell our story," he said. "We want to say thank you, thank you, thank you." He spoke to rising applause. "God depends on you," he added, "and that's a theological statement." This election was, he said, a "miracle come to pass."

Once in the presidency, Mandela sent an emissary to Nomavenda to determine whether she was her own person and not a front for some political cause. Satisfied with the answer, Mandela invited Noma to chat with him. He said he had followed her writing for years and welcomed her insights even when they challenged the ANC. "We need constructive criticism," he told her. He had read her stringent criticism of Winnie Mandela.

"You are a celebrity," I told Noma.

"Yes," she said timidly.

I asked her about Winnie Mandela's strong arm tactics. "All her 'boys,' the armed bandits posing as security lads, have been killed," she said, adding, "Live by the sword, die by the sword."

I said, "You were courageous to take on Winnie at the height of her power and ferocity."

"Not courageous," said Noma, "stupid."

There had been many changes. Some South Africans, black and white, were beginning to laugh at themselves. A popular white comic was telling mixed audiences, "Mandela got the Nobel Prize for spending thirty-one years in prison, and de Klerk got the Nobel Prize for letting him out!"

But in 2000, Nomavenda Mathiane told the South African Commission on

Human Rights studying racism in the news media that it was still unbearably hard to be black and a woman and advance in journalism. The commission's preliminary report had charged that mainstream newspapers stereotype blacks, particularly emphasizing their corruption and ineptness. During apartheid, there was vastly more corruption practiced by whites, but it was impossible to publish it, for fear of imprisonment or worse. Phillip van Niekerk, editor of the liberal daily *Mail and Guardian*, said, "I faced a situation where I believed I was being dragged before a statutory inquisition, under pain of imprisonment, to answer unsubstantiated allegations about the content of my publication." The commission, at first, subpoenaed him and some thirty journalists but then relented and took their replies voluntarily. The *Mail*'s editor read a brief roll of courageous white journalists. Under threat of imprisonment or banning, they defied the harshest apartheid laws, he said, "going far ahead of their readership and moving it toward accepting new and sometimes revolutionary views." He recalled the defunct liberal *Rand Daily Mail* and its courageous editors Laurence Ganda, Raymond Louw, and Alistair Sparks; the *Cape Times* of Tony Heard; and the *Daily Dispatch* of Donald Woods, "who challenged the white paradigm of the time."

Van Niekerk declared that he has concluded that there is "no pleasing our critics." He said, "If we report suffering in Africa, we are accused of making out that the continent and black people are helpless incompetents. If we fail to report on their suffering, we are accused of being insensitive to their plight. . . . If we report on the savagery of the conflict in Bosnia and Kosovo, we are accused of Eurocentrism. If we report on the savagery of the conflict in the Democratic Republic of the Congo, we are accused of making out that all blacks are savages who cannot govern themselves. We are not, however, accused of making out that all Europeans are savages when we report on the Bosnian and Kosovan situation."[2]

The test of the freedom of the press in South Africa will be whether neither the government nor its commission plays the role of press monitor or censor, even in the name of quenching racism. In such freedom, however, well-trained black and white journalists working together would be expected to investigate and cover events with balance and integrity, no matter the race of the principal.

NOTES

1. Nomavenda Mathiane, *South Africa: Diary of Troubled Times* (New York: Freedom House, 1989), pp. 116–17.

2. Phillip van Niekerk, "*Mail and Guardian* Editor Phillip van Niekerk's Submission to the Human Rights Commission," *Mail and Guardian* (Johannesburg), March 9, 2000, http://www.mg.co.za/, pp. 1, 12.

27

HELEN SUZMAN
"First Lady" of South Africa

The first lady of South Africa was never—really—Winnie Mandela, ex-wife of Nelson Mandela, who in 1994 became his nation's first black president. Winnie Mandela became something more fearsome than the "Nation's Mother," as she was portrayed. She exploited her husband's imprisonment to build a power base with killing "boys" and a sizable estate at the heart of Soweto, the poor black township.

The true first lady throughout Mandela's imprisonment and beyond was Helen Suzman, the white politician who stood up in Parliament—year after year—demanding an end to racial segregation laws and the cruel practices that divided families as well as races, forcing all but Afrikaner and British whites to lower-class status, inhuman ghettoization, elementary education that forced millions into peonage, and that linked whites and blacks to a mutually dehumanizing system: apartheid.

Segregationist Prime Minister P. W. Botha called Helen "Mother Superior" in derision. For thirteen years, Helen was a lone opposition voice in Parliament. As she sat after her speech there would be a "deadly hush," she recalls, or shouts of "Go back to Moscow" or "Go back to Israel." In later years, when several liberal legislators joined her, she said in a letter home, "It's nice now to turn around and see smiling faces instead of those beady eyes fixed on me in a hostile stare."

During Mandela's painful years on the island prison, one of his few visitors was Helen Suzman. Mandela recalled his first meeting with Helen in 1963. While awaiting trial, he had been visited by the chairman of the South African Communist Party. A woman passed the Communist leader in the corridor. The man whispered, "almost in reverence," says Mandela, "Helen Suzman"—significant, Mandela says today, "coming from a man whose political views would not normally lead him to respect a liberal."

Helen visited Mandela on Robben Island from 1967 onward whenever permission was granted, and she managed to persuade the authorities to improve conditions in several aspects. In 1983 she visited him after rumors had arisen that he was being maltreated. He was, however, in good health, she reported. She was able to speak privately with Mandela only when they walked in the exercise yard and guards permitted them to stroll out of earshot. Mandela's family was not allowed to speak to him without a guard present. Helen reported that Mandela was exceptionally well informed on the debates in the white Parliament on proposed constitutional changes affecting blacks. She came to bear witness to the treatment Mandela was receiving. That at least could be a positive role for Helen in a parliament where for thirty-six years she was often the lone liberal voice. Yet she never failed to speak out against every new dehumanizing bill and to seek, however futilely, the ending of older cruelties. Helen says,

> When I became a member of Parliament in 1953, the National Party government had already laid the foundations of what was to become the most racially defined society in the world, in which whites and blacks were segregated by laws covering every aspect of their lives. The Race Classification Act determined the status in life of each person born in South Africa. Children of different races were forced to attend separate schools. Certain jobs were reserved for whites only. The rights of ownership and occupation of South African land and property were defined on racial lines, as was the use of all public amenities—separate but unequal. Sex and marriage across the color line were forbidden. The right to vote was virtually a white privilege. By and large, the relationship between white and black was that between master and servant.[1]

She listened in Parliament with disbelief as government spokesmen boasted that South Africa was enjoying peace and quiet while other nations were gripped with violence. Helen responded that "violence can also mean the unfettered use of the powers of the state against a citizen, so as to deprive him of his normal civil rights." She continued,

> In this sense we have a great deal of violence in South Africa, for mass removals of African people from their homes is violence. The thousands upon thousands of Africans in resettlement areas leading hopeless and helpless lives of poverty and unemployment is a violence. . . . The destruction of the Colored community . . . the uprooting of Indians . . . is a violence. . . . The pass raids are a violence. I say the uprooting of people at dawn on a wintry evening in a shabby town and bundling women and children into police vans is a violence . . . I say the fact that we are turning something like half a million people per year into statutory criminals in this country is a violence. The malnutrition and infant mortality rate in a rich country like South Africa are a violence. The denial of collective bargaining rights and the low wages that result are a violence. . . . Banning [i.e., denial of rights], home arrests, detention without trial, banishment are all violence.[2]

Helen's role frequently required quiet courage. During one election campaign she was repeatedly interrupted at dinner. A caller accused her of being a traitor and threatened to kill her. He had just viewed a recorded televised debate in which she opposed police action in the black townships. She patiently explained her position over the phone. A few seconds later, another caller . . . and another . . . for three hours. Some were simply abrasive, but others menacing. When one shouted obscenities, Helen picked up a whistle and sent a piercing shriek through the phone.

Helen received much hate mail, most anti-Semitic. A letter came one day from Marie van Zyl, president of the Kappie Kommando, a women's organization dedicated to retaining memory of the Great Trek of 1836, when the Afrikaners took their ox wagons across the velt to settle this land. The women wore a bonnet (kappie) to shade themselves from the African sun. Helen had made an off-the-cuff remark to a newspaper interviewer that the ladies "really belong to the days of witch-burning." Ms. van Zyl wrote Helen angrily, saying she was proud of her old-fashioned ideas, and said her ancestors had carried the Bible across the mountains to the savages on the other side. "And what," asked Ms. van Zyl in an anti-Semitic sideswipe, "were your ancestors doing at that time, Mrs. Suzman?" Helen replied in polite Afrikaans, "My ancestors were busy *writing* the Bible. Yours faithfully, Helen Suzman." That ended the correspondence.[3]

On a rare occasion, Helen was heckled by black youths. She was about to speak to a throng of one thousand people at a memorial service for an activist black couple murdered by a masked gunman outside their home. Black youths shouted down Helen, and a local antiapartheid group expressed understanding for the youths' action. They called on Helen's party to quit the legislature to protest the government's segregationist policies.

I visited Helen three times in South Africa—twice when apartheid was in full swing and, again, at the moment when the first all-race election would raise Nelson Mandela, miraculously, to the presidency of a predominantly black nation that was until then in the hands of the white minority.

That last time, Helen came to the airport at Johannesburg to see me as I left for the States. I was already in a cleared zone awaiting departure. The guards recognized Helen, of course, and allowed her to pass. No South African, black, white, or "coloured," could miss Helen's slight frame, large handsome head, and warm smile unlike that of a career politician. We chatted about her new role. She had quit the legislature after thirty-six years. Some wanted her to run for a national office under the new interim constitution.

"But they asked me to serve as one of several members of the election commission to monitor the fairness of the [first] presidential election," she told me. "Someone said they appointed me to this honorific job because they wanted me out of the race and unable to support any candidate." She added, "I rather believe that may have been in someone's mind." She was completing a difficult, tiresome schedule traveling to all parts of the country to assure the fairness of electoral procedures and to supervise the education of millions of blacks in the process of voting—almost none had ever voted before. Certainly not Nelson Mandela himself, then in his seventies and running for the top office.

Mandela won not only the presidency but the Nobel Peace Prize—for which, incidentally, Helen Suzman had been nominated twice over the years. Nineteen ninety-four provided several kinds of closure for Helen, as her letter to me in January 1995 suggests: "I am heartily grateful that 1994 is over. It was a particularly bad year for me what with the five months battling on the Independent Electoral Commission and thereafter the culmination of Mosie's long illness. [Helen had married Dr. Mosie Suzman in 1937, when she was nineteen and he thirty-three.]."

She continued, "We are very lucky to have Nelson Mandela to see us through the transitional problems of converting South Africa into a true democracy—not an easy task after more than forty years of enforced segregation and race discrimination. It will, however, be very difficult to convert all those pre-election promises into reality and so satisfy the astronomical expectations of millions of young blacks. But whatever the difficulties I, for one, would not choose to go back to the ugly years before the 'miracle.'"

A miracle? Yes and no.

I must admit that when I visited South Africa for the first time in the 1980s I believed only horrible bloodshed lay ahead. I met with blacks, coloreds (as Indians, Malays, and other "mixed races" were officially labeled), and whites who supported, and others who detested, Helen Suzman. At dinner at the Suzmans' home their friends described the latest plans of Pieter Koornhof, whose office was euphemistically called the Ministry of Cooperation and Development. The ministry was then engaged in evicting black squatters from lean-tos made of tree branches covered with sheets of plastic. The squatters had set up "homes" in Cape Town after leaving rural "homelands" when sheer hunger and poverty forced them to flee. Helen and friends were planning a counterattack on the Koornhof action.

After I returned home, Helen wrote me, "The sad Nyanga saga continues, with the government failing to appreciate that these people are not defiant illegal squatters, so much as refugees from the poverty, malnutrition, and want in the so-called black homelands."

At my urging, John Richardson sent a cable as Freedom House president to Minister Koornhof, deploring the "callous treatment accorded squatters in Cape Town," who, we said, were "refugees from poverty and the unviability of the so-called black homelands." The squatters, we said, "are being treated instead as defiant illegals."

Astonishingly, the white citizens of Cape Town were also appalled at the sheer inhumanity of Koornhof's actions. The South African government was forced to back down. As a result, the weary black squatters won a temporary reprieve. They celebrated by erecting a huge wooden cross and attending a large interdenominational religious service in the desolate open fields where they had been hanging on grimly for weeks. For the first time, too, they slept undisturbed under shelter in the weird constructions they had created.

Ironically, in that government Koornhof was regarded as a moderate and was therefore awarded the Ministry of Cooperation. I met him at an international conference in Cape Town called by South African intellectuals who wanted to find some solution for the terrible apartheid system. They invited me and others from countries where multicultural, multiracial problems were being faced. I spoke of changes in the American South since the 1950s. Koornhof wore his academic face during the conference and appeared to be moved by some of the recommendations for change, but not much happened in South Africa as a consequence, though our papers were later published by Macmillan.

Shortly thereafter, Helen marked her thirtieth year of service in the Parliament. She wrote me, "It is hard to believe that I have spent nearly half my life in the House; to what end remains to be seen."

The "end" has not yet come. The Mandela presidency generated astonishing changes, but the nation still faces great trials. Millions of young blacks must be educated for jobs that are not yet available, find housing not yet constructed, and integrate into a social and economic system not yet color-blind. Blacks and whites on the political extremes act as though they are ready to pounce. It is sobering to observe that the aging Mandela may remain the key to a further peaceful transition. F. W. de Klerk, the former white president who was Mandela's heroic partner in the changeover and then served in the second-highest post, may still be able to restrain some white extremists. Impatient, younger activists in Mandela's African National Congress and the Zulus under Chief Minister Gatsha Buthelezi are unhappy with the relatively small role they play in the new government. When I spoke to Buthelezi in Johannesburg and New York, he indicated he expected to sit at the bargaining table when apartheid was finally dismembered. Instead, he was finessed out of the process as de Klerk and Mandela decided the fate of the interim constitution and government.

Later, de Klerk quit to move into an opposition-party stance. The South African Broadcasting Service (SABS) was reorganized with ANC people in key posts. A new national constitution was devised, though press-control laws remained on the books (but go unenforced). A delegation arranged by the South African embassy met with me at Freedom House to discuss methods the government might use to take full advantage of new communication technologies. I recommended a freedom of information law to provide public access to state information and extensive use of e-mail to release all manner of government information.

Helen would watch the internal struggle from the sidelines. At age seventy-nine she deserved an easier life, especially after a bad year. She was still very active in 1995 "despite my so-called retirement." She left her spacious, handsome house and moved into smaller quarters close to Houghton, her old campaigning district. She was born not far off, in Germiston, a small mining town just outside Johannesburg. Her birth date: November 7, 1917, the day of the Russian Revolution. Helen says her father had emigrated from Klykoliai, a *shtetl* in Lithuania on the border with Latvia. He left to avoid being drafted for twenty-five years of service in the czar's army, to escape the pogroms, and to seek a better life than the one with restricted opportunities that Russia offered to Jews.

Helen went to a Catholic school and the University of Witwatersrand. She considered a postgraduate degree in law, but never attempted it. Instead, she served in the legislature and received numerous honorary doctorates from universities around the world.

She worked hard even in retirement but told me in 1991 she was learning to live a simpler life: "I spent ten super days fishing for trout in the Eastern Transvaal and then went on to a private game park for New Year. I shall remember forever the wonderful sight of an open savannah dotted with acacia trees, under which were grazing peacefully seven different species of game—wildebeest, impala, waterbuck, kudu, warthogs, zebra, and giraffe. If the animal kingdom can manage such peaceful coexistence, why, I wonder, can we humans not do the same?"

In 2000, Helen gave me her latest view of the current political climate in South Africa and, incidentally, the role of Communists during apartheid. She commented on the Communists after I had mentioned a new book describing their activities:

> The Communists were the only people, apart from the small Liberal party, which soon disappeared, who actually were prepared to give full rights to blacks in South Africa; not even my party was prepared to give franchise without qualifications until 1978 when we changed our policy. But for the rest, of course, I have never understood how Communists could retain their dedicated attitude to that awful [Soviet] regime after the knowledge of the Gulag and the slaughter of millions of people by Stalin, and when the invasions of Hungary and Czechoslovakia were known. Here in South Africa . . . the Communist Party is alive and well, though it does not have thousands of adherents, but it is part of the ANC Government alliance, together with COSATU, the big Trade Union movement. I must say I am rather anxious when I see these Communist members promoted to the Cabinet. By and large, however, I must admit that the fiscal policy is fairly conservative, and there is no talk of the nonsensical policy of nationalization which first emerged with the triumph of the ANC. . . .
>
> Politically, this has been a difficult year, though we privileged folk continue to enjoy a very pleasant life. However, the ever increasing incidence of AIDS, the high rate of unemployment, the alarming amount of violent crime, and the introduction by the government of unwise labor legislation that inhibits job creation and foreign investment do not engender a very optimistic view of the future. South Africa, with its democratically elected government, is certainly the most stable of the African states. . . . However, none of this whining should be construed as my wanting to return to the old way of life or as plans of imminent emigration.

In January 2002 Helen wrote that the new year could "hardly be worse" than the last, "what with the dip in the Rand, which results in overseas visitors going on shopping sprees and coming back with the exultant cry 'it's for nothing.'" That she wrote, is "maddening to us locals, who watch with despair while our currency becomes worthless. . . . No one seems to know what it's all due to, though my old-time training in economics leads me to one conclusion—lack of confidence—and no wonder, what with [President Thabo] Mbeki's weird ideas on the HIV-AIDS pandemic and his failure to restrain the mad Bob Mugabe before the next election in Zimbabwe."

A further disturbing note: an Apartheid Museum has opened, financed by the proapartheid whites who operate a highly profitable casino next door. The museum, however, hardly mentions white participation in the antiapartheid struggle. No mention of Alan Paton, the Liberal Party, the Democratic Party, any NGOs, the liberal English press, or the English-language universities. And no mention of the First Lady of the Opposition, Helen Suzman.

When Helen married Mosie Suzman he was already an eminent physician from a distinguished family in Johannesburg. On one visit, I spent time with Mosie's brother Arthur, as distinguished an attorney as his brother was a doctor. Arthur commented on the similarity of our names. I said my family, several generations back, had come to the States from Germany, probably to escape the revolutions of 1848. I said I could not trace my origins accurately.

"No matter," said Arthur Suzman, "all the Suzmans and Sussmans are related." I rather like that thought.

NOTES

1. Helen Suzman, *In No Uncertain Terms: A South African Memoir*, with a foreword by Nelson Mandela (New York: Knopf, 1993), p. 3.
2. Ibid., pp. 5–6.
3. Ibid., p. 116.

28

PERCY QOBOZA, KOW BONZIE BROWN, AND THE HEART OF A JOURNALIST

Early in 1997, the *New York Times* verified a phenomenon I had viewed for a decade: streets of Chinatown, along my walking route, were more crowded each month. Hundreds of faces such as I had seen in China and across south Asia formed a phalanx moving west on Grand Street as I marched east. The *Times* said immigration to New York, especially from Asia, was at an all-time high. I wondered whether I had seen at least one of these mainly earnest young people on a street in Shanghai, Hong Kong, Jakarta, or Seoul. Given Ithiel Pool's "seven degrees of difference" (see chap. 12), chances are I had.

Later that same day, I was astounded by exactly that phenomenon. Kenneth Y. Best phoned to say he'd visit Freedom House that afternoon. Ken is one of the best journalists in all of Africa—and has searing memories to prove it. He escaped repeated bloody coups in his native Liberia and gained political asylum in New York. From 1981, Ken edited and published the *Daily Observer* in Monrovia. Master Sergeant Samuel Doe, who killed his predecessor to become president, repeatedly closed the *Observer* and finally burned it down in 1985. Best was twice imprisoned in a subsequent coup. In prison, his tormentor—tortured and stripped naked—apologized to Best. "By the grace of God," says Best, "I escaped." He was the only one with pants on that day and could walk out of prison.

He left Liberia, practiced journalism in freer Senegal, and recently trained journalists for a paper in the Gambia. But just hours after Best visited us, he phoned to say that five of his journalists in Gambia—all citizens of Senegal—had just been ordered to leave the country; our help was sought. The infamous cycle continues.

Best revealed one of Pool's "seven degrees," and we hadn't even moved out of New York! Discounting his own record, Best spoke of the courage needed to edit in a dictatorial country. It soon developed we had a mutual friend, widely separated from both New York and Monrovia: Hilary Ng'weno in Nairobi, Kenya, who created the *Weekly Review,* once one of the most respected publications in Africa.

Hilary and his wife published a unique children's paper as well. I had visited them in Nairobi and discussed the role of the press. I wondered whether a state press can be free enough to provide diverse views, even dissent from government policies. Then, twenty years earlier, few journalists had the courage or the funds to build independent magazines such as the *Review.* A diversified government press might be an interim advantage, I had suggested.

That is the "third world dilemma," Hilary said. "Theoretically," he added, perhaps pondering the future of the *Review,* "there is no contradiction in the concept of a state press which is also free." But, he mused, "nothing has really changed from the bad old days of colonialism." Before independence, Africa's nationalist leaders used the printed word to bring down colonial governments. There was no military struggle. The new rulers "in virtually every third world country" made sure when they assumed power that "the most potent instrument of propaganda—radio—was invariably controlled by the state." And newspapers, too.

"Investigative reporting is looked upon as a sign of disloyalty, antistatism, dissidence, or even treason, and it is a foolhardy editor, indeed, who will encourage investigative reporting," whether or not the paper is owned by the state. That seemed to place Hilary among the handful of courageous African journalists at that time. He had written that "investigative reporting tends to challenge the legitimacy of the power structure. It tends to hold up the bitter reality against the rosy image painted by those in authority. In short, it tends to make the ground underneath the feet of those in authority somewhat unsteady."[1]

Hilary admitted that during factional fights within a party there may be momentary descriptions of corruption or other damning realities. But when the party closes ranks, the journalist is clobbered or shut down. I held Hilary as a model of journalistic courage even after I heard that the *Review* had come under government financial control. Ken Best told me the depressing story.

The *Review*'s spectacular revelations of governmental failures, said Best, were leaked to Hilary by a high-placed official with his own agenda. When the political tide turned—even as Hilary had described to me years before—the ruling party took over the *Review.* Hilary was permitted to edit it, but I suppose on a short leash.

That seemed to be borne out in 1991, Ken Best told me. Hilary still had a respected reputation across Africa. When UNESCO arranged a historic press-freedom conference at Windhoek, Namibia, that year, Hilary was asked to give the keynote address. At the last moment, he did not appear but sent a text to be read. To the scores of African journalists yearning for greater freedom, Hilary's sermon mainly criticized *journalists.* Don't act irresponsibly, he told them—clean your own house. Hardly the proper message to support the still-feeble movement toward press freedom in sub-Saharan Africa. The Windhoek Declaration created at that conference is, indeed, a landmark for the transition to independent, pluralistic journalism in formerly dictatorial countries.

The Windhoek Declaration was embodied the following year at UNESCO's press-freedom conference for Central Asians in Kazakhstan, which I attended, and repeated at similar meetings in Latin America and in the Arab states. This was a far cry from UNESCO's decade-long assaults on press freedom in the 1970s and 1980s.

I had seen the dilemmas firsthand—forced by threat of fearsome assaults—that African journalists faced every day of their working lives. Ken Best reminded me of Percy Qoboza, who escaped physical and psychological assaults in his native South Africa by spending a year in the United States. Percy, too, turned up in that political haven, New York. We appeared together at an international conference run by the Fletcher School of Law and Diplomacy of Tufts University. The subject: press freedom then under assault at UNESCO. Percy was a Neiman Fellow at Harvard that year, shortly after leaving prison for editing the *City Press,* a black newspaper published under grave restraints during apartheid's fierce racial separation and oppression.

Years later, with Nelson Mandela still in prison and hardly headed for the presidency of his country, I sat with Percy in Soweto, the large black township near Johannesburg, as he edited his newspaper. It carried news of black South Africans not covered in the large white dailies. Editing the news, Percy had a lawyer at his side at all times to weigh every word destined for publication. The seething discontent of blacks was forced underground. Reporters could not even be near places where confrontations might occur. It was a criminal offense to publish information on political unrest, detention cases, the treatment of detainees, and many forms of political activity.

Most sources dried up out of fear of reprisal by the government. Officials preferred to be attacked for censoring rather than for repressive police activity, which was increasing. Severe press regulations were issued in 1986 and strengthened further over the next two years. In 1987 I met privately with editors of the "alternative" papers and the black press. Each had on his desk many complaints from the Home Ministry, sufficient to close down the papers and imprison the editors. One editor, Zwelakhe Sisulu, had been in detention without charge for more than a year when the paper was closed down for three months. He was released after two years, still not charged, placed under virtual house arrest and forbidden to work on a newspaper. Days after the closure, a rival newspaper, the *Weekly Mail,* itself threatened with a similar ban, published stories that could not appear in the banned *New Nation* that week. The *Mail*'s headline read, "What the *New Nation* Would Have Said." The editor of the *Mail* told me he had a difficult problem dealing with the government's warning because "I cannot even understand it."

Sitting with Percy Qoboza I watched these dilemmas unfold, story by story. Percy was grim, frustrated, depressed, and unhappy with the owners of his paper, a large Afrikaner press chain. He sought to buy the paper but could not. In my presence, he asked Katherine Graham, then owner of the *Washington Post*, to bring ten *City Press* staffmen to the States for training, but that did not happen.

At that moment, Percy faced two serious charges by the police. For each he could be fined twenty thousand rand and imprisoned for ten years. He had already served six months in prison. Even the lawyer at his side could not be certain of many implications of the draconian rules. Percy would often employ oblique language that enabled his readers to read between the lines. If discovered by the ministry, that could be disastrous. His sources dried up. If called to defend a story he could not in good conscience produce the source even if his freedom or his paper's future depended on revealing the source. He may have inadvertently covered a story or an area blacked out for security reasons, but he would not have been told in advance that it was a forbidden area.

He knew children as young as four years old who were beaten by the police. He had eyewitnesses, but it was forbidden to reveal police action not announced by the authority. If he asked the police to confirm the facts, Percy told me, in an hour he'd get a telex denying the whole story. "Then," he added, "the fun begins!"

I delivered to Percy the last Freedom House support check for *City Press*. These funds financed a series of two-page articles on democracy, including the full text of the United States Constitution and Bill of Rights. We hoped that the Afrikaner owners of the paper and their friends would read those pages. Not long after I left the country, the *City Press* was shut down, and Percy Qoboza died of a heart attack. The strain of editorial judgments in the face of daily oppression had taken its toll.

The words of Percy Qoboza that I published in 1977 sounded both a warning and a call for interracial negotiation that seemed still ages away, if ever possible. Yet in 1995 the first universal election in South Africa brought in a black president. Percy wrote eighteen years earlier,

> I have not come across any responsible black leader who has advanced the theory that whites are expendable and must be thrown into the sea. . . . [W]hites are South Africans and have the right to exist in a common fatherland; and all of us, around a conference table, must devise a formula acceptable for future coexistence. . . . [Yet] all those with whom the government should be talking in the black community have been subjected to punitive actions. The danger is that the time may come when the authorities are forced to talk to somebody, and there will be nobody to talk to. When that happens, our troubles will indeed have started.[2]

Fortunately, nearly two decades later, one white leader adopted Percy's formula, released Nelson Mandela from prison, and began negotiations. President F. W. de Klerk may have remembered Percy Qoboza's conclusion: "The price of keeping power is sharing power; and the price of independence is interdependence."

From my New York vantage point, late that same year (1995), I received a disheartening call from another "seventh-degree" contact, an investment banker who had also done a stint at Harvard. He was still trying to help a reformist party come to power in his native Ghana. He asked whether that insurgent leader could visit Freedom House to tell us his story. I assured the man at the other end of Wall Street that we would welcome his friend. That meeting never materialized, though, because the man could not leave Ghana. But during the course of several conversations I discovered that my Wall Street contact had known Kow Bonzie Brown, called "the best journalist in sub-Saharan Africa" by my late friend Stan Swinton, then director of the Associated Press's international service.

I met Brown in Accra when he was editor in chief of the Ghana News Agency (GNA). While his country was run by leftist dictator Kwame Nkrumah, "K. B." found exile in New York at the AP. After the dictator was overthrown— I saw his heroic-sized statue smashed where it toppled in a major Accra plaza— K. B. returned to head the GNA. It was an impoverished agency. I watched one day as his sole functioning teleprinter received Reuters dispatches from London. The machine was so decrepit it printed only numbers, no letters. At first, it seemed to me like a secret code, but K. B. laughed and explained that this was his only contact with the rest of the world. His agency served all of Ghana's newspapers and radio stations. He assigned young staffers to transpose every number into a letter and rewrite the news for distribution. I was reminded of my daily pre-dawn stint, years before, rewriting United Press copy from cablese into full-length stories for publication.

Brown commanded 350 reporters to cover that small country. Salaries, of course, were low. The GNA, nevertheless, was a model of small-agency integrity: in fact, K. B. was called on to train journalists in Liberia, Sierra Leone, and Nigeria, and run courses for journalists in the Gambia. But K. B.'s professionalism became his undoing—that was the word from my Wall Street contact.

Flight Lieutenant Jerry John Rawlings mounted a military coup in 1981. He crushed opponents, outlawed political parties, and clamped down harshly on the press. By November 1984, Rawlings could no longer abide K. B.'s independence and professionalism. Rawlings branded him a traitor to the revolution and summarily dismissed him from the GNA. From then on, K. B. was a pariah—even when he fled to Nigeria to work as a journalist. He was frequently detained and questioned by the Nigerian police. He later returned to Ghana and held several temporary jobs. He drove a truck. One observer says, "K. B. was this kind of journalist: If told to broadcast a news item he didn't believe, he would walk away from the microphone."

Unfortunately, K. B. suffered increasingly harsher treatment. Government persecution became so intense that even those who offered to help K. B. eventually became targets themselves. As a journalist, K. B. was a frequent visitor to the holding pens of the national security agencies. Torment and torture became his constant companions. He died December 15, 1995, in a small town outside

Accra. Ironically, in memory of the journalist pariah abandoned in his own lifetime, the Ghanaian journalists' association established posthumously the Kow Bonzie Brown scholarship for young journalists.

The horrific years and painful death of K. B. meant a profound loss to the people of Ghana. Rawlings eased his oppression and sought the mantle of democrat with democratic elections. Press controls became more subtle, but journalists were still cowed. And the Rawlings government owned and operated the major radio and television station—and raided independent broadcasters. Ken Best and Hilary Ng'weno would recognize this pattern. They have so far escaped K. B. Brown's terrible fate. From New York, it is easy to feel empathy for all the Browns and even the compromising Ng'wenos; far harder to place oneself in their stead and fashion a life as journalist.

I recall a letter Elie Abel once showed me. The former NBC-TV correspondent, later dean of Columbia University's journalism school (my own alma mater) had received the letter from an African student whom Elie described as "extraordinarily good." The writer had gone home in a rather triumphant glow, said Elie, to take charge of an important news organization in his country. Elie later received this word: "You taught us all too well. . . . This, as you know, is a one-party system and the things I learned in America have made it difficult—probably impossible—for me to function in such a system. . . . The system lays upon us an affirmative obligation to praise the regime and above all to glorify the head man. The dilemma of adhering to professional ethics and at the same time trying to satisfy the whims of politicians is a headache." That letter was written from outside the country. The man had given up journalism, as well as his country, to prepare himself for a new career in another field, another place.

With the collapse of the Soviet Union, a fresh wind from the East shook the olive trees of Africa, one aging African leader asserted. The Windhoek Declaration and other glimmers of hope have moved several African countries to originate democratic electoral procedures—political and financial corruption notwithstanding. Haltingly, they permit some independent newspapers, even a few non–government-owned broadcast systems. Glimmers of hope, yes, in Benin. Declines in Niger and Zambia. Outside of South Africa, one finds little press freedom on the continent. Ironically, apartheid—by precisely defining the points of suppression and oppression—demonstrated where freedom can flourish if such controls are removed.

NOTES

1. Quoted in Leonard R. Sussman, *Power, the Press, and the Technology of Freedom* (New York: Freedom House, 1989), p. 131.

2. Percy Qoboza, "South Africa: A Black View," *Freedom at Issue*, September–October 1977, p. 4.

29

ALLARD LOWENSTEIN
Political Rocket, Falling Star

W alking past Central Synagogue on New York's Lexington Avenue, I recall a muffled PA system carrying eulogies to a thousand mourners on Fifty-fifth Street who could not enter the overflow service for Allard Lowenstein, murdered by a deranged acquaintance in Al's own law office on Fifth Avenue. I had recently taken Allard to Zimbabwe to monitor an election that would eventually place Robert Mugabe in power after years of killing in the bush. Allard had survived the risks of an African insurgency but not the violence on Fifth Avenue.

He had survived much in his extraordinary lifetime. Few Americans could move as freely, and walk with such trust among blacks and whites—in Africa as in America—as Allard Lowenstein. And few have had as significant a role in determining the future both of America and embattled areas of southern Africa.

Al had been a one-term Democratic congressman from Queens, New York. As a freshman in the House he chose to defy his party's sitting president, Lyndon Johnson, over fighting the war in Vietnam. Al traveled the country with the message, "Dump Johnson!" That was without precedent. He called for a peaceful coup. More than that, he organized it. David Hawk, with whom I was to work after the horrendous Pol Pot genocide in Cambodia, was one of the first youths persuaded by Al in 1967. Hawk believed Al had a political strategy as well as reformist motives. "Allard was not only extremely articulate about how they're lying to you, . . . he [also] had an idea how to stop it," Hawk recalls.[1] With Al's help, Hawk opened a small office at Union Theological Seminary in New York to mount an antiwar movement.

Al's insurgency gained momentum. College campuses picked up the challenge; even some fellow congressmen reluctantly joined. Most Democrats regarded Al's drive as crazy. The first reaction of fellow New York congressmen (wrote William Chafe) was to ask what kind of mushrooms Al had been eating in Africa—the idea of upsetting a sitting president with the power of Lyndon Johnson!

Al's amazing energy alone seemed to win converts. He was at once the peerless college debater, still young and persuasive, and the mature visionary who took on Goliath with the deftness of a David. Al moved into established political arenas and by small margins coopted leaders—Americans for Democratic Action (ADA) and Gus Tyler, articulate spokesman for organized labor—for his antiwar movement. Finally, Al persuaded Eugene McCarthy, Democratic senator from Minnesota, to run against President Johnson in the 1968 New Hampshire primary. McCarthy garnered about 40 percent of the vote, but that was widely deemed a victory against an incumbent president of his own party. Johnson similarly read the returns. He mournfully addressed the nation. At the end, he dropped the bombshell: he would not seek reelection to a second full term. He had been dumped.

Al's success in putting together the movement that defeated Johnson was one of the most remarkable political achievements of the century—but it did not save Al's seat in Congress. He was a one-term representative, never again elected to public office. But he retained his right of access to official Washington as long as he lived. And he used that limited power—which I occasionally shared with him—to fight for causes he deemed worthy, at home and abroad. Al's genius enabled him to reunite with opponents from one arena to do battle in another. For instance, I did not share his unlimited anti–Vietnam War position; I was principally concerned with the effect of wartime divisiveness on America's long-term civility and political discourse.

But we could work together for other objectives. Al was, as I, a Roosevelt "baby," brought up on the political credo we shared: the social-democratic commitment to compassionate government that would assure the least fortunate some livable access to food, housing, and health care; and for every citizen, the protection of civil and political rights.

Al had a spectacular apprenticeship. After graduating from the University of North Carolina he served as an aide to Senator Frank Graham (his former mentor at UNC), became president of the National Student Association, earned a law degree at Yale (though rarely appearing in class), served briefly in the army, enrolled students nationally for Adlai Stevenson's two presidential campaigns against Dwight Eisenhower (Stevenson was the only presidential candidate for whom I mounted soapboxes and sound trucks), spent a year at colleges generating support for the new United Nations, and earned the friendship of Eleanor Roosevelt.

She answered his call in spring 1963. Al had become deeply involved in the civil rights movement. Eleanor Roosevelt went to the University of Texas, at Al's request, to help desegregate a theater showing *Sunrise at Campobello,* a movie about Franklin Roosevelt. Al continued fighting for civil rights after he returned to UNC as an assistant professor of social studies. Though most of his students pursued careers in engineering and agriculture, Al mixed "civilization and science" with the imminent objectives of the civil rights movement. He created support networks at UNC and at Yale and then took on the most perilous task of all: helping create a social movement in the heartland of racial segregation, Mississippi.

Lowenstein faced tremendous hurdles in helping to organize Freedom Summer 1964. He wanted to bring a thousand white students from the north to join black civil rights demonstrators at peaceful sit-ins and marches. Some black organizers feared that the northern whites, ignorant of local customs, would trigger violence from southern whites. Blacks were already being killed, whipped, or arrested for entering white-only restaurants and stores, drinking from white-only water fountains, or using white-only restrooms. When attacked, blacks could seek refuge in black neighborhoods, but northern whites, including Allard, retreated to segregated hamburger joints—a tactic opposed by blacks. Al also refused to accept legal help from the National Lawyers Guild, because it had been infiltrated by Communists. To anti-Communists such as Lowenstein and Norman Thomas, the Lawyers Guild represented Stalinism. William Kunstler was a prominent Guild lawyer. "You cannot expect liberals in this country to support the civil rights movement," Al wrote, "when you are using people who don't really believe in freedom."[2] Despite Al's campus reputation as a "flaming liberal," Chafe reports, he was in fact a mainstream kind of person. He brought in Bayard Rustin, deep in NAACP civil rights projects (see chap. 18 and appendix C), to oppose the locals who accepted the Lawyers Guild and employed dilatory tactics delaying the summer activities. In the end, Al left the summer project disillusioned with its local leadership. He had insisted unsuccessfully on playing the pivotal role.

There was a second aspect to America's liberal consensus: a sophisticated anti-Communism after World War II that flowed logically—and morally—from a concern for social reform at home. As few others, Allard Lowenstein and Freedom House, of which he was a board member, represented both aspects of this liberal consensus. As the Vietnam War bloodied on, that liberal consensus was sorely split. But Al did not allow his anti–Vietnam War stand to alter for long his commitment to anti-Communism as both a moral and geopolitical imperative. He moved in and out of South Africa several times to oppose apartheid, the cruel separation of blacks, whites, and "coloreds." I had visited South Africa three times on my own and could not believe there would be a relatively peaceful end to apartheid in my lifetime, let alone the election of a black president.

Allard visited other countries of southern Africa to persuade black leaders to pursue a democratic course. He accepted such a mission when I invited Al to join the Freedom House group monitoring the first election in Southern Rhodesia (now Zimbabwe) in 1979. Jimmy Carter was president at that time; Zbigniew Brzezinski, his national security adviser, was a long-time Freedom House board member. It was Zbig who had quietly prepared Carter while still campaigning for the presidency to stress human rights concerns as a new element of American foreign policy. Zbig was joined in this by Richard N. Gardner, whose son attended

St. Bernard's and Exeter with my son Mark. Dick, who became Carter's ambassador to Rome, had long been on the Freedom House board. The election in Rhodesia was highly controversial. White colonialists still ruled the country, though their power was clearly diminishing. The election would feature several black candidates running against the white incumbent. To speed his departure, the United States and Britain had put in place sanctions on goods and services going into the country. The boycott had been only partially effective. The official U.S. position was to ignore the election and stiffen sanctions; let the British take the initiative.

I didn't agree. I felt there was a middle course represented by the imminent election. This would not only provide Rhodesia with the first exercise in democratic processes, but the sight of a white minority permitting the overwhelming black majority to vote in a free election would also provide a historic precedent for South Africa, just a short flight away. Both countries had similar settler histories: white violence was pervasive, but black violence had risen in both places. Indeed, two military insurgencies now were tearing Rhodesia apart. Robert Mugabe and Joshua Nkomo each had well-armed fighters invading the other's homeland, occasionally fighting one another and threatening to attack voters and the polls on election day.

Under such conditions, I believed it was important to observe whether the voting was indeed free and fair. This Freedom House election observer team was the first of its kind. Since then, many other groups have engaged in such activity. Jimmy Carter's center at Emory University, created after he left the White House, has become a regular monitor of elections on several continents. But our first mission set the pattern for our future observations in Africa, Asia, and Latin America, and for other groups that followed. Some say election monitoring overseas has become a cottage industry.

But not yet in 1979. Allard and I shared one basic premise: that the democratic process—elections—was essential to any future settlement in Rhodesia. We acknowledged that these particular elections had been organized by the white government of Ian Smith. Clearly, he wanted to retain power but recognized that times were changing. He sought the perception abroad of a democratizing process if sanctions were to be lifted. Allard and I believed that a democratic process, once begun, would take on a life of its own among the intelligent black population. The land, moreover, was rich in resources with a productive agriculture. In short, we had faith in the process.

The Carter administration, on the other hand, believed that the black leader likely to win the election, Bishop Abel T. Muzorewa, would become a puppet of Smith. The Carter people, led by Andrew Young, a longtime black friend of the president and his ambassador to the United Nations, supported the rebel leader Robert Mugabe, then fighting in the bush. Allard and I regarded Mugabe as a Marxist who had military and political support from the Soviet Union. Before leaving for Rhodesia I spoke to Zbig Brzezinski and got the impression that he shared my view of Mugabe's Marxist attachments but that he stood by the administration's continuing support for sanctions—and leaving the final decisions to the British.

Before we flew to Africa, Allard, too, made the rounds in Washington. But in typical fashion he had his own agenda. He would meet with African leaders to try to work out a settlement of the Rhodesian question. He began by pressing for an elimination of sanctions and concentration on elections, as did I. But he found no takers at the White House or the State Department—or from Andrew Young, with whom he had marched in the American South for civil rights. There, voting rights and elections had made a significant difference for black citizens. Even acknowledging that white America, with all its prejudices, was still a long-functioning civil society, it seemed that the process of democratization in Africa should begin with similar assumptions: that a long-victimized people should begin the journey to freedom by employing that most elemental tool—free and fair elections, even if conducted under less than favorable conditions.

To his credit, Allard recognized the connection between the development of a democratic black government in Rhodesia and changes elsewhere in southern Africa. On that premise, in Johannesburg he discussed the situation with Foreign Minister Pik Botha of South Africa. And one day in Rhodesia, as I was about to fly in an old British warplane with Bayard Rustin to a distant voting place near the border where Mugabe's fighters were concentrated, Allard informed me he was flying in a different direction. He was going to see President Kenneth Kaunda of neighboring Zambia, which accommodated some Rhodesian guerrillas. Al would try to enlist a black "frontline" leader to help negotiate a moderate settlement to the Rhodesian question. Kaunda had been receiving U.S. aid as a buffer against further Soviet military and other encroachments in southern Africa. Allard also spoke to Smith, the white Rhodesian leader, on terms of settlement that he might accept. Bayard and I later talked to Smith and found him mainly suspicious of our intentions. I never discovered what Allard had found, but I believe Smith played as clever a game in private as he did in public. He offered to share power with an elected black leader provided his white constituency (some twenty or so votes in a one-hundred-seat parliament) would be guaranteed election for ten years by a separate white voting list. That is what ultimately happened. When the ten years passed, the black government of Mugabe wiped out this arrangement. By then, Mugabe had also eliminated any vestige of black opposition. He ran a one-party government that controlled radio, television, and newspapers as well. It was not a Marxist, but a Mugabe one-party government, dominated by his Shona tribe.

When we returned to the States after the first Rhodesian election, several of us addressed many forums urging a change in American policy. We called for "a constructive middle course." President Carter had already faulted the election and the constitution under which the polling took place. Despite the flaws, we believed the voting had been a significant advance toward multiracial and majority rule, freer than most elections in developing countries. Blacks then comprised 85 percent of the security force and 75 percent of the police force. We said that by his statement the president had missed an opportunity to reinforce these movements. We said it was not constructive to hold up to a developing country the standard of current political practice in the United States.

Allard made the rounds in Congress; he was quickly involved in the political debate in both houses. Those who wanted to lift sanctions immediately circulated word that Allard Lowenstein had called for just that. He had not; in typical Allard fashion, he had taken a separate course from both the Freedom House position and the administration's. He induced eight congressmen, Democrats and Republicans, to circulate a letter to *all* members spelling out the Lowenstein position. He was quoted as repeating our finding that the election "was a significant step in the ongoing process toward majority rule in Zimbabwe Rhodesia." That process, he said, "should be acknowledged and encouraged." He did not support lifting sanctions at the time, nor did we. But he proposed waiting until the fall, when the British would play their hand. Thus, Allard had mapped out a "Lowenstein position" just a degree or two different than Freedom House's—and quite different from the administration's, which refused to acknowledge any change on the matter in Rhodesia.

Sanctions had been put in place originally by a Case-Javits amendment in the Senate. Javits was a member of the Freedom House board, and Clifford P. Case was by then our organization's president. Senator Case and I testified before the Senate that the Case-Javits amendment was never intended to put U.S. policy in a permanent straitjacket but would apply sanctions only until events in Rhodesia had adequately changed. We argued that they had. Similarly, I drafted an op-ed article published in the *New York Times* under Senator Case's byline.[3] The first sentences told our story: "Should the United States lift the sanctions on Rhodesia? Yes, but gradually, as Zimbabwe is further democratized by its new black government." I wrote that Zimbabwe had made racial discrimination illegal. A majority of black voters had spoken eloquently. The new black leader had called on insurgents to come back and help run the society. If the United States moved too fast in lifting sanctions, the Soviets would step up aid to the guerrillas. But if the United States moved too slow, white South Africa would gain. The Senate voted for a resolution calling for lifting of the sanctions. The president ignored the resolution; the sanctions remained.

The British moved by setting up the Lancaster House (London) meeting, which called for new elections and a commitment to the whites to have twenty seats in a black majority parliament for ten years. This agreement paved the way for Mugabe to win. He represented the Shona, the tribal group comprising 75 percent of the population. His victory would lead to de facto one-party rule, even with the white presence in Parliament.

Bayard Rustin and I foresaw this when we interviewed Mugabe in 1980 after the second election, which he won. Allard had been murdered earlier. We were on the scene to monitor the second proceedings. Again, we found the election to be relatively free and fair, though all candidates used intimidation to bring voters to the polls in their own party's interest. By then, the British agreement had virtually removed Bishop Muzorewa from power. Several black fringe candidates made easier Mugabe's ascension over Nkomo's second-largest tribal group. Muzorewa suffered for failing to end the fighting—the insurgents would not comply—and being open to the charge that his election had been under terms set by the Smith government. Though not openly argued by Muzorewa, Mugabe's election was engineered by whites under the Lancaster deal designed by British prime minister Margaret Thatcher. She apparently wanted to rid herself of this colonial burden: a laudable objective, but achieved in a fashion likely to undermine democratic development in Rhodesia. The electoral process became merely a contrivance in international geopolitics.

In 1980, the day before Mugabe's victory was announced, Bayard and I met him privately. As we waited in a large, empty room Mugabe was speaking with three "journalists" from the Soviet Union, who were criticizing him for promising democracy. Said Mugabe, "Wait until afterward." He was a man of his word!

Twenty years later, Zimbabwe's one-party state, under strong central control, is among the worst of Africa's oppressive nations. Several other African countries have advanced toward democracy, but leading up to elections in 2002, Mugabe confiscated most lands of white farmers. Unexpectedly, despite his use of thugs to occupy some farms, a widespread display of black protesters blamed Mugabe for the corruption and the depressed economy, supporting an opposition candidate and thus offering the first real challenge in twenty years to Mugabe's rule. His militias murdered, pillaged, and raped in areas in which oppositionists resided. Mugabe won another election, this one so flawed that international observers condemned it, and American and European governments withheld support.

Fortunately, South Africa—the great potential freedom machine on the continent—did not follow the Zimbabwe model, as had been hoped during Zimbabwe's first election.

Allard, I believe, would be pleased with South Africa, unhappy with Zimbabwe.

NOTES

1. Quoted in William H. Chafe, *Never Stop Running: Allard Lowenstein and the Struggle to Save American Liberalism* (New York: Basic Books, 1993, reprint 1995), pp. 262–63.

2. Quoted in Chafe, *Never Stop Running*, p. 191.

3. Clifford P. Case, "Lift the Sanctions, Gradually," *New York Times*, June 1, 1979.

30

MARIE-ELAINE AND THE SLAVE-HOLD OF SENEGAL

To the northwest, nearly a whole continent away from Zimbabwe, lies Senegal. It should be idyllic: it has balmy weather year-round, excellent harbors, a 250-mile seacoast on the Atlantic, and a forested plain in the interior. But Senegal, as Marie-Elaine showed me, has had a grim history, even into the 1980s.

Marie-Elaine is a young journalist I met at a conference arranged by a Canadian university with a press-training center in Dakar, Senegal's capital. She is one of the few Senegalese who speak English—most citizens, overwhelmingly Muslim, speak only native languages, with a smattering of French. The French occupied Senegal from 1814—although only formally from 1920—until independence in 1960. But some things don't change with the lowering of a colonial flag.

Senegal has seen the worst of times, as Marie-Elaine demonstrated. She took me on a small ferry to the island of Gorée, off the coast of Dakar, where she has an apartment. It is on the second floor of an apartment building, just behind a window box of bright, colorful flowers. The largest of three rooms is a sitting room, where she left me and an associate while she prepared lunch. She spoke of a high point in her life: an American named Robert Kennedy had come through the island of Gorée, and Marie-Elaine had met him. When he returned home, he sent her a thank-you note on White House stationery. She had never forgotten.

Kennedy took that small ferry for the same reason I had: to see with our own eyes the very place where thousands of Africans had been held in inhuman conditions while awaiting transports for the New World—and slavery. Marie-Elaine presented lunch. It was bouillabaisse, a whole fish with vegetables in a great pot of soup. The three of us sat on low stools with the pot on the floor. Marie-Elaine used bare hands to squeeze off a piece of fish. My colleague followed. I gingerly did the same but felt queasy. I spent the rest of lunchtime moving about the apartment, admiring and photographing the furniture as well as views of the island.

Gorée played an ugly role in the slave trade from 1535 to 1848. We went to the old slave area. A tall guard stood at attention at the heavy wooden door of the Maison des Esclaves (French for "Slave House"). In slave-trade days, the human merchandise was kept in the basement of the merchants' grand houses. On the upper floors, airy rooms and a balcony overlooked the Atlantic. Down below . . .

We entered the narrow passageway of the basement. It was abysmally dark. A small electric bulb lit part of the way. Then, the area remained just as it was during slave days. Cold, dank mud walls were broken only by heavy metal bars. Slaves wore around their waist a 10.3-kg metal weight, linked to their ankles with a heavy lock to prevent escape. Anyone who tried to escape was shot. There were no toilet facilities or wash basins, and the only light from outside was a sliver of sky far down the tunnel. That was the cruelest signal of all. While it may have provided a flicker of hope for the hapless victims, they soon discovered that the light came through the earthen passageway that fed human bodies onto wooden planks. The planks rested on the deck of the ship that would carry the roped men and women to slavery—if they did not perish at sea, as many did.

Importation of slaves into the British colony of Virginia began in 1619. Slaves from Africa had already been introduced in South America and the Caribbean by the Portuguese and Spanish. The dehumanizing process began in Africa itself, where bellicose tribes swooped down on less warlike blacks and carried off slaves for themselves or for trading to Europeans. Hundreds of thousands of men and women passed through the Gorée hellhole and onto overcrowded sailing ships. All that remains today is this fearsome, sinister reminder of inhumanity. Just a hundred yards from my office in New York is a large sailing ship permanently docked at South Street Seaport. It was the last of the line of ships engaged in the triangular trade: from Africa (with slaves) to the Caribbean (for sugar) to New York (for gold), and back again.

Exploitation has not ended in Senegal, though it has a modern veneer amidst the tall, white buildings and the jacketed, French-speaking elite. Many have gone to lycees in Paris and, like Marie-Elaine, attempt to report present-day problems. Exploitation today is not as obviously brutalizing as the dingy prison of Gorée, but no less dehumanizing, even life-threatening in the long term.

I walked alone along the sandy beach near the center of Dakar. Boys of about twelve or fourteen carried heavy canoelike boats to the water's edge. These traditional boats were hewn from a single tree. They were so finely balanced they could not only float but could also hold five or six boys who paddled the weighty vessel through incoming waves. Once seaborne, they would clamber aboard. They used shells to bail and a net to snare fish. An hour or so later, they would return with several dozen brightly colored fish that would enhance an American aquarium.

But that was the beginning of a deeply disturbing sequence. I watched boys beach their craft and carry the fish, many still flapping, onto the sand. They placed the new catch atop a huge pile of dead fish. I looked down the beach for a quarter-mile. There were dozens of piles of fish like the one before me. Each pile rose higher than my head. Tens of thousands of fish lay rotting in the tropical sun. At that moment, just a few miles inland, men, women, and children were hungry, or at least starved for protein.

When I asked about this, I was told there was insufficient freezing equipment to preserve the fish and an inadequate distribution system. The numerous newspapers, mostly linked to political parties, seldom tackled this sensitive subject of pervasive corruption. But times would change, I was assured.

Now, ten years later, a colleague has just returned from Senegal. He discovered the saga of the fish "shortage." The sea still teems with fish, but only a small number of native entrepreneurs are licensed to fish and sell the product of their labor. Licenses go to a few French marketers and the inevitable Japanese. The Japanese, however, fish the plentiful stock and take the catch back to Japan. There, they either use the fish for Japanese consumption or sell the product to the Senegalese at inflated prices—which the French also do. Few Senegalese can establish a fish industry along their lengthy coastline. Young boys, I assume, still carve boats out of trees, as their ancestors did; and, like them, waste fish, a staff of life, while malnutrition persists not far off.

More than a decade later, ties with France are still strong. Unemployment and diminished income have served to strengthen mainstream opposition politicians and Islamist groups. Armed insurgencies have increased in the south. The dominant socialist party prevents the rise of a democratic opposition. Former president Leopold Senghor, authoritarian in his time, one of Africa's leading poets, was then under house arrest. He has since died, with eulogies for his poetic accomplishments. Marie-Elaine, who prefers her full name not be known, is twice victimized: as a journalist she must practice self-censorship, and as a woman Islamic laws restrict her further—and spousal abuse, a common fact of life, is her additional burden.

There are several degrees of colonialism, Marie-Elaine points out: between different nationalities and cultures, as well as between political, ethnic, tribal, or religious classes. Senegal suffers from them all. In the 1990s, there was significant movement toward a democratic polity. Across her small island of Gorée, however, looms the grim monument to the long tradition of exploitation that continues to this day.

31

LUDOVICK NGATARA
Dangerous Journalism

J ournalists in developing countries, particularly those in Africa, have my limitless admiration. I have met scores over the years. I marvel at their courage
in coming to work every day despite physical, psychological, and occupational
hazards. If they trim reports to avoid instant harm—if they, indeed, practice self-
censorship—I understand, and I take to task their government all the more for
their cowardice in denying their people the right to diverse information.

Long before there were faxes and e-mail—only hand-carried "snail-mail" and
unresponsive telephone circuits—Ludovick Ngatara, a courageous journalist in Dar
es Salaam, Tanzania, and I began an acquaintanceship that blossomed into friendship over a quarter-century. We seldom met, but we corresponded with increasing
frequency. We have quite different personal histories yet remarkably similar values,
which drive us to think and act in tandem—even without advance knowledge. Each
in our own, unlabeled way is a middle-roader. The great difference: that has always
been easy for me; terribly difficult, even life-threatening for Ludovick.

Ludovick was twenty-six when Tanganyika got its independence from Great
Britain in 1961; two years later it joined with the island of Zanzibar to become the
United Republic of Tanzania. Almost from the beginning, Tanzania was a one-
party state, ruled by Julius K. Nyerere. He flirted with both Soviet and Chinese
Communists and professed to establish an African socialist state. Ludovick, a journalist, dissented. But there was little a single journalist could do. Ludovick
expressed disagreement, particularly in international conferences and in writing for
serious journals in the field of communication. That brought us together, early on.

The Tanzania Journalists' Association was just an arm of the government for
many years. Members were government operatives. They worked for the newspaper, news agency, and radio controlled by the government and the Revolu-

tionary Party. In September 1987, for example, the association convened a meeting of journalists from southern African countries and the liberation movements of South Africa and South-West Africa (later Namibia). The purpose: promoting socialism in Africa. All journalists were required to be well versed in the party's political ideology and had to attend a school for indoctrination.

To ensure continued obedience in Tanzania, the government news agency, Shihata, licensed journalists. Without that credential, one could not work in the mass media, on pain of prosecution. Shihata, moreover, was the sole gatekeeper for all news entering or leaving Tanzania. Editors had to satisfy objectives set forth daily by the Ministry of Information. Criticism of government policies could result in dismissal or even detention without trial. Once denounced, journalists were severely reprimanded, and their editors warned or replaced. Foreign journalists on arrival had to report to the ministry and disclose the purpose of the visit. Even so, foreign newspersons were harassed by local officials, the police, or even the military. Movement about the country and access to news were extremely limited.

In the face of such controls and threats, it took great courage for Ludovick Ngatara to come to Dubrovnik, Yugoslavia, in 1978 and speak his mind freely. Addressing the International Institute of Communication he said, "In the two decades since various third world countries, especially those in black Africa, started emerging as independent states, the masses in these countries witnessed all media instruments, which were supposed to be their voices, being utilized by one regime or another for swaying them like helpless willows to all corners of the political winds."

The emerging regimes, he said, "have opted to use the instruments of mass media as a means or shield to protect [the regimes] on their unpopular thrones." Ludovick continued, "A regime which opts for dictatorship or totalitarianism in the guise of socialism employs the mass media instruments to achieve its end. Other unpopular regimes take different courses to justify their ends." When a new regime takes over, Ludovick added, "the media instruments also change hands to usher the masses to yet another ideological cause."

Ludovick Ngatara came out of the third world and expressed rational opposition to the problems he faced at home, while criticizing the so-called free world's journalism for valid errors of omission, commission, and unbalanced emphasis—but not for ideological bias or "cultural imperialism," the buzz words of the day in his sphere. I welcomed Ludovick's analysis of Western journalism for its rational examination, but I sharply attacked the exploitation of criticism of the West by authoritarians such as Nyerere, who controlled the very lives as well as the reporting of domestic journalists.

Both of us, coming through the middle range of ideas in our respective societies, found ourselves sharing fundamental conclusions. These endpoints, given a more profound title than either of us employed, were *universal* imperatives, which many sought but no one would accept; they would not, because to do so demanded compromise, the tool of democracy, which even democrats reject when overheated in public debate. And the international debate over the flow of information had become blistering, even counterproductive for all participants. The authoritarians turned off Western advocates and welcomed little constructive change. The democrats rejected every criticism, no matter how valid, and deprived their own audience of sensible reforms in Western journalism. It was easy for me to share a view with Ludovick. It was difficult, even courageous for him to do the same.

Ludovick was more than a writer. As a few independent weeklies appeared, Ludovick headed the Journalists' Organization of Tanzania. The nongovernmental JOT faced the most difficult times when the president of the country could ban any newspaper if he concluded such an action to be in the "national interest." Government approval was also required to create a new publication. The government owned and ran the major daily and the principal news agency. At his own peril, Ludovick could complain about injustice to journalists and the public—but power resided elsewhere. Yet complain he did; clearly, and in journals and periodicals abroad, where his calm words were read. Authoritarians say such criticism does not influence them, yet they often charge such critics with "incitement" or, worse, subversion. Ludovick trod carefully and repeatedly through such minefields.

With the retirement of Nyerere in 1986, there was the promise—but little fulfillment—of a real multiparty system of government and pluralistic newspapers, radio, and television. The state continued to monopolize the news media and, in fact, Nyerere remained in the political domain, occasionally propounding desirable policies. Ludovick maintained a continuous analysis in the domestic and international press. In our correspondence, he chronicled the intricate game of promises and deceit among the Tanzanian leaders: averting freer openings for the news media one moment, and withdrawing simple freedoms the next. As each sequence ended, he would write precise analyses for *Intermedia*, journal of the International Institute of Communication in London, or other papers of record. Meanwhile, as head of the JOT he would try to improve the lot of working stiffs in Tanzania—a challenge not felt as critically, say, by the leaders of the U.S. Newspaper Guild in their daily job.

Early in February 1994, Ludovick wrote me that his health "has been on the lowest ebb," but "I am keeping on in fulfilling my mission as long as there is still some strength in me." Only then did I learn that Ludovick had suffered from diabetes for many years and needed daily shots of insulin, that his eyesight was failing, and generally that he felt his age—then sixty. In that same message, however, he sent me a perceptive backgrounder that began, "With a thick tongue in the cheek, Tanzania government has at last given in to allow the establishment of private TV and radio." He continued, "After ensuring that all the instruments of media control are securely in place, the government recently issued licenses to two private TV broadcasting companies and one license for a private radio broadcasting firm."

Wrote Ludovick, "Having held the monopoly of radio broadcasting for over thirty years since independence in 1961, and also having completely barred establishment of television in the mainland on the pretext that it was a capitalist luxury for propagation of alien and capitalist cultural norms, the government has since the introduction of multiparty democracy less than two years ago defied all internal and external appeals to release Radio Tanzania from the clutches of the ruling party and turn it into a public corporation." He then described the intricate conditions set forth to control private news media. The main purpose in the government's "delaying tactics," he held, was the ruling party's determination to continue using Radio Tanzania as its mouthpiece mainly for keeping at bay the sweeping tides of multiparty opposition.

When the two private TV channels finally operated, however, the only competition they were allowed was over which would carry the world soccer championships. The government settled the brawl by letting them both carry the games. Foreign investors did not rush to support the new TV outlets, Ludovick reported, because "Western donors are wary of financing a network which, indicators have shown, might be utilized for antidemocracy purposes, as is the case with the government-owned Radio Tanzania."

In responding to Ludovick, I quipped at his "feeling old" at sixty, and said I had passed that mark without harm. He said that "the worry which was expressed in my last letter was caused by diabetes" and the knowledge that "here in Tanzania one is considered old after fifty or fifty-five, because that is the official retirement age." Referring to my age, he said that "most of us in Tanzania would have already turned to useless cabbages"—a frightful thought.

Some months later, in May 1995, after the genocide in Rwanda, he set out to cover the story himself. He made a laborious safari to Kampala, Uganda, and went on to Kigali, Rwanda, and Bujumbura and the western regions of Tanzania—Kagera and Kigom—where thousands of Rwandan refugees were camped. He understood that the warring Rwandan and Burundian ethnic groups, the Tutsis and the Hutus, could no longer live together, either in Rwanda or the neighboring countries. He proposed rearranging the borders between Tanzania, Burundi, and Rwanda into a single federal state. "Such a rearrangement," he said, "would bring about a unity which was once enjoyed by these three states during the German colonial days before World War I. Then this area used to be known as German East Africa." Ludovick sent this recommendation to several journals, but it merited wider consideration. He hoped the idea would be noticed by international bodies.

Ludovick was enjoying the hospitality of Baganda friends in Uganda. Hospitality is "very special" with the Bagandas, he said. They are a separate ethnic group whose kabakaship (kingdom) within Uganda has been wisely restored by President Yoweri Museveni. The wars of his predecessors, Oboto and Idi Amin, were largely directed against the Bagandas.

Ludovick returned home in July to write about his trip as well as the condition of Tanzania. Characteristically, he pulled no punches. The headline over his major article in *The Guardian:* "Tanzanians Go Hungry While Sitting on Vast Riches." He cited his country's economic isolation after thirty years of socialist rule. Having been resigned to being "users of finished goods from the industrialized countries," on which the Tanzanians spend what little they earn, "they end up becoming poorer and poorer," Ludovick wrote. The aim, he said is to "roll back the state of semiclosed society and strive to catch up with the rest of the world as full partners in international trade and commerce."

Later in 1995, Ludovick told me his government had just signed a multimillion dollar agreement with the People's Republic of China. The Chinese would assist Tanzania to meet its "educational and cultural commitments" for two years. The Chinese would establish a national television network and train Tanzanians to run it. The West had refused to help, fearing the network would be used to undermine the new multiparty system. China had been a partner in Ujamaa, Julius Nyerere's brand of Communism.

Soon after, a sad note came from Ludovick. His older brother, much like a father, died. But Ludovick pressed on. He still ran the journalist association, giving aid and comfort to others, but the latest word from Ludovick was grim. When the American embassy in Dar es Salaam was bombed in August 1999, Ludovick published a lengthy analysis placing the blame on Islamic fundamentalist extremists. Immediately afterward, he discovered that a *fatwa*—a death contract—had been issued in his name. He fled Tanzania with his ten-year-old son and found refuge in Uganda, but no source of employment. Ludovick was in dire straits. I tried unsuccessfully to secure some funding from American and European press groups.

Still, he wrote, "I happen to be a great admirer of Joseph Pulitzer, who has been my source of inspiration whenever I feel like laxing in my responsibilities. Like Pulitzer, my sight is diminishing rapidly due to diabetes, but I am able to keep on in order to fulfill that which I strongly feel is the cause of the Creator in bringing me into this world at this particular time."

For Ludovick Ngatara, this was a harsh time. Yet, for those for whom he labored, in all of Africa and beyond, that paragraph reveals the inner spirit of the man. He died in 2002, leaving behind an extended family decimated by AIDS.

A footnote: I have my picture taken sitting at Joseph Pulitzer's great roll-top desk. It stood at Columbia University's Pulitzer-endowed school of journalism when I was a student there. Pulitzer, also my idol, was included in my university teaching. Like so many other things we discovered we had in common, Ludovick and I had never discussed this before. More degrees of separation were erased.

32

MUHAMMAD ABDEL GAWAD
Mystery Journalist of Egypt

O ne of the most important journalists I've ever encountered flitted briefly, even mysteriously, in and out of my life, and never seemed available for recall. Muhammad Abdel Gawad and I met in several countries when he was director of the Middle East News Agency (MENA), an Egyptian government agency, but because it carries news from all Middle Eastern countries it is more balanced, less propagandistic than any of the solely national news agencies. Gawad tried to run MENA with as little interference as possible from Egyptian officials. He was to play an important role in the Arab region's first breakthrough with the state of Israel. I did not know until later that I was on the scene at the time.

Indeed, Gawad's historic role in June 1977 helped change the adversarial political climate in both Israel and Egypt. That made possible President Anwar Sadat's negotiation visit to Israel. Subsequently, interviews by Barbara Walters (ABC-TV) and Walter Cronkite (CBS-TV) signaled publicly that both national leaders were ready to talk. But it was two other journalists—Israeli Ari Rath and Gawad—who had already set the stage. And they did not receive the public plaudits that Walters and Cronkite did.

In the spring of 1977, the Murrow Center of the Fletcher School of Law and Diplomacy at Tufts University convened a two-day conference on the press and the third world. The year before, a bitterly divided UNESCO conference had placed on the international agenda the framing of "a new world information and communication order" (NWICO, see chaps. 42–44). The Fletcher meeting was designed to hear moderate spokesmen for developing and industrialized countries (commonly referred to as the "South" and "North," respectively) discuss workable solutions. The crux of the matter: the overwhelming volume of global news and information originated at headquarters in New York, Paris, and London (the Associated Press and United Press International, Agence France-Presse, and Reuters).

Gawad was invited as president of the Arab News Agencies as well as chairman of MENA. He and other major players in the news-flow controversies read papers for discussion. My contribution was "Developmental Journalism: The Ideological Factor." I tried to show the impact of political objectives on the content of news and information in diverse societies. For some years thereafter, I became the most prolific American writer on NWICO and related issues. Muhammad provided a history of the development of literacy and news writing in the Arab world.[1] He chided those who suggest that citizens of the Middle East are innately backward, instead attributing underdevelopment to centuries of oppression by foreign powers.

The discussions turned from theory and history to pragmatic steps that might be taken to improve coverage of the South, and enable it to provide more of its news for the worldwide flow. Roger Tatarian, former editor in chief of United Press International, produced a lengthy study of the history of free-flow controversies. Roger and I had served together on many panels discussing these subjects. He was then professor of journalism at California State University, Fresno. Roger's paper concluded by recommending the creation of a Multinational Pool, which would carry South and North news and would be directed by prominent journalists from all regions; a later version renamed the idea the North-South News Agency. Roger nominated Muhammad Gawad as one of the first directors of the new enterprise.

Several historic events then intervened. There were rumblings of fissures in the Arab bloc over ending the state of war with Israel. Terrorist attacks continued on both sides of the decades-old conflict. The chief Arab belligerent, Yasir Arafat and his Palestine Liberation Organization, was a shadowy figure constantly on the move to avoid assassination by Israeli security forces.

Shortly after the Fletcher conference I addressed press-freedom meetings in South Africa and Kenya. En route to Oslo and the annual sessions of the International Press Institute, I stopped in Cairo to see Muhammad Gawad at MENA. As it turned out, we were both headed for the IPI meeting on the same plane. Muhammad drove me to the airport in his black limousine, deposited me in a large VIP waiting room, and took my passport to be processed painlessly, help that I welcomed. On arrival earlier at Cairo I had confronted thousands of passengers, the absence of clearly marked lines, and general chaos.

Muhammad returned and sat next to me in the large, completely empty assembly room with a hundred chairs. Suddenly, from the rear came the sound of many booted feet marching in unison. As we sat alone on the center aisle, the military contingent marched past us. It disappeared through a door at the front of the room. A few moments later, an arm and then a headdress appeared from that door, beckoning Muhammad. He excused himself, walked to the front, and entered the other room. My momentarily slowed nerve endings replayed what I had seen: Yasir Arafat had called Muhammed for a brief meeting in the adjoining room. When Muhammad returned I asked some discreet questions and was told that Arafat with his guard was on his way by private plane to his secret headquarters in Libya.

Muhammad and I went on to Oslo, where the main event of this historic trip was to take place. At the IPI meeting, Muhammad was approached by Ari Rath, a prominent Israeli journalist. Ari and I had met at several IPI meetings. Here, with great secrecy, Ari raised with Muhammad the possibility of Israeli prime minister Menachem Begin welcoming Anwar Sadat to Israel. Muhammad was concerned: Arabs were not supposed to meet with Israelis. But Muhammad had decided to speak to Ari and then report the conversation at home. During an hour-long talk, Ari told Muhammad, "If you have access to President Sadat, tell him not to be afraid of Menachem Begin. Begin is a powerful man with whom Sadat can do business."

Muhammad said later he went home "trembling" and reported to Sadat what Ari had said. Sadat told Muhammad not to be frightened and added, "From now on we will not hide. We are going to do what is good for our country."

Ari's question set in motion an elaborate exchange over many months. Sadat consulted Nicolae Ceausescu, the Romanian dictator, who knew Begin. (Ceausescu and his wife were later executed as Communist rule ended in Romania.) The Romanian said that Begin's public statements were not the same as the views he expressed to friends. There was then contact between Begin and Ceausescu, and then with Ceausescu and Sadat. Sadat, said Muhammad, informed the Shah of Iran and the Saudi Arabs that he intended to go to Jerusalem. Both agreed. A few weeks later, Sadat made a public announcement about the historic meeting of the two former combatants.

In 1979, President Jimmy Carter persuaded Anwar Sadat and Menachem Begin to sign the Camp David Accords. Israel agreed to return the Sinai to Egypt and negotiate Arab autonomy in the occupied West Bank and Gaza. (The latter was not accomplished until 1995.)

But from the moment the meeting of Sadat and Begin was bruited in the Arab world, the Middle East News Agency was ruled *persona non grata* throughout the region—even in Saudi Arabia, which knew in advance of Sadat's trip to Jerusalem. Thus MENA had access only to Egypt, its headquarters, destroying any possibility that Gawad or MENA would even consider further the North-South News Agency proposed at the Fletcher conference two years earlier.

Several times in the ensuing years I tried unsuccessfully to reach Muhammad Gawad. In 1992 he was listed as a consultant to MENA. He remains on my list as one of the stalwart journalists in the developing world, who struggled against the daily pressures of government control. He always tried to bring to MENA the practices he learned as a young journalist representing foreign news agencies in Egypt. When MENA was started in 1956, he became chief reporter. He resigned in 1959, he told me, because the government brought in an army officer to run the agency. So he took a job as Egypt's press counselor in Chicago. He returned to MENA in 1965 and ran it for the next eighteen years. Within restrictions that were still serious, he sought to provide the most informative, most accurate reports possible. That is not easy in a free country; it is far harder, far more dangerous in an unstable society such as Egypt was and remains.

When Egyptian president Gamal Abdel Nasser was murdered, Gawad successfully urged Sadat to ease press controls. Gawad broadened MENA's scope, though still within the range of some explicit presidential desires. That is still the fate of Egyptian journalists: indeed, the freer Egyptian press of the late 1980s was restricted again in the 1990s with the rise of Islamic fundamentalist terrorism. But by then, Gawad was a consultant, no longer the prime mover of the Middle East News Agency. And by then, the president of Egypt going to Israel to mourn the assassination by a Jew of Prime Minister Yitzhak Rabin was not nearly as historic a sight as Sadat's first visit to Israel.

Late in 2002, Freedom House honored the first recipient of the Bette Bao Lord Award for Writing on Freedom. Bette Bao Lord, former chairman of Freedom House, is a best-selling novelist. Dr. Saad Eddin Ibrahim led the Idn Khaldun Foundation, a think-tank focused on political and economic reform that documented human rights abuses as well as government and electoral irregularities. Ibrahim's wife accepted the award in his name. He could not attend the Washington ceremony—he was in an Egyptian prison at the time.

NOTE

1. Muhammad Abdel Gawad, "Attempts of the Arab World to Participate in Balancing the Flow of Information," in *The Third World and Press Freedom*, ed. Philip Horton (New York: Praeger, 1978), pp. 173–86.

33

THE PRESS OF "TOMORROW" IN VIETNAM

I n South Vietnam, less than a year before Communists swept into Saigon (now Ho Chi Minh City) and Americans left by helicopter from a midtown roof, I spent a week addressing one hundred Vietnamese journalists. I stood beneath the banner that read, *Truven Thong Hien Tai Tuong Lai*. Translated: "The Media— Today and Tomorrow."

But there has been no tomorrow for most of those journalists who eagerly sought to work in a free press. When the Communists rolled in, they sent to "reeducation camps" anyone who had contact with Americans, especially journalists. Some remained in those camps for fifteen years; many died. Some escaped by boat to exile in Hong Kong or wherever the South China Sea would take them. Many drowned or perished from hunger at sea.

I still recall my last meeting with the journalists. They invited me to a sumptuous lunch at a Saigon restaurant. I drank their explosively potent vodka-like liquor—in Russian style, in one swallow. I was especially moved at the end of the meal. One of the men rose, offered a toast, and made me an honorary member of the Vietnam Journalists' Association; I was given a plaque to commemorate the election. I expressed my thanks and admiration for these journalists' integrity, pausing after each word for translation: "spirit . . . humor . . . and, above all, courage."

It was a memorable moment made all the more searing for me when within a year the country collapsed, and my thoughts turned immediately to those men around that luncheon table in May 1974.

I remembered with no less anguish the striving of those journalists to secure the freedom dangled before them briefly by visiting Americans. We had come because the Saigon government had passed Press Law 007, placing stiff restrictions on the Vietnamese journalists. Indeed, a government representative sat in the front row as I spoke each day, making copious notes, including responses from the journalists. That, of course, was most fearsome for them. Yet the questions still came, and the discussion flowed freely.

One query seemed philosophical in form, not unusual in that culture: "Is there a relationship between imitation and communication?" I did not respond immediately. The questioner, a prominent editor, repeated his query in Vietnamese and English. Frankly, I still did not understand the question. I whispered to the moderator that we might meet the man at tea and discuss his point privately to avoid embarrassing him (or us) by asking for another formulation.

The seminar was already extraordinary. Not because artillery exchanges were raising gray clouds thirty miles northwest of Saigon; nor indeed because acts of war are cited by the government to justify diverse controls over the press. The seminar was notable because Vietnamese journalists themselves challenged in that sophisticated fashion not only the Republic of Vietnam's press controls but also assumptions that universal standards of press freedom do not apply in developing countries.

As the seminar proceeded, we who were leading it gave little thought to the question of imitation and communication. We turned first to complex truths about third world journalism and particularly the status of press freedom in Vietnam. Presumably we had an abiding interest in seeing freer societies develop in Asia: was this not what the Vietnam War was about? And is it not true that free and responsible journalism is a major instrument in the development of political and civil liberties? We therefore felt it should be of some significance to discover whether (1) Americans can provide guidance that is useful and acceptable to developing nations in the expansion of press freedom; (2) standards of press freedom can be universalized beyond their Euro-American origins; and (3) indigenous journalists have the motivation and, above all, the creative subtlety to employ even limited opportunities to push for wider freedoms.

Sadly, we found the answers—all decidedly affirmative—but the military debacle within a year blasted any opportunity to test the favorable premises. But two decades later the United States government had committed hundreds of millions of dollars to assist developing journalism in Eastern and Central Europe as well as the new states of the former Soviet Union. I would be involved in that effort from its inception, but I never forgot my membership in the obliterated Vietnam Journalists' Association.

This group was composed of proud men laboring under wartime restrictions and the common paternalism of developing-country governments—as true in Africa and Latin America as in Asia. Those countries told journalists in effect, "You cannot be given greater freedom because you may misuse it." Yet journalists worked among the small permissive cracks of press controls.

I was moved by an unforgettable lesson: the Saigon newspaper told of a young girl in a small town in Vietnam who had died after eating cactus. Under censorship the newspaper could not report hunger. The story about the girl represented the idea of "writing between the lines," and readers knew how to read it: why else would she have eaten cactus if she had not been impelled by sheer hunger, unreported in the press? That was press freedom, of sorts. In many of the fifty-nine countries I have visited, reading between the lines is a daily necessity.

For thousands of years, during the long period when Vietnam was a satellite of China, the Vietnamese elevated their *si*, or educated men, to leadership. Since only a few could govern, the remaining *si* became teachers or, today, journalists (and sometimes also part-time teachers) to assure a livable income. One Vietnamese journalist told me that, just as his ancestors did, his colleagues "proudly think of themselves as members of an educated elite destined to a leadership role in an illiterate society. But because they are removed from the mainstream of activities many become frustrated critics, impractical, removed from reality, egocentrically proud, and incapable of cooperation, and therefore are ineffective and impotent in a changing society that needs their contribution."

This alienation of the brightest may have permitted a few corrupt leaders to dominate South Vietnam. North Vietnam, meanwhile, was run by highly motivated Communist ideologues who would overpower a far less committed though better-educated southern population.

To hold power, the southern leaders believed they needed more than American firepower. They wanted to appear to be moving toward postwar democracy—an objective Americans expected and pressed for—yet the South Vietnamese leaders had little faith they could hold their own against truly free journalism. The formula they devised is precisely the same as that followed *today*—years after the fall of Communism—in virtually every "new democracy" of Eastern and Central Europe and the former states of the Soviet Union, including Russia itself.

This formula was spelled out in South Vietnam's press laws of 1969 and 1972, which give and take freedom. They assert at the outset (as do all current laws in the new democracies) that press freedom is a fundamental right. The laws state immediately thereafter that "the exercise of press freedom shall not be harmful to personal honor, national security, or traditional morality." Also prohibited is insulting or slandering the president of the republic or representatives of friendly powers. Papers may not be "suspended," the next paragraph maintains, "except by due judicial process." The second article states flatly, "Press censorship is prohibited." But there are intricate and costly procedures for licensing newspapers, accrediting "qualified" journalists, requiring expensive bonds and specifying infractions of the law that may result in stiff penalties (including confiscation of entire press runs) or temporary or permanent suspension of publication. The euphemism "no censorship" is contradicted by the Ministry of Information's "advising" an editor that an article he plans to publish may be considered offensive. Copies of the day's newspaper must be given to the ministry before publication. In this cat-and-mouse game the editors often delete an article and print "self-censored" in large type in the white block but leave in the fringes of the deleted article, showing just a few words to tease and perhaps even inform the reader. "People become very adept at reading between the lines," one journalist told me.

Present-day leaders in the new democracies (and even the outright authoritarians) are more sophisticated but no less effective than the former rulers in South Vietnam. Today, new press laws in many former Soviet states also promise press freedom and "no censorship," but there follow intricate reservations that threaten reprisals if journalists defame the leader or the government, threaten national security (however defined), or favor a long list of social and political changes (however defined). As a consequence, self-censorship is rife in many of these countries, just as in the late South Vietnam.

One tended to forget that a generation of Vietnamese newsmen had observed close-up—and some had been trained by—American journalists who covered the war in Vietnam. Vietnamese reporters and editors learned the value of freedom perhaps even better than they absorbed techniques of reporting or electronic communication. This was an unheralded legacy of America's wartime partnership. One editor told me, "Your country has a responsibility to *ensure* freedom of the press in South Vietnam. You are a party to the Paris Accords, and one of the stipulations is that the Vietnamese press shall be free." After all, the journalist added, "the socialist states make certain that *their* allies are protected."

I found it difficult to reply and fell back on the assumption that the Vietnamese do not seek any new colonial relationship. They may have to win greater freedom by alerting and educating their fellow citizens, even within present restrictions, before they can persuade the regime that broadened freedom of the press is mutually advantageous.

That conversation led to clearing up the earlier mystery of the link between imitation and communication. I spoke with the young editor who had raised the issue. Without referring to his earlier question he asked me, "Why did you come here?"

I replied, "To discuss the press and its freedom in the United States."

"But why?" he insisted.

"Because we felt you might find it useful to have an example."

I broke into a broad smile: "Imitation as a form of communication." I now understood the point of his question. I got a sense of the high value *he* attributed to the uses of the American experience. His view clearly opposed the prevailing attitude I had encountered in dozens of third world countries. Rulers there routinely insisted that America had nothing to offer journalists of their countries, that we were too old, too rich, too powerful to be useful examples for their smaller, poorer, newer countries.

We discussed some of the specifics of my earlier talk. "What did you want to tell us?" he asked. "Were you saying that our press should come still closer to the government?"

I had spoken of the press in a free society consulting officials on the most crucial security questions; the press even then reserving judgment on whether or not to publish sensitive material it acquires. I had argued for a saner "gentleman's agreement" than had then prevailed in American press-government relationships. While counseling restraint by the press, my speech detailed the adversarial nature of press-government contacts. I described a dozen different areas of related controversies, from free press versus fair trial to leaks, subpoenas, and right of reply. Any one of these ongoing American debates would normally be unthinkable in South Vietnam. Yet the editor said sharply, "I shall publish the full text of your speech—without comment—just the speech."

"But what will your readers think?"

"That you delivered a talk on press freedom *in the United States.*" Was this the cactus story in another dimension?

A raucous, complex, confusing system, the American news media–government arrangement—yet worthy of "imitation"?

That was not the end of my relationship with Vietnamese journalists. American domestic support for the war collapsed, and U.S. troops were leaving. Just before the last Americans were flown out of Saigon, I cabled our ambassador there, with a copy to Secretary of State Henry Kissinger in Washington, urging that those journalists who had taken part in our recent seminar in Saigon be given priority in the last airlifts to seek a safe haven in the United States. It was almost certain they would suffer at the hands of the victorious Communists.

I never received a direct answer to my cable. I assumed that even if my cable had gotten through—not certain in those final hectic hours—crushing demands of the unsavory American departure would probably have buried my request. Weeks later, I received a cable from Guam—from four of the dozen Saigon journalists whose names I had put in my cable to the ambassador and Kissinger. They thanked me for getting them and their families to a holding camp in Guam. They said they hoped to thank me in person. I was gratified but felt I had heard the last of this group. Some months later, I received a phone call from a refugee camp in Pennsylvania. These journalists had made it to the U.S. mainland.

Marianne and I rented a car and drove that weekend to Fort Indiantown Gap where we were greeted warmly by the men and their families. Viet Dinh Phuang, the journalist who had hosted that final dinner in Saigon and inducted me into the Vietnam Journalists' Association, was the spokesman for this group in Pennsylvania. I asked him what he planned next. He said he wanted to start a magazine. I gave him all the reasons why this might be difficult. He smiled and was unshaken. Marianne and I left the camp, promising to retain our interest in their progress.

The refugees took this pledge seriously. Six months later I received a letter from the journalist I had spoken with. The International Rescue Committee, to which I referred the group, relocated the family to Cleveland, Ohio. The mother was working as a seamstress. A teenage son was employed. And the father had secured what he called temporary work before returning to journalism. The weekly income of the family was four hundred dollars—just a half-year after escaping Saigon.

Before the end of the family's first year in the United States I received a letter from them in California. Enclosed with it was the first issue of *Trang Din,* their weekly newsmagazine! It was a three-color publication in Vietnamese. There was a sizable Vietnamese colony on the West Coast, and this would be their weekly magazine. I received the publication every week for several years. The editor asked me to write a column in English urging readers to acquire the language as soon as possible. My words were published in English. Melting pot? Integration? Or communication *and* imitation?

34

ARISTEDES KATOPPO
Ghost in the City Room

My round-the-world travel to examine Fulbright scholarships took me to Indonesia in 1991. That is where I met Aristedes Katoppo, for the second time. In 1973, Katoppo was forced into exile from his native Jakarta, where he had been one of Indonesia's most distinguished editors. But that year the president of Indonesia, the minister of information, and the chief of security all agreed that they had read enough of Katoppo's journalism: they sent him out of the country for five years. Katoppo and I first met in 1974 in Kyoto, Japan, where the International Press Institute was holding its annual congress. I was among the speakers and protested to the Indonesian government over the exile of Aristedes.

His was not an unusual case. On the surface, Indonesia seems as idyllic as Western tourist promotion for the island of Bali before the horrific terrorist bombing there in 2002. It was, indeed, a becalmed, delightful, truly beautiful island—one among 13,500 islands in the Indonesian archipelago. This string of islands stretches 3,000 miles across the Pacific. Though some islands are sparsely populated and some are unpopulated, the main places are crowded. Indonesia is the fifth-most populous country in the world, and there are seething, even deadly political conflicts among the generally peaceful peoples of the archipelago.

East Timor, formerly colonized by Portugal, was harshly occupied by Indonesian troops until 1999. The western end of the island was firmly controlled from Jakarta. But an active insurgency demanded independence for East Timor. That repeatedly generated bloody massacres of East Timor's civilians by the Indonesian military. Australian journalists were periodically barred or expelled from East Timor. In October 1995, my colleague Brian Brown and six activists from other countries were summarily expelled from East Timor on the anniversary of a particularly bloody massacre by Indonesian troops. In 1996, shortly after the Nobel Peace Prize was awarded to two East Timor activists, Freedom House arranged for one—José Ramos-Horta—his first press conference in the United States. Freedom House briefly ran an office in East Timor to support its first election after the frightful slaughter of innocents ended.

Yet Indonesia has this near-saintly image of a peaceful people with a strong religious culture that permeates daily life. No high crime rate. No overweening materialism. No Western culture to offend or destroy fragile Asian sensibilities.

Moreover, Indonesia's president repeatedly promised democracy—Asian style. That meant strong government control over the political, economic, and educational systems to ensure that developments follow a preordained pattern and did not undermine the near-absolute domination of the ruling family and its friends. They did rather well in the growing economy since Suharto overthrew President Sukarno and slaughtered some thirty thousand of Sukarno's pro-Communist supporters.

Sukarno had been promising a "guided democracy"; Suharto continued to promise democracy but practiced "guided journalism." Aristedes Katoppo found it impossible after a while to play by those rules. He learned through the grapevine that he was about to be banned and exiled. Earlier, as a prominent journalist, he had been invited to spend a year in the United States on a Fulbright academic exchange scholarship. He accepted, just ahead of the banning. He spent a year at Stanford and afterward stretched his American visit further.

While still abroad, he missed one traumatic event at home. Rioting erupted in the streets of Jakarta, as his paper had predicted. Friends cabled Katoppo not to come home yet. A member of the Indonesian military, briefly in New York, told him, "Lucky you are here. I would have arrested you." The man later became chief of intelligence and security. So Katoppo then spent a year at the Center for International Affairs at Harvard. After two years, Katoppo "just walked back in" to his old paper. He had absorbed as much as he could from the American academic community and was ready to try new ideas at home.

Soon after he returned to Jakarta, we met again in his newspaper office. The virulence of the official attack on Katoppo had softened, Indonesian style. He was still banned but could remain in Jakarta—with certain unique provisos. He sat in his old office, but his name had been removed from the masthead.

"I've been beheaded," he told me. He could enter the newsroom and consult with writers and editors; they visited him for advice, "but," he said, "I'm a ghost."

Though a "ghost," Katoppo's influence on Indonesian journalism has been considerable, particularly after his exile in the United States. Stanford gave him the opportunity to do more focused reading and exchange views in many disciplines with knowledgeable people. After fifteen years in journalism, he told me, "one's knowledge tends to become fragmented, with too much emphasis on what is important today, though that may be quite insignificant tomorrow." That intellectual climate, "despite my skepticism then, led me to explain 'what it means.'" That experience altered his conception of journalism. He introduced it in Indonesia where it flourished—for a while.

He revived a failing magazine, building its circulation from 20,000 to 200,000 by a different approach to what is news. He covered crime, for example, not in isolation but by examining trends and recounting the "process" behind events. The authorities simply decried vandalism and rebellion among the youth. Katappo arranged and publicized meetings for young people to discuss problems on equal terms with adults and officials. He sought to change a basic aspect of Indonesian journalism. Many stories had only one source, the minister of information. "Good journalism," he told me, "should reverse that—one story with many sources." Indonesia, he added, "is a pluralistic, multicultural society. We needed to cover a broad spectrum, not a one-sided one."

Circulation soared, but the publication was banned in 1978 and again in 1986. Katappo was "beheaded" on the threat that the paper would lose its license to publish if he remained on the masthead.

"They banned me, but I had banned them," Katoppo said wryly. "I refused to publish pictures of the top three officials—in one-two-three order—as they appeared each night on state television, and as they once did in the Soviet press. No more ceremonial pictures, only photos of real life: developments in the marketplace, or on the bus. It's a different concept of news. We print it not only because the minister speaks, but we reverse it. Because we print it, the minister must speak out and answer."

Talking with his colleagues it was clear they regarded Katoppo as too advanced for his time. He doesn't deny that discretion is the better part of valor. He finds a certain advantage in being a ghost: "I'm not really here formally," he told me, "so the minister can't fire me again."

I met Katoppo several years later in Jerusalem, and we traveled together to Jordan. He was still a ghost at home but a lively camel rider at Petra, site of magnificent Greco-Roman carvings into rose-colored mountains.

And Indonesia's level of press freedom? In 1999, Suharto was booted out in a coup, his family threatened with loss of great fortunes, and Indonesian journalists set free. Symbolically, *Tempo*, the leading newsmagazine, which had suffered several bans starting in 1996, was allowed to publish immediately.

And Katoppo was no longer a ghost.

35

MAHATHIR MOHAMAD
Prime Minister as Editor

Beside my desk in New York is a poster that states in English, "DON'T JAIL JOURNALISTS!" The same message appears in Malay, Chinese, and two other languages. The editor of the major daily newspaper had given me the poster prepared by the Malaysian journalists' association,

The association asked me to speak to their annual meeting in Kuala Lumpur in 1985 to support their defense against Prime Minister Mahathir Mohamad. The Malaysian journalists were meeting with their counterparts from the other ASEAN countries: Brunei, Indonesia, Philippines, Singapore, and Thailand. It was a time of crisis—an ethnic crisis that could flare into a bitter crackdown on the press.

The government was already hinting at a harsh amendment to the Official Secrets Act. The repressive act had remained from the days of British colonial rule—along with the sparkling golf course and country club I visited, now frequented mainly by the Malay elite and the dwindling British. They were now a colony in their own former colony, though they enjoyed the perquisites of economic if not political power. Full political power was in the hands of the Malays—not the Chinese, whose growing numbers were fast overtaking those of the Malays in the overall population. And in Malaysia, as elsewhere in the Asian Pacific, the overseas Chinese were not only gaining population but economic power as well. The prime minister saw the rising numbers of ethnic Chinese as a threat to the fragile political settlement that enabled the two communities to share the geography, as well as some low-level posts in government. This deal had been fashioned a quarter-century after Chinese Communists terrorized the Malay majority. Fear was still just below the surface.

I sensed this when I met my host, an ethnic Chinese who was the editor of the *Star,* the major opposition daily in the country. He told me, "I come to work every day ready to go to prison. My bag is packed."

The tension was rising as much from the government's ambiguous praise for the role of journalists as from outright threats of new restrictions. The driving force of this tension was the struggle to define the role of the journalist: the Western mode versus the Asian or developing-country model. This struggle was proceeding with more or less fury in a hundred developing nations in Asia, Africa, and Latin America, it was the heart of the decade-long demand through UNESCO for "a new world information and communication order" (NWICO; see chaps. 42 and 43). I was invited to express the Western view. My friend Kaarle Nordenstreng (see chap. 44), head of the Soviet-funded International Organization of Journalists, was there to lend "foreign" support for the Malaysian-ASEAN restrictions known as "guided journalism." The debate in Kuala Lumpur was held in outwardly serene fashion, as befits the Muslim tradition and the unhurried atmosphere in this pleasant climate. The debate, however, mirrored countless overheated struggles for real power, coupled with real threats and just as real violations of rights in Malaysia and elsewhere. There, as in so many places, I had increasing admiration for that Chinese editor whose bag was perpetually packed, pending arrest—for being a journalist!

The head of the ASEAN journalists opened the congress by calling journalists "agents of change" who seek to be "free, independent, and responsible." He left it to politicians to practice their role. This innocuous format in the West was a challenge to authority in Kuala Lumpur, a fact that was immediately revealed by the first speaker, Datuk Musa Hitam, deputy prime minister.

Before he spoke, I met with him briefly. He asked that I be seated next to him at lunch. He was charming and knowledgeable about my views. As he addressed the congress, he used deliberate terms cushioned by polite obeisance to press freedom. He said, "We are leaders, as politicians. So are you, as journalists." But, he added ominously, "In a developing society, leaders lead; in a developed country, leaders are led." This suggested that electoral selection must be replaced by the imposition of leadership from the top in these countries. He temporarily included journalists in the "top," though rarely are they so regarded in developing countries. They are instead oppressed, because it is feared they may become too much the leader.

Musa insisted that ASEAN journalism is fashioned by the historic antecedents of colonial domination. He urged journalists to pay little attention to the blandishments of Western "liberals and progressives" who recommend "their mold" of journalism as best for ASEAN's. He agreed journalists should have "freedom of access to sources, freedom to criticize, and freedom to publish—call these democratic rights"—but they also have responsibilities "to educate, moderate, and restrain the leadership." Rights and responsibilities, he said, are subjective matters and "must be directed to the regional situation that demands ways to overcome the problems of development." Journalists must therefore strike a balance between regional and national interests, as well as between Western rights and ASEAN rights.

Then he became more specific, perhaps with me in mind. "Foreign journalists and observers come here and say 'your journalism is not free.'" But in the ASEAN context, he continued, the journalist needs to assist the development of society. "That," he said, "is the top priority, even over that ideal of democratic rights, if need be." He added, "History shows us that only when stomachs are filled would the people pay attention to and demand—and deserve—this concept of freedom as enumerated by liberals of the West."

I had encountered this argument many times, but not stated so clearly by someone in high position. To this argument I always reply, "History also shows that freedom and development must proceed together, else the country gets neither a full stomach nor political or press freedom."

"The clock is ticking," said Musa, implying progress in a democratic direction. But he warned that the government had to protect itself from agents of Communism, who would use force to shoot down its nascent democracy and replace it with something far more oppressive. Here, in the calm tones of a charming demagogue, he equated the traditional ethnic Chinese in Malaysia with "Chinese Communists." There were few inside the country.

Afterward, in a private session I attended, Musa was asked by a journalist what he could do to help them in the growing tension ignited by the government. "Nothing much," he replied. "You must do it yourself by the way you balance the risks." He was asking these courageous journalists to decide for themselves where the line was drawn between permissive reporting and what may be regarded as inimical to the regime, or worse.

Then another reporter drew a startling response. He said, "This is the first time we've heard that you are sharing power with us." The deputy prime minister replied, "Don't believe it!" He was clearly returning to the ambiguity that pervades the press-government relationship there. A third journalist, alluding to the deputy prime minister's earlier remarks, said, "I like the Western 'mold.' It's my model." The official replied, "That's your problem. I can't help."

The implications of this exchange were understood by my dinner companion, James Clad, bureau chief of the *Far Eastern Economic Review,* the prestigious London weekly. Clad recently published an accurate report of a secret cabinet-level discussion of how the Malaysian prime minister would bargain with the Chinese. Two high-level police visited Clad's home with a search warrant to discover where he secured his information. The Official Secrets Act was invoked, a serious matter. Clad gave only vague answers, saying "many" people had informed him. Clad was the first journalist arrested under the act, which dates to 1950. The British act was toughened in 1984 such that the mandatory life sentence was introduced for espionage (however defined). This new, harsh penalty was part of the motivation for this congress and my appearance. Clad pleaded guilty to avoid further criminal charges and was penalized $4,150. Ten years later, Jim Clad served on my panel in New York to examine our assessment of press freedom worldwide. He had quit the *Review* and was teaching at Georgetown University in Washington,

Jim's plight in 1985 was underscored by Bob Teoh, my Chinese host, who said that press freedom, "as in love, means you can go your own way without saying you're sorry." Not so in Kuala Lumpur, as Prime Minister Mahathir was about to explain. On his side of the argument, as Liew Peng-chuen, editor in chief of the opposition *Star,* told me, were the two annual licenses that newspapers must secure: one for publishing and another for printing. Losing either—for whatever reason—can put the paper out of business, which has happened in the past. The government had been trying to pass licensing of individual journalists, but so far the union had successfully resisted. The clash between press and government caused daily tension. The prime minister was about to address this fact in academic style, but with a clear political threat.

His style, in fact, caught me by surprise. He began by stating that "there never was this individual man, born free, living completely unfettered in isolated splendor." Thus "a code had to be developed and imposed by common consent . . . that could not but restrict individual freedom." Then, an "enforcement authority" was needed. The news media are actors in a human community, he said. But they have become "so powerful a force in fact that kings and presidents bow and scrape" before them.

Then Mahathir came to the heart of his talk. There are, he declared, four basic models of the role of the press: the authoritarian, Communist, libertarian, and social responsibility models. Each system, he said, has its own assumptions, and "none are completely without virtue, not even the Communist model." He added, "none are without flaws . . . not even the libertarian model that so many in the third world, unable to break the shackles of psychological and intellectual neocolonialism, sometimes aspire to with such wide-eyed enthusiasm."

He gave a back-handed jab to the democracies, saying he had "no negative assessments about the curbing of press freedom in Britain and the United States through the introduction of censorship during the First and Second World Wars." It should be "plain to the inventors of the doctrine of 'clear and present danger' [the United States Supreme Court] that [many societies today] have no choice but to do what needs to be done." Yet he declared himself "a firm believer in the greatest freedom consonant with the vital interest of society."

By that last statement, he had placed himself in the company of angels. He snuggled still closer by systematically demolishing authoritarian, Communist, and even libertarian journalism, and embracing the social responsibility model. About this time I began to sense a familiar pattern in Mahathir's text and reasoning. I was impatient to check his words against the popular U.S. volume by Frederick Siebert, Theodore Peterson, and Wilbur Schramm.[1] The prime minister used a major portion of his address to quote—without attribution—the American authors. In other contexts this would be called plagiarism; here, it was political exposition with an academic patina.

He attacked libertarian (Western) journalism because, he said, man is an irrational animal, and even the wisest "have often consistently been led up the garden path." He asked, "Is it right that truth, the whole truth, and nothing but the truth, must always be told, at all times?" History, he said, "is littered with examples where it was justified not to tell the truth." He acknowledged that "the libertarian model in its unremitting advocacy of the adversarial role may be justified in the case of an authoritarian or Communist or evil government." (In which cases libertarians would not be allowed to function!) But, he said, the "basic assumption that government must always be corrupt and evil is also absolute and silly nonsense." He agreed that "power tends to corrupt and absolute power tends to corrupt absolutely" but asked, "by what magical formula is the media itself, with all its awesome power, exempt from this inexorable tendency?" Freedom, too, can corrupt, he added, "and absolute freedom can corrupt absolutely." (Nowhere, of course, is absolute freedom practiced, possible, or advocated. To do so, one would have to eliminate pricing for acquisition of property, payment for labor, and even traffic signals from highways). He charged there is no "free marketplace of ideas in the United States where concentrated power [of the media] is in the hands of a select few." Finally, he termed it a "childlike assumption" that the media will generally, if not always, "adhere to ethical practices and aspire to the public good."

The prime minister then turned to national instability as the most vital part of his argument. "For a society precariously balanced on the razor's edge," he declared, "where one false or even true word can lead to calamity, it is criminal irresponsibility to allow that one word to be uttered." This was a surprising admission that Malaysia was, indeed, "on the razor's edge" of insurgency. The rising economic power of the ethnic Chinese did not suggest a violent uprising; rather, clear competition for the Malays in business and finance.

Mahathir declared social responsibility the best model for the press. He was largely misreading the book. It favored social responsibility, as did the Hutchins Commission twenty years earlier. Both, however, saw press responsibility as *solely* the commitment of the free journalists. They did not suggest a role for government in supervising or monitoring social responsibility of journalism. Indeed, the American critics regarded the assumption of social responsibility of the press essential to avoid future imposition of controls or even influence by government over the news media.

But the prime minister took the academic argument one ominous step further into the political arena. He said the rights of the individual, including the individual journalist, cannot override the rights of society. "It is a question," he added, "of quantitatively and qualitatively balancing the two rights." Then, the key question: "Who is to decide on the balancing of the two rights?" He answered, "In a democratically elected government, it is the task of the democratically elected government." Then he bore down: "So long as the press is conscious of itself as being a potential threat to democracy and consciously limits the exercise of its rights, it should be allowed to function without government interference. But when the press obviously abuses its rights, then democratic governments have a duty to put it to right." A clear directive to the press to continue regular self-censorship.

Almost slyly, the prime minister ended, "Now let us see how this little speech of mine is treated by the media."

The coverage was indeed instructive. The major Malaysian daily, which has significant financial support from individuals in the ruling party, carried four-inch-high front-page headlines over a report that began, "Datuk Seri Dr. Mahathir Mohamad said today the media must be given freedom but stressed that this freedom must be exercised with responsibility." The headline read, "Media Must Act without Prejudice and Malice—Freedom with Responsibility."

The less party-dominated paper, under a five-inch banner headline—"Limits of Press Freedom"—began the story, "Datuk Seri Dr. Mahathir Mohamad assured the press today that it will be allowed to function freely if it conscientiously limits the exercise of its rights and is conscious it is a potential threat to democracy."

The subtle differences in the headlines and reporting were an indication of the partial freedom under which the Malaysian press operates. Both reports were accurate summaries of the prime minister's talk; one stressed press freedom, and the other, press responsibility. The full text was published in the *New Straits Times*, which is strongly influenced by the party. But there was no editorial comment on the speech in either paper—and I was told there would be none. Too risky.

I took the opportunity the next day of responding to the prime minister. My remarks were not published in the *Times* but did appear in the *Star*, the less government-dominated paper. I welcomed the prime minister's discussion of the classic four models of the press and said,

> I have long favored the social responsibility model—but with a difference: Social responsibility, by definition, involves the responsibility of the journalist to *society*, not the government. The government is in no less need of watching than other organs of society. The watchers over the press, to answer the prime minister, are a more diversified press and an informed citizenry—both of which will monitor press infractions. To expect government to monitor the press—any government, even the most democratic—is to tip the scale inevitably in favor of government overpowering the press. For only government—not the press—has the power of the police, and the threat of a call in the night. The openness of a free society promises not everlasting truth, but the freedom to pursue it; not absolute freedom, but a balancing of power, particularly brain power. The canons of professional press conduct—based on a social contract with all of society, not just the government—is the surest way to strengthen both democratic government and social stability.

I spoke at an afternoon session, responding to the prime minister. I was quoted in the *Star* the next day. Not a word was carried in the *New Straits Times*, which reported in detail every session of the conference except the one at which I spoke. I was interviewed for the evening news program over government television. I pushed the free-press issue. At the end, the young reporter said she was not sure whether the camera had been taping properly. Apparently, it had not; or something else intervened. Next day, she engaged me in a long conversation about her future in government TV. In addition to content control, there was the problem of racial discrimination. She is an Indian. Her Irish mother contributed the trace of a lilt and an entrancing smile, but skin color obviously set her apart.

Some months later, the prime minister pressed a bill through parliament that toughened the Official Secrets Act. Prison terms were provided for passing "state secrets," which were only loosely defined. Soon afterward, major newspapers were temporarily shut down, and journalists arrested. The *Asian Wall Street Journal* was temporarily banned, and its correspondent expelled. A 1988 amendment to the Printing Press and Publications Act (1984) gave the prime minister "absolute discretion" to ban or restrict the publishing or importation of any publication deemed "likely to alarm public opinion." The minister's decision shall be final and not called into question by any court on any grounds whatsoever. I was quoted in the *New York Times* saying that "the climate for press freedom in the whole [ASEAN] region [had] deteriorated" at that time.

This is the strong arm of "guided journalism," hardly advancing the social responsibility of the journalist. The Malaysian journalists' union, in response, widely circulated posters headlined, "Don't jail journalists!" But they did, and they still do.

Yet, in 2002, Mahathir was warmly received in the White House by President George W. Bush for the prime minister's assistance in the new antiterrorism campaign.

NOTE

1. Fred S. Siebert, Theodore Peterson, and Wilbur Schramm, *Four Theories of the Press: The Authoritarian, Libertarian, Social Responsibility, and Soviet Communist Concepts of What the Press Should Be and Do* (Urbana: University of Illinois Press, 1956).

36

KIM SANG-MAN
Press Freedom, Asian Style

A surprise letter arrived for me in October 1987 from Dr. Kim Sang-Man, publisher of *Dong-A Ilbo* (Far East Daily), then the most prominent daily in South Korea. He said he was reminded of "the support that Freedom House and you personally gave us at *Dong-A Ilbo* when we were striving to maintain our independence and editorial integrity. I cannot tell you how much we valued that vote of confidence, and I think of it often to this day." He invited Marianne and me to visit his country as guests of the newspaper during the spring of 1988—just before the Olympic Games.

Fourteen years earlier, Dr. Kim and *Dong-A Ilbo* had been in desperate shape. Dr. Kim had long resisted the dictatorships of presidents Park Chung-Lee and Chun Doo-Huan. The repressive government in 1974 retaliated for Dr. Kim's editorial resistance. The paper's journalists went on strike to demand the lifting of censorship restrictions and the removal of agents of the Korean Central Intelligence Agency (KCIA) from newspaper offices throughout the country. As a result, Dr. Kim's passport was confiscated, and his movement severely restricted.

I prepared a citation for the Freedom House board, signed by Sen. Margaret Chase Smith (see chap. 48), that drew international attention. Part of that message follows:

> For 54 years, despite periodically grave governmental restrictions of the press, *Dong-A Ilbo* of Seoul has struggled to publish an independent newspaper in Korea. During much of that period—under foreign occupation as well as authoritarian Korean regimes; in war, peace, and the present protracted absence of a formal armistice with the North—*Dong-A Ilbo* has sought to inform the citizenry, strengthen democratic reforms of government, and enhance the cultural development of the Korean people. *Dong-A Ilbo* was singularly suppressed. . . .

in 1920, for criticizing the government-general and rousing its countrymen; in 1922, for attacking press controls; in 1936, for opposing the Japanese occupation's press laws; and in 1955, for resisting the Syngman Rhee regime's reprisals against the press. . . . *Dong-A Ilbo*, its publisher, Kim Sang-Man, and its enlightened editorial staff are again reflecting the highest universal traditions of journalism.

Following this protest President Park withdrew the KCIA but ordered a complete commercial boycott of *Dong-A Ilbo*. This created a severe financial crisis. The paper appealed to readers and drew a remarkable response. Thousands of factory workers, taxi drivers, and ordinary readers bought advertising space to help the paper survive. That year of travail, Great Britain—where Dr. Kim had earned his graduate degree at the London School of Economics—awarded him the title of honorary Commander of the British Empire. Several years later, when his paper was again under ferocious attack, Queen Elizabeth made him the first Korean Knight of the British Empire.

The paper was in trouble again in 1980. Several of his reporters who had protested against martial-law censorship were summarily dismissed by President Chun in the name of "social purification." Dr. Kim found many of these reporters jobs in a special "research department." They are now among South Korea's most respected editors and columnists.

Our first morning in Seoul, that spring day in 1988, we met with Kim Sang-Man in his office. He was eighty then and still worked from ten to six every day. We had not met since Oslo many years earlier. Then, he and his paper were under the gun from an oppressive government. I recalled that he had come to Oslo with a secretly written account of the repression, but asked someone not from South Korea to report orally on his government's press controls. Such actions resulted in his passport being confiscated by Seoul authorities. But Dr. Kim's acts at home over the years had a cumulative positive effect.

His paneled office had large leather chairs and was dominated by a larger-than-life portrait of Dr. Kim's father, the founder of the paper. Tea was served almost immediately. I described my visit earlier that morning with South Korea's new minister of information, a report that clearly pleased Dr. Kim.

Chung Han Mo was minister of culture as well as information. I had the impression he was far more interested in art and literature than in the newspaper business. He was himself a poet—the first academic to hold that post; usually it had been filled by an ex-journalist turned censor. That change in itself was a good sign for South Korean journalism. Chung said he had great respect for Freedom House. He hoped we would continue to watch political developments, because much was happening there, quickly. That year, he said, began a new era, turning from reconstruction to a democratic future. I noted that in the National Assembly elections earlier that week the party of President Roh Tae Woo (and the information minister) lost control of the legislature to several opposition parties. There were now four "ruling parties," he said, and that was good because "we must build a consensus."

I said I believed a free press could play an important role in this. Not just the legislative change, but his appointment, he said, signified a complete separation of government from the newspapers. I asked whether the "guidelines" system still was operating. Under previous regimes, the ministry would put on paper for its own personnel instructions to be relayed to the newspapers for covering or not covering certain stories or for slanting some in accordance with government policies. These guides were not given to the press but were phoned to editors. The year before, one dissident censor leaked the contents of these guides and was sentenced to a year and a half in prison. I had with me copies of many of these guides. The minister told me that since President Roh's declaration of democratic development the previous June there had been no such guides issued to the press. I checked this later with the president of *Dong-A Ilbo*, who had frequently received such calls in the past. He confirmed that only one call had been made since June 29—and that, he said, was advice from the ministry that the newspaper's ad for a political party violated the election law. *Dong-A Ilbo*'s lawyers decided this was true and pulled the ad.

Now, said the minister, it is the media's responsibility to fashion its own role. He asked what Freedom House had to say about the news media serving the society responsibly. "Shouldn't you watch whether the press violates human rights?" he asked explicitly. I said we are aware, and state so frequently, that responsible journalism is the other side of the coin of press freedom. The individual journalist must be aware of this and must act with professional integrity to serve the society. The primary function of press freedom, after all, is to ensure that citizens have accurate news and information, as well as access to diverse views. But this can not be regulated by government without destroying the freedom inherent in responsible journalism.

He said he was reassured by this statement and added that another democratizing factor was the unionization of reporters and the pressroom staffs. I recalled that an earlier government ordered seven hundred journalists fired, and most never got their jobs back. Some of these men were now establishing new papers that would compete with *Dong-A Ilbo*. When I discussed this with that paper's managing editor, he said he could not have held the jobs open all those years while the men were blacklisted. The minister said that some twenty new papers were being registered and that registration was now merely a formality and did not affect the content of the papers. *Dong-A Ilbo*'s editor told me, "We'll see how this affects us." I had the feeling that *Dong-A Ilbo*, with an established, solid tradition and exclusive publication rights to *New York Times*, *Times* of London, and other features, would hold its large audience. It was important that South Korea had dropped press licensing as a content-control mechanism.

Dr. Kim was pleased to hear this report. He said there had indeed been a distinct improvement in press-government relations. We talked about problems that publishers face elsewhere in the world. He recalled the bad time he had in 1974 and pointed across the room. There, in prominent display, was the glass-enclosed Freedom House citation, the letter I had written, and Dr. Kim's response. They were set in a large, three-section frame. I discovered later that the citation and my letter were reproduced in a glossy promotional brochure describing the progress and history of *Dong-A Ilbo*.

I was taken through the plant just as the presses started rolling for the first edition for that day. The paper was sixty-seven years old. Dr. Kim's father, Kim Songu, the founder, was also vice president of South Korea under Syngman Rhee but then broke with him and left the government. The newspaper building was one of the few structures in Seoul not destroyed during the war in the 1950s. The forty-year-old presses still functioned, and all type was hand-set. The Korean alphabet has twenty-four characters but many variations. I saw batteries of type-setters plucking metal letters from the traditional wooden type cases. *Dong-A Ilbo* would soon skip the "hot" linotype process, however, and go directly to "cold" computer typesetting; the coming competition from new dailies had probably spurred the changes. It was amazing to see how fast the paper was being assembled under archaic printing conditions. It took some seven hundred employees to turn out the paper.

We were driven to the Inchon Memorial House, built by Kim Songsu. As with most prominent men of his time, out of respect his real name was never spoken. Instead, his pen name, Inchon, the name of the second-largest city, was used. The memorial house had traditional Korean architecture, with slanted roofs held by large bamboo-like struts. Typical floral designs and animal objects were crafted into the corners of the roofing. The house had wooden panels and narrow platforms above ground on all sides. Inside, each room was small and low with exquisite furnishings, hand-painted screens, elaborate hangings, and tea services. There was, most important and valuable, a wall-sized map about ten feet square, acquired by Dr. Kim. This map was a national treasure.

The memorial house was a private building decorated by a loving son, so we felt particularly honored to be led through. In other rooms hung the clothing worn by Kim Songsu, but the only sign in the house of the present Dr. Kim's mother—women were accorded far less stature then—was a photograph of Dr. Kim's father and mother together. There were also photos and a sculpture of the grandfather in traditional dress; the sculpture stood in a beautifully landscaped garden near a bronze of the present Dr. Kim's father (depicted wearing a business suit). The contrast of the two statutes was striking. One photo in the house, about five feet wide, showed the father's state funeral. The cortege was surrounded by thousands of people lining the streets. I was again surprised to discover, in a prominent part of that room housing memorabilia, a framed copy of the Freedom House citation, my letter, and Dr. Kim's response.

After a two-hour pause, we went to dinner with Dr. Kim and James R. Lilley, the U.S. ambassador to South Korea (with an editor, there were five at our table).

The ambassador spoke of the week's election. He admitted that neither he nor his political section had predicted the result accurately. Nor had the journalists present. Clearly, the voters kept their intentions well hidden until they entered the voting booths. Then they divided power between the ruling party and the legislature. Not much different from the situation in the United States then.

The ambassador regarded that week's election as historic and as likely to speed the move toward democracy there; he was correct. He faulted the U.S. press, particularly the Associated Press correspondent, for interpreting the success of the opposition parties as likely to lead to chaos. Instead, said the ambassador, it was democracy.

I said that when I was last there, fourteen years earlier, I saw a developing country, and now it had developed; fourteen years from now, I said, we would find it a developed democracy. The ambassador responded, "Four years would be more like it." In 1989, the Freedom House survey of political rights and civil liberties for the first time called South Korea "free." (By comparison, the 2002 survey called the country "free" though beset by a sputtering economy, corruption scandals involving top government officials, and a lack of progress in relations with bellicose North Korea.")

Ambassador Lilley said he greatly admired the Freedom House–sponsored book *Big Story: How the American Press and Television Reported and Interpreted the Crisis of Tet 1968 in Vietnam and Washington.*[1] He liked it because it revealed the damaging misperceptions and, in some cases, the ideological preconceptions of reporters. He knew the author, Peter Braestrup, from their time in Laos together. I mentioned Ambassador William Sullivan, with whom I had gone to China, because Bill had been the top diplomat in Laos. Ambassador Lilley was Bill's deputy in Laos and served in China for two years with the elder George Bush, when he headed the first U.S. post there after the Nixon "opening." Lilley was at Yale with Bush, though three years behind him.

He was interested in my meeting with the information minister, and wondered whether I had discussed the Olympics with him. This was after I said it would be important for South Korea to prepare for the influx of television and other media people—not so much for the period after the games begin, but in the week or so beforehand. That is when the cameras would be in place, the big-time correspondents arriving, and the networks committed to highly expensive daily feeds. They would look for hard, spot news, I said. Chances are, they would seek political controversy, particularly student demonstrations, and they would doubtless be provided. I suggested that someone should prepare in advance to provide a series of broadcast ideas of a positive nature. Recent political developments would certainly qualify, along with rich cultural-historical material. At that point the ambassador wondered whether I had mentioned this to the minister. I hadn't, but maybe the ambassador would.

The ambassador said several times he had resisted strong appeals from the State Department to show U.S. support for one of the South Korean opposition leaders. He did not do so, saying that this was something for the South Koreans to work out. I told him what Jimmy Carter had said when I was in Atlanta earlier—that as president, Carter had gotten Kim Dae Jung, then a major dissident and later a legislative leader, freed from prison and a possible long-term sentence. Carter mentioned this as an example of the successful use of quiet diplomacy (a tool he derided as insufficient when promoted by the Reagan administration). The ambassador said Carter's version of Kim's release was no more accurate than the explanation the Reagan staff had given for the same man's release to come to the United States. Actually, the ambassador said, the Koreans decided to send Kim Dae Jung off to the United States to reduce the man's irritation quotient at home.

Years later, in 1995, future president Kim Dae Jung invited me to Seoul to participate in the creation of an organization called the Forum of Democratic Leaders (FDL) in the Asia-Pacific. The FDL attracted several hundred former heads of state, ex–foreign ministers, and other big-name personalities from the Asia-Pacific region, as well as a few from other regions. This was to gain the international spotlight for Kim Dae Jung shortly after he lost a run for the presidency of South Korea.

I spoke at one session on news media issues in the region. I probably irritated many in the audience: I described the criteria we use to determine the level of press freedom in a country. I stated that most Asian countries had partly free, not free, news media. There was a stirring in the seats. Most of the audience came from places I regard as having partly free news media. Several questioned my assessment by saying that they were free to complain in their countries. I pointed out that those complaints against their governments's press policies made them better than not free but still not completely free. The point seemed to satisfy, eventually. I was strongly supported by Emily Lau, legislative counselor of Hong Kong, who described dramatically the steps already being taken to rein in the free news media in Hong Kong in anticipation of the takeover of the Chinese government in 1997.

I had the opportunity at this conference to chat again with Raul Manglapus (see next chapter), former foreign minister of the Philippines, the real organizer of this meeting, along with the former president of the Philippines, Corazon C. Aquino, as well as former president Oscar Arias Sanchez of Costa Rica. Arias had spoken at a conference I ran in his capital. Freedom House was helpful to him years later, when he mediated the road to peace in Central America, for which he was awarded the Nobel Peace Prize.

Before a second annual meeting of the FDL could be held—to which I was again invited—the political system of South Korea burst wide open. There were charges of great scandals and corruption in high places, and former presidents and other leaders were implicated. The second FDL conference was held in 1996 in Manila, where I spoke on ways nongovernmental organizations can help bring down the dictatorial regime in Myanmar (Burma). In 1998, Kim Dae Jung, who had barely missed execution years earlier, was elected president of South Korea and began a sweeping reform of the government. His creation of the FDL had played some role in his ascendancy to power.

On Dr. Kim Sang-Man's twenty-nine-event schedule for Marianne and me, we went to the Changdok Palace and Secret Gardens, the largest of the three palaces remaining in Seoul. In one small part of this palace two widows of former kings still resided; one was eighty-seven, the other ninety. The fabled past was not all that far behind and remained quite real. The widows had thirty servants to care for them at government expense; one occasionally took part in a public ceremony; otherwise, they were seldom seen. We walked through the vast grounds. Flowering trees were beginning to bloom. Nothing but open space remained inside the palace, however. Some furnishings had been taken to museums, but the rest had disappeared. One imagined that the North Korean occupation of Seoul in the 1950s destroyed or removed whatever was left. Similarly, much of the real treasures of Beijing and other parts of China were carried with Chiang Kai-shek to Taiwan when he left the mainland (museums in Taipei testify to this). And, of course, Hitler raided the museums and private art treasures of Europe and took them to Germany. Many of these priceless pieces later were transferred by the Soviets to Moscow and Leningrad.

This was a memorable visit, not just because of Dr. Kim's limitless concern for our welfare and interests, but also because this was a turning point in South Korea's postwar history. This was not the beginning of chaos, but of a democratic opening. It belied the contention that economic development had to precede democratic reforms, as was argued then—and still—in Singapore, Malaysia, and wherever authoritarians are afraid to trust people with democratic power. Democracy and economic development can proceed in tandem.

As we prepared to leave South Korea, we received Dr. Kim's farewell visit in our hotel room. He gave us a wall-poster–sized replica of an old Chinese map of Seoul and also handed us, with obvious pride, a book of mounted color photographs taken of Marianne and me when we visited his father's Inchon Memorial several days earlier. The photos showed us examining many of the most important pieces; it was a unique and thoughtful gift. I prepared to give Dr. Kim a hand-carved glass piece from Tiffany we had carried from New York. I made a brief speech about how our appreciation for his hospitality was expressed in this American symbol and its American workmanship. As I was about to hand the statuette to Dr. Kim, Marianne saved me frightful embarrassment. She took the piece and surreptitiously removed a small sticker. I thought it was a price tag. It said, "Made in Japan."

Dr. Kim Sang-Man, KBE, died in 1994 at the age of eighty-four.

Late in 2002, I visited South Korea again to speak under the auspices of the Korea Press Foundation. At that moment, South Korea was in the throes of multiple crises. North Korea had just revealed it was working toward a nuclear capability. The presidential election was about to replace Kim Dae Jung. And the

Korean news media were deeply split over the prosecution the year before of the three most influential publishers on charges of tax evasion. All three had been convicted, served a brief prison term, and were released pending their appeals. They still faced extensive jail sentences.

I was asked to address the issue of press responsibility and the media's relationship with the government. I supported neither the foreign press associations' claim that censorship of criticism of the administration was the reason for the prosecutions, nor the claim of smaller publishers and many in the public that the large publications should be reined in for their biased reporting and dominating circulation tactics.

I recommended creation of a small commission composed of civic leaders of indisputable integrity, drawn from several fields of Korean society, to examine all the relevant charges. Their study should be transparent and their findings fully publicized. I stressed that the tax issues were a legacy of older press-government relationships that have ended. This tax issue should be treated as a special case—as a civil rather than a criminal procedure—because it involved essential news media.

I met personally with publishers and editors of the political left, center, and right, as well as far-left press-reformists and members of the retired correspondents' club.

Most moving, on my final evening I dined with *Dong-A Ilbo*'s senior executive managing director Kim Jaeho, the great-grandson of Kim Songsu. Kim Songsu was prominent in the modernization and democratization of Korea: he created educational institutions and was a prime mover in the civic reform movement, as well as the father of the daily newspaper. He fought the Japanese occupation and led the movement advancing cultural nationalism.

His son, my friend Kim Sang-Man, had consolidated *Dong-A Ilbo* and fought the Korean military oppressors. In turn, his son, Kim Byung-Kwan, moved the newspaper's office to a new high-rise building in central Seoul and established a museum on the history of the Korean press and *Dong-A Ilbo*. In 2001, Kim Byung-Kwan was indicted and convicted of tax evasion and spent time in prison pending his appeal. His wife committed suicide shortly before I met their son Kim Jaeho. It was a tragic moment in South Korea's modern history.

I met privately with President Kim Dae Jung in the magnificent Blue House, the presidential offices and living quarters. He spoke frankly, somewhat emotionally, of his decision to prosecute. He said his predecessor had uncovered the tax evasions but did not prosecute. He told me that his conscience and his sense of official duty could not allow him to ignore the audits.

It was indeed, a multiple tragedy. Two of the president's sons had just been convicted and faced prison terms for bribery.

South Korea was in the throes of a traumatic, divisive domestic crisis exacerbated by the nuclear threat from the North. "Reformists" called for laws to ensure "balanced reporting" and an end to press-circulation wars—a formula for new press controls. The president had rejected that approach, he told me. But corruption had clearly been dealt a major blow; once the turmoil ended, a stronger South Korean democracy seemed likely.

NOTE

1. Peter Braestrup, *Big Story: How the American Press and Television Reported and Interpreted the Crisis of Tet 1968 in Vietnam and Washington*, with an introduction by Leonard R. Sussman, 2 vols. (Boulder, CO: Westview Press, 1977).

37

RAUL MANGLAPUS
From Correspondent to Foreign Minister

P hysical appearance can be deceptive. There was no mistaking General
Douglas MacArthur, even in adversity during World War II. He was tall,
angular-jawed, crisp of speech. And when he returned to the Philippines after the
Japanese had tortured his troops, forcing him to fight his way back, he was every
inch the certified hero.

Not so Raul Manglapus. He was just over five feet, trim, soft-spoken, not
quickly recognizable as having heroic potential. Yet Raul may have adopted
some of MacArthur's qualities while serving as a war correspondent at the general's headquarters in the Pacific. Raul, too, had had life-threatening experiences
at the hands of the wartime Japanese.

When they attacked his country, the Philippines, Raul Manglapus left law
school and joined the American armed forces as a broadcaster. He was imprisoned by the Japanese in 1942 and escaped two years later. He joined Hunter's
Guerrillas, attached to the U.S. Eleventh Airborne Division, where he served as
captain, and then at MacArthur's headquarters. He covered the Japanese sur-
render to MacArthur aboard the USS *Missouri* in Tokyo Bay.

Well before Raul and I met under less than heroic circumstances, he had
made a notable mark in the Asian region and in his own country. After the war,
he was driven by the possibilities for democratizing his homeland as well as the
Pacific rim. He became secretary-general of the founding conference of the
Southeast Asia Treaty Organization (SEATO), which was to be the NATO of
Asia. The following year, he was vice chairman of the Philippine delegation to
the Asian-African Conference at Bandung, Indonesia, which was the founding of
the nonaligned movement.

That hardly became a path to democratization, though it did provide a mouthpiece for what later came to be known as the third world. Sadly, it was "nonaligned" only in its anti-American, anti-Western politics, never in opposition to the Soviet Union's policies in the bipolar Cold War. Raul would say that America could take care of itself, but the weak developing countries could not. They had to play the best game they could manage. What may have seemed best for them, however, could be counterproductive in the longer run.

Raul was pragmatic and energetic. At thirty-seven, he became the youngest secretary of foreign affairs in Philippine history. He won a Senate seat with a record number of votes and was named most outstanding senator for two consecutive years. After leading the senatorial list six years later he was chosen as a delegate to the constitutional convention and became leader of the Progressive Party and later of the Christian Social Movement.

I was attracted to Raul because he sought to blend the highest spirit of the traditional world with the tested democratic implements of developed, industrial lands. When Ferdinand Marcos made political freedom untenable in the Philippines, Raul Manglapus escaped once again—this time to America, and to meetings with me at Freedom House.

We discussed ways Raul could make his anti-Marcos voice heard even at a time when American policy supported the status quo in the Philippines. The long-established U.S. military bases in the Philippines were a great influence on American policy there and throughout the Asian-Pacific region; it was unthinkable that U.S. naval forces should be withdrawn from that vital area. Marcos played this card successfully. His corruption and violations of human rights were swept aside by Washington in the interest of sustaining naval power. It would be argued that American military strength, especially in the face of implicit Soviet threats, was an indirect support for the stability of the region, and therefore even in the long-term interest of assuring human rights. Manglapus did not accept that argument. As a Philippine nationalist he wanted the United States out of the bases, but with strong economic ties between the two countries. Then he foresaw unencumbered friendly relations.

I could understand his nationalist view. But I believed this was shortsighted in a bipolar world in which neither of the two superpowers would understand or accept a Philippines that did not demonstrate "nonaligned" positions that disfavored them.

As Raul formed the anti-Marcos Movement for a Free Philippines I introduced him to other émigrés fighting despots in their homelands from sanctuaries in America. Raul found eminent sanctuary teaching at Cornell University and American University, doing research at the Carnegie Endowment for International Peace, running a development-policy center in Washington, and accepting a fellowship at Harvard.

I arranged a round-the-world trip for Raul that took him to Asia, Africa, Latin America, and parts of the United States. Raul designed the trip to study non-Western democratic traditions—his longtime theme. He sought to demonstrate that it is possible to accommodate traditional culture to the needs of modern societies by enhancing human freedom without the loss of particular mores—economic, social, or political—that distinguish one people from another. I wrote the introduction to and published his book *Will of the People: Original Democracy in Non-Western Societies.*[1] Arthur Schlesinger Jr., historian of the Kennedy administration among others, quotes Raul: "Human rights are not a western discovery." Schlesinger continues, "Perhaps human rights are less culture-bound than some Americans, in an excess of either humility or vanity, like to believe."[2] Or as some Asians such as Lee Kuan Yew of Singapore, Mahathir Mohamad of Malaysia (see chap. 35), and Suharto of Indonesia profess in the name of "Asian values."

Raul returned—rather triumphantly—to the Philippines. Marcos had been ousted by direct action in the election and the streets of Manila, assisted finally by President Ronald Reagan. Then Marcos, too, sought refuge in the United States.

Raul returned by plane, not sloshing through waves on a beach as did Douglas MacArthur. But Raul was quickly acknowledged by the new president, Corazon C. Aquino, who was elected soon after her husband was assassinated on the Manila tarmac as he returned from exile in America. Raul became foreign minister of the Philippines in the Aquino administration. He had dedicated his book "To that 'inexperienced housewife,' Corazon C. Aquino, who has shown the world that democracy is a native human right to be experienced, not a lesson that needs to be learned."

Early in his new post, despite his earlier calls to close U.S. bases in his country, Raul unsuccessfully resisted his administration's effort to end the American presence on the great bases in the Philippines; before Aquino's term was up, U.S. forces had left. Raul also played an active role in bringing together ASEAN countries for greater mutual security. There was some talk of inviting a new American presence after the Cold War ended.

Raul's most ambitious effort once Aquino left power was his leadership (under the direction of Kim Dae Jung, South Korea's opposition leader) in creating the Forum of Democratic Leaders (FDL) in the Asia-Pacific (see previous chapter). On Kim's behalf, Raul invited me to the 1994 inauguration of the FDL in Seoul, South Korea. This was an assembly of internationally known democratic politicians from all parts of the Asia-Pacific region. Most had had key positions in their countries but were now in retirement or in active opposition. The moving spirit was Kim Dae Jung, who had been jailed for his opposition voice in the years before South Korea turned democratic. He had lost a free and fair election the year before, partly, I believe, because he favored—prematurely—movement toward reunification with North Korea.

Other participants included former president Aquino; Nobel laureate Oscar Arias Sanchez of Costa Rica; Sonia Gandhi, widow of the late prime minister of India; and former officials from Malaysia, Mongolia, South Korea, Japan, Russia, Canada, and the United States. I spoke on a panel with an editor from

296 A PASSION FOR FREEDOM

Hong Kong, UNESCO's regional director, and the vice chair of Indonesia's human rights commission.

At the conclusion, a formal structure for the FDL was set in place. At the 1996 follow-up meeting of the FDL in Manila I broached to Raul—now CEO of a national oil company—the topic of a joint Freedom House project for assuring privacy on the Internet in Asia. The Web was becoming the new touchstone of the degree of censorship in a country. In Asia, China, Singapore, Russia, and other governments were restive as their citizens went online and threatened to practice freedom as the Philippines was demonstrating.

Unfortunately, Raul Manglapus died in 1999, just three years later.

NOTES

1. Raul S. Manglapus, *Will of the People: Original Democracy in Non-Western Societies* (New York: Greenwood, 1987).

2. Quoted in Theodore de Barry, "Multiculturalism and Human Rights," *Freedom Review*, March–April 1994, p. 31.

38

SERGEI GRIGORYANTS
From Gulag to Typewriter

It was easy for the plainclothes police to observe the activity outside the isolated apartment building on the perimeter of Moscow. This was the summer of 1987. Mikhail Gorbachev was still running a centrally controlled Communist state. He was trying, however, to loosen some bonds so that economic progress, desperately needed for an increasingly restive people, could proceed. My son Mark and I were there to observe a major test of Gorbachev's *glasnost*, Russian for "openness." It would come through the courage of a slightly built, deeply serious, and committed man, Sergei Grigoryants, just released after ten years in the dreaded gulag, convicted on trumped-up charges for expressing his opinions. To come to Grigoryants's apartment Western reporters had to leave their own ghetto to converge on this small flat where Grigoryants would launch—in his words—"the most important magazine created in the Soviet Union since 1918."

It was 4:00 P.M. on Friday, July 3. Mark and I had just attended a Fourth of July celebration at Spaso House, residence of the U.S. ambassador. Former president Jimmy Carter had left the house earlier to make favorable comments about Gorbachev. The most "humanitarian" of today's world leaders, Carter had called him. Elsewhere in Moscow, Vernon Walters, U.S. ambassador to the United Nations, was discussing ways to cool the Iran-Iraq war. And in and out of the Kremlin came Prime Minister Gandhi of India on an elaborate state visit, to be followed by President von Weizacker of West Germany.

Perhaps the most important event of that day, however, was in the toughened hands of Grigoryants, a prison-scarred literary critic who released the first copies of a magazine significantly named *Glasnost*, after the current Gorbachev policy. Grigoryants held up a copy of the fifty-five-page publication, which had been hand-typed, single-spaced, on onionskin paper. Fifty copies were laboriously made using carbon paper. This was the main "press run." Yet it was an important moment—for Gorbachev as well as for Grigoryants and his thirty writer-colleagues. The significance of *Glasnost*, the magazine, could have been seen in the bitterly courageous life of Grigoryants and the tenuous hope posed by the present policy of glasnost. All of this converged in that crowded room of reporters. Below is a timeline of events in that year that led to the publication of Grigoryants's journal.

February 7, 1987: Sergei Grigoryants was released from Christopol prison after serving 3½ years for writing *samizdat* (unauthorized publications). Freedom House, for many years, had published his *samizdat*—sometimes these messages arrived scrawled in tiny letters on toilet paper. Vestiges of Grigoryants's recent hunger strike could still be seen in July in his sunken eyes and general pallor, though his vigor and determination were no less obvious.

At the university in the late 1960s he had made "bad friends," in the words of his first prosecutor. Those friends were Andrei Sinyavsky and Yuli Daniel, the first writers who had been imprisoned for sending their books to the West to be published. Grigoryants, too, served his first of three harsh prison terms then.

Returning home in February, however, was different. Gorbachev promised a new opening to further *perestroika* ("restructuring" of the economy). The production and distribution system of the massive nation had all but failed. In an age of high technology, the Soviet Union was unable to move beyond the stage of lesser development. Though a military superpower, the USSR seemed destined to become a vast third world country for most of its 280 million citizens. The policy of glasnost was not to introduce Western-style democracy but to loosen the reins so that public discussion and even limited criticism of domestic policies could support the changes in the economy and the mindset of Soviet citizens— all needed to raise productivity.

April 19: Grigoryants and his friends regarded glasnost as a historic opportunity to democratize the writing and eventually the thinking of Soviet citizens. He would create a magazine that would not be *samizdat* but an openly published, officially authorized periodical.

In Paris, Alexandr Ginzburg heard about the plan. He, too, in 1966 had involved himself in the fate of Sinyavsky and Daniel by protesting their arrest. By then, Ginzburg had already served time in prison for editing an underground publication called *Sintaksis*. Two years later he was rearrested for publishing his "white paper" on the Sinyavsky-Daniel case. We at Freedom House supported Ginzburg by drawing international attention to his plight. At his trial, a codefendant falsely implicated him in illegal activity. Ginzburg then spoke words that made his case widely known in the West: "A patriot should be ready to die for his native land, but not lie for it."

Ginzburg was, of course, convicted—all accused were. That touched off the "year of human rights" among dissenters in the Soviet Union. The sentencing of Ginzburg politicized the "cultural opposition." In time, this aroused further attention in the West. Finally, in 1979, Ginzburg and several other dissidents were traded for two Soviet spies. He took up residence in the West, occasionally visiting us at Freedom House. He continued to support efforts of other Soviet dissidents striving for openness in their homeland. No surprise, then, that Ginzburg greeted warmly the report that a new form of writing was developing inside the USSR: a magazine of commentary and documentation that, for the first time, would be independent and yet seek official authorization.

June 19: The twenty to thirty men and women around Grigoryants worked steadily to devise the format of *Glasnost*, a direct link to the policy of Gorbachev, yet a challenge to it. Their most important decision was to print openly and seek official approval for publishing. They decided that Gorbachev's policy could become successful only if all citizens could write "the truth about life in their society," particularly those who had already spoken and written the truth "despite prohibitions and repressions." They acknowledged it was "not so simple" that there was "active resistance from those in the political and economic apparatus who have brought the nation, directly or indirectly, to this 'precrisis' situation."

The first editorial would spotlight those who "continued to occupy numerous key positions [and who] actively stand in the way of restructuring." The editors noted, "We are aware of the danger of acting, but inaction is intolerable." On this day, therefore, Grigoryants called a press conference to announce that *Glasnost* was being sent to the Central Committee of the Communist Party. He asked formally for permission to publish and attached the text of commentary and documentation. That began an extraordinary sequence of events.

There was no abusive response, as in the days of Sinyavsky and Daniel. Instead, Aleksandr N. Yakovlev, second in command to Gorbachev, passed the request to a Kremlin deputy for agitprop (agitation and propaganda). Years later, I was to write extensively about Yakovlev, who had come to the United States on an exchange fellowship funded by the Fulbright program. Indeed, when I interviewed Senator Fulbright he repeatedly mentioned Yakovlev as a model of the Fulbright academic exchanges. Yakovlev was not only at the seat of power in the Kremlin but also often demonstrated a liberating policy that was then unusual in Moscow. Indeed, Yakovlev was credited with persuading Gorbachev to release the world-renowned human rights activist Andrei Sakharov from internal exile and return him to his home in Moscow. I met Sakharov at his apartment in Moscow shortly before he died.

The agitprop man turned over Grigoryants's request to his deputy, who handled press matters. In the days following, after his repeated phone calls, Grigoryants told me, they treated the request with benign bureaucratic silence. That was a far cry from the official response, which until recently would have been a three-year term in a work camp.

June 27: When no official response came, Grigoryants called another press conference to announce they would begin releasing *Glasnost* openly in July whether or not they heard from the Kremlin. This announcement was reported in the Western press. This turned the spotlight on the Kremlin, which wanted a global image of openness and concern for human rights issues.

July 3: Grigoryants issued the first fifty copies of *Glasnost* to a packed room of Western reporters. The official press, though invited, did not attend. One of its representatives phoned and asked a few questions about Grigoryants's literary work, but no one appeared. Many articles were published the next day in the Western press—still, it was felt, a necessary protection for the writers and editors. The editors were quoted as stating that "a large part of the country is biased against official publications," and therefore official acceptance of *Glasnost* would provide "serious evidence" that "democratization is beginning to take place."

July 6: Mark and I interviewed Grigoryants in his apartment with only a translator friend present. It was a relaxed afternoon; Grigoryants made tea and served thickly sliced ham and cheese, apologizing for the hard black bread. It was clear that this was an important time for one who spent ten years in various prisons, had left the last one only five months earlier, and yet was energetically leading a dispersed group of men and women through an unexplored field. One might expect that keeping such a group together and making decisions acceptable to all would be no easy task. Indeed, there were divisions among the group, and Grigoryants's personality could be abrasive.

He told us he did not know all the contributors across the country. Some were friends of other writers but all, he said, would be specialists in their field. The first number had an article by Andrei Sakharov, as well as discussions of press issues and political pressures. Subsequent issues would include articles on the secret police, demonstrations in Lithuania, Jewish emigration, and problems of the Russian Orthodox Church. Clearly, such subjects did not appear in critical form in official journals.

Grigoryants said he would act the next day to form a "press club." This, he hoped, would be a loose association of dissident writers, former prisoners, official journalists, and Kremlin officials who deal with the press. An utterly clever and idealistic conception! Grigoryants phoned one Kremlin office in advance and was told they would be glad to participate, but the seven invitees were all "on vacation" the day of the "press club." Very polite, very civil.

As the tea was steeped again, Grigoryants spoke more of himself. He began writing in the 1960s and was trained as a specialist in Russian literature. His great-grandfather was a director at La Scala in Milan and had many friends in Italy who were Russian émigrés. Grigoryants studied in the Department of Journalism at the University of Moscow, and wrote literary criticism for *Youth*. He was expelled from the university after his arrest for supporting Sinyavsky and Daniel. He was rearrested in 1975 on a trumped-up charge and spent five years in various camps and prisons. The secret police tried unsuccessfully to persuade him to cooperate with them. He was released in 1980 but three years later was imprisoned again for publishing *V*, which contained information about arrests. He was sentenced to two years in prison, five years in a labor camp, and three years of internal exile. Grigoryants was among the first prisoners released in February 1987 in the Gorbachev amnesty. Secretary of State George Shultz had brought a letter to Gorbachev appealing for Grigroyants's release. He became a "special case," largely the result of international pressure that groups such as Freedom House had generated.

We asked whether the Central Committee would ever grant permission to publish *Glasnost*. He did not know but said it depended on the quality of the publication and the interest it aroused abroad. The magazine did attract international attention. Indeed, Grigoryants was invited shortly afterward to address an international press association meeting in Paris, but the Kremlin refused to grant him a visa to attend.

Clearly, times had not changed completely. Mark and I prepared to leave the Soviet Union. We spent the final evening walking on Red Square. It was almost empty in the dusk, but the red glow in the western sky gave the Kremlin a setting of beauty and mystery. As we walked, we were approached by a small man with a leather briefcase who said he had an important question to put to us: Would we carry to the West a paper he, a scientist, had prepared on the dangers of nuclear power? I said we could not do so. He persisted, saying many lives were at stake. I suggested he take the paper to the U.S. Embassy. He said he didn't know how to approach the embassy. I offered to give him the phone number. He backed off and disappeared. I was certain this had been an effort to plant a document that would be found the next day as we passed through the airport. At that time, our room was bugged, the hotel was under twenty-four-hour surveillance, and one could be certain that local contacts of foreigners were watched.

My fear surfaced the next day. Mark preceded me through the last stage of security checks at the airport and disappeared. I stood alone before the barred window of the uniformed official. He took my passport, looked sternly at me, and examined a large ledger before him. Some minutes passed. Then he picked up the telephone, and engaged in a spirited conversation for another five minutes. I was glad I had not taken with me the first copy of *Glasnost*. Instead, I had left it at the embassy to be forwarded to me in New York. After what seemed a long, tense time, the official took my passport and with great vehemence stamped it and thrust it through the window. I snapped it up and walked to meet Mark and mount the steps of the plane for Paris.

On the way home, Mark and I wrote an op-ed article for the *Wall Street Journal* and published alongside it the full text of Grigoryants's editorial in his first edition.[1] This was the first exposure in the United States of the actual writing in *Glasnost*.

In the months following, with funds provided by the National Endowment for Democracy in Washington, *Glasnost* appeared as a printed magazine with a colorful cover. For several years, Grigoryants provided critical analyses and documentation not found anywhere else. In 1989, he was brought to New Orleans to receive the Golden Pen award of the International Federation of Journalists. He was hailed for providing uncensored journalism in the Soviet Union. My associate, Lucia Thorne, served as interpreter (see chap. 52). No problem with a visa this time.

Times had indeed changed—so much that daily newspapers in the new atmosphere became increasingly critical of domestic policies and eventually of leaders themselves. After a failed coup, Gorbachev was replaced by Boris Yeltsin, who then suffered increasing opposition. The broadcast services remained under general government control, but the press became lively, unpredictable, contentious though still dependent on government or the banks for newsprint and funds to operate. The Russian mafia refined corruption almost into a science. Many Russian journalists were killed or otherwise intimidated—a mark both of their partial independence and their travail.

By 1996, Grigoryants had folded his magazine and replaced it with a foundation that watched the operation of the Russian security apparatus. He now holds conferences and speaks on this sensitive subject; his health has deteriorated. His wife and daughter live in Paris; his son was killed in what was called an accident but probably was an act of vengeance against Grigoryants's independent journalism. He suffers physical pain from hypertension—possibly a form of paranoia. But not without real cause, even in an era of greater openness, but also one of unquestioned turmoil and bitter vindictiveness.

The interpreter for our meeting with Grigoryants and Andrei Sakharov was Yevgeny Yakir. Mark and I were led to him by a mutual friend in New York who knew Yakir as a longtime *refusnik*, a Jew denied permission to emigrate to Israel. When I met Yakir in his tiny Moscow apartment he looked at my card and said, "I know you. I've heard you on the Voice of America."

His story, too, illuminates the horrors of the Soviet Union. Yakir remembers the Stalinst terror: he was six when men burst into the apartment and dragged his mother and father off to prison. His grandmother, watching helplessly, fell into a coma. The child sat for hours, transfixed over the body of his grandmother until neighbors rescued both. Yakir's father and uncle, both military officers, were executed; his mother was imprisoned for ten years; his aunt was sent to her death in the same prison; and, much later, Yakir's own son, Alexasandr, was taken to a prison camp. He had been released shortly before we met Yakir.

I said tentatively, "Prison has become a family tradition." Yakir said I must understand then why he wanted to emigrate. He had seen too much. He applied in 1974 for permission to go to Israel. As a consequence he was fired from his job as an engineer, and his wife, Rima, deprived of work as a computer programmer. Rima became a cleaning woman in a gymnasium. Yakir made an "unofficial" living repairing tennis racquets. The floor of his small living room was cluttered with racquets to be restrung. Some high officials were among his clients. Despite repeated appeals to emigrate, however, the Yakir family became one of the longest-term refusniks.

They waited fourteen years. When I returned from the Soviet Union I told Max M. Kampelman about the Yakirs. Max, in addition to serving as chair of

Freedom House, was ambassador to the CSCE meetings that stressed human rights. Max assured me he would press Yakir's case. When presidential summits or other high-level diplomatic meetings were held by the Soviets and Americans the U.S. delegation frequently urged their Soviet counterparts to make some human rights gestures. Soon after, September 1987, the Yakir family was granted permission to leave for Israel. The *New York Times* said the release of the Yakirs "appeared to be part of a general Soviet effort to reduce foreign criticism of its human rights record."[2]

NOTES

1. Leonard R. Sussman and Mark J. Sussman, "*Glasnost*, the Magazine, vs. Glasnost, the Policy," *Wall Street Journal*, July 31, 1987.

2. Philip Taubman, "13-Year Wait Ends for Family of Soviet Jews," *New York Times*, September 25, 1987.

39

PAUL ANASTASI AND THE DEATH OF *PRAVDA*

A n international news packet I created led me straight to a Communist-front mystery that took more than ten years to unravel.

Shortly after the National Endowment for Democracy (NED) was funded by Congress, I secured an NED grant to create an international service to reprint and distribute articles to promote democracy. Each week, I sent a packet of articles to several hundred writers and editors in developing countries. The reprints were often republished abroad or served as themes for local articles and editorials.

One regular recipient of this service was Paul Anastasi, the Greek stringer for the *New York Times* and the *Daily Telegraph* of London. We became active correspondents. One day, an urgent phone call came from Paul. He was being sued and needed help. He wanted us to publicize his problem. The *Times* carried a three-paragraph story from Athens, apparently written by Paul, but the newspaper did not want to become involved in the lawsuit.

I decided to publish as much of the story as our mail packets could bear. For many weeks, we described the charges and then the actual proceedings in Athens and later in London, based on telephoned reports from the courthouse. The story: Paul had written a book based on extensive investigative reporting of the clandestine funding of a new, flamboyant Athens tabloid, *Ethnos* (The Nation). Soon after it was launched in 1981, *Ethnos* became the largest-selling daily in Greece. Apart from the color and sparkle of its pages, *Ethnos*'s editorials and news coverage unerringly followed the line set down by *Pravda*, Moscow's Communist guide for the press.

Paul's well-documented book followed the laundered money that moved from the Soviet Union to its press puppet in Athens. This ploy had serious implications far beyond the obvious issue of press freedom, and even the cuckolding of *Ethnos*'s readers. For Greece was a fragile outpost of Western Europe at a still-indecisive period in the Cold War. Clearly, the Kremlin was reenergized after the stagnation of the Brezhnev years. The Soviets were stepping up their challenge to NATO and their support of the European Left. It was increasingly anti-American and favored neutralism. *Ethnos* obediently reflected all this, cleverly masking Moscow's propaganda aims.

Paul's book quickly became a bestseller and caused a scandal that reached high in the Greek government. Many officials were close to the owner of *Ethnos*. Indeed, the Papandreou government was then anti-American and pro-Soviet. The scandal spread to London and Paris, where the *Economist* and *L'Express* carried articles reporting Paul Anastasi's revelation that the KGB, Moscow's secret service, had hired the Greek publisher and his editorial staff and provided the money to publish the tabloid.

With further support from Moscow, *Ethnos*, charging libel, sued Paul Anastasi, *L'Express*, and the *Economist*.

I received a call from the editor of the *Economist* urging more coverage in the United States of the issue. He promised to keep me informed.

At the court proceedings, the Greek government gave overt and covert support to *Ethnos*. Papandreou's people assured the court that *Ethnos* and its staff were good democrats. Officials forced one defense attorney to withdraw during the case, and officials refused to assist Paul when KGB operatives unlawfully bugged the office of the *New York Times/London Telegraph*.

Paul phoned me with the sad news: he had lost the case. But the judges agreed there was something mysterious about *Ethnos*'s funding, even questionable, and its political attitudes seemed odd. Paul's original sentence of two years in prison was reduced to one and was then settled for a monetary fine. Similarly, in London and Paris, *Ethnos* won against the *Economist* and *L'Express*. There seemed to be no "smoking gun" to make an absolute connection between Moscow funds and *Ethnos*'s money and editorials. On the contrary, the accusers, using the KGB's wiretapped conversations, forced the court to hear Paul boast he had "bombshells," new evidence. He called it "the heavy artillery." But that ending fizzled.

Paul was counting on testimony by Yannis Yannikos, a former Greek Communist and guerrilla fighter. Yannikos was ready to say in court that he had been a party to the whole gambit in Moscow. He was originally tapped to be the KGB's key man at *Ethnos* and claimed that he had the idea to set up the tabloid and that he had discussed it with the Kremlin. The KGB went ahead, however, and named a Greek millionaire, George Boboulos, to run the show instead. Obviously, he presented a better "front" than did the old guerrilla fighter. Yannikos, miffed, threatened to defend Paul Anastasi.

Yannikos's description of the actual deal made in Moscow to launch and control *Ethnos* could have been persuasive, but he never testified. A high-level official, sent from Moscow to persuade Yannikos, drew on the old guerrilla's faithful adherence to party discipline. Earlier, it had cost him years in prison, and even a death sentence. Another deal was struck: Yannikos walked away with $625,000. What kept Yannikos off the witness stand in Athens: party discipline or monetary gain?

Apparently both. The KGB mediator promised Yannikos that he would be called on later for similar duty. No one, least of all Yannikos, probably believed that.

But this strange case had an even stranger denouement. Soon after the collapse of the Soviet Union there appeared a short item deep inside the *New York Times*, date-marked Athens. The story said that *Pravda*—the key Russian daily, the newspaper founded by Lenin himself, the mouthpiece of the Communist Party—was near bankruptcy. But a generous benefactor in Greece had rescued it. His name: Yannis Yannikos.

Mel Lasky, my friend and longtime editor of *Encounter* magazine, tells the near-final act. Some relevant confidential documents have been uncovered. Moscow's decision to send millions of dollars to its Greek "agents of influence" was recorded in a high Politburo policy paper, says Lasky, "which bore the signatures of both Chernenko and Gorbachev, the two last heads of the Soviet Empire."

Papandreou was back in the premier's office when this news broke. He was still "helpful," says Lasky, by insisting that he could not "confiscate and return" (as the Yeltsin government had been demanding) the fortune in old "Moscow gold" that had been transferred for KGB operations—since it had been a "private transaction" between the Bolshevik Party in the Soviet Union and nonofficial Greek citizens.

Lasky concludes, "Millions are still swishing around, conveniently usable for old-style active measures and new-style disinformation." But Papandreou would know nothing more. He slipped into a coma and, after a long illness, died—still the premier.

Pravda lingered on. Its readership in 1996 was just over 170,000—down from 11 million. A large statue of Lenin still dominated the entrance to *Pravda*. Its editor, a twenty-year veteran, Aleksandr Ilyin, was heartened by the favorable showing of Communists in the December 1995 election. The day after, a banner headline in the newspaper read: "HOLD FIRM COMMUNISTS!" One Muscovite commented, "I remember that for important job interviews in Soviet times, you were expected not only to have read but memorized that day's editorial in *Pravda*. I hope it won't come to that again."

It would not. On July 30, 1996, *Pravda* died. "Soviet Dinosaur *Pravda* Extinct," front-paged Toronto's *Globe and Mail*. "Owners Pull Plug on Lenin's Oracle," the headline added.

40

HUMBERTO AND GLORIA RUBIN

In Defense of Radio Nanduti

W hile the longtime dictator Gen. Alfredo Stroessner still ruled Paraguay with an iron fist, I was invited to hold a press conference in Asuncion, the capital, to support the leading radio station that the general had shut down two years earlier. Radio Nanduti was built and operated on and off the air by a charming husband-and-wife team, Humberto and Gloria Rubin.

In the language of the indigenous Guarani Indians *nanduti* means "spider web." Humberto became a personal as well as a professional target of the government. His ample physical appearance, sport shirts, and full beard drew vicious caricatures, as well as such references as "that ungrateful Jew." Anti-Semitic catcalls were mixed with other vulgar shots, shrill blasts, and the sounds of gunfire and rocks aimed at Radio Nanduti.

The Rubins were repeatedly threatened with imprisonment by Stroessner's people. I had been helping Radio Nanduti for several years by providing funds that Freedom House secured from the National Endowment for Democracy (NED). The NED was run by Carl Gershman, its first president, who came to the NED after serving for several years on Jeane Kirkpatrick's staff when she was U.S. ambassador to the United Nations. Before that, Carl was on my staff at Freedom House.

I would stop off in Paraguay, en route from Rio de Janeiro to chair a two-day conference in Santiago, Chile, where another dictator, General Augusto Pinochet Ugarte, held forth. Pinochet was about to put his career on the line through a referendum—citizens would vote yes or no for him—that he believed he would win (see next chapter). After all, the economy was strong, and who cared so much about human rights? The news media were mainly under his control, with several significant exceptions. The CIA had poured some money into the leading newspaper to assure "stability" in Chile. The Freedom House conference, flying in the face of current reality, would discuss the democratization of the hemisphere. Significant participants included Patricio Aylwin, the future president of Chile.

Landlocked Paraguay, to the northeast of Chile, was a poorer model of one-man control. It was ironic as I landed in Asuncion to be greeted by a sign in the customs area, "Welcome to the land of peace and prosperity." A three-year state of siege had just been lifted. I was met by a U.S. embassy representative, the former Paraguayan ambassador to Washington, and Humberto Rubin. I gave an impromptu interview to four press people, who asked how I rated press freedom in Paraguay and, say, Marxist-controlled Nicaragua. I said it was strange that a Marxist-Leninist state such as Nicaragua could permit oppositionist *La Prensa* and Radio Catholica to operate while here *ABC Color*, the most important independent press, and Radio Nanduti, the most critical radio, had been shut down. These tapes were played and replayed on the radio, in English and Spanish. A few feet off, a camera flashed. It was the secret police taking pictures of the scene. I met them later under less pleasant circumstances.

The Paraguayan constitution was an advance model for some press laws passed after the Cold War in Eastern and Central Europe, and the former Soviet states. The Paraguayan constitution states, "Freedom of thought and of opinion are guaranteed on equal terms to all inhabitants of the republic." It continues, however, "It is forbidden to preach hatred or class struggle." Then the other shoe drops: "Press organs lacking responsible direction shall not be permitted." That was used to silence dissent; one to six years in prison could result.

Humberto and Gloria Rubin were personally popular, highly sophisticated broadcasters. They interspersed daily radio schedules of mainly entertainment shows with gutsy news and opinion programs, which attracted the largest audiences in the country. Humberto was arrested in 1984 and again the next year, and he was threatened with expulsion from the country. In April 1986, a mob of fifty government sympathizers attacked the radio station with stones and shot firearms, breaking most of the outside windows. When I arrived, I saw the debris and the bulletholes in the facade. The government had also created radio interference that was loud enough to drown out 90 percent of Nanduti's broadcasts. With the station near bankruptcy, I was asked to come down and help.

A widely publicized press conference had been scheduled for me at 6:00 P.M. at the sizeable studio-auditorium of Radio Nanduti. I decided to make an early foray to the station. It formerly employed seventy people, but now only twenty could be retained. They were mainly engaged in transcribing tapes going back twenty years to provide a record of press-freedom violations in Paraguay. Freedom House funding paid for part of this project. Government agents had sabotaged the broadcast equipment. I brought to Asuncion the replacement for a stolen element used by the government that enabled it to reply on the air whenever Humberto made a statement the Stroessner people didn't approve. They simply tied into his frequency. They called him a Communist and his wife a homosexual—not a very sophisticated attack, and utterly without foundation.

I visited the auditorium that seated more than 250 persons. A large banner across the stage declared, "You may have this meeting . . . [but] no one may attend." That was the official catch-22 decision regarding my press conference. Nanduti people could enter the building with their IDs, but no one else. They could not broadcast, of course, but they could put on a "meeting"—but no one could come!

We drove up in a taxi at about 4:30, and the three of us walked quickly into the building. Five armed police were chatting across the street. Within minutes one guard with a walkie-talkie summoned others. They blocked off the entrance to the street from the avenue and remained in position while others came up to the building door and blocked the entrance.

We remained inside and took phone calls from journalists and other radio stations. They wanted to know whether the press conference was still scheduled; we said it was. As we chatted in Humberto's office, another radio station carried my airport interview in Spanish and English. A few minutes before 6:00 the Catholic radio station carried a live report from its reporter in a car driving toward Nanduti. He described the ban and said he was now six blocks from the station, and still driving. He pulled up in front, was held back, and described his bout with the military on the air. And then they played my airport interview again in both languages.

Just then, Jack Martin from the U.S. embassy appeared outside Nanduti, angrily demanding to see me. I photographed him. He saw me, but the police did not. Later he said he couldn't believe his diplomatic credentials were not respected. The soldier told him, "My orders are to keep everyone out." When Jack told him I was inside, the soldier said that was a mistake, and the officer concerned would be reprimanded. Meanwhile, I did several interviews by telephone from Nanduti.

I tried to leave Nanduti to go to the hotel where the press conference had been rescheduled, but I was detained by troops. They covered the entire visible area. They took my passport and demanded other identification. I showed them my Freedom House card. "Casa de la Libertad" had been mentioned repeatedly all day on radio. The soldier examined me suspiciously for some time. I did not know what would happen next. The soldier finally returned my card and passport and made an ominous sound, which I was told was mainly for the benefit of my translator, a Paraguayan citizen with a history of torture inside police headquarters.

I held the conference at my hotel. We taped an hour-long interview. I spoke of the methods of press control in many places, which reflected the rulers' lack of faith in their people. Among the correspondents was the man from EFE, the wire service of Spain that serves all of Latin America. His report that I had been detained was published in Chile, where Freedom House staffers were awaiting my arrival next day. They worried, not knowing I had been released. At that moment, I was at dinner in Asuncion with Aldo Zucolillo, owner of *ABC Color*, whose paper was still banned. The BBC correspondent served as interpreter. She regarded my incident as significant for the transition from the absolutist control of General Stroessner.

This was a thoroughly corrupt and corrupting society, but most people knew it. Stroessner ran a mafia-type organization. He would tell a colonel after many years' service to become a farmer. Although the man may not want to farm, Stroessner commands it. The man gets a government loan, buys the land, uses soldiers as indentured workers—and is a farmer. Another man may have "family problems"—his income has dwindled. Stroessner makes him a border control officer, where he can extort money at will and recoup his losses. The system worked two ways: you did Stroessner's bidding, and he granted plums to help you when you needed it. The basic law enabled an officer to earn money on the side. But another law said that if an officer did something that irritated the commander in chief, the man could be court-martialed. Similarly, trade unions were licensed by Stroessner so that they could be used against big business if needed, and vice versa.

But perhaps the most important factor was Stroessner's dependence on Brazil. As I saw from the air, the great dam at Itaipu is a major boon to Brazil. The hydroelectric potential is enormous. The dam, at the confluence of the Paraguay and Parana rivers, is six times the size of the Aswan dam that the Soviets built for Egypt on the Nile. The power generated there goes overwhelmingly to Brazil. Moreover, the river, which winds hundreds of miles across Brazil, is Paraguay's sole link to the ocean. There is a free port on the Atlantic for Paraguayan traffic; if that were closed and the bridge removed, Paraguay would be entirely landlocked and would wither economically.

I tried to speak to the interior minister but was refused. Stroessner's people were disconcerted by President Reagan's reference to the general as a dictator. They had expected that from Jimmy Carter, but not Reagan. The U.S. ambassador was almost unwelcome. Several generals were high on the list of drug-trade accomplices, but Washington's demand for their extradition would be refused.

I went to the building of *ABC Color* with its owner. He was refused entry, despite word the day before at a meeting with Stroessner that the ban would be lifted. The evening paper appeared with a three-column story and a photo. The caption read, "Leonard Sussman, executive director of Freedom House (Casa de la Libertad), of the U.S., at the moment when he is queried by the police about his documents, though he was not able to enter the radio station."

The next day, I rode beside my interpreter in a taxi to Nanduti. The driver called our destination "the police nest." When we stopped at a traffic light, an unidentified driver in another car shouted, "Keep it up!" We passed the police station where my interpreter had been tortured. He said, "Funny, I don't mind passing this any longer. I used to avoid it." We passed a man reading a newspaper on the street corner. "That's a secret policeman," said the interpreter. I said it must be strange to meet your torturer like this. He said, "Many people pass their torturers and say nothing. That's their problem. Too little civic education. We haven't had democracy for more than six months, eighty years ago. And many generations have known only fear." He paused. "Funny, I don't have the Paraguayan fear any longer." Perhaps living in Washington for nine years wiped it out. We reached Nanduti. It was entirely ringed with heavily armed police—to prevent the launching of a book, for which I was to appear. There would be no softening of news media policy, no "new opening," no easing of restrictions in preparation for a presidential transition.

But the transition came several years later. My friends had their newspaper back. And Radio Nanduti, once again, was the most popular voice on the airwaves. We closed the traumatic period with a warm *brazo* (embrace) from both Humberto and Gloria at an appropriate show-and-tell meeting in Washington run by the NED.

The moral for press controllers of all stripes is clear: Stroessner demonstrated the utility as well as the futility of press censorship. The news media have no direct influence on the government. A dictator does what he believes he has to do to maintain power. The news media serve as an irritant, yet they provide a clue to actual public opinion. The government strongly, often violently influences the content of the news media; yet the more successfully it does this, the less credible the news media become in the eyes of the public. Indeed, once the public understands that news and comment are under government control, people usually conclude they have not been told the whole truth—no matter how much a courageous journalist may risk in revealing some truth. This disbelief is sustained by the iron hand of dictatorship clad in the velvet glove of journalistic self-censorship.

41

NO TO PINOCHET

With Gloria Rubin of Radio Nanduti (see previous chapter), I went to the airport in Asuncion, Paraguay, for the flight to Chile. She had disturbing news: the night before, a prominent leader of a liberal party went to a small town about seventy kilometers from Asuncion to meet with friends in a private home. Paramilitary forces dragged him out, beat him severely, and forced him to lie prone on the road for all to see. They threatened him further and then released him in wounded condition. Nearby, the paramilitary attacked another politician and threatened to rape his wife. Gloria also reported that her husband Humberto—after I left him at Radio Nanduti—was roughed up by police and was told to stay indoors. He had come out to see me.

He said the police seem to be getting more nervous. This worried Gloria, who was accompanying me to Freedom House's democracy conference in Chile. I had taken an extra copy of her speech, in case she was detained or searched at the airport. She told me she worried, too, because the police had rented the house three doors from theirs to watch Humberto's movements. The police had a drinking party earlier that week, and one said, as Gloria left her house, "Humberto will drive into the country and have a bad accident, from which we shall see he doesn't return."

We arrived at the Asuncion airport, but our 707 was in shambles. Paraguayan Airlines (the plural is a euphemism) owned two 707s and one DC-9. The other planes had long since flown to distant places. There was no alternative flight. We sat for four hours while sixteen men clamored over the dismantled engine. A supervisor held the repair plan, and a fire truck stood by.

There was time for stories about voting in Paraguay. Gloria said that during the last election she was told by a highly placed friend that he had just come from the

315

vote-counting process. He had advised officials not to announce an 85 percent victory for Stroessner. "It's not credible," he said, worried. They called it 87 percent.

An Argentine, an American, and a Paraguayan were boasting of their electoral systems. The Argentine said they could have results in only five hours after the closing of the polls. The American said the electronic system made possible instantaneous results. The Paraguayan said his country knew the result two months *before* the election.

I heard intimate stories about Stroessner: one son, given papa's encouragement of the narcotic trade, was an addict who spent much time in hospitals. The president's daughter, I was told, said her father cannot understand why men he's made millionaires through corrupt deals eventually want to leave the government and enjoy life. Stroessner was also quoted as saying that Paraguay is a model democracy and that other countries should come to see how a splendid political system works.

Eventually we were airborne and breathing easier. This was indeed a beautiful country. The sadness and fear do not show at thirty-one thousand feet. The repaired engine worked, though we had a few breath-holding moments at take-off. The Andes loomed ahead. Except for the tallest peak, which stands majestically above a high plateau of snow-covered mountains, the picture is not as spectacular as the Mexican Cordilleros, the Rockies, or the Alps, but the Andes stand among the world's tallest and evoke a feeling of cold, utter loneliness. Clearly, this is no place for a sputtering engine.

Now, said Gloria, "we go to the land of a nicer dictator." It was, however, only a matter of degree.

It was November of 1987. General Augusto Pinochet Ugarte was still very much in power, but I believed that a hemisphere-wide conference on movement toward democracy could speed constructive change in Chile. With Bruce McColm, my deputy and later successor at Freedom House, we produced prominent democratic participants from Latin America. It would take two more years before a referendum would vote, by a 54.7 percent margin, a resounding "No!" to Pinochet's reelection for eight years. He was deeply surprised by that vote and left the presidency while retaining his hold on the military. I would return in October 1988 to monitor that referendum.

Years before, I had learned more about Chile than I expected. Shortly after President Nixon began his first term in the White House I arranged with Henry Kissinger, then national security adviser, to hold a private briefing in his office for members of the Freedom House board. Henry owed me this boon because he had been scheduled, some months before, to chair my two-day conference on Soviet affairs, but immediately after the Nixon election, Henry cancelled, saying he would have other plans. At his briefing for us, I expected Henry to discuss the Vietnam War, then on everyone's mind; instead, he gave us an hour-long talk about Chile, which no one in the room understood. Years later, we learned that at that moment Henry was masterminding the 400 Committee, an offshoot of the

CIA attempting to force from office Chile's Marxist president Salvador Allende. Long after that, at dinner with Jeane Kirkpatrick, then ambassador to the United Nations, I reminded Henry of that Chilean discourse. He raised his arm, finger pointing directly at my face, and shouted, "I was right, wasn't I?"

He was right about Allende, who had already begun to nationalize major industries, but I believe Henry did not expect General Pinochet to become dictator for the next fifteen years. By 1987, Pinochet was showing signs of tolerating "illegal" opposition parties. It was time to run our democracy conference in Santiago.

I shepherded my Paraguayan group to the Hotel Carrera across the street from Pinochet's palace, called La Moneda. It is an imposing square four-story building occupying the space of two football fields. The center entry through a tunnel-like passage used to be open for pedestrians to walk through, from the broad park in front of the palace to the busy plaza at the rear. But when we were there, that passage was blocked by soldiers in the "popular" green uniform, with less than popular snub-nosed automatic rifles at the ready. The park and surrounding areas were patrolled by soldiers with automatics, and in the "garage" beneath the park were army vehicles ready to move out.

On the broad mall some four blocks from the palace was the city's sole "alternative" place, except for occasional minor outbursts at the university. At this alternative spot, young people produced street theater, observed by some two hundred viewers. The actors mounted steps of a public building shut for the night, carrying on a subtle dialogue with one another. The lines were spiked with humor. The crowd responded: some men and women sprinkled through the audience would spontaneously shout comments, and the actors would instantly respond, usually followed by a great roar of laughter from the crowd.

Down the street, two men dressed as clowns performed a bawdy Punch-and-Judy act, beating one another crudely but not painfully. This was far from subtle. Off to one side, a man with no tonal attributes whatsoever sang loudly, but no one stopped to listen or cross his palm. Though it was near midnight, children no older than five or six sprang from one person to another in the open mall, begging for money or offering to sell a single red rose. They were mostly attractive children, not in tatters, and obviously well trained for this demeaning profession. The police made no effort to stop them.

Yet Santiago was an orderly, sedate city with handsome, vintage Madrid-style buildings—solid and dignified. The people seemed much the same, dignified. Yet it was not long before I sensed the same fearfulness I had just left behind across the Andes. There were similarities in these two countries, though Chile was more sophisticated in its repression. Yet repression it was.

This mall had been the site where some sixty people died when Allende killed himself inside the palace. Pinochet, with the firm backing of the military, established a state of siege, practiced the bloody art of "disappearance"—kidnapping people who were never heard from again—arbitrary arrest, torture, exiling of opponents, and other human rights abuses. In a 1978 referendum Chileans were said to have supported Pinochet's policies by three to one, though the opposition was not permitted to mount an effective campaign. In 1980, a new constitution was endorsed by the electors, again with little chance for debate, leading to a "slow and gradual evolution" toward a democratic order.

That vision is what brought us to Santiago.

The newspapers carried bold statements from politicians calling for future change, but nothing much happened. Demonstrations across from our hotel, a few years earlier, were broken up by tear gas, and worse. Pinochet was now saying he would grant free and open presidential balloting ten years later, saying, "We would betray the Chilean people if we returned to a formal and hollow democracy." A forty-eight-hour general strike some months before our arrival had been called by twenty professional, student, and labor groups, endorsed by all political parties, including the Communists. That, of course, gave Pinochet "proof" that he was the defender against a Communist takeover. He arrested many prominent centrist politicians and cracked down again. Some weeks later, he survived an assassination attempt. He said he expected to be the junta's choice for president in 1989; the choice, he said, was him or "chaos."

When Pope John Paul II visited Santiago a few months earlier, he called the regime "dictatorial" and urged church leaders to continue supporting reform. Next to the cathedral is a nameless building that is distinguished for the work it does and the attention it draws from the police. A police van is regularly parked in front of the Vicaria de la Solidaridad, observing all visitors and threatening reprisal. The Vicaria is the social service agency of the church. It helps the victims of political repression and economic depression, assisting some 120,000 "marginal" people: the homeless, the hungry, those searching for disappeared or imprisoned relatives. Outside, the green van with well-armed soldiers and communications equipment waited. The eyes of soldiers follow as you pass. Those who enter, as we did, were photographed. Occasionally, there were arrest sweeps there.

Inside, we were told how the church tried to help the poor and the victims of political oppression. To be poor was to be suspect in Chile. For Marxism lured the poor; hence the poor—who beg, who go to soup kitchens, who plead to the church for help of many kinds—must be Marxists, and enemies of Pinochet. Indeed, many poor rose in thanks when it was rumored that Pinochet had been assassinated. When he survived, the military went through poor districts, killing and wounding at random. We saw some desperate-looking families waiting to hear about relatives. We bought some woven pieces made by prisoners. The money from sale of their goods is repayment for the help they receive. We walked back through the mall, where people seemed totally unconcerned about the "marginals" of oppression. But were they really unconcerned about their own possible marginality? That is the insecurity that a dictatorship brings in the name of stability.

I was supposed to visit the local prison to meet Manuel Bustos, the Chilean labor leader who had been arrested without charge two weeks earlier. He was to have been a speaker at our conference. We kept his name on the program even after his arrest. Our lawyer-consultant arranged for our prison visit—but Bustos was released early that morning. We would never know whether our featuring Bustos at our conference helped secure his release or led to his arrest. A strange system.

The U.S. ambassador to Chile, Harry Barnes, came to our conference. Like his counterpart in Asuncion, Barnes was almost unwelcome in Chile. Both must have been doing something right. They were about to visit one another's home ground. An "exchange of pulpits," I called it.

I opened the conference by describing my experience in Paraguay. Many were interested because the Reuters story about my detention had appeared in the local press. I concluded by playing on the highly amplified PA system a cassette Humberto Rubin had given me of the physical attack on Radio Nanduti. It began with the sound of gunfire, the screams and chants of the mob, and continued with the breaking of glass and intermittent shots and rocks hitting the building. Humberto and Gloria were inside the whole time. One can also hear the muffled cry in Spanish, "Get the Jew with the beard." Gloria was in the audience as I spoke, but Humberto was not, because the Paraguayan police had taken his passport.

Gloria spoke impressively. She has a doctorate in psychology and was a university professor before directing Radio Nanduti for fifteen years. Her forebears included a general in the Paraguayan army. She discussed education for democracy.

Robert Eisenmann of Panama, whose newspaper *La Prensa* had been closed and occupied by the government, and Emilio Filippi, the most distinguished independent journalist of Chile, discussed the watchdog function of the press. (Eisenmann had visited me in New York just before founding *La Prensa*.) Filippi stated that twenty reporters were still under police charges, and one reporter had to spend every night in jail for eighteen months. One was recently murdered. When Filippi finished, a progovernment writer stood up in his "personal capacity" and tended to negate Filippi's report, including the claim that the murdered journalist was really a politician affiliated with a terrorist group. Filippi's report was applauded at some length; the second received not a single clapping hand.

Vladimiro Saez described the work of the Vicaria. Other speakers were from Cuba, Uruguay, Brazil, Mexico, and Latin American organizations.

Marta Lagos, wife of the university professor who helped plan this conference, took my colleague Barbara Futterman and me for a drive into the country. She drove along a highway constructed as access to an $18 million home General Pinochet built "for future presidents." He had many different architects design different rooms, so no one had the full plan for the estate. It is at least three stories with a ballroom that accommodates hundreds, and several floors underground. Some eighty-five acres were needed to provide security separation and cover, but Israelis later said the plan was an easy target for terrorists. It can be seen all the way from Argentina, across the Andes. The house was built at a time when Chile was seeking $180 million in emergency funds from the International Monetary Fund, producing a scandal even in this tight-lipped country. Pinochet insisted he didn't live in this house, though no one believed it.

The charade continued in an area behind La Moneda, the presidential palace. That area has an oil-burning eternal flame set into the street, surrounded by stone decoration. But *beneath* the eternal light is a bunker that can be reached by a tunnel from La Moneda. One way for a dictator to go out in flames.

But Pinochet, to his utter surprise, went out by democratic ballot.

I returned to Chile in October 1988 for the referendum to decide whether the general could stand for another eight-year term. On that question, the people would vote either *Si* or *No*. On the Sunday before the Wednesday polling, the last demonstrations were held before La Moneda and down the broad avenue leading to it. I watched hundreds of cars, trucks, and other vehicles draped with Pinochet's face, as well as large flags and posters for the *Si*. A plane dropped hundreds of thousands of leaflets for the *Si*. The avenue was two inches deep in paper. A few came down as parachutes with a stone tied to them. Children ran to catch them. So did Barbara and I, but we lost out to the children—to the laughter of several soldiers.

There was a disturbing incident. Four cars and pickups stopped along the parade route. The occupants, all young men, had been waving white flags with a black insignia that resembled crossed swastikas. The men shouted slogans, then with precision lined up before their vehicles. At word from the leader, they shouted the first word, then completed the slogan. Next, they raised their right arms in a Nazilike salute. This was the FNLP, or Fuente Nacional Patria y Libertad (National Front for Motherland and Freedom) representing some twenty groups on the far right, including the death squads. As a warning, they put dead cats on front doors, wrote graffiti, and wore shirts saying, "Be careful." The leader was the former head of the DINA, the secret police, who was fired by Pinochet when accused of plotting the assassination in Washington of Chilean diplomat Orlando Letelier. The DINA leader was indicted by a U.S. court, accused by one of his men, but not extradited by Pinochet when the United States requested it. The incident still soured U.S.-Chile relations. The crowd on the street cheered. The men mounted their vehicles and drove off.

The opposition had fifteen minutes a night on television for twenty-seven nights. Though the *No* was overshadowed greatly by the government's control of television, this arrangement tended to legitimize the electoral process. The *Si* used all regular news shows and speeches by Pinochet to stress "anti-Communism," "antiviolence," and "antipoverty." The Monday morning TV news was filled with shots of the Sunday demo—all *Si*.

I went to the briefing of the Chilean teachers association, the most active organizers of the *No*. They were assisted by my friend, David Dorn, the shrewd representative of Al Shanker's American Federation of Teachers. The opposition political parties could not come together, so apparently the teachers did it for them. Most of the foreign visitors were mainly from U.S. teachers' unions. Some forty thousand Chilean teachers served as watchers at the polls. One teacher said,

"In fifteen minutes of television we destroyed fifteen years of government publicity for the dictatorship."

I also attended an ad hoc conference called by families of eleven victims of
violence, including survivors who saw others murdered. The victims were
among the most famous Chilean martyrs. The ostensible purpose of the meeting
was to state opposition to the death penalty, but it was clear from the timing that
the intention was to remind Chileans of the torture and killing in the Pinochet era.
They read a 125-word statement and signed it before television cameras.

I spoke briefly to the widow of Orlando Letelier, killed in Washington. One
of the victims present, Carmen Gloria Quintana, was badly scarred on most of
her face. She wore gloves to hide hand scars. Two others, Don Bernardo
Leighton and Ana Freco de Leighton, were attacked with a bomb in Rome. He
was a former vice president of Chile. I spoke to the youngest of three daughters
of General Carlos Prats, killed by the DINA with a car bomb. Also present was
the widow of a slain journalist, Jose Carrasco.

Next day, to observe the actual voting, I went to Concepcion, the second-
largest city, and Talcahuano, a poor port town. The voting was orderly, though
the marines at Talcahuano were stern and fully armed. At the women's site in
Concepcion, some waited in line for three hours, starting at 7:00 A.M. One
woman gave birth to a child while in line. By ten o'clock, there were two lines
extending for a quarter-mile in two directions. The military let only two or three
women in at a time and then slammed the gate shut. This soon destroyed the lines
around the gate, and a formless mob resulted. I was in the midst of several hundred women becoming rapidly impatient. Pushing, shoving, shouting began. A
high-ranking officer appeared, and the women applauded good-naturedly but still
pressed against the gate. I squeezed through, with women trying to follow, but
they were held back. I had to show my passport as well as my press card.

I interviewed an editor of *El Sur*, the major independent newspaper in Concepcion. The publisher was head of the Chilean publishers' association. I also
spoke to the head of the national Colegio de Periodistas, the journalists' association through which the government controlled the licensing of journalists. The
editor indicated there are government threats to withhold government advertising
as well as pressure on commercial advertisers to kill ads when the paper carries
coverage too critical of the regime. Yet, he said, there had been an easing of other
pressures on the paper since the state of siege was lifted before the referendum.

The editor said he must use "common sense" to decide how much controversy to publish. He gave an example of tracking a major story despite government involvement. In 1984, three men were executed in the streets. The paper carried the story, but the editor believed there was more to it than a casual multiple
murder. The government denied any knowledge of the killings. But just weeks
before we talked, four years after the crime, the paper said the killing was done
by the CNI, the secret police. Since the case was heard in the military court, the
paper did not have the same access as in a civilian court. Journalists, too, were

tried in the military courts. The editor said this case showed some added degree of freedom, but he was not certain how long this "Chilean spring" would last.

There was to be an ominous event for journalists two days after the referendum. But first, there was exaltation for the supporters of the *No*.

I watched the votes being counted at a *mesa* (voting board) in Talcahuano. From the start, the votes were running 3 to 2 in favor of the *No*; it was about the same in Concepcion. It was eerie, if not farcical, to watch state television in the early evening. By carefully selecting the returns, the television news had *Si* in the lead. By 10:30 P.M. the official figures were still claiming a *Si* lead, but with only 100,000 votes counted—so they said. By then, the Christian Democrats were claiming 60 percent for the *No*. The streets were quiet in Concepcion. But groups of TV watchers in the hotel laughed at the official returns. There was the question, though, whether there would be an attempt to impose those false numbers as the official result.

Next day, the papers reported the victory of the *No* by about 11 percent, with 98 percent of the electorate having voted. Shops reopened. At 11:45 A.M. the streets filled with normal traffic in Concepcion. At noon, a crowd of fifty youths began chanting and waving flags at the east end of the Plaza de Armas. As I moved through the plaza, crowds converged on the cathedral from all sides. At the steps of the cathedral there were some two hundred young people. I climbed on a bench and watched the crowds converge. All ages clapped, chanted anti-Pinochet slogans, and raised signs. A young mother took the tiny hands of a two-year-old in a sailor suit and clapped his hands for him. The crowd swelled to three thousand. No police or soldiers. The armored cars on the side of the plaza did not move. After fifteen minutes, the crowd performed a giant arm-moving "wave," then popular at sports events in the United States. They chanted, in Spanish, "Where are those of the *Si* who were going to beat us?"

As the crowd marched off, arms upraised and waving, they engulfed the mobile water cannons. The soldiers emerged and stood outside but did not speak. Slowly, an armored car moved out of the plaza—symbolically. The crowd applauded. It stopped briefly in front of the Intendencia, military headquarters. Some of the top officers looked out of the fourth-floor window, but nothing further happened. A far cry from earlier years.

Two days later in Santiago, foreign journalists covered the last event of the week, a victory rally at a large arena. As they left, they were suddenly set upon by uniformed officers. Some reporters were brutally beaten. Others had equipment shattered. I saw the bloody heads moments later and knew some of the victims. Several of us helped find bandages. The most wounded went directly to hospitals. I prepared an immediate response: a statement for Freedom House decrying the "totally unprovoked attack" on a score of journalists, "mostly non-Chilean, professionally engaged as reporters and photographers, brutally assaulted by police." I said that "we were particularly concerned because we heard a rumor early this week that once the plebiscite ended just such an assault would target journalists." I said that we discounted the rumor when the police and military acted with great professionalism during the voting. "This brutal attack," I added, "is all the more disturbing." I asked the authorities to investigate and punish those responsible.

I spoke to Governor Bruce Babbitt, cochair of the U.S. observers' group. He told me how much he appreciated Freedom House and the election-monitoring process. The correspondent for the *Guardian* of England asked him to comment on the role of the United States in the 1973 overthrow of Salvador Allende. Babbitt said he was not there as a historian or analyst. But I recalled Henry Kissinger's long discussion of Allende while the late president still occupied La Moneda. Allende, the Marxist, had been elected by a minority coalition in a democratic balloting. After fifteen years of Pinochet's brutal dictatorship, another democratic vote was starting the downfall of a right-wing dictator. It was now up to Patricio Aylwin to meld the coalition of democratic parties into a viable government. In the years afterward, he did much that he promised at our conference on democratizing the hemisphere.

Pinochet remained a shadowy force among the military in the first few years of the democratic Chile. The citizenry, still in shock after years of Allende's left-radicalism and Pinochet's right-radicalism, preferred to avoid recriminations—until Pinochet went to England in 1999 for medical treatment. A Spanish judge called for Pinochet's extradition to Madrid to stand trial for tortures and executions in Chile during his rule. Through most of the year his lawyers fought in British courts. Early in 2000, the aged dictator was released by the British, judged to be physically incapable of standing trial. He flew to Chile and received a mixed reception. Finally, the public was forced to consider his fate: he was considered too old and ill for further trial. This would be the last *No* for Pinochet.

42

NWICO, PART ONE
Amadou-Mahtar M'Bow

Amadou-Mahtar M'Bow, the first black man to head a United Nations agency, took ten years to change his impression of me from villain to friend. During that time he promoted the ideological struggle that was to bring him down. As the most prolific American writer and speaker in the information-order debate, I opposed him most of that time. M'Bow called me the chief American villain. But toward the end, I believed it was wrong for the United States to withdraw from the agency he headed—the United Nations Educational, Scientific, and Cultural Organization (UNESCO)—either because M'Bow ran it or to protest programmatic or administrative deficiencies. I believed the United States should stay in and fight. M'Bow only then called me friend.

The organization has a sizeable bureaucracy that operates worldwide in diverse intellectual fields, yet its annual budget is smaller than that of most major American universities. The United States withdrew in 1985, fulfilling the life-time opposition to the United Nations itself by Ronald Reagan's California conservative backers. For seventeen years, UNESCO would be denied the universal support for educational, scientific, cultural, and communication programs that benefit Americans as well as others. But by withdrawing, the United States spurred reforms within UNESCO.

M'Bow is a complex man who does not fit the stereotypes created by news writers or politicians anywhere. How could he be otherwise? He was born and grew up in Senegal, the former French colony on the west coast of Africa. Just offshore, as I have seen, is the island of Gorée, where slave merchants shackled thousands of black men in dungeons—I have photographed the site (see chap. 30)—before shipping the suffering humans off to the Americas. To be sure, Arabs and Africans consorted with whites to assure the functioning of the slave trade. The legacy is still horrendously apparent in Senegal.

M'Bow grew up with that legacy, as well as the language of the colonizer, France. He became a teacher and then minister of education. He attended the Sorbonne and later taught at the National Diplomatic Academy in Paris, became his country's ambassador to UNESCO, a member of that organization's cabinet and, in 1974, its director-general (DG).

The new DG sought to do more with UNESCO than publish definitive books or hold conferences on language, history, science, and the like. He would continue those endeavors but would also raise world consciousness of the interests of developing countries, especially those in Africa. When M'Bow left UNESCO, the Senegalese education minister said, "M'Bow's first achievement was to affirm a principle of paramount importance, the principle of the equal dignity of all cultures." This, he said, was not obvious. "Our languages were considered dialects; our medicine called pharmacopoeia; our science, magic; our laws, customs; and our peoples, tribes."

The minister credited M'Bow with advancing the idea that all cultures are valid and should be developed by people on the scene, rather than by standards set abroad. This would require economic support managed locally, not controlled by international agencies. Most important, he praised M'Bow for promoting the "new world information and communication order" (NWICO), which, said the Senegalese minister, "definitely led to the freedom of the press." NWICO, he added, informed "the elites who, most of the time, are the agents that equally create favorable conditions for domination and alienation."

However, this claim for NWICO's information-order success is not justified. As a UNESCO program, it was an utter failure. In 1976, the idea surfaced in Costa Rica and then Kenya. In 1987, it was officially buried by M'Bow's successor in Paris. In those ten years, NWICO fractured UNESCO, almost caused its downfall, and persuaded even liberal Western news media to support the American and British withdrawal from the organization.

Though NWICO will never receive even limited credit, it did, however, bring to wide attention some valid objections to Western journalism. Some of these criticisms were quietly addressed over the years while NWICO was still being attacked for raising them. The *New York Times*, a bitter opponent of NWICO, slowly increased its "soft news" or "process" coverage of developing countries (as distinct from "first-day" or "hard news")—and placed such stories regularly up front. The Associated Press heard charges that it only transmitted exotica, coups, and earthquakes from developing nations. The AP subsequently sent Mort Rosenblum, its chief roving editor, to third world countries for background features as well as hard-news coverage. The AP noticeably beefed up its third world coverage, thereby altering its criteria for "news" from those countries.

Such benefits aside, the information-order debates probably delayed for at least a decade the sober analysis of international journalism, an analysis long overdue. Every effort to discuss valid criticisms of Western media policies and the obvious numerical domination of global news flows by four Western wire services, indeed all such valid examinations, were disparaged and foreclosed by charging that NWICO's proponents sought to censor the content of domestic and international news for their own dictatorial purposes. Indeed, most active proponents of NWICO represented countries that already controlled domestic news flows, hampered foreign journalists, and sought to create such standards globally. In brief, while there could be reasonable discussion of the symptoms, the proposed "cures" were unacceptable to press-freedom advocates. Consequently, NWICO embittered and polarized the participants, paving the way for the United States and the United Kingdom to leave UNESCO.

There were other objections. M'Bow had deftly used patronage to assure support in the secretariat and on the board of UNESCO. He created programs designed to advance third world, particularly African, cultural interests. He enjoyed elaborate travel and housing facilities. His accounting procedures were less than transparent, though he was not charged with misappropriating funds—just extravagance. These factors helped the Reagan administration insist that NWICO was not the only reason for withdrawing. Nevertheless, it was both the first and last straw in the U.S. withdrawal—the charge that the press, in its self-interest, understood best.

That was the issue that brought me to examine UNESCO in June 1976, four years before Reagan had even won the White House. I had heard that the next month in San Jose, Costa Rica, there would be a UNESCO regional conference on news flows. To get the background papers for that meeting, I called the UNESCO office in New York. I was told they did not have the papers, though they had been prepared in Paris after "expert" meetings in Bogota (1974) and Quito (1975). I cabled UNESCO in Paris and was told the papers were classified. That startled me; I thought UN materials were in the public domain, particularly on a nonsecurity subject such as news flows. I persisted by engaging a friend who had recently resigned from UNESCO. He secured both texts—labeled "confidential."

Reading these texts, I was astounded. These were not academic exercises but policy papers intended to change the way news was prepared and transmitted worldwide. Particularly, news distribution—its content and international flow—would be influenced, perhaps controlled, by governments and intergovernmental officials. There were serious, extensive discussions of "the ideological context of communication policy: role of the state in the formulation of a national, coherent, and corrective policy." After elaborate analysis of present and future policies, the papers discussed "the difficulty of applying a national communication policy without participation of the government and institutions: creation of 'National Communication Councils.'" The papers, of course, led up to "the role of UNESCO in the communication sector"—applying intergovernmental oversight and its control mechanism.

The clear implication came in this conceptual shift: "instead of emphasizing the *right to inform* the accent is currently being placed on the *right to be informed.*" This shift would apparently confer on government the "right" to determine the information intended for the "receiver" (the report's word for the citizenry). For, it was added, "communication is a necessary public utility." And, of course, governments even in democratic countries regulate public utilities!

Some Quito experts urged that "the respective government take the necessary steps to ensure that the national news agencies are *exclusively empowered* to disseminate news from outside the region referring to the internal affairs of each country, in order to avoid the distortion of news that is so frequent on the part of international agencies" (emphasis added).

A majority of experts at Quito opposed this recommendation, but it nevertheless reflects the attitudes held by a significant number of media consultants to UNESCO at that time. And, of course, many countries in Africa and Asia—then and now—do indeed control all incoming global news before it is circulated to local newspapers and broadcasters. The simple procedure: the government-owned news agency contracts to receive the Associated Press, Agence France-Presse, or Reuters wire and then edits (censors) it for transmittal through local news media.

Director-General M'Bow put his and UNESCO's imprimatur on the Quito meeting by declaring, "News agencies obviously have a fundamental part to play in the building of modern society in its economic, social, and cultural aspects. It is, moreover, illogical that such an important phenomenon as the flow of information should, to a great extent, pass through a small number of channels which are, in addition, determined by an ideology and a technology not necessarily suited to the region." He called for a "balanced and objective flow of information."

M'Bow must not have realized that he was opening a virulent, decade-long debate that would nearly destroy UNESCO and would ultimately bring down his own office. I shared my finding with the Freedom House board. UN Ambassador Daniel Patrick Moynihan (soon to be senator) egged me on (see more on Moynihan in chap. 9). I called a press conference in June 1976. This alerted the American news media to the conference, scheduled for San Jose, Costa Rica, in two weeks. Copies of our Freedom House statement went to every president and prime minister in Latin America. A large contingent of correspondents covered the proceedings. Opposing forces set up a press camp across the street from the UNESCO conference. There were frequent briefings from both sides as the conference debated. Ultimately, the San Jose recommendations were softened and sent on to Nairobi, Kenya, for final voting at UNESCO's biennial conference that fall.

There the Soviet Union took over the press-control struggle from the non-aligned movement and the UNESCO bureaucracy. The Soviet's draft resolution on the news media stated baldly in a separate, one-sentence paragraph: "[S]tates are responsible for the activities in the international sphere of all mass media under their jurisdiction."

This provision theoretically would require Washington officials to bear responsibility for international reporting by, say, the *New York Times* or the AP, and assure another government that it could have equal time or space to rebut or offset a press report that a government might challenge in the American news medium. The idea is patently ridiculous, even for democratic countries without a First Amendment. But this Soviet draft drew serious attention in a hundred national capitals for many months. The challenge served to place NWICO on the global agenda for a decade.

Scores of international conferences were held to discuss NWICO. I addressed many meetings and met with journalists and officials in some forty-seven countries. I wrote three books on the subject, many op-ed articles in leading newspapers, chapters in some twenty-five books, and many magazine pieces published around the world. I was cited countless times in the press, magazines, and textbooks. Ultimately, M'Bow told Leonard Marks, a leader of the World Press Freedom Committee, that the "chief villain" in the United States was Leonard Sussman. The other Leonard had been trying to alter UNESCO communication policies by dealing directly with M'Bow on a friendly basis. They had many private dinners in Paris and elsewhere, as well as considerable private correspondence. Marks, former director of the U.S. Information Agency under President Lyndon Johnson, had considerable political clout in both Democratic and Republican administrations in Washington. I had mainly a sizable volume of publicly expressed views and, for five years, membership on the U.S. National Commission for UNESCO. I was its vice chairman for the last three years of American membership in UNESCO. Consequently, on his infrequent trips to the United States M'Bow met with me and a few others to assure us he meant no harm to the free press. He merely wanted fairness and "balance" in the press coverage of third world countries and their interests. He was indeed persuasive in one-on-one discussions.

I had a record of supporting the reasonable examination of Western news media policies—analysis by the media themselves, not by governments. I had agreed there were valid criticisms of Western coverage of third world news. But I clearly opposed many of the "cures" recommended for improving that coverage, including the licensing of journalists, creation by governments of journalistic codes of procedure, policing those codes, and ultimately penalizing journalists and media who break the codes.

M'Bow insisted that UNESCO had never officially urged the licensing of journalists. This was correct; but the organization had, however, held meetings at which such methods were espoused.[1] Sadly, I often reminded UNESCO, participants at its communication meetings were almost always limited to government officials and never included third world journalists, the chief victims of NWICO.

As the NWICO debate intensified, I testified repeatedly at the invitation of U.S. congressional committees. I twice debated Gregory Newell, President Reagan's assistant secretary of state assigned to plan America's withdrawal from UNESCO. I was invited several times to Paris by M'Bow to advise him and his associates. But the fat was in the fire: years of threatening the news media had turned even the liberal U.S. press against UNESCO. M'Bow now regarded me as a friend because I had urged the United States not to withdraw from the organization but to stay in and fight for reforms.

In November 1983, I was placed publicly in a thoroughly conflicted position. I was in Paris as a member of the U.S. delegation to UNESCO to negotiate the reform of communication programs. American troops had just gone ashore in Grenada, but journalists were completely barred from the first thirty hours of this Caribbean adventure. Reports of the invasion came only from official sources. I was about to address UNESCO on behalf of press freedom, opposing governmental controls of news media, when the State Department cabled to me the official rationale: "The Grenada operation [not "invasion"] was launched at very short notice and in strictest secrecy in order to ensure the safety of not only the American citizens in Grenada but also our military forces. In order to maintain this level of secrecy, only those persons with an absolute need to know were involved in the planning of this operation. No members of the press were included."[2]

I was quoted in the *New York Times* saying that I thought the controls were wrong, but I intended to respond to any criticism by noting that the controls were less restrictive than those routinely imposed by other nations and that they were finally lifted after an "uproar in the press of the kind that only happens in a free society." I added that the issue would be raised "more as a matter of rhetoric by countries that are year-round censors themselves."[3]

And so it went. I subsequently negotiated a major modification of the NWICO scheme. The ambassador of our delegation, a long-time Reagan supporter and intelligence operative, felt we had achieved several significant breakthroughs at this UNESCO general conference. He and I would recommend staying in the organization.

I took this position at some risk. I held a press conference as vice chairman of the U.S. commission opposing the announced Reagan policy of withdrawing. Freedom House Chairman Max Kampelman, a former Carter and Reagan ambassador, said I was "declaring war on the administration." A major conservative foundation cut off some $200,000 in grants to Freedom House, largely on the basis of my stand on UNESCO. At a small dinner given by then UN ambassador Jeane Kirkpatrick I was met by Irving Kristol, father of neoconservatism, who asked angrily, "How could you?" He didn't wait for the reply.

The United States left UNESCO in January 1985. In 1995, President Clinton hailed UNESCO's fiftieth anniversary and said he wanted to return if he could find the funds to pay for membership. Earlier, the State Department and the General Accounting Office (GAO) of Congress had given UNESCO a clean bill of health. President George W. Bush, while addressing the UN General Assembly in September 2002 to urge action on Iraq, announced that the United States would soon reenter UNESCO; this step, he implied, would display America's faith in the world body. In fact, the United States did return to the organization in October 2003.

M'Bow was voted out of office in 1987. His successor, Federico Mayor, a natural scientist from Spain, reversed—indeed buried—NWICO. He has held a series of conferences on four continents to assist the development of pluralist, independent news media. He involved the organization in World Press Freedom Day and has taken many opportunities to display UNESCO's completely changed attitude. Several times he brought me to Paris to consult on these issues. I welcomed the invitation to write a major chapter on press freedom in a book marking Mayor's second term in office.

In retrospect, the NWICO era represents far more than a challenge to the Western news media, although that challenge was not entirely undeserved, even if badly conceived and wrongly placed in governmental contexts. The larger meaning was the impact of the Cold War on the increasingly vital flow of news and information. The Soviet Union quite accurately regarded the free press as the ultimate enemy of a closed society. The nonaligned countries—coalesced by Yugoslavian Marshal Tito and Indian Prime Minister Indira Gandhi, with aid from Fidel Castro—became Soviet pawns in the geopolitical struggle with America and the West. News and information controls were vital accessories to Marxist policies. Embarrassing the West over news flows was more important than providing "balanced" news, especially if balancing meant assuring critical as well as favorable coverage of Marxist and Soviet affairs. The international news flow had thus moved into the big-time arena at UNESCO. That organization, the news business itself, and Amadou-Mahtar M'Bow would never be the same again.

NOTES

1. Alex S. Jones, "UNESCO Reported Turning from Issue of Licensing Journalists," *New York Times*, November 6, 1984. Report based on letter to the author from Director-General Amadou-Mahtar M'Bow.

2. See Department of State memo 320722, November 9, 1983, to missions abroad regarding military action in Grenada.

3. Quoted in Jonathan Friendly, "U.S. Press Curbs in Grenada May Affect International Debate," *New York Times*, November 8, 1983.

43

NWICO, PART TWO
Turnabout in Guyana

T he New World Information Order (NWICO) controversy challenged me, of all places, in Guyana. (See chap. 42 for background on NWICO.)

Poor-country leaders are not like the movie primitives cowering at the sight of a lighted matchstick in the dream sequence of *A Connecticut Yankee in King Arthur's Court.* Yet third world officials say they are sufficiently aware of the power of modern communication to fear the uncontrolled flow of information from abroad. But some fear more, it seems, the unrestricted access of their own people to domestic news and information. I have argued that two-sided question in many places, but nowhere have I been more directly confronted than in Guyana.

It should no longer be news that the world order (or disorder) is critically influenced by Byzantine politics and economics; firefights in the Persian Gulf, Palestine, the citadel of Panama; or disputes over fishing rights in Tuvalu or the Caribbean. The question arises: What is the relationship between national development and the expanded use of communication for political purposes?

That question was intelligently discussed by Frank Campbell, former minister of information of Guyana, writing in *Intermedia* in March 1984. We had met many times at international conferences. At the time, he was out of office and was writing more freely for the International Institute of Communication's audience. He described the "development approach to communication" in postcolonial Guyana. He had been a key administrator of programs that he says "yielded somewhat mixed results." His analysis, however, is valuable not only for other poor countries but for rich-country observers who often misunderstand or denigrate the relationship of communications to national development.

I contributed some confusion. Campbell quotes my friend Narinder Aggarwala of the United Nations Development Program, who wrote,

There is a general tendency in the Western media to confuse development journalism with developmental journalism. The latter term was coined by Leonard
R. Sussman, executive director of Freedom House. . . . One very often finds
Western media leaders condemning development journalism when in fact what
they have in mind is *developmental* journalism as defined by Sussman. It is of
utmost importance that we distinguish between development journalism and
developmental journalism, or what in United Nations circles is referred to as
Development Support Communication (DSC) programs. The UN term,
although a bit more cumbersome than "development journalism," is more con-
venient and descriptive of the use of various media—not just mass, but any
media—for promoting economic and social development. Development news
reporting is only a very minor element of DSC, which in recent years has won
many converts among third world planners and leaders.[1]

Development news may have been only a minor concern of the United
Nations, but it is a major instrument by which many regimes control the flow of
all information to their populations. Consequently, when these regimes carry
news flow debates to UNESCO and other international forums, Western media
spokesmen and governments respond. To be sure, as Aggarwala indicates, these
free-press defenders did not distinguish between the "good" and the "bad" terms
for journalism-cum-development.

I regret having coined the term *developmental journalism.* Unless one reads
Mass News Media and the Third World Challenge, the book in which I first used
the term in 1977, one can easily misunderstand my putting down of developmental journalism.[2] I rejected the politicization of communications under the
guise of economic development. I did not attack—indeed, I applauded—straight-
forward applications of "development news" and journalism to improve skills,
services, and infrastructure.

Campbell, in the careful recounting of his experience with communication
development in Guyana, acknowledges that "the government's socialist program"
as well as the use of the media for development purposes resulted in the politicization of communications. Former independent publishers and broadcasters sold
their holdings to the government when socialist policies dried up advertising
income. Says Campbell, "As part of its campaign to correct the global information imbalance . . . and the imperialist information deluge, the government established the Guyana News Agency [as] a monopoly on the flow of foreign news to
the government-owned media." Campbell quotes Guyana's late prime minister
Forbes Burnham: "The government has the right to own sections of the media,
and the government has the right, as a final arbiter of things national, [to mobi-
lize] the people of the country for the development of the country."[3]

Campbell warns, however, of the damage done to journalism, the country,
and the government by a "pathologically narrow interpretation and implementa-
tion of a government-supporting development-oriented media policy." He
referred to "the withholding or distortion of the truth; an apparent fear that the

criticism of inefficiency in even a single government agency would cause the agency, if not the entire government, to crumble; and an exclusion of the opposition voice from the media, especially the print media."[4]

There were other consequences. Campbell reports,

> Strict, day-to-day political control of the media led to the geographical or professional exile of some of the best journalistic brains. Apart from the bias, which was sometimes very obvious, whole editorials and feature stories occasionally disappeared from the newspapers. Some of this was a function of the brain-drain and, in some cases, the mind-drain. Some, however, resulted from a fear of antagonizing the government; or from confusion about what the government media policy was. In times like these, governments seek refuge in—speeches! Almost every news story began with a minister's declaration that something was being done, had been done, ought to be done, or would have been done.[5]

The public, says Campbell, "reacted with creative and understandable cynicism. A new culture developed among our people—a culture of disbelief, especially in the traditional or progovernment press. Sometimes, in fact, people longed for underground media, especially when the traditional opposition wasted the opportunity by overplaying its hand."

To his credit, once Campbell was given ministerial responsibility for information, he campaigned within both government and party for a new media policy—"one that would promote the use of the media for development without the kind of abject onesidedness which had made a mockery and a failure of the entire exercise." He argued that to be effective the message must match reality and be tested "in the crucible of debate rather than forced through in the exercise of our virtual media monopoly."[6]

Campbell won his battle but lost his war. The policies he proposed were finally adopted; but, he reports, "After more than a decade of the old policy, the professionals [government bureaucrats] refused to accept the new as anything but a politician's rhetoric." For example, "Accustomed to altering photographs to create the illusion of a crowd, some colleagues continued this practice even where the crowd was so large as to make it unnecessary."[7] Much of the "journalistic skill, self-confidence, courage, and breadth . . . had disappeared or had been subdued." Campbell was removed from his post and was made editor in chief of Guyana National Newspapers. There, he says, he assisted professional colleagues who considered themselves politically vulnerable. "The irony," says Campbell, "was that a political appointee was apparently required to depoliticize the newspaper, in the sense of making it less partisan."

One of the lessons from this, Campbell said, is that the media should help national development but not become "developmental," i.e., politicized. He adds, "I reject the Eurocentric idea of men like Leonard Sussman, who argue that press freedom as practiced in the North must be transferred to the third world, complete with its mechanisms and its methodology. However, third world leaders should resolutely resist the temptation to use the nontransferability of these myths as an excuse for eschewing the ideas of freedom."[8]

But Campbell misreads me. I never argued that it is either desirable or possible to transfer the mechanism of the "North" to journalism in the "South." Yet, no matter how impoverished, no matter how underdeveloped a country or its mass media, it is possible to separate "news" from "information," development-oriented or otherwise. Of course, the primary business of developing countries is development. Every available technology, mass or other, should be engaged. But news is an element apart. It delivers the realities of each day to citizens who need to know what is happening in their village, their capital, and the world outside. News, then, is the intelligence of life. Development news may convey word of the process and progress of national change. To be an effective carrier, however, mass news media must be perceived as balanced in reporting and reliable in reflecting over time the full range of a citizen's interests; beyond that, they must provide an adequate context from which citizens may fulfill their civic responsibilities. This, admittedly, is a tall order for a poor information system in a developing country; but no technology is too small to be deployed for these purposes.

A copier in a tiny village can begin to share news of the neighborhood and indeed the world—if central authority will allow. A single radio transmitter can further enlarge the circle of knowledge. It should, however, reflect diverse views, whether covering nearby or distant events. These are not "myths" but minimal examples of press freedom that are transferable anywhere. I have promoted in several countries the use of solar-powered transmitters for FM radio broadcasts. I found a lonely technician in Paris who builds wooden cases to hold solar screens that turn the sun's rays into stored power for a small transmitter. That, linked to a turntable and a microphone, creates a broadcast "studio" in places where no electric power is available. Such FM broadcasters function in isolated areas of Haiti and several African countries. The broadcasts can be heard within a thirty-mile range, providing hills or buildings do not intervene—and, most important, provided central authority does not shut down the system or harass the broadcaster.

Campbell himself struggled vainly to provide some diversity and critical reporting in Guyana. Yet he labels my similar approach "Eurocentric." We come together at the end, happily, when he warns his colleagues that they should not use "any excuse for eschewing the ideals of freedom."[9]

NOTES

1. Quoted in Frank Campbell, "The Practical Reality of 'Development Communication,'" *Intermedia* (International Institute of Communication, London), March 1984, p. 24.

2. See Leonard R. Sussman, *Mass News Media and the Third World Challenge* (Beverly Hills, CA: Sage, 1977), p. 11.

3. Quoted in Campbell, "The Practical Reality of 'Development Communication,'" p. 25.

4. Campbell, "The Practical Reality of 'Development Communication,'" p. 26.

5. Ibid.

6. Ibid.

7. Ibid., p. 27.

8. Ibid., p. 28.

9. Ibid.

44

KAARLE NORDENSTRENG
NWICO Point Man

M y memorable visit high above the Arctic Circle in Finland was arranged by Kaarle Nordenstreng while he headed the Soviet-funded International Organization of Journalists (IOJ). Kaarle and I were regular antagonists at international communication conferences around the world. We were probably the most prolific writers on the New World Information and Communication Order (NWICO; see chaps. 42 and 43). The controversy raged bitterly for fifteen years, starting in 1976. We held basically opposite views on many issues. He started from a fundamental Marxist premise and supported the news media philosophy of the Soviet Union as well as the press-control policies of third world rulers.

Kaarle was also a widely published, conference-circuit academic who headed the journalism department of the University of Tampere, Finland. This academic post and the presidency of the IOJ gave Kaarle double the clout. He spent most of the year traveling to international academic conferences and initiating IOJ projects that trained (IOJ claimed) some one hundred thousand journalists in Eastern and Central Europe, Africa, Asia, and South America. The IOJ was the parent organization for "journalist unions" in countries that had Soviet ties, were open to Marxist persuasion, or accepted IOJ assistance still without intergovernmental commitments. The IOJ, at its peak in the 1980s, was the world's most active producer of journalism texts, guides, and polemics—all flatly opposing Western-style journalism and linking Soviet objectives and procedures with daily news reporting. All of this was projected as anti-imperialist journalism destined to supplant the "merchandising" of news by nongovernmental Western media.

Kaarle and I had this in common: we both fully understood the other's position; neither attacked the integrity of the other; and each quoted the other for his own purpose and used tones argumentative but rational.

Once we even discussed joint efforts to end the seemingly pointless debates in UNESCO over the information-order controversies. At the end of a conference in Kuala Lumpur I invited Kaarle to breakfast and proposed that, after returning home, we urge our major supporters to meet for the stipulated purpose of ending the confrontations. Kaarle "happened to be going to Moscow" a few days later. I would sound out Dana Bullen at the World Press Freedom Committee in Washington to estimate the reactions of his numerous affiliates. Dana was not enthusiastic but was interested in Kaarle's response. It came shortly: there was no interest on the other side.

Kaarle continued to visit me in New York; it was always a friendly meeting. He would tell me mainly about his academic work. I could read in his publications the more strident efforts of the IOJ.

There was a tragic note I've never forgotten. For many years I would meet at conferences around the world Oldrich Bures, director of the IOJ who worked under the direction of Kaarle. Bures had been a Czech sportswriter before World War II. I had the impression that sportswriting was the high point of his career, though he was a devoted Marxist bureaucrat. Each time we met abroad, he was cautious the first day and avoided direct conversations with me. There were always Communist watchers and enforcers nearby. But later we would meet and have rather free conversations about our differences over journalism.

One unusual occasion was our luncheon discussion at a beautiful open-air restaurant in Athens, at which Marianne and Mark were present. Bures and I slipped into a comparison of the different systems under which we lived. I was perhaps too frank in expressing my view of the Communist states. Suddenly, looking pained, he simply broke off the conversation. I never returned to that again with him. But several days later, as he and I walked alone in a garden, he told me this story. His voice broke several times as he spoke. "I am still a young man, you know." He may have been in the early fifties. "But," he said, "I am told I must retire from the IOJ. So I applied for an information job at the United Nations in New York. I was successful, and they said my government must agree. I thought it would be routine, but I was warned in Prague that if I go to New York I must leave behind my fifteen-year-old daughter."

I was shocked, as he knew I would be. But not nearly as shaken as he must have been. His only comment to me: "Bureaucracy! Bureaucracy!"

Of course it was worse than that. It was hostage-taking by the Communist government of Czechoslovakia. The story had a still more tragic ending. Not long afterward I learned that Bures was dead; suicide was suspected. I wrote a condolence letter to his wife but did not receive a reply. When Kaarle Nordenstreng appeared in my office some months later I asked him about Bures's death. Kaarle said he thought it was heart failure.

It was Bures, incidentally, writing for the IOJ in 1977, who had signaled the opening of the decade-long debates over NWICO. The developing countries, he said, had challenged the West, "the centers of world capitalism," to do more than "understand" the third world, as Western resolutions in UNESCO had promised. The West must provide "normative" new standards for changing the content of the worldwide news and information flows. American and other Western journalists regarded this as tantamount to censorship, whether self-inflicted or by oppressive governments. Bures concluded in 1977, "By now it is clear that western industrialized countries have no other alternative than to yield under the pressure of the new forces on the world scene—a front of the developing and socialist countries."

It was always clear to me that such polemic by Bures interpreted the broad mandate from Moscow. Kaarle did not need special briefing—as a dedicated Marxist he could analyze objectives and opportunities without specific directives from the Soviet Union. Indeed, he was probably well ahead of most Soviet ideologues in devising tactics in UNESCO and other international forums, as well as writing polemical and scholarly articles for academic journals, speeches for diplomats (especially from developing countries), and perhaps, on occasion, a speech for the president of Finland on international communication.

Kaarle was also a prime mover in the creation of the UNESCO Commission to Study International Communications (the MacBride Commission of 1980). He recommended some of the sixteen participants (those favorable to his positions) and produced voluminous memoranda on the content of the two-year study. He also actively attacked the secretariat of UNESCO for soliciting from me a paper on how the commission should handle its main work. At that first meeting in Stockholm in 1978, Kaarle joined a few ideological friends in submitting a strong memorandum to UNESCO, hand-signed by all, deploring the presence of Paper 18 by Leonard R. Sussman. UNESCO ignored the protest.

My paper was listed in the appendix of the published report. I had recommended that the commission produce not one final report, but two. One would analyze and recommend specific improvements for news media owned and run by governments; another would do the same for news media independent of governments. I sought to avoid the commission's setting forth some universal standard presumably to be applied to both free and not-free journalism. The commission opted for a single report but included in every sentence, every paragraph, every chapter an allusion to both free and not-free media. The book fully satisfied no one, though a careful reading provided a detailed outline of several sides of hundreds of issues in international and national communications. Perhaps because of this multi-ideological approach to heated issues, the MacBride Report was never adopted as a UNESCO document but remains the special project of then director-general Amadou-Mahtar M'Bow. The report was filed for "study" and was quietly published as a book, *Many Voices, One World* (UNESCO 1980).

The report became one of Kaarle's standard tools to convert the new information-order campaign into the status of customary international law. Another implement was UNESCO's Mass Media Declaration (1978). Kaarle worked closely for two years with M'Bow, the Soviet delegation, and numerous developing-country representatives to advance the Soviet Union's draft resolution. That text, set forth in December 1975, served as the official draft for all delegates at the UNESCO General Conference in Nairobi (1976). That draft stated flatly, "[S]tates are responsible in the international sphere for all mass media under their jurisdiction." (I describe that struggle in chap. 42.)

It was clear to me early on that Kaarle was a tireless operative, with easy access to all third world delegates and the full array of Soviet-bloc representatives as well. He was a master of defining and redefining the minutiae of "UN-ese." He cleverly used the UNESCO procedure of voting by consensus to veto words and tactics.

His goal was clearly to link the selected record of intergovernmental institutions—the League of Nations (from 1925 until World War II), the United Nations (from 1945 on), and UNESCO—with the nongovernmental organizations that supported his main theses. The resolutions, some not approved by a UN majority, covered such matters as measures to be taken against "supporters of war," false or distorted reports, the international right of correction (of false reports), sovereignty over natural resources (the press being a national resource), rejection of unacceptable cross-border television, and many other special issues that could be said to have implication for press coverage. The purpose was to use this link to support the claim that the "international community" already subjected news and information media to some regulation and standard. Would it not follow, then, that customary international law was already applicable to the content of cross-border journalism?

Kaarle believed so. He was the most influential politicoacademic in framing and riveting the link between the Soviet Union's global communication policy—a Cold War strategy to undermine Western influence over international news flows—and support for third world demands on the West. The developing countries sought communication infrastructure and an end to the "free flow of information" as the ideological basis of Western news content. Kaarle expressed the confluence of these goals and commitments in appearances before hundreds of conferences worldwide over several decades, on all continents. Kaarle devised or coauthored scores of resolutions and declarations for African, Asian, Latin American, and UNESCO meetings, where communication policies were formulated. He took such formalized statements to the next level of meetings as "authoritative" expressions of the will of the attendees at previous meetings. Thus would be created an aura of movement among "peoples" and nations for "a new world information and communication order" (NWICO). That title was not Kaarle's; it has been attributed to Mustapha Masmoudi, when he was minister of information of Tunisia. But Kaarle was always the prime mover, wearing hats as an academic and as president of the IOJ.

Kaarle got on the NWICO bandwagon early, though he refused at first to accept the *W*—for "world"—in the program's name. He used instead the *I*—for "international"—which the nonaligned summit employed in Algiers in 1973.

"International" implied that nations or governments would somehow control and resolve global communication issues, even for independent news media not owned by governments. This concept, of course, raised the specter of censorship. Kaarle was defeated later in UNESCO when, on the demand of Western governments, UNESCO adopted "world" as the more unbiased term for the information-order controversy.

Kaarle nevertheless gave full opportunity for the most extreme anti-Western views to be heard. In Kaarle's sourcebook on NWICO (1986) he had Enrique Gonzales Manet, a communication professor at the University of Havana, Cuba, provide the book's opening chapter. Manet writes, "The heart of the matter is that power centers need unrestricted global acceptance of the imperialist 'free-flow' doctrine emanating from the First Amendment to the U.S. Constitution—to survive and maintain supremacy. It is a vital component of domination considered as being of priceless political value."[1]

No credence is given in such analysis to the two-century struggle of Western news media—in England, France, and the United States—to free themselves from the controls of government. Milton, Locke, and Hume in England; Voltaire and Rousseau in France; and Franklin and Zenger in the American colonies were not fighting for imperialist gain but for freedom from state control of news content. Such controls existed in more than one-third of the countries of the world in the 1970s, especially in places where Kaarle derived state support. This was the origin of the free-flow concept. Although it was indeed influenced by international news conglomerates in the twentieth century, the struggle to preserve diversity of information remains a burning issue. Developing-country criticism of Western news domination is a valid complaint and must be addressed—but not by the "cure" of implicit or explicit censorshop, either run from national governments or induced by intergovernmental organizations.

Kaarle has never ceased pressures for structural changes in the international news flow. Such change would require formal standards of press conduct and some machinery for policing and correcting "misconduct" of journalists as defined in the code. Kaarle repeatedly recalled League of Nations and UN efforts to frame such codes, all of which failed to gain consensual support. The closest he came to seeing approval for such a broad code was the 1978 Mass Media Declaration of UNESCO. I, too, was involved for two years in the drafting of this resolution.

The starting point had been the horrendous Soviet draft for the Nairobi general conference of UNESCO in 1976. Several Americans and I had repeatedly softened the tone and content of the drafts, but then each staff revision toughened the paper still more. Late the night before the draft was to be voted on, an American delegate, a spokesman for Director-General M'Bow, and several others completely gutted what was basically the Soviet version. By morning, a respectable draft was tabled. It drew not only unanimous approval but also a standing, boisterous ovation. Everyone was relieved that three years of bitter debate over the Mass Media Declaration had ended. My analysis stated that the worst had been avoided and that the spotlighting of third world communication needs—without the implication of state censorship—was appropriate. Kaarle later published the full text of my analysis, along with many others, in his book on the mass media declaration. The *Washington Post* disagreed. By what right, it editorialized, did U.S. officials even debate issues of news content?

With great persistence and highly sophisticated tactics, Kaarle worked to turn a significant defeat into the first stage of a victory. The defeat was the withdrawal of the United States and Britain from UNESCO in 1985 and 1986 partly, at least, in response to UNESCO's communication program. That cost the organization about one-third of its annual income and resulted in the election of Director-General Federico Mayor, who ended the NWICO program. Kaarle did not take this institutional change as a rejection of information-order objectives; instead, he cleverly linked the old objective (guarantees of third world access to mainline Western news and information flows) as more urgently needed in the new era of cyberspace and electronic communication. Kaarle packaged this timely target by creating a series of meetings piggybacked onto major conferences called by other agencies such as the International Association for Mass Communication Research (IAMCR), of which he was already a prominent member (I myself was one as well, though less prominent). He created at these meetings a MacBride Round Table, whose purpose was to advance those issues that the MacBride Commission examined but never resolved. Kaarle and his group of like-minded academics would now pursue NWICO objectives under this new umbrella. Year by year, on several continents, the roundtable expanded, drawing a new body of papers on updated NWICO issues.

By 1995, the seventh Round Table was able to hold an international meeting of seventy-four participants from twenty countries in Tunis to discuss the topic "Africa Faces the Information Highways." The conference organizer was Mustapha Masmoudi, a member of the MacBride Commission and father of NWICO, the old information-order controversy. That now decades-long debate originated in Africa in 1973 at the Algiers summit of the nonaligned movement, which was only theoretically neutral in the Cold War. The nonaligned nations systematically supported—and were supported by—the Soviet bloc on virtually every issue.

The Tunis Round Table concluded that "now would be the time to show honest and active solidarity with the hard-pressed peoples of the continent, starting from their real needs and not from the global strategic needs of the corporate-driven North." The introduction of an information superhighway may only magnify the gap between the information-rich and the information-poor, said the Round Table's chair, Richard Vincent of the University of Hawaii. This is a valid concern: how to structure a global news and information flow that provides fair access to everyone, rich or poor, within countries that are rich or poor. Almost 70 percent of Africa's population lives in villages with no electricity and no telephone connections. There is indeed the opportunity to define an information society that is relevant to real African needs, not just debate broad national access to global information flows.

Kaarle Nordenstreng's strategy for creating a new institutional base for the latest debates over global communication is thus gaining ground, even as his old International Organization of Journalists disappeared. (The IOJ was created after World War II in a split-off from the International Federation of Journalists [IFJ], the Western association of journalist unions. The split was along Cold War lines—the IOJ went east.) When the Cold War ended abruptly, Czechoslovakia turned immediately toward a democratic polity, a free press, and a market economy. The Czechs discarded vestiges of the Communist control mechanism. The government asked the IOJ to leave its international headquarters in Prague. Kaarle resigned the presidency; his successor also resigned shortly afterward, saying that IOJ bureaucrats were still pressing a Communist line, even in a non-Communist world.

Kaarle had moved on, working through IAMCR, the MacBride Round Table, and other academic and activist groups in communication. We remained in contact. I was fascinated by his annual letter, describing each year's travel and the progress of his lovely wife, son, and daughter. Mark and I met them when we traveled to the Soviet Union. We stopped in Finland for a memorable visit to the Nordenstreng country home in Tampere and then went by air to a point far above the Arctic Circle. Kaarle arranged to put us up at a journalists' union lodge in Lapland, and he and his son Markus accompanied us. It was June, the time of the midnight sun. At such a moment, we walked on the treeless terrain and saw in the distance a herd of reindeer. (I was later squeamish when drinking reindeer soup with bits of meat.) On the horizon, circling the herd, was a perfect rainbow—all of this in the brightness of an Arctic midnight. My photograph of the reindeer and rainbow is a reminder of that moment.

On the political forefront in 2003, under the aegis of the International Telecommunications Union (ITU), was the first of several global conferences on communication in the Internet age. The ITU traditionally dealt with technical spectrum assignments on Earth and in outer space; now the organization was poised to examine the flow of information—implying some oversight of the *content* of messages—to assure fairer dissemination of information among the rich and the poor, inside nations and between them. This was the objective of the MacBride Round Table.

Yet when I read Kaarle's Christmas tale of his latest activist travels in the world of global communication—soon to appear, I assume, at the ITU—I recall the reindeer cavorting under the midnight sun.

NOTE

1. Enrique Gonzales Manet, "Issues and Development," in *International Information and Communication Order Sourcebook*, ed. Enrique Gonzales Manet, Kaarle Nordenstreng, and Wolfgang Kleinwachter (Prague: International Organization of Journalists, 1986), p. 44.

45

YURI BATURIN
OF THE KREMLIN

During the Cold War, shame was a common weapon of Western diplomacy. Even the most brutal totalitarian countries called themselves "democracies"—or worse, "peoples' democracies." Authoritarian rulers didn't want "their people" to know that other peoples saw them as pariahs.

Though it was difficult to document, some improvements occurred after oppressive regimes were sharply prodded at international meetings. Such countries had been shamed into signing documents that pledged adherence to commonly recognized civilized behavior.

Getting oppressors to live up to their promises was more difficult. Serving with the U.S. delegation to the Information Forum in London in 1989, I saw that no delegate liked being treated as the representative of a pariah government. And no matter how he raged during the conference, he had to report home that he and his government were the butt of international opprobrium. Even if he and his colleagues then chose not to reform their system, they had to weigh the costs of rationalizing fact-based criticism. At the very least, the bureaucrats received a lesson in real life beyond their restricted borders.

The Information Forum was part of the Helsinki Process, begun in 1975 under accords creating the Commission on Security and Cooperation in Europe (CSCE). Signing the Final Act were thirty-five nations of Eastern and Western Europe (including the Vatican), the United States, and Canada. For fourteen years before the London meeting, CSCE meetings had been held to review progress in military and economic affairs and human rights. Now, for the first time, the CSCE would address problems in international communication, especially journalism. My contributions to the approved CSCE agenda were the following formal proposals:

- To remove restrictions on independent journalists
- To guarantee openness and diversity of information and to regulate only to maintain the diversity of content
- To remove restrictions on the importation of equipment by journalists for cross-border transmission of audiovisual information and data
- To remove licensing of satellite television reception dishes by individuals and organizations
- To simplify procedures for television and radio news organizations to obtain a permit
- To limit the need for assignment of a government telecommunications operator for each use of satellite uplink flyaway terminals
- To reduce administrative obstacles to greater use of satellite and cable television and open architecture in computers and other communication devices
- To encourage development of globally accepted common standards for telecommunications and computers
- To provide nearby telephone service to all citizens by 2010
- To remove administrative and criminal restrictions and penalties on independently obtaining, reproducing, publishing, and distributing printed and photographic materials
- To permit private ownership, use, and access to typewriters, word processors, copying machines, and related instruments, while respecting intellectual property rights in the use of reproduction technology[1]

Shortly after these formal recommendations were distributed to all thirty-five countries, I was visited by Dr. Yuri Baturin, from the Soviet delegation. He was interested in my copious proposals because he was working at an institute in Moscow on many of these same issues. I welcomed this conversation; indeed, it was the beginning of an extraordinary relationship that continued for several years. When I wrote Yuri later, however, I addressed him at the Kremlin. He became President Boris Yeltsin's administrative assistant for security affairs after serving in a similar capacity for Mikhail Gorbachev.

The road to the top of the political mass was difficult for a scholar. Yuri, it seems, has retained his personal integrity and avoided the appearance of a power-seeker. One Russian journalist sought to discover from Yuri why "an independent critic takes the risk of turning into a target of criticism. What brought [him] to the office in the Kremlin?" Yuri's response focused particularly on interests like the one that brought us together years before.

When Yuri approached me in London I recalled that there had been leaks from the Soviet congress that it was debating a law of the press. This interested me, but I had been unable to discover the nature of the draft legislation. It could be important not only for the Soviet Union but for the Central-Eastern European bloc as well. There had already been significant deviations in Hungary, Poland, and elsewhere from the old hardline Soviet treatment of the news media. That was apparent at the London forum, and it caused me to write those complex recommendations for changes in technical as well as editorial controls of news and information.

Yuri told me that he worked in the sector of political systems at the Institute of the State and Law. Most interesting to me, he was working—privately, he said—on a draft for a law of the press. He was well qualified: he held separate doctoral degrees in law and journalism, did research in cosmonautics, and wrote a thesis on the European Parliament. After the Soviet congress tussled for three years with its own press law, it took Yuri's draft and embodied 80 percent of his ideas in the official text.

I was with Yuri in Washington when the congress approved the law of the press. Yuri was completing a stint at the Kennan Center, a Washington think-tank, and would return to Moscow—but not before we toasted him. The law had been approved on his birthday. I made clear, though, that I did not have high regard for the law; it was too lengthy and tried to be too precise. I had urged Yuri several times to limit the issues covered in the law. There were regulations certifying a journalist and a publication, as well as elaborate rules regarding libel and "permissible restrictions" of coverage (no harm to national security, health, well-being, etc.). All of these, I said, provided loopholes for bureaucrats to restrict journalists or their coverage.

Sergei Grigoryants, editor-publisher of *Glasnost*, the first major unofficial magazine in the Gorbachev era (see chap. 38), was wary about registering under the new law. He said, "I will only register if it involves a single declaration of our existence." He said he would not respond to innumerable "clauses and conditions." Lev Timofeyev, publisher of the independent *Referendum*, said, "Before we always had a certain room for maneuver when our journal was a symbol, an act of protest against the lack of press freedom." Now, said Timofeyev with a touch of nostalgia, "we must operate normally, but the economic conditions do not exist for it."

Yuri said he recognized this, but I should remember that the Soviet Union did not have two hundred or even seventy-five years of civil freedom, with a tradition of self-regulation by journalists. Yuri clearly understood the role of the U.S. First Amendment, but he could not envisage such freedom with journalistic responsibility coming soon in the Soviet Union. He was, of course, a pragmatist; and in current political terms, correct.

The first law of the press was a significant milestone in the Soviet Union, even though it would require an independent judiciary and government-free news media to monitor press freedom. Yet the law provided the first legal guarantee, though limited, of *glasnost*. Perhaps the most important gain in the passage of the law was its fiery legislative history: the cauldron in which fundamental precepts of Soviet governance and society were successfully challenged. It would take revisions of the law in a new Russia, years afterward, to improve on this first effort.[2]

In August 1991, Yuri returned to Moscow to work on Gorbachev's staff. The coup followed, and Yuri said, "I left the Kremlin and thought, thank God, I'll have a rest at last." But shortly afterward he was asked to work on the popular Itogi television program. About that time, Yeltsin was looking for a bright assistant to write decrees and oversee national security matters. Yeltsin probably remembered that young man he had met at the first Congress of People's Deputies. Yuri had handed him the draft of the law of the press and, says Yuri, "we walked together from the Congress to the Kutafya Tower."[3] That was all.

They met for the second time when Yuri participated in a meeting in Novo-Ogaryovo. Recalls Yuri, "One day a friend of mine asked me to deliver to Yeltsin a packet of papers on relations with Japan. After some hesitation, in violation of all apparatus regulations, I did it directly. [Yeltsin] looked at me, hesitated, but reached out and took the packet. After that, coming to Novo-Ogaryovo, he began to shake hands with me, as he did with those he knew personally."

Yuri became responsible for drafting presidential decrees. Many hands approve the final version, so discovering responsibility for formulations is difficult. "This is the weakness of the system," he says, but "I can try to change it." But he could not allow circumstances to dictate his role: "During my preliminary conversation with Yeltsin I said I shall be frank even if he would not be pleased to hear certain things from me. If I come to realize that my presence in the Kremlin is meaningless I shall resign, and he would be the first to be notified about this. There must be some degree of trust between people who work together, even in politics. It is impossible to live permanently thinking of some dangerous, dirty trick from outside as well as from inside [the Kremlin]."

About his future? "From time to time I feel the need to be alone and think. I don't want anyone to disturb me." He also feels the need for a home. He is divorced, with a twelve-year-old daughter. "For a year and a half," he says, "there has been a bathtub lying in my corridor. It is to replace the old one. There are a lot of books and papers lying around." But, he says, "the main thing is to know the work I am doing is useful."

After Russia's runoff presidential election in 1996, Yuri's life in the Kremlin seemed more complex. In the final days of the campaign, Yeltsin had coopted former opponent Gen. Alexander Lebed and installed him in the Kremlin as national security adviser. That had been Yuri Baturin's job. Yuri was named "adviser to the president"—duties not spelled out. Yuri reminded Yeltsin of his remark to the president in June 1993, just before he started work in the Kremlin. Said Yuri, "When you don't need me anymore, tell me straightaway, I'll pack my briefcase and leave." Now, in 1996, Yuri asked, "Maybe that time has come?" Yeltsin responded, "No, you're staying on the team."

Yuri later told a newsman, "I'll hardly do whatever it takes to stay in the Kremlin. I have some experience and knowledge. I would like to use them to maximum effect. If the work isn't interesting I can look elsewhere."[4]

Yuri invited me to visit him in the Kremlin. But President Yeltsin's and

Yuri's time in office ended. Soon after, Yuri, forty-nine years of age, blasted off from the Bankonur cosmodrome and two days later docked with Mir in space. The former defense adviser became the first bureaucrat in space. Television footage at the launch showed him dressed in a spacesuit, prepping from a flight manual. A lucky stuffed animal, attached by a string to the ceiling, started to float as they entered weightlessness. Yuri was a qualified cosmonaut. "We can teach anyone to become a cosmonaut as long as he is not an idiot," said the deputy flight director.

Returning to Earth, Yuri may have become a qualified plumber to install that waiting bathtub.

NOTES

1. Leonard R. Sussman, "Who Controls Journalism? The London Information Forum," *Freedom at Issue*, July–August 1989, p. 24.

2. See Leonard R. Sussman, "The New Press Law of the USSR," *Freedom at Issue*, September–October 1990, pp. 34–36.

3. Quoted in Natalya Gevorkyan, "Yuri Baturin: 'I Came to Walk with President Yeltsin,'" *Moscow News*, July 23, 1993, p. 11.

4. Ibid.

46

MILOVAN DJILAS
Half a Life in Prison or in Disgrace

Heroic leader and rebel—his reason and conscience turned him against tyranny.
—Freedom Award plaque inscription, 1969

It seemed unworthy and inhospitable to crowd Milovan Djilas, this frail man then in his seventies, into a smelly freight elevator in a New York hotel. He had just received the Freedom Award, and I was leading him for security protection through the kitchen and out the back exit of the hotel. With him and his wife were his old friend and publisher, William Jovanovich, and his wife, as well as Marianne and I. I had arranged elaborate security for Djilas because he was a target of Communists and anti-Communists alike: of Croatians who hated Montenegrans (Djilas was one), and others who remembered that he had been vice president of Communist Yugoslavia under Marshal Tito and had broken with him. Countless Balkan sharpshooters could target Milovan Djilas.

Indeed, we had just seen a threat in the ballroom of the hotel. As Djilas rose to accept the award from Freedom House, a man in the rear shouted epithets and promised death. Police hustled the man out of the hotel. Moments later, the event ended and Djilas was escorted to a service elevator. Jovanovich, also a Montenegran and publisher of several of Djilas's books, half Djilas's age and twice his size, was visibly shaken. Djilas put his arm around Jovanovich's shoulder and said, "Bill, don't be frightened. This happens all the time."

Far worse had happened to Djilas in the past. He had spent thirty-six of his eighty-four years either in prison or in disgrace under house arrest in Belgrade. When Marianne and I visited him there in 1980, we had to take a far more circuitous route to his apartment than he followed in leaving that hotel in New York years earlier.

We had gone to Belgrade for the general conference of UNESCO. I vowed to see Djilas and had written him in advance. I could not phone him from my hotel room because all the lines were tapped. The hotel itself was the "unsafe house" in which foreign visitors were put for complete surveillance by the Communists. I phoned Djilas from a street phone and announced we were on the way. We took a taxi across the Danube and left it several blocks from Djilas's house. We entered the small vestibule of that building on Palmoticeva Street, where a man with a dark fedora, obviously a state security person, asked whether he could help us. We politely refused the offer and took the elevator to the second floor.

We pressed the bell, and Milovan Djilas quickly appeared and invited us in. As I crossed the threshold I asked, quietly, whether we could talk freely. "Oh, yes," said Djilas, as he pointed to the ceiling light fixture. Next, he went to the window of the small living room and drew the blinds.

We talked for more than an hour about conditions in Yugoslavia. Toward the end of Tito's reign, he said, Communism was still controlling even those aspects of life that had been theoretically removed from centralized direction. In effect, the "new class," Djilas's major contribution in 1957 to an understanding of the Communist state and its dehumanizing mentality, was still in control despite "reforms" of unions, the press, and other institutions.

Djilas, in his own words, had "traveled the entire road of Communism." He had been a Partisan guerrilla fighter against the Nazi occupiers of Yugoslavia. He became an ardent believer in Stalinism. But he was disillusioned and repelled by the "all-powerful exploiters and masters" it produced—particularly Stalin himself. Djilas was the trusted second in command to Marshal Tito—in the resistance to the Serbian monarchy, in the Partisan struggle, and in the building of the Yugoslav Communist state. Djilas organized a purge of the Serbian intelligentsia. That was never forgotten, and it may have resulted many decades later in the shouted threats against Djilas in New York.

In January 1948, Tito sent Djilas to Moscow on the historic mission to tell Stalin that Yugoslavia would break with the Soviet Union and develop its own form of Communism independent of Moscow. That was the first fissure in the Communist monolith. As a consequence, Yugoslavia received aid from the West. Tito also slyly created the nonaligned movement to profit from Western fears of the Eastern bloc. But Djilas began to doubt the entire Communist structure, inside as well as outside Yugoslavia. In 1954, Tito expelled Djilas from the Communist Party and all the posts he held. Djilas became a dissident and thus a nonperson in the eyes of the government. The following year, he was put on trial for "hostile propaganda" for an interview in the *New York Times*. He began writing *The New Class.* In 1956, he was imprisoned for writing in French and American magazines. He spent much of the next thirty-six years in prison or under house arrest. That was how Marianne and I found him.

It was significant that the prison to which Tito sent him, Sremska Mitrovica, was where he had served three years, just after law school, for demonstrating against the monarchy. As a youthful prisoner he learned Russian; as a mature prisoner he learned English.

Before entering prison, Djilas smuggled his manuscript of *The New Class* to an American publisher. The book was more than an anti-Communist tract at the peak of the Cold War; it revealed the corrupting motives, privileges, and self-serving defenses of bureaucrats who had come to power under the promise of egalitarianism, public service and, above all, utopianism. Wrote Djilas, "In contrast to earlier revolutions, the Communist revolution, conducted in the name of doing away with classes, has resulted in the most complete authority of any single new class." He referred to its "high priests" who, he said, "are simultaneously policemen and owners of all the media which the human intellect can use to communicate thoughts—press, movies, radio, television, books, and the like—as well as all the substance that keeps a human bring alive—food and a roof over his head."[1]

Djilas served five years in prison for writing *The New Class*; he was released only after international pressure targeted Tito. But then Djilas wrote *Conversations with Stalin* and was imprisoned again. In it he wrote, "Every crime was possible to Stalin, for there was not one he had not committed. For in him was joined the criminal senselessness of a Caligula with the refinement of a Borgia and the brutality of a Czar Ivan the Terrible." Djilas said he could not understand "how such a dark, cunning, and cruel individual could ever have led one of the greatest and most powerful states, not just for a day or a year but for thirty years."[2] One might also wonder how so many intelligent, even intellectual citizens and publications of free countries could for so long have regarded the Soviet Union as the "wave of the future."

Djilas told me that, weak as it was, Marxist-Leninist ideology was not dead. "It is ossified and rigid, but not dead," he said. Rather, it created and still fueled the Soviet system. The Soviet leaders still behaved as if they were the incarnation of "irrefutable truths," Djilas added. All of that—ideology, irrefutable truths, and laws—free the Soviet leadership of "all moral and contractual obligations," he said. In addition, he pointed out, the Soviets had a monopoly over information. They make "generous use of both lies and disinformation." But, he added, the Soviet system, with its secrecy and closedness, keeps its motives and intentions from the ordinary citizen, as well as from the international publics. Thus the system is based on "spiritual foundations that are deeper and more dangerous than the lie itself; a system of perverted values." And that secrecy and ideology perpetuate the "ideal" image of the Soviet Union in the eyes of "those poor countries that are without rights and often feel jeopardized by many nebulous internal and external forces."

When he met Stalin in Moscow, Djilas said the Soviet leader was "in tears as he spoke of my 'attack' on the Red Army for raping women in a devastated countryside." At every turn, Djilas later wrote, "Stalin would drink a toast, crack a joke, feed the fire, weep, and kiss my wife 'because you're a Serb,' all the while jeering that 'I'll give you a kiss even if the Yugoslavs and Djilas accuse me of rape.'"[3]

Djilas's *The New Class* was the first exposure from within that society—leading to Tito and Stalin himself—by one who had unimpeachable credentials. More than that, as my friend Mihajlo Mihajlov points out: "Djilas was the first high figure of the Communist party who, after having clashed with the party and been expelled from the system, continued to live in his homeland while speaking out openly against the system, publishing articles, and giving interviews to the world press. He was the first person to suffer imprisonment and then, after being released, to continue to talk and write openly, and to repeat the process again, all the while refusing to leave his country. This was a new phenomenon for the Communist system: an opponent who did not go underground or emigrate."[4]

Mihajlov was also imprisoned repeatedly for his writing. He had published *Moscow Summer*, describing conversations with Russian authors and scholars. Mihajlov was a university professor in Zagreb. The Soviet ambassador officially protested to Tito, accusing Mihajlov of "Djilasism," lifted his passport, expelled him from the university, and leveled a prison sentence. Mihajlov wrote about Djilas for a New York magazine and received another prison sentence. During one of his "free" periods, Mihajlov prepared to publish a magazine, which we discussed at some length. But that was quashed, and he received another prison term. In the face of renewed international uproar, Mihajlov was imprisoned, but Djilas was freed! I had tried to help Mihajalov repeatedly during the dark years to obtain support in America, as well as permission for him to join his family in the United States.

Mihajlov points out that Djilas set the pattern for fighting totalitarianism employed by other Communist dissidents—Solzhenitsyn and Sakharov in Russia, Havel in Czechoslovakia, Walesa in Poland, and many others. Mihajlov notes that Djilas and later other dissidents elsewhere confounded Communist authorities by insisting that they were violating their own constitutions. Communist constitutions promised, but never allowed, freedom of expression, among other freedoms.

It was this contradiction that became the centerpiece of Western criticism of Soviet bloc policies in meetings with the Communists at the Conference on Security and Cooperation in Europe (CSCE). Starting in 1975, the thirty-five nations of the CSCE regularly discussed human rights violations. These meetings placed Soviet bloc governments on the defensive. They were challenged to live up to the proclaimed "freedoms" in their national charters—just as Djilas had done for three decades in Yugoslavia. In 1980 in Madrid, I observed the American delegation at the CSCE "name names." Every day for three years, Max Kampelman—on leave as Freedom House chairman—and others in the West challenged the Soviet bloc to cease specific cases of human rights violations. And each time the Soviet bloc bureaucrats would have to acknowledge, at least to themselves, that they were violating their own proclaimed principles. They would, of course, rationalize their actions and make counterclaims, but we may never know how such tactics corroded support for hardline Communism within its own ranks. That, over the years, was Djilas's tactic.

In 1995, Mihajlov spent two hours with Djilas shortly before he died. They agreed that as long as nationalists are in power in Croatia and Serbia peace will never be achieved, no matter what agreements are signed as a result of international pressure. "Only a supranational, antiwar, democratic movement offers any hope for the peaceful coexistence of the many different ethnic, national and religious entities that exist on the territory of the former Yugoslavia," Mihajlov said. This despite the presence "for one year" of some sixty thousand NATO forces separating the belligerents.

Prison transformed Djilas, he told us, "from an ideologist to a humanist." He feared that ethnic separateness would follow the demise of Communism. Communism has ended in what is left of Yugoslavia—interestingly only Serbia and Montenegro remain together—but ethnic violence has bloodied the region. Tens of thousands have died, and millions have become refugees. Djilas, fifteen years earlier, saw no humane future for ethnic divisiveness in his homeland.

I can still see Djilas seated in his darkened living room, dominated by a great picture of Faust, brooding on whether to become a man of action or a man of the book. Djilas was both—and also a man of history.

As we were about to leave, Djilas beckoned us toward a closet door. He opened it. Hanging alone on the inside was the bronze, specially sculpted Freedom Award we had handed him years earlier in New York, and which he had clutched to his shabby coat in that inappropriate freight elevator. He smiled, and said thank you.

But it is we who are indebted to that unique man. I tried to say this in an op-ed article in the *New York Times*, October 23, 1980. It was titled "A Story of 2 Belgrades." I wrote, "I have just visited two Belgrades—the unreal, where UNESCO delegates from 153 nations, mostly authoritarian, have been debating the 'democratization' of information; the real, the closely watched home of the writer Milovan Djilas. . . . He is, he says, a 'nonperson.'"

I concluded, "He has earned the [Freedom Award] many times over. He could easily have crossed [the Danube] into the other Belgrade and mouthed the 'democracy' litany of the authoritarian elites." But he did not.

NOTES

1. Quoted in Serge Schmemann, "Milovan Djilas, Yugoslav Critic of Communism, Dies at 83," *New York Times*, April 21, 1995, p. B7.

2. Ibid.

3. Milovan Djilas, *Fall of the New Class: A History of Communism's Self-Destruction*, ed. Vasilije Kalezic (New York: Knopf, 1998), p. 52.

4. Mihajlo Mihajlov, "The First Dissident: In Memoriam Milovan Djilas," *Uncaptive Minds*, summer 1995, p. 64.

47

SPRINGTIME IN CHINA

It was May 1983, shortly after China had removed strict Communist control over its farmers. It permitted them to sell produce to the state or individuals—after the farmers had completed their assigned quotas to be given to the state. This experiment in slightly more openness seemed to be working. China was still suffering from the decade-long Cultural Revolution, during which intellectuals were at least humiliated and turned to the countryside, if not killed outright. Since that debacle ended, the country had been trying to restore or create institutions on international relations.

In that spirit, China invited seven American think-tank directors to spend three weeks with Chinese civilian and military leaders, presumably to ponder creating think-tanks in China. Freedom House was invited.

Heading our delegation was William H. Sullivan of the American Assembly at Columbia University. He had been ambassador to Iran when all American diplomats there were held hostage. Bill was in Washington at the time. As he put it, "the chargé d'affaires was in charge." He and his staff were held in frightful conditions for 444 days.

Other colleagues were from the World Affairs Council of Washington, DC, the American Enterprise Institute, the Brookings Institution, the World Affairs Council of Northern California, and the Heritage Foundation.

In all of our meetings we sat in red-carpeted rooms with deeply upholstered chairs. The Chinese sat in a group on one side, and we on the other. Bill explained every day to each new group that we represented widely differing viewpoints and that we often disagreed. It was clear at every meeting, however, that no such diversity appeared on the other side. Usually, only one person spoke for the Chinese. At our first meeting he decried the United States going back on its word and taking "cheap shots" at the Chinese people. This was a reference to American support for Taiwan.

At every session, with different discussants each time, the issue of Taiwan was raised in combative fashion. Finally, Bill opened one meeting by saying that we understood the Chinese position on Taiwan and that nothing would be served by continuing this rhetorical ploy. Like magic, the issue was never raised again at any of the succeeding discussions (excluding formal speeches) in three cities, and before different civilian and military groups; so effective was the control.

In a substantive meeting with Yong Longgui, head of the state planning commission, we asked about the recent price reforms, together with work and salary incentives, which have immediate implications for creating a semi–market economy.

This was a preview of what was to come years later.

The Chinese had already realized that the socialist system simply was not working (as the Soviets were also discovering). Central control did not produce sufficient agricultural or industrial products, nor did it permit prices to fluctuate sufficiently with labor-created values. Instead, government subsidies grew enormously. One-third of China's expenses went to subsidies: twenty billion dollars.

After his description of the loosening of central planning, Yong showed us the sixth five-year plan already in the works. It had 110,000 items including all sectors of the national economy except the military.

By 2002, China was still struggling with the limited open market the Communist hierarchy was permitting, and the problems implicit for retaining central control of both production and the information flows upon which a Communist society depends.

We had lengthy discussions of nuclear power. The Chinese spokesman said China could never be blasted out of existence by nuclear bombs. We were shown through extensive underground tunnels in which whole cities and their services had been created. The implication: we can survive.

At one meeting with our host organization, each of us was asked to discuss his group's functions. I described our press freedom program as an integral part of any prodemocracy movement. I stated that the new demand by Congress that the State Department prepare an annual analysis of human rights deficiencies in all countries would make it more difficult for a nation to receive U.S. aid if it is a rights abuser.

We met with Han Xu, the impressive vice foreign minister. He lost no time in asserting that U.S. policy toward Taiwan was a burden for America and just another of its mistakes. If the United States hadn't erred in the past, he said, there would not have been a Korean War or a Vietnam War. Bill interrupted, "And China would still be under Japanese domination!"

At the Institute of International Strategic Studies there was extensive discussion of Arab-Israel questions. Bill said there was broad support for the Reagan plan to create a Palestinian state, but prospects were dim for its happening soon.

He said that the United States and Israel do not agree on Israel's security needs. General Jiang Yonshu said that China would cooperate with the United States on the broad Persian Gulf issues once the United States solved the Arab-Israel question. Bill asked (in jest) whether this institute, under contract from the United States, would tackle that issue. Silence followed.

En route to Xion, site of the six thousand larger-than-life terra cotta soldiers still only partially uncovered after centuries underground, we flew in a Soviet-built prop-jet. Only foreigners were permitted to fly the domestic air routes after a Chinese plane had been hijacked to Korea; the Chinese were not permitted to travel without an official assignment. From the air, it seemed primitive outside the large cities. Many roads outside Beijing have signs reading, "Forbidden to Travelers without Permission." They are seemingly innocuous roads leading to poor settlements. Almost everything is watched carefully, and the whereabouts of everyone are carefully noted. There are block monitors in the cities who watch every person in their apartment section. Some of the extensive surveillance used to check mail, phone calls, and other communication is hard to justify even in a police state.

At an extravagant banquet in Xion we feasted on dishes from the Tang dynasty, including a steaming, still rising soufflé with chicken broth. This is where the French discovered the soufflé, and Xion does it grandly.

There was a moment of silence when Bill described how he had learned army tactics from Mao and used them in Laos. Our host looked disturbed and said, "You must remember the Vietnamese were our allies at the time." Said Bill, "We all make mistakes." But the translator let that pass, and the evening was over.

We visited a commune, a university, an agricultural trading zone, the crowded city life of Shanghai, and perhaps most important, an institute where the democratic movement that in 1978 critically analyzed Marx held forth. The debate was on humanistic grounds: Should we follow the early or the late Marx? In a room once occupied by Chairman Mao there was a picture of Lenin flanked by Stalin and Trotsky. These two were then regarded as Lenin's deputies, and Marx was seen as a *Western* philosopher. In analyzing Marx's works in this fashion they were debating the relevance to *them* of this Western influence.

The philosophers at Fudan were actively writing on this subject, but their work was narrowly distributed. These debates were felt to be necessary to reach new conclusions about China. But the participants were instructed not to talk to Western diplomats or journalists. Clearly, some did even in this highly controlled society—else we would not have heard.

Yet the secretiveness was pervasive. One wondered how the closeness of family members in China could continue when its dissidents were maligned, marginalized, and even killed—all with seemingly little impact on the family structure. Dissidents were swept aside, their writings destroyed. Not so easily in the Soviet Union, where dissidents, even those in the gulag, had their writings transmitted to the West. And some Soviet dissidents even met with Western visitors. Not in China, until the new millennium; but even now, it is very risky.

Just before leaving China, one of our hosts asked me, "How do you know the Dalai Lama?" I had not mentioned him on this trip. I explained that Freedom House had arranged his first visit to the United States (see chap. 51). He asked, "What do the Tibetans want?" I told him that they wanted freedom to practice their religion. "They have that," Xu responded. Then I added that they also want their political autonomy restored. "China is one country," said Xu. I said that Tibetans were not satisfied with their treatment. I offered to give Xu a Tibetan pamphlet. "That won't be necessary," he said and walked off.

At our last meeting, at the Chinese Academy of Social Science I gave Li Shenghi, its director, a set of Freedom House's journal *Freedom Appeals*. This contained writings of jailed Chinese dissidents and a list of eighty-two Chinese dissident publications that recently had been closed down. I explained that such material circulates in the United States and influences Congress and the White House. Li took them without comment and walked off with the collection under his arm.

Seeds planted in hardened soil, sometimes even beneath concrete, somehow surface and thrive. Such conversations with Soviet bureaucrats during the Cold War helped speed the thaw that finally caused that hardened system to implode. Why couldn't it happen in China as well?

48

MARGARET CHASE SMITH
The Conscience and the Rose

W hen I signed on as executive director of Freedom House, January 1, 1967, I began thirty-seven years of association with extraordinary men and women. Some would be closely related to our organization; others would be widely diverse activists in many other countries. For me, none would be more inspiring than the lady from Maine, Margaret Chase Smith.

Sen. Paul H. Douglas of Illinois had become chairman of Freedom House when I joined its staff. He was a great boon for three years, accessible even when in the Senate. Most important, his political judgment was impeccable. It had been honed in both high-level academic politicking at the University of Chicago and the rough-and-tumble ward politics of that city's Democratic machine. It was indeed miraculous that one with Professor Douglas's integrity could get the Illinois senatorial nomination—or perhaps his selection was a stroke of genius in the revitalization of the old Daley political machine. In any event, Senator Douglas never compromised his personal integrity in all the years in the Senate. He put it to me once, "I decided early in my career never to accept a gift of more than a five-dollar necktie."

With Senator Douglas's retirement we needed a chair with similar public service and no less integrity. In the Freedom House pattern of maintaining political and other forms of balance I approached a Republican to replace a Democrat, a woman to replace a man, a New Englander to replace a Midwesterner, and the "conscience of the Senate" to replace "Mr. Integrity."

The choice: Margaret Chase Smith, longtime Republican from Maine. I visited her Senate office. She expressed admiration for Freedom House and especially for Leo Cherne, veteran officer of the organization, who had been among the first to challenge Sen. Joseph McCarthy in the 1950s. McCarthy's anti-

Communist campaign had generated widespread character assassination while putting anti-Communist liberals at risk, all in the name of patriotism—and it never nailed a single Communist spy.

In February 1950, Senator McCarthy launched his charge that there were card-carrying Communists in the State Department. He began a numbers game of just how many there were. When his first speech drew wide attention, he increased the numbers. Senator Smith asked McCarthy to show her the evidence. He produced some papers, but she proclaimed, "I don't understand the relevance of this to the charges." And those charges were destroying careers—and in several cases lives, by suicide. Senator Smith said, "I began to wonder about the validity, accuracy, credibility, and fairness of Joseph McCarthy's charges."

One day she confronted McCarthy on the floor of the Senate. He said, "Margaret, you seem to be worried about what I am doing." And she replied, "Yes, Joe, I want to see the proof. I have been waiting a long time now for you to produce proof."

"But I have shown you the photostatic copies, Margaret."

"Perhaps I'm stupid, Joe, but they don't prove a thing to me that backs up your charges."

Week after week, employing national television as well as the Senate rostrum, McCarthy enlarged his attacks, increased his charges against individuals in the army as well as the State Department. Dozens of veteran officials were pilloried under the cloak of senatorial immunity with unproved accusations and were smeared with guilt-by-association implications. Clearly, his anti-Communist fervor was casting doubt on the integrity and patriotism of major segments of the information and entertainment industries, as well as the national government. It was a period of political nightmare on a pervasive, national scale. As Senator Smith later wrote, "This great psychological fear even spread to the Senate, where a considerable amount of mental paralysis and muteness set in for fear of offending McCarthy." She added, "Distrust became so widespread that many dared not accept dinner invitations lest at some future date McCarthy might level unproved charges against someone who had been at the same dinner party." Later, even President Dwight Eisenhower, supreme Allied commander in World War II, cowered when McCarthy accused army generals of being soft on Communists.

Senator Smith was just a freshman senator. At that time, newcomers such as she were expected to hold their tongues and merely listen to their elders in the Senate. Senator Smith went home to Skowhegan for Memorial Day 1950 and returned to Washington with a speech that would be the first substantial blow against McCarthy and McCarthyism.

She had two hundred copies mimeographed and held by her assistant Bill Lewis until she started delivery on the floor of the Senate. On the way, as she stepped into the Senate subway train, Senator McCarthy appeared. "Margaret," he said, "you look very serious. Are you going to make a speech?"

She said, "Yes, and you won't like it."

He smiled. "Is it about me?"

"Yes," she replied, "but I'm not going to mention your name."

McCarthy frowned, "Remember, Margaret, I control Wisconsin's twenty-seven convention votes."

"For what?" she responded. Apparently, she supposed, he would keep her from getting his state's vice presidential nomination. That ended the conversation.

Once the Senate was in session Smith said she would speak as a Republican, a woman, a senator, an American of "a serious national condition," a national feeling of "fear and frustration that could result in national suicide." The Senate itself, she said, long known as a great deliberative body, has become "debased to the level of a forum of hate and character assassination sheltered by the shield of congressional immunity."

She noted that senators can "verbally attack anyone else without restraint" and yet "we hold ourselves above the same type of criticism." An attack by one senator on another is generally stopped. "It is high time for the United States Senate and its members to do some soul-searching—for us to weigh our consciences."

She referred to the constitutional guarantee of trial by jury. Character prosecution in the Senate, she said, can ruin a person's life. "Those who shout the loudest about Americanism in making character assassinations are all too frequently those who, by their own words and acts, ignore some of the basic principles of Americanism."

She said, "The American people are sick and tired of being afraid to speak their minds lest they be politically smeared as Communists or fascists." Freedom of speech has been so abused by some that it is not exercised by others, she added.

She said a Republican victory in the next presidential campaign was essential, but she did not want to see the Republican Party "ride to victory on the Four Horsemen of Calumny—Fear, Ignorance, Bigotry, and Smear."

She then released her Declaration of Conscience, signed by herself and six other Republican senators. The statement accused Democrats and Republicans of "unwittingly, but undeniably, playing directly into the Communist design of 'confuse, divide, and conquer.'" It is high time, the statement concluded, "that we all stopped being tools and victims of totalitarian techniques—techniques that, if continued here unchecked, will surely end what we have come to cherish as the American way of life."

Senator Smith's speech and her Declaration of Conscience were widely hailed by some and vehemently attacked by others. President Harry S Truman publicly ridiculed the speech but privately told her at a dinner, "Mrs. Smith, your Declaration of Conscience was one of the finest things that has happened here in Washington in all my years in the Senate and the White House." Senator Smith later wrote, "His public ridicule of the speech and his private praise of it were perhaps understandable by partisan political codes, even if conflicting by other standards."[1]

McCarthy mounted a vicious campaign against Senator Smith's reelection in 1954. He called her a fuzzy-minded, intellectualized left-winger and falsely said she was dying of cancer. Until having to undergo hip surgery, Margaret Chase Smith answered 2,941 consecutive Senate roll calls. McCarthy died several years later from cirrhosis of the liver and cancer.

All of this happened twenty years before I visited the senator to offer her the chair of Freedom House in 1970. But now there was a new national crisis—the divisive war in Vietnam. Margaret Smith had just written her Declaration of Conscience II.

Widespread discord over the war threatened once again to destroy the civility essential for a democratic society. She saw danger from the left and right. "Extremism bent upon polarization of our people," she warned, "is increasingly forcing upon the American people the narrow choice between anarchy and repression." This paralleled the Freedom House position on the war and the crucial absence of civility in the debates over national policy.

Sen. Hubert H. Humphrey, the liberal Democrat, wrote Smith, "Once again, you have said in your own quiet, concise, and persuasive manner what many of us have been thinking and all too few have been able to clearly articulate." And Richard Nixon, not yet the Republican president, said, "It was indeed fitting and timely that you should speak as you did on the twentieth anniversary of your Declaration of Conscience. Your counsel of renewed judgment was needed then and is needed now. I thank you."

Senator Smith told me she was inclined to accept the chairmanship because she saw it as "another opportunity to nurse our 'national sickness.'" She warned, however, that she was about to have two serious hip operations that would incapacitate her for awhile. I said that I would help her through that time, particularly since the operations would be at a hospital in New York City.

She later told me that she was impelled to accept my invitation because of the volume of mail she had been receiving from students around the country who challenged her "to do something about the words in [her recent] speech." I confessed that it was that speech, indeed, that had prompted our approach to her.

Shortly afterward, Senator Smith became chairman of Freedom House. I occasionally visited her in Washington on organization business, once introducing Mark and Marianne. She remembered them frequently and often asked how Mark was doing at school. She was 70 at the time, 77 when she retired as chair, and 97 when she died at home. Just a few months before her death she had written to me about Freedom House, where she was still chair emerita.

No matter how busy her Senate career, she managed to drive from Washington or from Maine to New York with Bill Lewis to chair board meetings. She came prepared for a full agenda of politically controversial subjects. Bill, too, was an extraordinary person. He had been Margaret's executive assistant since she started in the House of Representatives in 1940, replacing her late husband. She next ran for the Senate and became the first woman to gain election to both houses of Congress—with Bill's advice and assistance. He held degrees in law, business administration, geology, and mathematics and was decorated for service in the army, navy, and air force. Bill drafted much of Margaret's writing. Bill "ought to get a medal" for his literary work, said Edward R. Murrow, dean of American broadcast journalists.

Bill owned the house in Washington in which he and Margaret lived—she "on the second floor," she would say. They were inseparable, on and off the Senate floor. Bill never married. Their relationship in public was always professional. After months of driving Margaret to board meetings I urged the group to elect Bill to the board. He would no longer sit outside the room while the board was in session. It was a stunning loss for Margaret when Bill Lewis died, about ten years before she did. A room in the Margaret Chase Smith Library in Skowhegan is named for William C. Lewis Jr.

Interestingly, Mainers reelected Maggie Smith to public office knowing that "family values" for her and Bill meant something quite different than it did for straight-laced New Englanders. Yet that relationship produced not only declarations of conscience that the whole country came to admire, but Maggie Smith became the first woman to enter a primary for the presidency and the first woman to serve on the Armed Services Committee. She also held the rank of lieutenant colonel in the air force reserves—one suspects, with Bill's help. When she opposed the Pentagon's early proposal for an antiballistic-missile system, Mike Mansfield, Senate majority leader, said, "I never saw so many men publicly woo one woman."

She said, however, that she was not a feminist, but when she took her seat in the Senate for the first time, the women who had come to the Senate gallery from all over the country burst into applause. There was some buzz of "her vice presidential possibilities escalating into presidential fantasies," wrote Janann Sherman. When an NBC commentator asked her, "What would you do, Senator Smith, if you woke up some morning and found yourself in the White House?" She replied, "I think I'd go right to Mrs. Truman [then first lady], apologize, and go right home."

There was a decidedly feminine side to Maggie Smith. Her relationship with Bill was one mark. Another was her constant wearing of a red rose—whenever and wherever she went. Her desk in the Senate always had that single, fresh rose in place. And when Senator Smith came to Freedom House, Jessie Miller placed a fresh rose on the Senator's dress as she entered.

Early on the morning after President Kennedy was assassinated, Margaret Chase Smith walked solemnly across the Senate—from the Republican to the Democratic side—and gently deposited a red rose on Kennedy's former desk.

NOTE

1. Margaret Chase Smith, *Declaration of Conscience* (New York: Doubleday, 1972), p. 21.

49

EUGENE WIGNER
"Why Didn't You Tell Us?"

For more than sixty years, there have been widely known Americans on the board of Freedom House. One member won the Nobel Prize as well as many other honors in science and was most responsible for persuading President Roosevelt to build an atomic bomb before the Nazi Germans completed theirs. Yet Eugene Wigner was so self-effacing that his name had little public recognition. And in his years on the Freedom House board he rarely spoke without an apology that, to me, was deeply embarrassing.

Had the Nazis created the first nuclear blast, the world would have been dramatically changed, perhaps for the thousand years Hitler meant when he spoke of Germany's ascendancy for a millennium. Gene Wigner played a crucial role in forestalling such an outcome by alerting Franklin Roosevelt to the horrendous danger. But the names most often associated with that foresight are Albert Einstein and, to a lesser extent, Leo Szilard. Wigner and Szilard were world-class physicists. Wigner had a strong character but a self-effacing personality; Szilard was no less determined but had a sophisticated sense of promotion of a cause and of self.

I met with Gene frequently during the last twenty years of his life. I was as astounded at our first meeting as I was at our last by the utter modesty, extraordinary politeness, shyness, and deep sincerity of the man. Here was the recipient of every major European and international award in physics as well as the catalyst for the greatest scientific-cum-military development in human history—here was Gene Wigner apologizing whenever he rose at a Freedom House board meeting to address an issue under discussion. And, to the discredit of several fellow members, they even snickered over the mild tone of his remarks and, however pertinent they might be, regarded him as a novice in geopolitics. Wigner a novice? He had played a major role in transforming the military, and therefore the geopolitical, context of world power—and especially American power. What a novice.

In 1939 and 1940, Wigner had helped gain presidential support for the Manhattan Project, which split the atom and paved the way for succeeding nuclear developments. He also ran theoretical studies at the Metallurgical Laboratory in Chicago, which built a working nuclear pile for the production of plutonium. That yields atomic energy through fission. And Wigner, no less, designed the DuPont Company's engineering of an air-cooled atomic pile.

Yet I frequently cringed at the reception Gene Wigner received at meetings. Before he spoke, he would ask me all too politely whether or not he should address a particular national or international issue. I always encouraged him to speak. Generally, he did, drawing the demeaning reaction of several members.

He lived beyond ninety, still nearly erect, with a trim body—taking steps two at a time—and a boyish, self-deprecating smile.

Shortly before he died, I wrote Wigner, the Nobel laureate, the following letter:

Why didn't you tell us?

You heard us debate the crises in Europe, Africa, Latin America, and Afghanistan. When you did speak you apologized for your "inexperience." You always seemed extremely shy, painfully so. Now, you say, "I never wanted to be famous." An unlikely fate for a Nobel laureate, you acknowledge.

You never told us, until now, it was *you* who persuaded Albert Einstein in 1939 to write that historic letter to President Roosevelt urging him to construct an atomic bomb before Adolf Hitler built one. With it, Nazi Germany could have dominated the world. Einstein quickly agreed that Hitler must be stopped. Though Einstein was not a specialist in nuclear physics and had been a pacifist, you say, he quickly grasped the urgent need. Einstein's biographer Donald W. Clark quotes Einstein as saying in 1952 that the possibility of a chain reaction [needed for releasing atomic energy] "never occurred to me." In fact, he added, "I did not foresee that it would be released in my time. I only believed it was theoretically possible." At your meeting with him, you say, "Einstein spoke in German and I scribbled down his words." You translated the letter into English and Einstein signed it "without hesitation."

Yet Leo Szilard, by his account, stage-managed your meeting with Einstein. (Szilard, your old friend from Hungary and prewar days in Germany, had a far more outgoing personality.) Several meetings later, a secret U.S. government committee was set up, but Einstein was urged to prod for faster action. At your instigation, he wrote President Roosevelt (Einstein's biographer recalls) that the Germans were working intensely, secretly on the development of uranium.

Wrote Einstein, "I have discussed with Professor Wigner of Princeton University the situation in light of the [new] information available." The letter emphasizes how fear of Germany was the impetus for U.S. work in the field, and for the censorship in nuclear development.

Within two months. England and Germany were at war. Roosevelt started the Manhattan Project, the development of the atom bomb. But you didn't tell us, Professor Wigner, that you made the crucial contribution to the project. Your physical theories and applications influenced the basic design of nuclear reactors. You do tell us—now—that you were "quite conscious of an immoral element in my action": building a bomb. But you say you were "more concerned with the moral failure of . . . Adolf Hitler." Einstein, in his old age, expressed similar feelings. "I made one great mistake in my life," Donald Clark reports in *Einstein*, "I signed the letter to President Roosevelt recommending the atom bomb be made." But Einstein, as you, immediately added, "But there was some justification—the danger that the Germans would make them."

You did not tell us until now, Gene, of the moment the first nuclear reaction was accomplished. You stood beside Enrico Fermi on the squash court at the University of Chicago. You heard the recorder mark the first pit-a-pat of neutrons being absorbed and the first self-sustaining chain reaction. Afterwards, the bottle of Chianti you provided was opened for a toast, and all the participants signed the cork. *The cork was the only written record of those who witnessed this historic moment.* You could feel the silent prayers that building the atomic bomb was the right thing.

You never told us about your boyhood friends Edward Teller, Leo Szilard, and Janci von Neumann. They all garnered Nobel and other laureates. Self-effacing, as always, you say of the four child prodigies, "I was the slowest." Certainly the shyest and most modest. Together, your quartet reshaped mathematics and physics for all time. Your formidable group came to America and contributed greatly to this country's dominance in science and military power.

Among your contributions were your students. Of these, Frederick Seitz developed a theory of solids, was prominent in the Manhattan Project, and later became president of the National Academy of Sciences and president of Rockefeller University. John Bardeen did pioneering work in physics, helped develop the transistor, and was the first ever to receive two Nobel prizes.

In your self-analysis now, you write, "I very rarely sought an audience with the great physicists. . . . [I]t seemed unreasonable to ask Albert Einstein . . . to pay attention to Wigner. I was afraid of imposing. Looking back I suppose this fear of imposing was unfounded. But I felt it keenly at the time. I was content to be introduced to Einstein's *thoughts*." And so you were, by the power of your experiments and your writing; sufficiently so that Einstein quickly accepted your analysis of both the physics of atomic energy and the politics of building a nuclear bomb.

You exonerate your former German colleague Werner Heisenberg, judging that though he remained in Nazi Germany during the war he cleverly avoided developing the atomic bomb, which he had the capability to produce. You also do not believe that your American colleague, J. Robert Oppenheimer, a sturdy contributor to U.S. nuclear development, should have had his security clearance stopped and his career placed under a cloud.

I have come to understand you better through your conversations with Andrew Szanton, published as *The Recollections of Eugene P. Wigner*. You grew up in Hungary under a strict parental code. You were taught to be "correct and friendly, to follow others going through a doorway, and never to claim more credit than you deserve." (You still act as your parents taught you, to a fault.) You were expected to enter your father's tannery business. You did for a while but then decided to study science. In the 1930s, studying and teaching in Germany, you say you were a "distinctly *unperceptive* young man, absorbed in learning physics . . . wanting no part of national politics or warfare." Yet you say "it did not take any special perception to see the Nazi will to subjugate. It took a special perception *not* to see it."

Yet most Americans did not see it. And so you disliked being "pleasantly disagreeable," urging America to war only because you felt it was imperative. You never blamed Americans for resisting that idea. "Good people dislike waging war," you say. It was "refugees" like yourself, you add, who saw most clearly that war was coming. You learned, though, "that people do not like to learn from foreigners." Yet you persisted in the late 1930s and again in the 1960s and 70s (as Freedom House was doing) when aggressive Communism loomed. You concluded, "As foreigners, we knew Americans far better than they knew us." Americans, you say, "rarely had any meaningful contact with foreigners and hardly understood us." Yet, when war came and nuclear physics was crucial for America's survival, the United States called on its "foreigners," particularly your Hungarian quartet, to turn the tide.

Geopolitics were far more complicated in the 1970s and 1980s. You found no ready acceptance in America to understand the Soviet challenge. You were "dismayed." That is what brought you to Freedom House and the discussions we have had. There were "slogans and brutality on the Russian side; slogans and nonsense for the Americans," you say. You wanted the American people to think seriously about Soviet aggression in Europe—Berlin, Czechoslovakia, Hungary, Estonia, Latvia, Lithuania—"and the United States did next to nothing about it." The Russians vigorously practiced science, you say, "but science only in the service of their military." Yet, you are loathe to criticize "too sharply" the country that has "adopted me and given me a safe and pleasant home for sixty years."

"One thing that Americans do understand deeply," you say, "is freedom, and that is a very great blessing." That, I assume, is what brought you to Freedom House.

If only you had spoken more freely, less modestly.

Professor Wigner, perhaps modestly, never replied to my letter—he may have regarded it as presumptuous. He died soon afterward. His life and career are the best response.

50

JONAS SAVIMBI
From the Killing Field to Park Avenue

M any foreign leaders visit Freedom House: dissidents from oppressive governments, freedom fighters in bloody conflicts, journalists harassed by authoritarian regimes, parliamentarians in and out of office. They visit New York so that their words will reverberate at the United Nations and will be heard at the headquarters of international news media—or by an American president who has not yet offered an official visit.

For many, we provide a sympathetic hearing; for some, help in approaching Washington officials; for others, a press conference to air their stories. The most controversial of all such visitors—he required more attention and more protective security—was Dr. Jonas Savimbi, commander of UNITA, the National Union for the Total Independence of Angola.

Before I met him, Savimbi was the charismatic bush fighter who had been engaged for twenty-seven years in the struggle to free Angola: first from Portuguese rule, and then from the divisive battle with Angolan parties. UNITA's struggle soon involved inflammatory aspects: Savimbi, desperate for help, accepted Chinese arms and was called a Maoist. When the Angolan government welcomed weapons from the Soviet Union and troops from Cuba, Savimbi depended on a secret arms source in South Africa, whose white-racist government all of Africa opposed, though Washington must have winked at the UNITA relationship. UNITA was secretly regarded by the United States as a geopolitical asset because of Soviet support for the Angolan government and the thousands of Communist troops sent by Fidel Castro to fight Savimbi. His principal opponent was President José Eduardo dos Santos, whose MPLA (Popular Liberation Movement of Angola) controlled Luanda, Angola's capital, and its environs. Although Savimbi was in the bush and did not control a major city, the area held by his fighters was larger than that controlled by President dos Santos.

I was called one day by Jeremihas Chitunda, Savimbi's Washington representative, to discuss a proposed visit to the United States by the UNITA leader. The State Department had refused to designate Savimbi an official visitor. The department indicated, however, that it would like to speak to Savimbi informally. A number of people in both houses of Congress, in both parties, similarly said they would appreciate a visit. Chitunda spent many hours with me discussing where Savimbi would like to visit and how the trip might be organized. We had frank talks about the controversial nature of Savimbi himself, as well as UNITA as an embattled force charged with some particularly bloody forays. Chitunda had a degree in mining engineering from the University of Arizona. He was a highly intelligent spokesman clearly slated one day to be at least foreign minister in a Savimbi cabinet. Savimbi himself held several degrees from European institutions and spoke several languages fluently.

I faced a clear division on the Freedom House board. Some opposed any effort to sponsor Savimbi's visit. They felt he was a reckless warrior with no real democratic aspirations. Others believed that Savimbi held a key to the eventual pacification of southern Africa and the removal of Soviet influences from that critical part of the continent. Freedom House decided to take the public relations risk of serving as sponsor of the Savimbi visit.

With Chitunda, I arranged the kickoff press conference at Freedom House, which would be Savimbi's first encounter with the massive Western news media. I assumed we should expect a major press turnout for this shadowy figure, right out of the Angolan bush. I also arranged accommodations at a small but select hotel on Park Avenue South. I was dealing with a sizable contingent of armed warriors, and I understood as well that special arrangements were necessary for security at Freedom House—and all along Savimbi's U.S. itinerary. I spent considerable time clearing details with the FBI and the New York City police. The bomb squad and other special details were assigned. The visit would begin at a small feeder airport in New Jersey, a place kept secret from the press.

Dr. Savimbi alighted from the plane with an entourage of some twenty burly fighters, with Chitunda, slim and bespectacled, at his side. Chitunda introduced me to Savimbi, who gripped my hand, almost crushing some bones, and thanked me profusely for sponsoring the visit. From the first moment, Savimbi was an articulate exponent of his politics and his military plan. He looked the part of the military leader. He wore his version of an Eisenhower jacket; it was amply filled by his large and seemingly powerful frame. He carried a military crop. Clearly he was in command. His several levels of subordinates automatically fulfilled appointed chores the moment a need arose. Savimbi was accompanied by a young woman who was also a highly voluble spokesperson for UNITA.

Savimbi, Chitunda, and I rode in the lead car to the hotel. In that half-hour he described the military situation in Angola and asked me to outline questions the press might put to him. I mentioned the most controversial matters concerning his relationship with South Africa, his source of arms and funds, his estimate of the outcome of the armed struggle, and his plans for a government after fighting ended. In the next few days I would hear his answers to these questions several times. Clearly, he had mastered the art of political discourse and press relations.

Checking into a Park Avenue hotel with this band of fighters just out of the Angola bush was an unusual sight. I had arranged the reservation, so I was expected to see everyone properly housed. Assigning rooms based on various tribal and military distinctions was not easy. Nor had the hotel personnel (dressed in formal attire) ever coped with such problems. At checkout time, the question of sponsorship would turn serious. Chitunda was to have provided funds to cover the hotel bill, but he did not. I paid the nearly $10,000 bill and months later was refunded from a private donor in Texas who had been visited by Savimbi and was probably promised some interest in the considerable oil reserves in Angola. By 1996, however, the oil was still in areas under dos Santos's control, whereas the great diamond fields were under the jurisdiction of Savimbi's forces.

Savimbi addressed a large press conference at Freedom House while security people ringed the street outside. An opposition group demonstrated a block away, under police surveillance. Shouting supporters were kept at a distance from the opponents. Savimbi lectured the press on the intricacies of Angolan politics the past thirty years. He told the press, as he had told me, that he had gone to South Africa only to purchase arms, not to make any deal with the apartheid government. As a black nationalist, he told me, "I am against apartheid and have been for years." He said he was forced to buy weapons in South Africa because dos Santos was getting Soviet arms and Cuban troops. He said the Cubans had no idea what they were fighting for in Africa and were suffering heavy casualties in the unfriendly terrain.

I discussed privately with Savimbi the kind of government he would establish once he came to power. He said he favored a democratic government, with free elections. He denied he would form a socialist government, as some opponents had said. But I felt that he would blend some Western democratic forms with an African mode.

Savimbi held numerous private meetings in Washington and other cities before departing from the New Jersey airport. For the next two years, I heard frequently from Chitunda about progress Savimbi's forces were making in the bush. After returning from the fighting field himself, Chitunda carried a message to me from Savimbi. He invited me to join him in the field and observe the military advances he was making in Angola. I considered making the trip but decided against it.

Instead, in 1988, Savimbi asked me to sponsor another visit. We provided another press conference, and this time, there was greater interest in more public visits with officials in Washington. I did not have to provide housing or transportation. His discussions in Washington concerned the movement toward a negotiated peace that was deemed possible because of the advances of his forces in the field. There had been bilateral discussions between the United States and the Cubans over removal of the Cuban troops from Angola. The imminent independence of Namibia was also encouraging. Chester Crocker, a former contributor to *Freedom at Issue* and now assistant secretary of state for African affairs, was mediating talks among the Cubans, the Angolan government, and South African officials about resolving the conflict in Angola. Crocker had urged me to sponsor Savimbi's second visit so that the talks could be extended. This time, I set up Savimbi's presentation at Freedom House as a formal address.

He began by saying he was in New York because the potential for a peaceful settlement was "very great." He said the MPLA and the Cubans—after fighting him for thirteen years—realized "there is no military solution to the conflict in Angola." He said he did not seek a final victory in the field but wanted to get the MPLA to the negotiating table. He said that in 1987, the Russians spent $1.8 billion for military hardware to launch an offensive against him, which failed. He credited support from the United States for this victory. With the "new atmosphere between the Soviet Union and the U.S.," he said, "a peaceful change in Angola and Southern Africa is now possible." He added, "We are not Maoists, agents of the CIA, or puppets of South Africa. We are Angolan nationalists who have sacrificed much of our own lives for this struggle."

Then, in response to a question I had put to him privately several times, he addressed the question of democracy for Angola:

> A European friend who used to be close to me would say, "You need freedom in your country, you need democracy." He was invited to Luanda [the capital, occupied by dos Santos], and they gave him caviar, champagne, everything. Then when he came back he said, "No, democracy is good for the West, for civilized countries. For you in Africa, to begin with, you should content yourselves with dictatorship." I said that was wrong. If that was the fate reserved for our people, we would not have had enough courage to fight Portuguese colonialism. And for thirteen years we have been fighting the Cubans and the Russians.
>
> It is shocking to me that few of the groups I have spoken to in the U.S. have addressed the Cuban occupation of my country. Most have addressed only the South African issue. . . . My father died fighting for freedom. I have been fighting for freedom for years, and my life has not been easy. But I could feel comforted if those who attacked apartheid also attacked the occupation by fifty-seven thousand Cubans. But people tend to believe that Cubans are good guys by colonizing the blacks in Angola. The South Africans are bad guys—as they are!—by oppressing the blacks in South Africa. . . . We deserve a different destiny. We will achieve it.[1]

In the question period he described the negotiations then proceeding without him in Europe. He also revealed for the first time that, despite his South African relationship, he had support from black African countries, naming six of them.

He criticized Gulf Oil and Chevron for pumping oil in Angola and paying hard dollars to the MPLA, money that purchased arms used against UNITA.

Finally, he was asked the question I had put to him: What would be his role in a government after reconciliation? He said, "If I am not dead, my spirit will be there, even if I am not in the government. But I will be a candidate, but not before [reconciliation]."

In 1991, after the Cold War sponsors withdrew their support, dos Santos and Savimbi signed a peace agreement, and the war stopped long enough to begin negotiations. Savimbi sent Chitunda and several trusted friends to the bargaining table with the government. As the UNITA men entered under a truce, Chitunda and his colleagues were shot dead in cold blood. I felt a personal loss for this gentle man who dreamed of serving in a peaceful government, perhaps at some overseas post—maybe in Washington. Savimbi was angered and outraged; he lost all trust in MPLA negotiators.

But internationally sponsored elections were held in October 1992. Savimbi lost and faced a runoff election. He charged fraud, the war resumed, and Savimbi gained new ground fast, capturing Angola's second-largest city. But the government fought back, having purchased vast amounts of new weapons.

In 1996, Savimbi, a fighter for a third of his life, was sixty-one years old. Angolans generally were tired of war and blamed both sides for prolonging it. The war had indeed tapered off. Savimbi told aid donors, "I will never take my people back to war." A peace treaty signed the year before had brought 6,500 armed UN peacekeepers to Angola to receive surrendered weapons and to provide housing and twenty thousand beds for UNITA warriors. The first signs of reconstruction could be seen in parts of the country.

The transition had been slow, partly because of hardline subordinates on both sides. In years past, both sides had broken pledges and resumed fighting. Early in 1996, U.S. ambassador to the UN Madeleine Albright visited Savimbi in his bullet-scarred headquarters in Bailundo. He promised to deliver his troops soon thereafter. Then, using his silver-headed walking stick, he pointed to pictures on the wall of his dead nephew and others who had fought with him. "You can't let people go along with you, watch them die, and in the end let it all go," he said.

He doubtless pointed to a picture of Jeremihas Chitunda.

The war dragged on—too long for Savimbi. Early in 2002, he was ambushed and killed by government troops near his camp in the bush. His dead body was prominently displayed on government television.[2] A subordinate met with Luanda leaders to arrange a cease-fire. Certain, then, was Savimbi's statement to me years earlier that he would never leave the country. But at the time of his death, it was in disarray, partly due to his insurgency, partly to internal and external Marxist influences, and the ensuing corruption in Luanda.

NOTES

1. See Jonas Savimbi, "The Horizon of Peace in Angola," *Freedom at Issue*, September–October 1988, p. 13.

2. Henri Couvin, "Angola Shows Rebel's Body on Television," *New York Times*, February 24, 2002.

51

THE DALAI LAMA AND THE *TALIT*

Another troubled—but this time a pacifist—leader sought a visit to Freedom House as a gateway to America, its people, and its government. I was asked to arrange the first visit of the Dalai Lama of Tibet.

In 1959, China exiled from Tibet the fourteenth Dalai Lama, temporal and spiritual leader of six million Tibetan Buddhists. The Chinese government systematically invaded the Jokhang temple, beating and killing thirty monks and dragging their bodies "like dead animals and threw them in the back of trucks." More than eighty-seven thousand Tibetans were killed in Lhasa alone, according to Chinese sources. The slaughter continued for years, as did China's effort to obliterate the culture and religion of the Tibetans. Some 170,000 troops of seventeen divisions of the People's Liberation Army were stationed within striking distance of Lhasa. The center of the firestorm is the Dalai Lama. Tourists in Lhasa are surreptitiously handed bits of paper calling for Tibetan independence; said one slip, "Long live his Holiness the Dalai Lama." What manner of man is he, chosen as a child in an ages-old ceremony to lead all Tibetans?

In 1979, I would find the answer by arranging his first visit. Tibetans are a small but devout group in America. They learned after many years to blend their religious beliefs—contemplation, harmony with nature and other humans, and avoidance of violent speech and action—to integrate their traditional lifestyle, with the activism of American political life. In calm, almost defensive terms they would plead for understanding of the plight of Tibetans under the gun in China. They seldom gained public attention. Their troubles seemed a long way off, their civilization and religion just as distant. Most difficult, their leader, the Dalai Lama, lived in exile in India. Finally, they realized, only he could attract the interest of the American press and through the media generate some support from officials in Washington.

I was worried at first, because I knew little of the religious nature of Tibetan tradition. Freedom House had supported religious freedom and ecumenism but never addressed the particular practices of a religious denomination. Clearly, however, the central issue here was political. Tibet declared its independence in 1913, but Beijing claimed Tibet was merely an autonomous territory within China. Some six thousand Tibetan monasteries had been razed, and traditional practices forbidden. China seems bent on obliterating the small non-Han enclave on the 13,000-foot-high plateau in the Himalayas.

I arranged a press conference at Freedom House, advised the Tibetans on how media interest is aroused and sustained, and suggested other cities that the Dalai Lama should visit. I included Washington and tried to arrange an official reception at the White House. That was rejected, though President Carter had made support for human rights a centerpiece of his administration. Officials did not want to irritate the Chinese.

The arrival of the Dalai Lama at Freedom House was carefully choreographed in Tibetan tradition. He stepped from a car wearing maroon robes, rose-tinted sunglasses, and a warm smile. He seemed younger than his traditional title suggested. I met him at the steps of the building, escorted him inside, and introduced Whitney North Seymour, chairman of our board. Wit, in his own right, was an impressive personality, distinguished in the law and often considered for the Supreme Court. He was indeed courtly. We three chatted in my office before the press conference began. Without vindictiveness, the Dalai Lama reviewed the history of the Chinese occupation. Indeed, he avoided references to acts of cruelty. He said that a free Tibet would reflect the experience of Tibetans in exile as well as those who remained in their homeland. They had been exposed to many systems and ideologies, he said, but his people would put it all together under the main principle of compassion and altruism.

Some 150 representatives of major networks and newsmagazines appeared at the press conference. That day, the Dalai Lama received his first national publicity originating in America. Coincidentally, that same week, Pope John Paul II drove past Freedom House and waved to us. His entourage did not stop. Press coverage for his New York visit, as expected, saturated the media.

The Dalai Lama was soon forgotten, except on those annual days of remembrance when several dozen Tibetans and a few hardy folk from Freedom House demonstrated across the street for the United Nations. I spoke from a soapbox one year, and others succeeded me. On the fortieth anniversary of the United Nations in 1985, some three hundred Tibetans celebrated the day in Lhasa and were attacked by police. Eighteen were killed, and more than 150 seriously wounded. That drew little press attention in the United States, despite our best effort.

By 1991, the untiring work of a few hardy Tibetans in America persuaded the Dalai Lama to return to the States. On that occasion, Freedom House would present him with its Freedom Award; and we would do so in Washington this time—at a luncheon cosponsored by the Congressional Human Rights Caucus. I was particularly moved by his opening remarks after receiving the award: "I have a special relationship with Freedom House . . . because it was at Freedom House in 1979 that I held my first press conference here in the United States." He said he was "extremely happy . . . to be here with some of [his] old friends." He greeted me warmly after the speech.

His words were a challenge to those in power. "I am a monk," he said, who comes from "the roof of the world." Tibetan civilization, he added, "is quite useful" to humanity as a whole. On behalf of his "unfortunate people" he said "we are passing through what really is a critical situation. We are facing a situation where one ancient nation with a unique cultural heritage may disappear from this planet. So this is a question of life and death."

He said he always prays for "all sentient beings, and in particular for all human beings." But, he added, "prayer alone is not sufficient. . . . The prayer should transform itself into action." He urged those present to fight against human rights violations, and for democracy. That, he said, "not only saves human rights [but] helps human progress."

He added, "Within humanity, those people who have a deeper or greater creative nature and more intelligence, these people usually become more critical of the existing system or government. So when you see these people's rights suppressed, then essentially the entire progress of that country or that community has been stopped. Without freedom, the human creative nature cannot he utilized fully. And without utilizing creative human nature there is no progress."

After the speech, the Dalai Lama was ushered to the White House, where for a few moments he met—informally—the elder President George Bush. For the sake of the Chinese government, to which Bush had served as ambassador, this was not a planned meeting, just a happenstance. And there were no photographs taken; that might embarrass the present U.S. ambassador to Beijing. The worldly wise Dalai Lama understood: the United States was having it both ways. At least this time, though, a president bowed ever so gently toward the Dalai Lama, the embodiment of a religious leader bearing witness to men defiling not only spiritual houses and artifacts but the flesh and blood of religionists.

The Dalai Lama is a remarkable man. Soon after receiving the Nobel Peace Prize he invited to Dharamsala, a remote town in the Himalayan foothills of India, eight rabbis and Jewish scholars, wanting to discover the mystery of Jewish survival for two thousand years. Presumably that history could help Tibetan tradition prevail, despite intensive assault.

The Dalai Lama wanted to learn about the "inner life" of Jews. He wondered how Judaism provides for transforming the human being, for overcoming "afflictive emotions" such as anger. Clearly, during this critical period for Tibetans, anger and violence could be a predictable response. The rabbis found the Dalai Lama a man of humility and kindness, with a "quiet mind." They admired the Buddhist practice of meditation; it seemed to make its practitioners "calmer, wiser, and more capable of dealing with difficult emotions," one rabbi recalled.

The Dalai Lama wondered about the equivalent in Judaism. He was told by Rabbi Rodger Kamenetz from Los Angeles, "The work of transformation, for us, is a holy path. But more and more people who seek transformation don't go to a rabbi. They go to a psychiatrist, who will teach them not enlightenment but self-satisfaction."[1]

They addressed the sensitive issue of Jewish converts to Buddhism. The Dalai Lama said he never urged anyone to change religions, but to honor all faiths. Many monks and nuns around the Dalai Lama had Jewish roots, including the great-granddaughter of Henrietta Szold, founder of Hadassah, the American women's Zionist organization. The rabbis changed their opinion of these former Jews; they were no longer regarded as "cultists" but "witty, even radiant in some cases, certainly not brainwashed zombies." The converts said they had found something valuable in Buddhism that they had not found in Judaism.

Rabbi Kamenetz left the Dalai Lama saying, "I realized how I had undervalued what was precious in my own tradition, especially prayer and study. I was also entirely ignorant of Jewish meditation. My contact with the Tibetan Buddhists deepened my expectations of Judaism."

That author noted some similarities in the two religions. He likened the monk's robe to the *talit*, the Jewish prayer shawl. I have a memorable token of my meeting with the Dalai Lama. As he left Freedom House in 1979, he handed me a clear-white scarf. It was a traditional greeting from an honored guest. Coming directly from the Dalai Lama, the scarf has the quality of a *talit*.

NOTE

1. Rodger Kamenetz, "What I Learned about Judaism from the Dalai Lama," *Reform Judaism*, summer 1994, p. 21.

52

LUCIA THORNE
AND THE *MUJAHEDEEN*

I n my travels to dangerous places I never worried as I did when Lucia Thorne took three secret trips in 1983. My Soviet specialist would go inside Afghanistan, where Soviet troops were conducting the "dirty war" against the *mujahedeen,* "holy fighters" against Moscow-implanted Afghan Communists. Lucia, moreover, had been born in Russia, escaped as a child with her parents, served for two decades as an active anti-Communist, and would almost certainly have been imprisoned, or worse, if caught by Soviet troops.

No Western journalists had been allowed inside Afghanistan. After months of negotiations with rebel fighters, Lucia found a way inside the country. On four trips (her last in 1986), she would lead into Afghanistan photographers and journalists from ABC-TV's *20/20*, Australian TV's *60 Minutes*, *Life* magazine, and a Canadian newspaper. Each foray would require elaborate decoys, secret codes, and great stamina. The purpose: to interview Soviet soldiers held captive by the *mujahedeen*, to try to secure their release to the West, and to show Western citizens the utter degradation and slaughter by the Soviets in Afghanistan.

Five years later, Lucia met President Ronald Reagan in the White House to plead for help in bringing her "boys" to asylum in the United States. Several men still in Afghanistan had written heartbreaking appeals to the president; one had questioned whether the president believed in God. Lucia handed the letters to the president. Sergei Busov wrote to the president. "Is it possible that after all this, my friends and I are destined to live a life of anguish and suffering, without freedom? Can it be that this is all we deserve?"

The president seemed moved and said, "When you write, tell them I do believe in God." Lucia gripped Reagan's hand and said, "Please do your best."

384 A PASSION FOR FREEDOM

He said he would. Within a few weeks, the last of eighteen men Lucia rescued were on their way to safety.

It was hard for me, knowing each time that Lucia was entering a war zone totally unprotected and without lines of communication. It was a land where both sides killed at random and Soviet gun ships aimed especially at places where Soviet POWs were known to be held. Not to mention, where women were treated as chattel, and Western women clearly were suspect by Pakistani border gunmen.

It is ironic that before this cruel war began in 1979, the term *Afghanistanism* was used by journalists to describe anything in the world that went unreported. I had also hired Rosanne Klass to concentrate on resistance to the war in Afghanistan. For years before the war, Rosanne had been a teacher in Afghanistan and knew some of the current players. She parlayed these contacts into several dramatic press conferences when Americans knew nothing of the conflict, and cared even less. She also wrote a widely publicized book, which I published: *Afghanistan: The Great Game Revisited.*[1] Rosanne became an indefatigable opponent of the Soviet invasion of Afghanistan, appearing before congressional committees and in radio and television interviews.

By 1983, journalists were eager to see the war but could not get inside. The Soviets did not even tell their own people that Soviet ground troops were fighting in Afghanistan. Only Soviet bombers were admitted to be aiding their "Socialist allies," the Communist puppets in Kabul. Body bags came home in metallic boxes sealed to hide the terrible wounds, not nonbelligerent accidents suffered by Soviet ground troops. The Pakistanis closed their Afghan border to journalists because they did not want retaliation from Moscow. Iran's border with Afghanistan was already closed to Westerners. Lucia learned through a Soviet émigré in Paris that the *mujahedeen* were holding—some said as many as two hundred—Soviet POWs.

Lucia began months of negotiation with several different *mujahedeen* leaders. Some were political or religious moderates, others extremist and wildly bloodthirsty. Eventually, Lucia dealt with them all. Each group held some POWs. Her anti-Communist credentials got her past the initial suspicions. Then, with great patience, she persuaded the rebel leaders that their general cause would be helped by the humanitarian signal of releasing some POWs. Their political objectives would be advanced by allowing Western journalists to tell the Afghans' remarkable story of poorly armed resistance to a formidable superpower.

When Lucia arranged her first crossing she put her case to me bluntly as a fait accompli. I had great misgivings. I knew the usual journalistic drill, that no story is worth the life of a reporter. Yet this was Lucia's determined decision. She knew the risks. She shared them only with me; her parents were told she was going to Europe. I asked her why she would do this. She said her father had emphasized all her life how badly POWs had been treated. He himself, an engineer-lieutenant in the Red Army, had been captured by the Germans. On a second try, he escaped while still in Soviet territory and went back to Rostov for his wife and Lucia, then about three years old. They made their way out of the Soviet Union and into a detention camp in postwar East Germany. From there, they escaped the East German Communists and made it to West Germany.

After the war, many Soviet POWs still held in Western Europe were returned to the Soviet Union by a British-Soviet agreement. Tens of thousands of these Soviet POWs were slaughtered on their return by the Soviets or died in the gulag. Lucia never forgot those events and how close she came to them. She wanted to save Soviet POWs then in the hands of the *mujahedeen*; I understood, and I worried every day of her long, repeated immersion in Afghanistan.

Lucia's anti-Communism was deeply ingrained, not the result of indoctrination in America or solely her commitment to Freedom House's Soviet program, for which I had retained her. In 1934, her maternal grandfather, a militant Baptist preacher, was arrested in the middle of the night by the Rostov secret police. He returned home after a year and a half with all of his fingernails pulled out and died shortly afterward. Lucia's paternal grandfather was arrested in 1937 and sent to the gulag; the rest of her father's family was exiled to Siberia. The last word from her aunt said they were living in a small hut in the forest, surrounded by howling wolves.

In 1983, Lucia knew that the Soviet military was still playing by the same rules. Even in peacetime, some five thousand Red Army soldiers died each year from beatings of recruits by their officers, and officers in turn were killed by infuriated privates. Lucia was to hear such reports firsthand once inside Afghanistan. The men she would interview had been pushed beyond human limits and had defected to the Afghan rebels.

To get inside Afghanistan Lucia faced great tests of endurance and deception. She entered from Peshawar, Pakistan, but only after early-morning briefings with *mujahedeen*, silent drives through dark alleys toward the border, through seven Pakistani checkpoints before leaving vehicles behind and trudging on foot across the border. To pass these checkpoints, Lucia wore a *burqa* that loosely covered her body from head to feet, leaving only room for her eyes, which were covered by a netting so as not to be visible by others. She removed all red from her toenails, because her feet might be visible through the sandals. She seemed pregnant because she carried under her costume the portable cameras the men would use. When asked by a border guard where she was going, she would answer in Urdu, "Ask my husband." That was a fittingly demure response for an Islamic woman. She had practiced these words and uttered them in reply to every question put to her.

Once across the border, they walked southeast along rocky ridges and forded streams, came upon grassy valleys, and reached rockier bluffs and moonlike surfaces devoid of vegetation. They would dash for cover in that sparse landscape when Soviet gunships roared above. After a wearying trek, Lucia and her band came to a secret *mujahedeen* training camp. One trainee was fifteen years old, with "peach fuzz on his gentle young face," Lucia said. Two weeks later, he would be sent with a captured Kalashnikov rifle to face the heavily equipped Soviet military machine. Years and thousands of deaths later, the *mujahedeen* would have CIA-provided handheld surface-to-air missiles, which made the war too costly for the Soviet Union. After ten years, it withdrew.

Almost from the beginning, as Lucia observed, Soviet soldiers were thoroughly disillusioned. One young blue-eyed Russian boy of nineteen who had deserted from the Russian army in Kabul said, "The Soviet Union should pull out its forces because innocent people are dying on both sides." The POWs were under constant guard. Some held by Islamic extremists were kept in dank underground holes. Most would sit in a small room built into a quadrangular stone wall that made up the guerrilla stronghold. From a distance, it seemed a small medieval fortress standing in the middle of nowhere. Two prisoners, kept together, would spend time talking or reading and rereading the few magazines Lucia could provide. They were allowed brief walks under the watchful eyes of an armed guard. For amusement, they caught snakes, lizards, and scorpions, said Lucia, of which there were plenty.

The Soviet troops were told before they were sent to Afghanistan that they would protect the Afghan border against American and other mercenaries. Once in Afghanistan, there were no Americans, but mainly defenseless Afghan men, women, and children to be bombed, their houses invaded and looted, and horrible treatment meted out to captured *mujahedeen*. Twelve were tied and forced to lie on the ground while three armored personnel carriers drove over them. One POW told Lucia, "I had to clean the remains out of the tank treads." After he and other privates were forced to dig a shallow grave for the remains, the drunken lieutenant pulled one severed head from the ground, poured benzene over it, and placed it in a pot to boil. Igor Kovalchuk, the POW telling this account, wrote poetry in captivity. Of that incident, he wrote of the drunken officer carrying on a conversation with the severed head:

> Allah is great;
> Make him connect
> A body to your head
> So you can become my buffoon.

Igor's job was to fire the machine gun on an armored personnel carrier, equipped with a laser. It wasn't supposed to kill people, but blind them, Igor explained. "The gunner would look for a suitable target, usually a group of villagers, and then I would have to shoot," he told Lucia. "After I pulled the trigger and looked through the viewfinder I could see people's heads rolling off like watermelons and their bodies ripped apart, like pieces of raw meat," he grimaced. Although he had less than six months left to serve, he couldn't take it any more, he said. He defected.

Atrocities were also committed by the Afghans. One group of Soviet soldiers, ambushed at night, were killed in cold blood and their bodies mutilated. The Soviet officer laid the bodies on the ground to excite his soldiers' anger and enmity.

One of Lucia's saddest experiences was returning to these desolate young prisoners, time and again—some after six years—and finding their bodies deteriorated, their spirits low, and hope all but gone. They would plead with her to take them to the United States. She would leave, haunted by their faces and their pleas, and increase her visits to American officials. She testified before congressional committees and met behind closed doors with administration as well as legislative leaders. One senator said it was strange that one young woman could find these POWs, but the CIA insisted it was too difficult for the agency to do so. We held press conferences, and she wrote articles for major U.S. publications. Slowly, the tide was turning in Washington, very slowly. Officials expressed some desire to help but cautioned that it would be difficult to save these men without endangering relations with Pakistan (good relations were needed by the United States for other geopolitical reasons), or without exacerbating the Soviets directly in the supposedly secret surrogate war both sides were playing.

Lucia's persistence paid off. One by one, the guerrilla groups agreed to release some men. The first three came out in December 1983. Lucia never asked the *mujahedeen* how they made their selection, and she did not ask the U.S. government how it managed to bring out these men. The "secret railroad" had to remain secret. One day, Lucia was phoned and told, "Your men are coming." She met them at their arrival with overwhelming joy on both sides. The men hugged "Mama Luda." They appeared soon after at our press conference, and there began a five-year battle to keep the flow coming. The men were the best spokesmen not only for the release of their fellow POWs, but for the education of Americans to the terribly bloody war that had already created four million refugees, hundreds of thousands of dead Afghan civilians—Lucia in a *Wall Street Journal* article called it the "War of Innocents"[2]—and the killing of thousands of raw Soviet recruits.

Soviet officials offered the POWs amnesty if they returned home, but most refused the offer as a ruse. One who accepted the bid was sentenced to twelve years in prison upon his return to Moscow. (He was later released when word of the deception got out.) Another who returned was killed in an automobile accident in Russia. Most telling was the response of Khadzhimurad Suleimanov, twenty-five, a sergeant who defected in 1982. "They make this offer now when it's too late," he said. "I was held captive 5½ years and the Soviet government offered no help, no interest." This was part of the gigantic cover-up inside the Soviet Union. To allow the POWs to return would have revealed to the Soviet people the nature of the war in Afghanistan. This cruel rejection of the plight of Soviet soldiers was best uncovered in documents Lucia secured inside Afghanistan.

The Hezb-e-Islami guerrillas who had kidnapped and executed Evgeny Okhrimyuk, the Soviet Union's top geologist stationed in Afghanistan, gave

Lucia the man's briefcase. Okhrimyuk had pleaded with Soviet officials as high as President Leonid Brezhnev to save him, a civilian. "It's very disappointing that during this long period [seventy days in captivity] no one has even tried to put himself in my place as a human being, and no one has cared to send me a single word through the Red Cross." Letters were forwarded to Moscow by the International Red Cross, but the Soviets never responded. "I'm already sixty-eight years old. I have honestly devoted all of life to our homeland. I don't want to believe there are no ways to save my life," he wrote Brezhnev. To release Okhrimyuk would reveal there had been more to the Soviet invasion of Afghanistan than sending help to "Socialist allies." Okhrimyuk's elaborate notes contained statistics on the extensive losses to the Afghan infrastructure inflicted by "counterrevolutionary elements"—those opposing the Communists—and the Soviet Union's major plans for the future industrial development of Afghanistan under Soviet control. Neither the present losses on the ground nor plans for future Soviet exploitation would jibe with then current Kremlin propaganda on the nature of the war. Okhrimyuk was left to die.

The viciousness of the war did not end at the borders of Afghanistan. Lucia was repeatedly attacked by spokesmen for the Soviet Union, in the United States and, of course, in Moscow. The link between Soviet journalists and the KGB, the secret service, was never clearer than in their treatment of Lucia Thorne. We who regularly monitor press freedom had always known that at least half of all Soviet journalists were in fact KGB agents using journalism as a prop. One of these turned up at our press conference at which we introduced Soviet POWs whose release was secured by Lucia. Iona I. Andronov, representing the *New Times* and the *Literary Gazette*, made loud disparaging comments. In his article, he charged that Lucia was receiving $1,000 a head for every POW she brought out, and that she was also engaging in sexual activities with the young ex-soldiers. Andronov denied he was a KGB agent. He left the United States when Lucia threatened to sue him here for libel and slander. Years later, in 1993, after the collapse of the Soviet Union, Lucia's friend Vladimir Bukovsky turned up evidence in Communist Party archives in Moscow on Andronov's activities. Documents revealed that the Communist Party had set up the office of *New Times* in New York to release anti-American disinformation during the Cold War.

One "top secret" document stated that KGB Chairman Yuri Andropov opened foreign *New Times* bureaus in New York and Lima, Peru, "to step up activities of the KGB locally." Another document recommended sending Andronov to New York, where he remained for fourteen years. He became notorious for spreading anti-U.S. propaganda. In addition to his articles disparaging Lucia, Andronov published disinformation pieces alleging CIA biological warfare experiments to develop lethal mosquitoes and that it was the CIA in 1981 that attempted to assassinate Pope John Paul II. Andronov returned to Russia and became a member of the Supreme Soviet and a close adviser to Russian vice president Alexander Rutskoi.

Lucia Thorne—finally—also returned to Russia. She was a member of the U.S. team monitoring the April 1993 four-question referendum that would test support for President Boris N. Yeltsin. She was back in Rostov, where her family had suffered greatly, and where she had lived as a small child but had no memory of it. She found the very house where she had lived, a large Czarist-age mansion divided by the Communists into tiny apartments for whole families. The only family left was a distant cousin whose correspondence had stopped twenty-five years earlier. The KGB had "advised" him to stop writing to foreign relatives, especially one like Lucia who was engaged in "anti-Soviet" activities. Lucia was relieved to discover that her cousin was working for reforms in Russia. "Our Cossack genes were pushing [my cousin] in the right direction," Lucia wrote later.

I asked Lucia for her reaction when she reentered her homeland after so many years, so much bitterness and turmoil, so much fear of intercontinental annihilation. Her one word: "Bittersweet."

What of Afghanistan following the Soviet war? Rival *mujahedeen*, Islamic fighters, killed one another at random. A Kalashnikov rifle is this generation's only access to the modern world. The war the Soviets started, a conflict stalemated by American covert weaponry, destroyed all life-saving and governmental institutions.

The Afghan Taliban brought "order" by banishing women to their homes, destroying television sets, and controlling every word in the information flow, imposing the most severe form of Islamic "justice" and rooting out perceived enemies with utmost cruelty. Osama bin Laden, the wealthy Saudi Arab exile, exploited the Taliban and employed Afghan caves as headquarters for his international al-Qaeda terrorist network. After the September 11, 2001, terrorist assaults on New York and Washington, American armed forces with Afghan allies routed the Taliban and destroyed al-Qaeda's arms, training assets, and headquarters.

A consensus government was formed in Kabul, but warlords still controlled other parts of Afghanistan. Women, however, were liberated, and scores of schools opened to educate a new generation of Afghans.

What of Lucia? She continued to assist the democratization of the former Soviet Union, returning frequently to Moscow. During the years of the Cold War, Lucia Thorne accomplished the impossible. Whereas all Soviet dissidents and their Western friends were sharply divided between supporters of Andrei Sakharov and Alexander Solzhenitsyn, Lucia was an active spokesperson for *both*—no small accomplishment. The deep split between the liberal-modernists (represented by Sakharov) and the religious traditionalists (headed by Solzhenitsyn) goes back to Czarist days and continued through the Communist era. Statements by Sakharov in internal exile and by Solzhenitsyn in American exile were frequently handed to Lucia for release through Freedom House. After the demise of the Soviet Union, Lucia worked closely with Sakharov's widow to create the Sakharov archive and museum in Moscow. In her recovered homeland, Lucia also organized conferences to assist journalists and arranged for a television series on democracy to be shown to an audience of 200 million.

Lucia had heartbreaking days even in the post-Communist era. In the spring of 1996, *60 Minutes*, the popular CBS-TV newsmagazine, led with a segment on the tenth anniversary of the Chernobyl nuclear disaster. I watched and was appalled when a spokesman for the World Health Organization (WHO) repeatedly downplayed the magnitude of the nuclear explosion. He said "hundreds" of children were affected, perhaps more in the years to come. He was asked about estimates that thousands, tens of thousands had died. He said this was a myth. The interviewer for *60 Minutes*, despite being known for aggressive questioning, let it go at that.

Next morning, I told Lucia about the program. She was furious. She had attended a meeting just that week in which specialists on Chernobyl spoke of one hundred thousand deaths or more. Some six to seven thousand men who rushed in to clean up the debris after the 1986 explosion had subsequently died, according to reliable Ukrainian and Soviet sources. But *60 Minutes* allowed the WHO spokesman's belittling of the disaster to stand largely unopposed.

That next morning, Lucia faxed *60 Minutes* a strong criticism of its Chernobyl segment. Within the hour, Don Hewitt, creator and still producer of *60 Minutes*, phoned in a blistering attack on Lucia. As this was happening, the official U.S. congressional committee of the Commission on Security and Cooperation in Europe was holding hearings to commemorate the tenth anniversary of the Chernobyl disaster. At those hearings these Ukrainian government statistics were cited unopposed by U.S. and other specialists: (1) there has been a 15.7 percent increase in population mortality in the most affected Chernobyl region, and (2) Some twenty thousand to thirty thousand people had died so far as a result of the Chernobyl accident.[3]

Hardly support for *60 Minutes*.

NOTES

1. Rosanne Klass, ed., *Afghanistan: The Great Game Revisited* (Lanham, MD: University Press of America, 1987).

2. Ludmilla (Lucia) Thorne, "Afghanistan War and the Innocents," *Wall Street Journal*, September 21, 1983, p. 32.

3. "Anniversary of Chernobyl Nuclear Disaster Focus of Hearing," *CSCE Digest*, May 1996.

53

AISHA SEYTMURATOVA
The Diminutive Tatar

Aisha Seytmuratova, at the age of forty-two, was a diminutive refugee carrying a few pitiful belongings as she stepped onto the tarmac at the airport in New York on January 25, 1979. She came to relate a cruelly violent story and plead for her people, the Crimean Tatars of Russia. A colleague, Musa Mamut, had recently immolated himself in the Crimean city of Simferopol. Lucia Thorne and I met Aisha, settled her in an apartment, and several weeks later introduced her to the press at Freedom House.

The Tatars are a Turkic people whose medieval khanate controlled Russia for almost three centuries. Ivan the Terrible captured Kazan, the Tatar capital, in 1552 and absorbed Tatarstan into Holy Russia. To mark this victory, Ivan built St. Basil's Cathedral just outside the Kremlin's walls. Just as that colorful landmark today is a symbol of Russia and its capital, so the striving of the Tatars for greater autonomy reflects the stirring within many minority nationalities in Russia for greater freedom—or, as the Kremlin fears, national sovereignty. This would mean the further disintegration of Mother Russia's eighty-eight republics and regions, a factor in Boris Yeltsin's bloody resistance in 1995–96 and 1999–2000 to the claims of Chechens for greater sovereignty.

I met Aisha several times after her arrival in 1979. The following year, I took her to Madrid to plead her case before the Conference on Security and Cooperation in Europe. I had also brought to the CSCE Maj. Gen. Petr Grigorenko, who had been one of the most acclaimed heroes of the Soviet Union in World War II. Yet when the general spoke on behalf of the Crimean Tatars, he was arrested, stripped of his military rank, and sent to an insane asylum. He eventually was allowed to emigrate and came to Madrid to assist the Tatars once again. Aisha and Nadia Svitlychna, another former political prisoner of the Soviet Union, addressed the American press in February 1979.

Aisha was seven years old on May 18, 1944, when her story began. On that day, all Crimean Tatars in Russia were subjected to prolonged intimidation, murder, and deportation. A few among them had capitulated to the Nazis; overwhelmingly, however, the Tatars remained loyal, and many died patriotically fighting for Russia. Yet all Tatars, including war heroes, women, infants, and the elderly were loaded onto cattle cars and expelled from their traditional homeland in the Crimea. The ministry of defense simply labeled all Tatars "traitors to the Motherland."

In the first year of exile in Central Asia, 60,634 Tatar children out of 112,700 died. Of 93,200 women, 43,085 died. Of 32,600 men, 15,061 died. This was 46.2 percent, or almost half of the group. During the deportation, classics of Crimean Tatar literature and the Koran (Tatars were Muslim) were burned in public bonfires. Bulldozers and tractors obliterated ancient Tatar monuments. In Bakhchisarai, the ancient capital of Crimea, entire architectural complexes including Gazi-mansur and Aziz-dzhami were destroyed. Most Muslim cemeteries and mosques were devastated.

In 1945, the Crimean Communist Party decreed that "all names with Tatar origins" be changed. The Crimean Tatars, with a history fifteen hundred years old, was on the brink of extinction. The Crimea had been annexed to Russia in 1783. A nation with a population of about 7 million in the eighteenth century was reduced to just over 500,000 in 1945, scattered throughout Central Asia. The Soviet government had finished what the czarist regime had begun generations earlier. Almost half of the Crimean Tatars starved to death, and the survivors in the mid-twentieth century subjected to intense russification.

Aisha Seytmuratova was the first Crimean Tatar to come to the United States. Her mother and six brothers and sisters had been deported to Central Asia, but her father died fighting the Nazis. In 1966, she was taken to Moscow's fearful Lefortovo prison, and tried for "fanning nationalistic feeling." She nevertheless worked ceaselessly to enable the Tatars to return to their homeland in the Crimea. She arranged a 3½-hour meeting in the Kremlin with the head of the KGB and the minister of internal affairs. That was unproductive; so, too, was her fourth effort to do graduate work at the History Institute of the Academy of Sciences. Eventually, she was accepted at an academy in Tashkent, where she researched the growth of education among the working class in Uzbekistan, where she had been exiled.

But shortly before she received her doctoral degree, Aisha was arrested and tried under the criminal code for "defaming the Soviet state and social system." She was sentenced to three years in a labor camp, was shuffled through six prisons, and ended up in a camp reserved for common women criminals. When released, she was refused permission to resume her studies but was allowed to continue her education abroad. That brought this diminutive woman to New York and the beginning of her ceaseless efforts in the United States on behalf of the Crimean Tatars. The KGB then began a campaign of intensified harassment against Aisha's relatives. Aisha asked the UN Commission on Human Rights to investigate the Soviet Union's official policy of genocide against national minorities in the USSR. She said that in protecting the Tatars the United Nations would assist all national minorities in the Soviet Union. Nothing was done at the United Nations. Aisha therefore continued her one-woman crusade in the United States.

When she arrived in America, Aisha spoke not a word of English. When I last saw her, in May 1993, she was fluent in English, had an apartment in Brighton Beach, and was still devoting her life to the Tatar cause—she was en route to the Crimea. In 1967, the Soviet government politically rehabilitated the Tatars and admitted they were unjustly treated. By 1988, a Soviet commission reviewed the rights of Tatars after they staged an extraordinary demonstration in Moscow's Red Square. The commission ruled that Tatars may return *individually* to the Crimean peninsula, but they would need the same work and residence permits required of all citizens. This effectively denied the reestablishment of a Tatar homeland in the Crimea. Aisha would return again and again to the Crimea to assist the returnees and press for the restoration of their homeland.[1]

When I last saw her, Aisha told me that Tatars were moving back to the Crimea at the rate of five thousand a year. The movement was slowed by the need to build housing, difficult in the present economic climate. She was collecting boxes of clothing in the United States to bring to her people in the Crimea. She was proud that the government had made the Tatar language one of three official languages of the country. That had been denied them all those years by the Soviets. I told Aisha I had recently visited Kazakhstan, one of the Central Asian states where the Tatars have lived in exile. She invited me to visit her in her new homeland.

I would see signs of separateness in Tatarstan, Aisha told me. The Tatars have their own airline, constitution, parliament, and license plates. Their green, white, and red flag flies on public buildings. There is not an extremist Muslim return. Islam has little political content; intermarriage, as for generations past, is common. Even devout Muslims dress in Western styles, though modestly. But there is a significant Tatar cultural revival. Tatar schools are now operating. The new state symbol is a griffin, a fabled monster having the head and wings of an eagle and the body of a lion. Interestingly, in India and the east, a "griffin" is a newcomer from an eastern country. The Tatars have, indeed, returned from the east, but not as newcomers.

It is not often that dissidents see even part of their most devout wish fulfilled. Aisha said her case proved the value of using all methods except violence. "I always told my people not to use violence," she added. But much violence had been used against her people. She said it didn't matter to her what religion one followed, whether one crossed oneself (as a Christian) or covered the face as a Muslim (which she is). Half of the population is building churches, half is building mosques. "There's just one God," said Aisha Seytmuratova.

St. Basil's Cathedral, however, continues to symbolize not only the religious diversity of Russia but also its traditional political control over diverse nationalities.

NOTE

1. See Steven Erlanger, "Heirs of the Golden Horde Reclaim a Tatar Culture," *New York Times*, August 13, 1993.

54

ISAAM SARTAWI
He Knew His Assassin

On a March day in 1976 a conservatively dressed, soft-spoken heart surgeon visited my Freedom House office across from the New York Public Library. "I've come to make a house call," he quipped. But Isaam Sartawi was far more than a physician, and the meeting place was the "house" of freedom. Dr. Sartawi, in his youth an Arab fighter against Israel, had become the most prominent Arab "moderate." His specialty in heart surgery was learned in the United States.

He traveled the world to gain Palestinian recognition of Israel, as well as an Arab-Israeli partnership for the peaceful resolution of their decades-old differences. Sartawi was on his way to Europe to lobby tirelessly for a negotiated peace between Arabs and Israelis. Although Yasir Arafat of the Palestine Liberation Organization was then regarded officially by Israelis as a terrorist enemy, Dr. Sartawi was known in Jerusalem to be a close adviser to Arafat, as well as a confirmed "moderate" on Mideast issues. Dr. Sartawi knew of my moderating approach to Arab-Israel questions and wanted to discuss this.

Moreover, he knew that I planned to visit Algeria the following week, stopping there en route to a conference in Europe. I sought to meet with interesting people in Algiers. Dr. Sartawi volunteered to provide an escort for me. I expected to meet several like-minded Arabs who would discuss the possibility of peace talks.

So I went off to Algiers, where Dr. Sartawi said I would be met at the airport by "Mohammad," who would assist me. Only a dozen passengers left the plane at Algiers; I was the only non-Arab. The others were quickly whisked away by friends and relatives. There was no public transportation visible, and none arrived. The airport was quiet and virtually empty except for a cleaning woman.

It was early evening and no other planes were due. The city was four miles away. I stood alone waiting for some sign of recognition. None came.

Instead, a badly damaged Fiat appeared. The door on the passenger's side was missing. The car slowed and the driver aimed the vehicle in my direction. "Taxi?" he asked. I had waited forty-five minutes, and neither Mohammad nor any other escort had appeared. I haggled over price and lost; it cost about thirty dollars to reach my hotel in Algiers. That would have been normal in New York or Paris, cheap in Tokyo, but it was expensive in Algiers. I had little choice. I most regretted not being able to meet Dr. Sartawi's friend.

The next day, with the concierge of the hotel we drove some seventy-five miles southwest of Algiers to the Roman ruins at Tipasa on the Mediterranean coast. The towns as well as Algiers were crowded with cars and trucks impatiently pressing pedestrians and small carts to the side. President Houari Boumedienne, who had taken power in a military coup, was running for his first elected term, and campaign slogans were everywhere. "Militant" was his pledge. Newspapers were filled with stories of the struggle by OPEC (the Arab oil cartel) against the U.S. State Department. Vibrant was the tempo of towns and cities, but the concierge told me that spirit was creating a deep gap between young Algerians and their parents.

French culture is now too modern for an older generation of Algerians, the man said. "Parents and children want a different future in France and here," he added. "The new generation wants to move fast on the streets and in their minds. They forget their hearts. They want money, power, but that's not human, it's selfish. Our religion teaches us not to be selfish but to care for one another, for humanity." The miniskirts on youth in the streets, he said, are but an example of the great change. The drinking in Algiers is another. No liquor is permitted in the entire city of Constantine or in any village.

The National Liberation Front (FLN), the revolutionary party still in power, placed posters on street corners exhorting women to play a political role. Intended or not, such appeals would inevitably cause conflicts between the traditional and the new role of women. While miniskirts would not immediately sweep aside the female Muslim's bulging gowns with only eyes showing, the new dress was obviously a harsh break with the past. Counter graffiti told the story: "A bas la Bourgoisie" (Down with the bourgeoisie), "A bas l'Imperialism" (Down with imperialism), "Assez de Dictatur Boumediste" (Enough of the Boumedist dictatorship).

(This clash was apparently the early sign of the far bloodier terrorism that was to grip Algeria in the 1990s. The FLN permitted other parties to form for the first time in 1989, but after it fared badly in the first national elections in 1991, the results were cancelled, and Muslim extremists took to the streets. Barbaric violence ensued. Thousands of journalists, judges, police, and political leaders were murdered.)

The next day, in 1976, without the help of Isaam Sartawi, I tried to reach the

Minister of Information. I wanted to ask about the new third world press pool. But telephones seemed useless. One could understand the State Department's warning that "the fact of [an American citizen's] arrest may not be known to U.S. officials in Algeria for up to a month." I was sure that much of that time was lost on the phone.

I finally saw an assistant to the information minister. He pointed me to that day's *El Moudjahid*, published by the FLN. The dominant story was the president's ceremonial opening of what was claimed to be the largest cloth manufacturing plant on the African continent. It was obviously an important addition to the local economy. The press hailed it as a "new conquest of the agrarian and industrial revolution," since local wool provided the basic material. The minister asked whether this story would be carried worldwide by the major wire services headquartered in New York, Paris, and London. I explained it might make the business pages, but probably not the front pages of Western newspapers. The minister said that this, then, was another example of imperialist censorship of an important third world event.

After the conversation, I walked alone through the casbah, the old part of the city built by the Turks. There was the all-too-usual depressing sight of people living on a steeply rising hill of hovels. The most apparent factor, apart from the lack of sanitation and living space, was the unemployment of men and the great wave of children playing, shoeless, on filthy streets and pavements. This was not unusual. I had seen grime that year on smiling faces of youngsters in Saigon and Lisbon and, years earlier, in La Perla, outside San Juan, Puerto Rico. Children ran after me, asking for money to take their pictures. One asked if I wanted a guide through the casbah. I walked faster and they drifted off.

Except for one boy, about six years old. He turned up, street after street, asking for "bon bon." I was not sure of the way out of the casbah, but I did not trust the boy to guide me. Every so often I would meet that small, large-eyed boy, and every time he would say, "bon bon," and extend his small hand. Either he knew all the streets I would take and arrived ahead of me, or I was walking in circles. I kept the sun on my left and the hill ahead, and climbed whenever there seemed to be a dead end. I climbed steps equal to a ten-story building, and came upon a man sprawled on the steps. He looked like a beggar in a soiled, formerly white Arab cloak, but his limbs were seared and his throat reddened by what seemed to be marks of strangulation. Some passersby stopped to notice—the first time I had seen attention paid at a street scene. I climbed to the top of the steps and suddenly entered a very crowded street scene. It was a different world. An almost illegible sign pointing in the direction I had just walked read: "Casbah." I exited through the gate and took my only picture: the small boy who had tracked me for so long was at my side as I left his world. I gave him several coins.

Too soon, I moved on to Europe and a conference. I planned to question Dr. Sartawi about my visit to Algeria, but we never met again. Some years later, a Reagan peace idea gained support from Jordan and Saudi Arabia. They favored a negotiating conference, and Arafat seemed to agree. But events would take a deadly toll. With the peace possibility in mind, Isaam Sartawi went to Portugal to attend the annual meeting of the Socialist International. He was promptly assassinated at a hotel in Albufeira, Portugal.[1] The assassins were a PLO splinter group headed by Mazen Sabry al-Banna, also known as Abu Nidal, who had led the gang that murdered Israeli Olympic athletes and highjacked the cruise ship *Achille Lauro*, killing an American invalid and tossing him overboard.

Simultaneously, King Hussein of Jordan announced that Yasir Arafat had withdrawn his earlier agreement to the peace conference proposed by Washington. Presumably, the hardliners in the PLO had forced Arafat's withdrawal and had engineered the assassination of Isaam Sartawi. Arafat was warned he would be next on the hit list if he agreed to the Reagan proposal.

Months before he died, Dr. Sartawi said precisely who his assassins would be. He knew he was risking his life when he worked for peace. He knew the Abu Nidal gang had murdered other Arab moderates and, he said, was "carrying out a series of atrocious acts against Jews in Europe." Anthony Lewis noted in the *New York Times* that "men who rejected Isaam Sartawi in life praised him in death."[2]

Arafat blamed the murder on "Zionist intelligence" and added that Sartawi's death was a great loss to the Palestinian cause. It was; but, as Lewis noted, Arafat had failed the test of courage by not supporting negotiations with Israel about the West Bank. It would be eleven years and the death of thousands more before Arafat would shake hands with an Israeli prime minister—who, in turn, would be assassinated by a terrorist Jew.

Also in Portugal at the Socialist International was Shimon Peres, leader of Israel's Labor opposition and later successor to slain prime minister Yitzhak Rabin. Peres's latter-day reputation was dovish—as were his words I heard in Jerusalem in 1996. But not so his actions in 1983, when the early soundings for a "peace process" were made by Dr. Sartawi. The day before he was killed, Sartawi wrote to Peres calling for a negotiated settlement as "the only civilized solution for the Middle East." Sartawi spoke then the way Peres was to speak a decade later.

Peres responded by lobbying strenuously at the Socialist meeting to bar Dr. Sartawi from official participation. Anthony Lewis wrote, "The supposed alternative to Menachem Begin [Israel's hardline prime minister] was so spineless that he did not want to be seen at a Socialist meeting where a moderate Palestinian was a delegate."

Israeli fear of his moderate speeches was the reason Sartawi was barred for years from entering the United States. Prime Minister Begin's spokesman wrote off Sartawi, saying Arabs who talk to Israelis "are sometimes shot and killed." But then moderate Israelis and other Jews who sought Arab-Israeli reconciliation were demonized by Zionists, and in Prime Minister Rabin's case, assassinated by a fellow Jew.

"One of the sad things," said Sartawi shortly before he died, "is the failure of the peace camp in Israel to get enough recognition in the United States or Europe." It was such a mission that brought Dr. Sartawi to my office that bleak March day in 1976. He wanted to discuss ways to give peace a chance in the Middle East by broadening the discussion in America. He never returned to continue that conversation.

Flora Lewis, foreign affairs columnist for the *New York Times,* concluded her eulogy of Sartawi's assassination: "Perhaps if American Jews who still think in the old Zionist terms swing heavily to support Israeli peaceniks, that would make a difference and encourage Arab moderates. For now, the tide is running with the prophets of doom."[3]

Anthony Lewis had recently asked Sartawi whether Yasir Arafat and the Palestinians could support a two-state solution—Arabs and Palestinians living side by side in harmony. "Chairman Arafat will have to decide sooner or later," Sartawi replied. He concluded, "We live in worlds we create for ourselves." And sometimes we die in them.

I treasure a sprightly greeting card with five groups of men and women, Garden-of-Eden style, clasping hands above equally stylized pairs of fish. The handwritten message: "Best wishes for the new year. Sorry about Algeria. Isaam Sartawi, December 1976."

NOTES

1. See "Jordan Rejects Peace Plan; Says PLO Broke an Accord; Palestinian Moderate Slain," and "Backer of Peace with the Israelis Shot in Portugal," *New York Times*, April 11, 1983, front page.
2. Anthony Lewis, "Killers and Cynics," *New York Times*, April 14, 1983.
3. Flora Lewis, "The Frail Peace Camp," *New York Times*, April 15, 1983.

AFTERWORD

ASTRONAUT SUSSMAN

Finally, a story that could have ended this book before it began.

The title "Astronaut Sussman" was put on a file by Jessie Miller, my assistant, after I closed some personal correspondence. I did not see Jessie's title until years later. By then, the subject was momentarily depressing, yet comforting.

The subject involved the National Aeronautics and Space Administration (NASA), but the sequence began in no less likely a setting than the Office of Technology Assessment of the U.S. Congress. Until its demise in 1995, the OTA for twenty years had advised congressional lawmakers of both parties on technical issues to research and analyze. As the think-tank for Congress, it was the unbiased specialist in several dozens of fields each year. It was widely regarded by scholars and legislators as highly professional and productive.

To study any problem submitted to it by Congress, the OTA created a panel of diverse specialists from the field under analysis. The panel also included a few citizens whose peripheral expertise might enrich the quality of the final report. I was one of those invited to sit on an eighteen-month-long panel on cooperation and competition in outer space. At the outset, I explained my utter ignorance of—though fascination with—the science of space travel. I had followed the ballistics missile controversies and had written briefly about their geopolitical aspects, but that was all.

I was assured there would be adequate briefing, orally and in print, on the basic issues facing the United States in outer space in the decades ahead. There would be consideration not only of military competition from the Soviet Union and the French and British—in addition to still-unforeseen proliferation from less-developed countries—but, in the longer term, competition as well as cooperation in market, not military, control of space travel and satellite usage. The possibilities intrigued me, and I agreed to serve on the panel.

Several times a month for 1½ years I spent a day at the OTA in Washington, engrossed in outer-space technology and potentials. At the outset, that troubled me: I felt I could not add very much to the panel's work. We were given technical drafts prepared by the staff to critique and edit. My contribution inevitably concerned such issues as freedom and human rights projected from the earth to outer space. How unimpeded, for example, would satellites be thrust up by states that oppress others on this planet? What about unwanted cross-border communication via satellite? And even before "Star Wars," what about destroying mischievous carriers in space? There were, after all, ethical and political considerations along with the technical. I felt comfortable addressing these, but always with some hesitation.

The final report incorporated a few of my ideas. I still marveled at the high-tech company in which I found myself. But this sometimes exhilarating experience led me to another sequence.

On May 5, 1983, the *New York Times* carried a short report, "NASA Study Backs Space Shuttle Rides of Private Citizens." NASA said the first to fly in space, sometime in the mid-1980s, "should be writers, broadcasters, artists, poets, and educators." These professionals should provide the public with "insights into space flight and the role of a human in space." The report was the conclusion of a nine-man study group. It urged Congress to pass legislation allowing passengers to board NASA crafts. They would "provide a comprehensive visual mission history" as well as on-the-spot reports.

I kept that clip on my desk for some weeks and then began phoning NASA to learn how I might fly on a forthcoming mission. I felt I could make a case for my several "specialties." It took numerous conversations to locate someone who knew anything about the possibility. Apparently, the report in the *Times* did not generate a bureaucratic procedure. I located a William O'Donnell at NASA headquarters in Washington who gave me some encouragement; he suggested I send him a full biography, photograph, and indication of my interest.

I wrote a three-page biographical letter with an informal photo in a floppy sun cap. I stated that I had an interest in space flight long before the *Times* article appeared and that, indeed, my service still underway on the OTA panel on outer space spurred my interest in space matters. I said that since NASA's first mission I had watched its development with great interest and some optimistic expectation: I hoped from the first that progress would be fast enough to enable me one day to travel in space.

I described my "forty-year experience as a public communicator of events, ideas, and images." I said I offered qualities and skills beyond those limited solely by news-media communicating. I said, "I am sixty-two years old (there should be an older person in space in the eighties) and in excellent health." I noted that "I travel one hundred thousand miles a year, sleep anytime, anywhere when desired. After a twenty-hour flight from China this May I arrived home refreshed (see photo)." I mentioned my humanitarian concerns developed in two dozen countries on six continents. I added that I had a "strong commitment to American objectives in a peaceful world."

I also listed my international associations as well as my reputation among journalists worldwide. I stated that I broadcast frequently over international shortwave outlets and frequently discussed diverse issues on radio and television in the United States.

I also mentioned my religious background. Up to that time, no one of the Jewish faith had flown in a NASA spacecraft.

A month later, I received an acknowledgment from NASA's deputy director of public affairs. He said that a space shuttle passenger-selection process would consider such criteria as "(1) the degree of individual interest and motivation in this opportunity; (2) a willingness to undergo necessary training to assure adaptability to flight and mission requirements; and (3) ability to meet exacting physical standards."

He suggested that I keep abreast of news reports for future developments or decisions, including information on how applications should be made. Meanwhile, the *Times* in an editorial asked "why not expand the passenger function?" Why not, indeed? The *Times* headlined "The Citizen Astronauts."

On December 16, 1983, the *Times* reported that NASA would propose regulations "very soon" on how it would select private citizens to be passengers on the space shuttle. James M. Beggs, NASA administrator, said he hoped to select the first applications "by early next year" and expected the first flights carrying such passengers to occur "as early as 1985."

Beggs said, "We're thinking of journalists," among others, who would describe what they saw. One reason for taking such observers, he said, was that "the astronauts all come back from these flights and they all say, 'Gee whiz, we have these pictures and they look beautiful but they don't near do justice to what we saw.'"

So, he added, "We kind of like to send people up there who can translate the experience of what they see in space into real terms for the public." He said such observers would be assigned minor tasks for the mission such as "tending the galley or things like that."

He said he had already received some letters displaying interest, but formal applications would not be accepted until after the official "announcement of opportunity" in 1984.

On May 4, 1984, the Associated Press reported that "without any fanfare" NASA had issued regulations under which private citizens can fly aboard the space shuttle. The requirements don't seem too stringent, the AP said, "but don't pack your suitcase."

I was prepared to do so, however.

Obviously, interest in the possibility was mounting. Some suggested there should be a lottery to choose the passengers. But NASA rejected that because it wanted to select candidates who could best suit NASA's responsibilities under the Space Act. Ultimately, of course, the selection became a political decision at the highest level.

President Reagan personally announced on August 27, 1984, that an elementary or secondary schoolteacher would become the first "citizen passenger" to fly into space. In that presidential election year, both political parties had been vying for support from the two large teacher organizations, the National Education Association and the American Federation of Teachers. (Al Shanker, head of the AFT, was my longtime friend, but I was not then a teacher.) Beggs, of course, denied that electoral politics had influenced the president's selection.

Finally, I was disappointed, though NASA said there would be other missions the next two years, when two to four other citizen passengers would be flown into space. Though the odds against my flying had always been astronomical, I savored the long-shot possibility. And I had told no one about my correspondence—until after the first flight of a passenger.

The program moved ahead slowly; it was another two years before the first passenger went aloft. That was January 28, 1986. Just before liftoff, there was some concern about a small technical problem involving the "rings." A political factor: that evening, President Reagan was set to address the country and mention the first teacher in space. All shuttle systems were "go."

The teacher-passenger was Christa McAuliffe; the shuttle was the *Challenger*. The record book states simply, "Exploded 73 sec after liftoff; all were killed."

APPENDIX A

A SURVEY OF THE PROGRESS OF FREEDOM IN 1968
The Critical Year

I n the United States after World War II, 1968 was a historic year. Following are the introductory paragraphs of an annual Freedom House analysis, the "Balance Sheet of Freedom" drafted by the author. Later surveys of political rights, civil liberties, and press freedom provided a far more extensive annual analysis.

Shock waves of revolutionary social change rocked the world, affecting open and closed societies with equal force. Citizens on every continent took to the streets to force basic changes. In free societies, confrontational politics replaced orderly processes and threatened anarchy or repression. In closed societies, dissent produced immediate, harsh reprisal.

The painfully built disciplines of free nations were torn asunder in the escalating drive for change. In the United States, lingering racial injustice, growing dissent over the Vietnam War, the presence of poverty amid affluence, and the protest of youth against all three shook the nation's confidence in its leaders and its goals. Every human institution was challenged—from the manner of electing presidents to the fairer marketing of products and the revolt of liberal Catholics against the Pope's banning of the Pill.

Yet, even as America was engulfed by angers and fears, plunged twice into national mourning for assassinated Negro and white leaders [Martin Luther King Jr. and Robert F. Kennedy], rocked fitfully by political confrontations that split heads and divided the country—even as the planned and unplanned disruption of the society deepened, Americans kept working at the racial, social, political, and moral ills that needed curing. After a lengthy, critical national election campaign voters firmly rejected extremist appeals and the country avoided a constitutional crisis in the Electoral College. New laws and court rulings further bolstered minority rights to open housing and civil actions. For the United States, 1968 may yet prove to have been a bitter, costly turning point on the way to overdue improvements in race relations, urban rehabilitation, and broader economic justice.

(The full twenty-five-page analysis was attributed to the Freedom House Public Affairs Committee, composed of Leo Cherne, Paul H. Douglas, Roscoe Drummond, George Field, George B. Ford, Harry D. Gideonse, Mrs. Andrew Jackson, Francis P. Miller, Whitney North Seymour, Gerald L. Steibel, and Rex Stout; text by Leonard R. Sussman.)

APPENDIX B

PRESIDENT REAGAN AT THE WHITE HOUSE BEFORE HIS ICELANDIC SUMMIT WITH GORBACHEV

I was invited to meet with President Reagan on October 7, 1986, just before he departed for his summit meeting at Reykjavik with Soviet leader Mikhail Gorbachev. The subject was human rights and their role at the summit.

Each of us from human rights organizations spoke briefly. One man delivered a five-minute speech that drew glares from Secretary of State George Shultz and left the president scowling. The man concluded, "Don't give up SDI, Mr. President." SDI, the Strategic Defense Initiative, was Reagan's planned missile interceptor. Reagan smiled and said, "I'm married to two things: the SDI and Nancy." Laughter all around.

Entering the room was Yuri Orlov, the famed Soviet dissenter just released from the gulag (at the urging of Freedom House and others). Orlov said there can be no sense of national security if human rights are not sustained and trust between the powers is not displayed. There should be open contact between American and Soviet scientists, he said.

I spoke briefly to the president and to Orlov about our efforts to free him.

The president said he collects stories that show the cynicism of some people in totalitarian states toward their own government. "It was evening in the Soviet Union," said Reagan. "A citizen walking along the street. A soldier yells, 'Halt!' He starts to run. The soldier shoots him. Another citizen says, 'Why did you do that?' And the soldier says, 'Curfew.' 'But,' says the citizen, 'it isn't curfew time yet.' Said the soldier, 'I know. He's a friend of mine. I know where he lives—he couldn't have made it.'"

"You know something?" the president concluded, "in the summit meetings I tell some of these stories to the other side." Laughter.

After he left the presidency, Ronald Reagan, with great fanfare, delivered the Churchill Address at the Guildhall in London. He called for a prodemocracy program to assist the former Soviet states and used some material from my book *Power, the Press, and the Technology of Freedom: The Coming Age of ISDN* (New York: Freedom House, 1989). Reagan stated in his address: "In a book coming out this fall, Leonard Sussman, a senior scholar at Freedom House, writes that the speed, variety, and number of new communications tools defy control. At some point, Soviet citizens will be permitted to interact live and on-line with people in other countries. They will share information in a working relationship. . . . [W]hen that happens, the Goliath of totalitarian control rapidly will be brought down by the David of the microchip."

APPENDIX C

BAYARD RUSTIN ON THE CIVIL RIGHTS MOVEMENT
An Unpublished Interview

L ess than a year before he died in 1987, I interviewed Bayard Rustin, the least publicized hero of the American civil rights movement. It was the week the country was celebrating Martin Luther King Jr.'s birthday. I wanted to get Bayard's comparison of King and Roy Wilkins. Roy received the Freedom Award from Freedom House in 1967, and President Lyndon Johnson hailed him as one of the true leaders "of all time" in the struggle for human rights. Roy used the occasion to challenge Dr. King for having stated that the war in Vietnam was playing havoc with the civil rights movement. Wilkins said that "civil rights battles are going to have to be fought and won on their own merits, irrespective of the state of war and peace in the world." I had known and admired Roy for many years and regretted that he was almost completely forgotten, despite his historic contribution to the civil rights movement.

Bayard created the historic March on Washington for Jobs and Freedom in August 1963. "It was one of the few moments in American history," Bayard said, "when there was almost absolute unity within the black community." He added, "I don't think it will ever exist again." As the sun set on the Washington March one of its leaders said to Bayard, "Rustin, I have to hand it to you. You're a genius." Both Rustin and Wilkins were members of the Freedom House Board of Trustees. When I reread this interview nearly ten years later, I was struck by its importance. I have included it here virtually as the words can be heard on my tape; the transcription is in the Library of Congress. This is the first time the interview, or any part of it, has been published.

LRS: Freedom House has several historic connections with the civil rights movement, apart from our own programs in the early days of that struggle. The national headquarters of the NAACP was housed in our building from 1944 for twenty-four years. From that building, Thurgood Marshall (later a Supreme Court justice) and his colleagues worked on many landmark cases, such as *Brown* v. *Board of Education*, which ended school segregation. But most of that long record of patient court appeals, all over the country, of demonstrations accompanying such appeals, and of organizing the largest black organization in American history, the NAACP, that long record is overlooked in the remembrances of Martin Luther King Jr. Crowded briefly into such celebrations as we speak, February 3, 1986, was the presentation of a medal to the widow of Roy Wilkins, longtime executive secretary of the NAACP—the National Association for the Advancement of Colored People—and for thirty years a trustee of Freedom House.

It doesn't diminish the remembrance of Martin Luther King Jr. to recall Roy Wilkins's great contribution to the civil rights movement. No one can better discuss the two men than you, Bayard. You were colleague and friend to both. You participated in their public and private efforts to turn America around, not only in the 1960s but before and after. First, then, can you summarize ways in which Wilkins and King were similar, and how they differed? I refer here to their personalities, their methods of planning ahead, their ways of organizing.

BR: King was a person who pretended to be a responder. He responded to situations, responded to crises. Roy was a longtime planner and a great diplomat. Roy was an urbane, extremely careful person who knew each step of the way. Roy came to a position out of a conviction that he had a role to play. Martin, on the other hand, was thrust into a situation. I was at a meeting in Montgomery, Alabama, where he was asked to take over the leadership of the Montgomery Improvement Association. He refused on the basis that he had had no experience, hadn't been in town long enough, and didn't know enough people. Many of the ministers took the view that it was precisely because he had not been in town to make any enemies that he could probably lead the group, because everybody else had something against them.

LRS: When was that?

BR: That was in 1955. The boycott began in December, when Rosa Parks sat down [in a bus seat designated for whites only], and this was early January when King took over. He did not initiate the boycott, as many people think; it was initiated by E. D. Nixon. He was a member of A. Philip Randolph's Brotherhood of Sleeping Car Porters and a leader of the NAACP. So it was really the NAACP that started the Montgomery bus boycott. When you talked to Roy you had a feeling that he was, along with Thurgood Marshall, a person who understood that they were going to take years of piling one court case upon another throughout the entire structure until finally—as it did happen in 1954—the Supreme Court was going to have to say, once and for all, what the *Brown* decision says: in every respect blacks are citizens, and the law must be equally applied. *Brown* affected much more than education alone.

While Martin would respond when something happened, Roy was a master planner and knew down the road exactly where he was going. A church would get bombed, and King would rush into town, and something would happen. Roy Wilkins referred to him in what Martin took to be a derogatory term—I don't think it was—he said Martin is not a planner, he's an ambulance chaser. Roy had the ability to use words that way. I never felt that Martin needed to be the strategist and planner that Roy was, because the situation was largely determined by the violence of the South. That catapulted Martin from one thing to another.

One incident indicates how Roy's planning was so integral. I was in the courtroom with Martin one day. He was telling me before the court opened how things were getting bad. People had been marching for more than a year then. It was almost impossible to continue people-walking; something needed to happen. He was saying, "Well, I don't know just how long we can keep on going this way." This was a year after the Montgomery bus protest. While we were sitting there, somebody came in and handed Martin a note. He looked at it, grabbed me by the arm, and began to smile and shake my arm. "What's happening?" I asked. He said the NAACP had won the case—and that meant that the Montgomery bus protest had won. In other words, without the long-range planning that Roy had done we'd never have gotten through. That's an illustration of the differences between the men.

LRS: Did they understand the difference? As you tell it, one seemed to complement the other. Did they recognize that?

BR: I think they did complement one another. Roy understood it very well; I don't think Martin did. And Martin was never really comfortable when any civil rights leader of stature was present who might question his judgment. He was therefore very reluctant to be in a room with Wilkins. I don't think that was true of Wilkins with him. For example, I would notice that all during the great struggle, when the Leadership Conference on Civil Rights would meet, Martin would seldom come to the meetings; he would almost always send a representative. I spoke with him about this once, and he said, "I just don't feel comfortable with Roy." I think that Roy was more glib, more facile, more analytical. I think Roy had—not contempt for, but did not always trust—the judgment of the clergy, although he had largely to depend on them for a place to meet, and the like. But I think he had an unhappy feeling about the clergy, and I think this Martin knew.

LRS: An interesting comment, because Martin King certainly has the reputation of being a great speaker, a great sermonizer, and you are saying, in effect, that Roy had much more careful use of language—particularly in smaller and more confined situations.

BR: Yes, Martin had what many black ministers have, that is, a great gift of poetry. If you will analyze the March on Washington, very great speeches were made there. Rabbi Joachim Prinz, who spoke of his experience with Nazis in Germany—that really was a substantive document. A. Philip Randolph's speech was one of great substance; he essentially said this was the end of marching. We had moved from protest to politics, and within the realm of politics the problem of blacks from now on would be solved largely because of economic responses, and not responses to segregation or discrimination. The first two-thirds of Martin's speech is not really very important. When he begins to do the poetic thing that black ministers do—I don't care where they come from, all do it—"I have a dream that one day . . . ," and "the mountains this" and "the valleys that"—that sort of thing, that's what gets remembered. And I think to a certain extent Roy understood the necessity for carrying an audience along that way. But I think he also had considerable feeling that that was about the end of where black ministers went. That when it came to really analyzing the nature of the problem that we faced, they seldom did that.

LRS: Do you think this may be an explanation for what is regarded, I suppose fairly widely in the black community, as the falling off of attention and concern for the bread-and-butter issues that affect blacks as they do all Americans? That, in effect, the King approach, as you say, went as far as it could go; but there's been nothing else filling in for it in terms of leadership directed to the complex and substantive issues such as economics and politics?

BR: Yes, I think there's no question that that is the case, and that is the greatest challenge before the Urban League and the NAACP. Whether they can continue to carry a considerable number of blacks with them if they make clear to their constituents that it is not merely a matter of racial discrimination and segregation now, but basic problems having to do with production of goods and services; decline of American industries such as steel and automobiles, which are putting great numbers of people who are unskilled out of work; and the fact that labor-intensive industry is going overseas. Until the black community begins to tackle these basic problems we're going to be in very serious trouble.

LRS: One would expect that a Roy Wilkins would be tackling that kind of problem. But the King approach, it seems to me, tends to gloss over some issues. It's probably unfair to him, since he has been dead for many years, but let's turn back history a bit. In the period we're talking about, the time when both men were alive, Roy and King, what would you say was Roy's most lasting contribution to the movement, and thus to the country?

BR: Roy's lasting contribution is the fact that his decisive movement over many years led the courts to declare black citizens totally under the [protection of the] law, as they did in the 1954 *Brown* decision. It is quite logical that we who began in 1946 sitting-in in the South—in buses, restaurants, hotels—were not able to get any appreciable number of blacks to do it with us. But once Roy Wilkins and the NAACP got the 1954 decision and Mrs. Parks sat down following that decision in the beginning of 1955, a revolution was created. People were armed with the Supreme Court decision, and as Roy used to point out to Martin—"Stop saying that people are engaging in civil disobedience. We are not engaging in civil disobedience; we are upholding the highest law of the land. It is the Southerners who are disobedient in attempting to keep us out, when the Supreme Court says we can come in."

LRS: A fundamental distinction.

BR: Obviously, a very important distinction. And now, I think came Martin's contribution: Wilkins and company, Randolph and the others who helped, having created a situation in which the Supreme Court declared us citizens, Martin then said to people, "Your next moment is to get rid of your fear. Come and sit with us in these hotels, restaurants, theaters and get arrested." So Martin's contribution was not tactical but psychological. He helped people understand that going to jail was honorable, that they were joining the ranks of the great people merely by sitting. It was almost like Milton's sonnet on his blindness: they also serve who only stand and wait.

LRS: Do you think in those days whites understood this, or were they turned off by King? Today, it's obvious—he has a national holiday, and people are responding much after the fact.

BR: If you raise the question from my own experience, not from anyone else's, King was at the beginning looked upon as an absolute troublemaker by the great majority of whites in this country. Do you know what really saved King from that? The emergence of Malcolm X, Stokely Carmichael, and Rapp Brown. They so frightened people that many of the church people who had called Martin immoral for getting into politics embraced him out of their fear of those black radicals and black violence.

LRS: Suddenly, he was moderate.

BR: That's right. That was the great turnaround toward King. It took place with the emergence of those others.

LRS: On the question of getting into politics: that was a fighting issue at the time, not just domestic politics, but King moved from that into international politics—the Vietnam War and some other issues. And there, as I recall, he was distinctly different from Roy; Roy tried not to mix the domestic issues with international questions.

BR: Roy felt that blacks already had enough against them. They didn't need to take on what would be a triple-threat jeopardy by becoming left-wingers. Roy used to say to me, "I wish you would get out of the Socialist Party." He said, "I know Socialists are not Communists, but it's just another burden you have to bear." He said I would be much more effective if I were not a Socialist. He took the same attitude toward the peace issue. Now let me be very clear: Dr. King behaved in a way which caused Roy to be very frightened. Roy well understood that as a Nobel Prize winner, Dr. King had to speak out on war. What he was afraid of, what I was afraid of, what Phil Randolph was afraid of, and many others—Roy was not alone—was the combining of the two issues. Martin spoke about combining the civil rights movement and the peace movement—it was at that level, not at the level of his speaking out on the war, that Roy found so difficult—on combining these issues. Mr. Randolph and I had considerable experience with this, and that was the reason we agreed with Roy. Jim Farmer and a number of other young blacks formed CORE [Congress of Racial Equality] in

1941 when we were all working for the Fellowship of Reconciliation, a pacifist organization. When World War II came, young blacks in CORE increasingly declared they wanted to separate CORE from the Fellowship of Reconciliation. They did not want to be active in civil rights issues through the peace movement, and we had to separate them. Remembering that experience, Mr. Randolph and I tended definitely to agree with Roy. I wrote a long essay that appeared in a hundred black papers saying that King had every right to speak out for peace but that he was strategically wrong to try to bring the peace and civil rights movements to the same platform—that he would be doing injury to both.

LRS: You mentioned political issues. Was it Roy's feeling that King might be veering toward the left? We know that in later years J. Edgar Hoover and the FBI had very serious suspicions about how far left, if not King himself, certainly people around him were going. Did you ever have such a feeling?

BR: There was a very real feeling that many around King were Communists. There was a great debate over Stanley Levinson, who was one of King's advisers. I knew Stanley and worked with him; I never saw any evidence that he was a member of the Communist Party. Nevertheless, it continuously arose and frightened a person of Wilkins's background and temperament. I'll give you an illustration because this was a personal thing, and it indicates how much respect I have for Roy. When Mr. Randolph proposed the March on Washington and Roy finally agreed, Mr. Randolph also proposed that I be the director of the March. Roy hit the ceiling. But what I admire about Roy is that he called me in first and said, "Look we can't have you as director." I said, "Why not?" And he said, "Well, there are several reasons. There are all sorts of stories going around about you, and we don't want to bring them into the movement." He said, "First of all, you're a Socialist, and why would you bring that in?" He said, "Second, you were once a member of the Young Communist League, why do we bring that in?" He said, "I want you to know that I'm going to oppose you." I said, "O.K., Roy."

When the meeting took place, Roy did oppose me. When the leaders met he said he didn't want Rustin. He said, "Mr. Randolph, you started the March and you have to be the leader of it." Mr. Randolph said, "Roy, if I am the director of the March I'm going to need Bayard to be my deputy. What do you say to that?" And Roy said, "Phil, you were always a hard bargainer, and I guess there's nothing I can do if you want to make him your secondary, but keep him out of the public view." Well, that was why I appreciated that Roy called me first. It was nothing he did behind my back, and he had very logical reasons. Not only did Strom Thurmond bring up those two things when he spoke before the March for forty-five minutes in the U.S. Senate, but he also accused me of being a homosexual. Roy was fearful that that was going to happen. It did happen. When it came time to decide what to do about it, Randolph consulted Wilkins, who said, "I'll tell you what to do, Phil. Don't haggle these ten civil rights leaders at the press conference; they'll all want to talk, and they'll all say something silly. You have the conference and speak for all of us, and say only two things, and close your mouth. One, gentlemen and ladies of the press, we have absolute faith in Bayard Rustin's character; second, we have faith in his ability to carry on this March as we have planned it." And, he said, if they ask you anything else, say this had been agreed upon by ten leaders. Nothing more to say. That's exactly what Randolph did. Three days later the *New York Times* carried a fabulous article about how black leadership and the Jews and the labor unions were standing firm against character assassination.

LRS: That's an interesting story. I remember seeing your picture in the front line of the March, so obviously you were right out in front. And you are credited frequently now, in effect, with having organized the March. Is that the way it went?

BR: Under Randolph's direction I surrounded myself with a group of some twenty-five young people who did most of the hard work for the March. To show the difference between Randolph, King, and Wilkins: Mr. Randolph called me in and said, "Now you've got to go to Roy, to Martin, and the other leaders and get the money to put this March on." Mr. Randolph couldn't ask anybody for money—it was just out of his character. I went to Roy, and within fifteen minutes he said, "You and Randolph are always thinking up these things and coming to me for money, but it's important and I'll give $10,000 to start out." When I went to Ralph Abernathy and King they were both sympathetic, but to this day we never got a penny from the SCLC [Southern Christian Leadership Conference] to put on the March. Now, it's called Dr. King's March. Well, Randolph, who conceived it, and Roy Wilkins, who helped to pay for it, are almost never mentioned.

LRS: That was one of the facts that motivated me to have this conversation with you, because I felt keenly during the Week of Remembrance of King that it blacked out other sides of the story. I would hope that in years to come somehow that would get filled in.

BR: It is important to get it filled in for two reasons. First, it would avoid an injury to Dr. King. His stature is there. But second, it would show what is a fact: that no movement is ever the result of a single individual behaving in a particular way. It is always a combination of factors. For example, when Martin Luther King needed taxis, cars, to get people to work it never would have occurred to him how to get them, but Randolph knew immediately. Randolph had a different experience. Randolph said, "Get Dr. King on the telephone for me and ask if he's having trouble getting cars. I know exactly how to handle that." And Randolph called the head of the steel workers and said, "We have the largest group of black trade unionists in Birmingham amidst the steel workers there. Why don't you just call them to make seventy of their old cars available to Dr. King and say the union will stand by it?" He got them overnight. You had Wilkins in the courts, you had Randolph working with labor, and at a crucial time they could provide something. And you had King saying to people, don't be afraid, come with me and we'll break this thing once and for all. So it's for that reason that I want the real history to be written.

LRS: I think this is probably a start. It will take a lot more than this. Are there some remembrances that you have of working with King? Did you work closely with him at any time after he became the great national figure?

BR: I worked with King for almost seven years altogether, and he had definitely become a national figure at that time. Martin was a man who was hounded by apprehension that perhaps he wasn't doing enough, or that he would be misunderstood by the press, or that he might not be liked by some of the other civil rights leaders. He had that sort of dark side to him. And I think that to some extent it helped him in making judgments that were less than his judgments would have been without that. He surrounded himself with people, by and large, who would say, "Yes, Martin, your proposal's a good one." For example, the two major things that he proposed, I was against, and that led Coretta King to feel that somehow or other I was letting Martin down. That was the poor people's campaign and moving north. At the meetings, I made it clear to Martin that his moving north had to be a major mistake, because his popularity in the South was the result of the fact that blacks could not vote. Therefore, no citywide or statewide leadership was present. I said that if he went north into Chicago, he ought not to go unless he was willing to fight the Daley machine, all of its black constituents, and unless he was prepared to fight the Chicago police. "Stay out of there," I said. Consequently, when he came north it was Daley's blacks and to some extent the Catholic Church that defeated him, because he got in the way of both. When he went to New York, Adam Clayton Powell gave him twenty-four hours to get out of town. Now I'm telling you this in relation to what I felt was a defect in Martin. That is, surrounding him with people, whether it was Andy Young or Fauntleroy, who largely because they were religious, got trapped by their religiosity. Well, if Martin was called upon by God to go north, why should we stand in his way? Well, called upon by God or not, if there was no basis for his having a political base there, he was going to be defeated.

LRS: Do you think he regarded himself by then as a legend or as having Messianic qualities?

BR: You had only to listen to some of his speeches toward the end to discover that that was so. He was in a sense predicting that he would be killed. He was comparing himself at one point to Moses—like Moses I will get to the mountaintop, but I will never get into the promised land. Obviously, that is the language of someone who has a [Messianic] view of himself. Wilkins would not for a moment have [such a view], but if he had he would never have expressed it. That's the difference.

LRS: It wouldn't have occurred to him. Do you think that influenced King's judgment?

BR: I think it did. An illustration: I talked at length to Mr. Randolph about the poor people's campaign, and we came to the decision that the campaign could only be successful if we could get all poor workers, Catholic, Protestant, Jewish, black and white to cooperate in a campaign. But since the trade union movement spent millions of dollars a year trying to bring that same coalition together when it was in their interest to come for higher wages and better working conditions—and that the trade union movement was failing while spending all that money—how could Martin Luther King pull remnants of this group to Washington and start a movement that the trade union movement couldn't start with all its millions and power and political strength? There again, his followers said that if Martin is moved to go to the poor people's campaign, he should go. As you well know, it was a disaster.

LRS: The interesting thing is that several such failures are forgotten, and what are remembered are the romanticized acts and, of course, the very great speeches. There's a difference, however, between form and substance in the movement. I wonder whether today the movement is still affected by that. Is it waiting around, in a sense, for someone to issue the call from on high to come again with that approach? There are times when Jesse Jackson, for example, seems to be borrowing very much from that theme and from that heritage. Yet, while he has a momentary impact, it doesn't seem to catch on.

BR: I don't think it can catch on, because most of the black leaders today are failing to understand the difference between what I would call the period when Martin was vital, and now. For example, if you look at what Martin King attempted to do with Roy and Randolph, and all their help, there were three things: the right to vote, the right to use public accommodations, and the right to send your children to a school of your choice. Now, if you will examine these three things—although many people died and were brutalized to achieve them—their achievement was very simple as compared with the achievement of things today. Today, if you ask blacks what they want, they want a job, they want a decent house, they want medical care, and they want education for their children. Getting the three things we got in the early period did not cost this society a penny, except for police protection. To get jobs, housing, medical care, and education will cost billions—that is a great difference. Furthermore, many white people felt that blacks deserved the earlier things because they had been mistreated.

LRS: How can one proceed now?

BR: When it comes to jobs, housing, medical care, and education there are numerically more whites who need these things, even though blacks may need them more grievously. Therefore, you've got to build a major class base in the society to bring about these changes, which are going to require billions of dollars.

LRS: That kind of coalitional effort is much more difficult.

BR: It is much more difficult for two reasons. First, because the society now gets the view that blacks and others are not prepared to put any limitations on their ethnic demands, and that divides rather than builds the coalition.

LRS: And ethnic demands along ethnic lines?

BR: Yes—instead of demands of "we want all these things for everybody." Second, the problems are complicated by the fact that in the 1960s, when the great progress was made, the American business decline vis-à-vis Japan and others had not begun. Now, great numbers of people are put out of work because we cannot produce steel and automobiles as cheaply and efficiently as other people. The labor-intensive industry had not left this country. Now, you can scarcely find anywhere where shoes, clothing, electronics, televisions, radios, etc. are made here. There's the whole question of automation. There's the business use of robots, which has thrown poor people out of work. One of the tragedies is, you don't hear that kind of problem discussed by civil rights leaders. They are still discussing the conditions of black people as if segregation and discrimination were the only problems. In fact, the discussion of discrimination and segregation, even though they still exist, tends to obscure the major problem. For every black who is out of work today because he is black, there are ten out of work because of the things I have been mentioning. But you don't hear those things discussed by civil rights groups.

LRS: When Jesse Jackson, for example, discusses some of these things on his own turf in Chicago, does he not raise some of these questions of economic problems, or are they generally couched in terms of discrimination and segregation?

BR: They're almost always couched in two terms now. Number one, in those terms [I've mentioned]; and number two, in terms of the black family, which is going to have to revive itself if something [good] is to happen. We have to get rid of teenage pregnancies, men leaving women head of households, dope, alcohol, with all of which I agree. But on the other hand, many of these things will be with us until the family has some basic way of making a living by its wits. So I don't think Jesse emphasizes building the kind of coalition we are talking about. And in the meantime, while he does talk about the Rainbow Coalition, he simultaneously says and does all kinds of things that he knows would not bring Jewish people, Catholics, and poor ethnic whites into the coalition. He never speaks for them.

LRS: When he speaks of the Rainbow Coalition, do you think he's mainly speaking of a political coalition?

BR: Yes, purely political. He's trying to say that there are white liberals largely on the left who will vote for him, and I think that's true. One black newspaper says his Rainbow Coalition has only two colors in it, one is black and the other is red.

LRS: Roy Wilkins has somehow got the reputation of not being interested in direct action. What is your feeling about that?

BR: People are wrong; Roy was always interested in direct action. In fact, at the same time the Montgomery bus protest was going on, there were several protests by the NAACP. For example, there was a major one during the time of the Montgomery bus protest in Wichita, Kansas, a major confrontation with lunch counters; another one in Oklahoma City that Roy financed and encouraged.

But I'd like to go back a bit. In 1946, the Supreme Court passed the *Irene Morgan* decision. That said if you held a ticket for an interstate carrier, bus or train, once you get to Washington [going south] they cannot force you out of the train or bus into a segregated one because that is the burden of interstate travel. I got a call from Roy because I was then field director of CORE. He asked me to visit him in his office [in the Freedom House building]. Roy looked like the cat that swallowed the mouse and said, "Now we've got them, but I need your help." I asked what he meant. He said, "I want you to set up a major group, black and white, to go all over the upper South with blacks and whites sitting together, in the front and the back The reason I can encourage you to do this is because I will pledge you three things: whatever money you need, NAACP lawyers in every town where there is a possibility of your being arrested, and our whole publicity outlet."

This developed through the years until the 1954 decision; it was almost a ten-year period. We redefined the effort in the early fifties more finely than this. Roy would say to me, "Well, it's time for CORE to go into Norfolk, because we've been negotiating with them in Norfolk for two years and they don't intend to move. If you guys go in and threaten to sit down and act very radical they're going to come to us and say they're ready to talk." And for years that's exactly what we had going. He knew that the NAACP's major job lay somewhere else. But anybody who thinks Roy Wilkins was against direct action . . . was ridiculous. He paid for it for CORE any time we needed it.

Another illustration: in 1947, a group of us were arrested in North Carolina in one of those first sit-ins. Roy was elated and gave us a lawyer. We turned over all our material to the lawyer, and a year later when we came to trial I got a call from Roy saying, "Oh, my God, I'm sorry to say but our lawyer was a son of a bitch. He turned over interstate travel tickets to the opposition and claimed that he had lost them."

LRS: Why did he do that?

BR: Because he was selling out. Roy said, "I'm sorry, but you poor fellows have got to go to the chain gang." And I said, "Why don't we fight the case?" Roy answered, "You can't win that case when the guy has destroyed the tickets." He said we would stand trial, lose, and set a very bad precedent. He said, "I wish you'd go to jail." We went to jail for thirty days. It was pretty tough. We were chained and had to work on the highways, breaking rocks in North Carolina. But as a result of that Roy called me and told me to write up the case for the *New York Post*. I did and he got it into the *Post*. The University of North Carolina, Department of Penology, called me to come and lecture there. They invited the key state leaders of the legislature, and three years later the chain gang was destroyed in North Carolina—as a result of Roy Wilkins working under the table.

LRS: And your working on the chain gang . . .

BR: But this was an indication of the kind of thinking that Roy did.

LRS: Was there any similar coordination with King at any point, or did that never come about?

BR: Not really. I think it was very sad, because it could have been [similarly effective]. But we were in a different period. There were great conflicts between the SNCC [Student Nonviolent Coordinating Committee] and NAACP, between

SNCC and SCLC, between Malcolm X and all the rest, between Elijah Mohammed and all the rest; and this was a period of great internal confusion. It reminded me, in a sense, of South Africa. The closer you came to achieving something, the more groups you were going against, each struggling in its own way. But as I look back upon it—for example, in the March on Washington, it was [successful because of] the NAACP's money and the great majority of the people who were brought in by NAACP buses and trains from all over the country. The NAACP had a very real, established structure in every one of these cities and a constituency. SCLC did not have a membership, it had chapters. But they were largely key individuals who were doing things and calling King in occasionally when they needed to get a mass meeting.

LRS: Is anything left of SCLC?

BR: There's very little visible of SCLC except in a few places where they get people to register and vote. Martin must have known that by turning things over to Abernathy he was not turning them over to anyone who was taking things in the direction that [SCLC] would need to go. But I think he felt so indebted to Ralph that he could not name anyone else to take over.

LRS: There is no hierarchy, is there? You don't hear of Abernathy much. Andrew Young, of course, is deeply in politics. But there's no likelihood of Young coming out again in the civil rights uniform, I wouldn't think.

BR: Oh, no. In fact, I suspect that the civil rights movement, as we have known it, is no more. It sounds very strange, but if you were to go to Harlem tomorrow—if it is true that blacks need jobs, medical care, housing, and education—if you went to Harlem and changed everybody up there to white, there would not now be more jobs for them, nor housing, nor medical care, nor education. I think the movement now has got to rethink in class terms, instead of race, how to proceed.

LRS: Of course, if it does that, it is no longer a civil rights movement.

BR: That's right. And that's one of the reasons it hasn't proceeded, because I think people are afraid that if we really educate people to see what the new problems are, they are not going to have the same constituency with the same expectations. It has to be. It's going to take a new and different, and a more courageous leadership to do that.

LRS: Do you see anything on the horizon that seems to point in the right direction?

BR: Yes, I see a great number of young black intellectuals who are beginning to raise very serious questions. Some ask the right questions and come up with the wrong answers. Others are asking the right questions and come up with the right answers. There are people like Thomas Sowell, as others, with whose answers I do not necessarily agree, but who are raising serious questions, such as whether the welfare system has harmed or benefited. They think it has harmed. Black communities are now ready to listen to Pat Moynihan's basic assumption about the nature of the black family—twenty years later [see chap. 9]. But the very fact that they are now willing to listen to him indicates to me that something has begun to happen.

LRS: Do you think that the sudden attention the civil rights groups are giving to South African issues tends to hold back the reevaluation you call for?

BR: Yes. Deep black concern for South Africa is the feeling that any group has when "somebody like me" is being pushed around. In a deeper sense, I think the [civil rights groups] are clinging to [South Africa] because they do not have real answers for their constituencies in racial terms. So they substitute South Africa. Why? An illustration: whenever black leaders go to the State Department they discuss only South Africa. They do not discuss with the secretary of state the loss of labor in intensive industry, which has brutalized blacks in America. It is not only an economic measure but a decision of America's foreign policy. We give labor-intensive industry to other people who have no hard currency. All they can give us back to pay for the hard currency is utensils and other things that are made by their labor-intensive industry. That's not discussed, nor is there discussion of the effect of the decline of American industry and what it is doing to the blacks. [In this context], even . . . retraining for jobs for blacks should be discussed at the State Department. South Africa is always discussed. The last two times I have gone, I said that "unless you guys are willing to discuss some of these important issues that the State Department should be concerned with, I don't think I want to go again."

LRS: These are also subjects for the Commerce Department, and others.

BR: Exactly.

LRS: I imagine it would be refreshing to go to a new battery of officials and get new attention.

BR: No, they want to be able to tell the black constituency, "We held those white folks off on segregation and discrimination."

LRS: One further word about Wilkins, Bayard . . .

BR: From 1955 to 1965, Dr. King seemed the central figure who was getting attention. But I want to call attention to five or six events which took place that could not have happened without Roy Wilkins. One was a prayer pilgrimage of 1957 that Phil Randolph called. It brought sixty thousand ministers to Washington on the question of integrated schools. The next was in 1958, the Youth March for integrated schools; 1959—some forty thousand to fifty thousand youngsters coming to Washington. Then, in both 1960 and 1964, Mr. Randolph called for demonstrations at both political party conventions. Nineteen sixty-four was vitally important, because that was when Lyndon Johnson ran and SNCC went halfway into the Democratic Party. Mr. Randolph called all of these demonstrations—1957 to 1964—and I organized them, but Roy Wilkins and the NAACP paid for every one of them. Roy griped all the way—"You and Randolph put on these things, and then you bring me the bills"—but he paid for them.

LRS: Without which they probably wouldn't have happened.

BR: They couldn't have happened, because neither Randolph nor I had the prestige to raise the amount of money that was needed. It's interesting to note that the first really prominent moment with Dr. King outside the South was his "give us the votes" speech at the 1957 prayer pilgrimage, and the thing that really solidified him was his 1963 speech at the March on Washington. So the major events at which King was projected are the two major events that Roy Wilkins put the most money into seeing that they occurred.

LRS: And which Randolph and you were instrumental in organizing.

BR: Mr. Randolph, who was very charitable, used to say, "You know, Bayard, it was just inevitable that they would want to say the 1963 march was 'King's March.'" Then he'd say, "I think we were lucky, because Martin Luther King has become so important that if they think it was his march they'll never forget it; where if it had been our march I don't know if it would have been remembered." That was the kind of man Randolph was.

LRS: It just about turned out that way.

BR: That's the history. Anything that's been written is not necessarily true, and therefore by deduction history is sometimes [only] reflections of the truth.

BIBLIOGRAPHY

Amalrik, Andrei. *Will the Soviet Union Survive until 1984?* New York: Harper and Row, 1970.

"Amalrik: Changing the USSR." *Freedom at Issue*, November–December 1979.

"Anniversary of Chernobyl Nuclear Disaster Focus of Hearing." *CSCE Digest*, May 1996.

Barnes, Joseph. *Willkie: The Events He Was Part of, The Ideas He Fought For.* New York: Simon and Schuster, 1952.

Barry, Theodore de. "Multiculturalism and Human Rights." *Freedom Review*, March–April 1994.

Bellow, Saul. "Writers, Intellectuals, Politics: Mainly Reminiscence." *The National Interest*, spring 1993, p. 131.

Berman, Howard A. "The Faith of Classical Reform Judaism." *Issues* (American Council for Judaism), summer 2001.

Bickel, Alexander M. "Press and Government: Aspects of the Constitutional Position." *Freedom at Issue*, September–October 1973.

———. *The Morality of Consent.* New Haven, CT: Yale University Press, 1975.

Braestrup, Peter. *Big Story: How the American Press and Television Reported and Interpreted the Crisis of Tet 1968.* With an introduction by Leonard R. Sussman. 2 vols. Boulder, CO: Westview Press, 1977.

Brownfield, Allan C. Review of *Why Should Jews Survive?* by Michael Goldberg. *Issues* (American Council for Judaism), spring 1996.

———. "It Is Time to End the Doomsday Rhetoric of a 'Second Holocaust.'" *Issues* (American Council for Judaism), summer 2002.

Campbell, Frank. "The Practical Reality of 'Development Communication.'" *Intermedia* (International Institute of Communication, London), March 1984, pp. 24–29.

Chadwin, Mark Lincoln. *The Hawks of World War II.* Chapel Hill: University of North Carolina Press, 1968.

Chafe, William H. *Never Stop Running: Allard Lowenstein and the Struggle to Save American Liberalism.* New York: Basic Books, 1993, reprint 1995.

Coleman, Peter. "Books: Civility, Edward Shils." *Quadrant* (Australia), March 2002.

Djilas, Milovan. *Fall of the New Class: A History of Communism's Self-Destruction.* Edited by Vasilije Kalezic. New York: Knopf, 1998.

Epstein, Jason. *The Great Conspiracy Trial*. New York: Random House, 1970.

Frazer, James George. *The New Golden Bough*. Edited and with a foreword by Theodor Gaster. New York: Criterion Books, 1959.

Gable, Neal. *Winchell: Gossip, Power, and the Culture of Celebrity*. New York: Vintage, 1994.

Gawad, Muhammad Abdel. "Attempts of the Arab World to Participate in Balancing the Flow of Information." In *The Third World and Press Freedom*, edited by Philip Horton, pp. 173–86. New York: Praeger, 1978.

Glickman, Mark. "One Voice against Many: A Biographical Study of Elmer Berger (1948–1968)." Thesis for ordination, Hebrew Union College–Jewish Institute of Religion, 1990.

Goldberg, Michael. *Why Should Jews Survive?* New York: Oxford University Press, 1995.

Hamilton, Nigel. "Inga Binga." Part 9 in *JFK: Reckless Youth*. New York: Random House, 1993.

Hawes, Elizabeth. *New York, New York: How the Apartment House Transformed the Life of the City, 1869–1930*. New York: Knopf, 1993.

Hook, Sidney. "*Bakke*—Where Does It Lead? The Triumph of Racism?" *Freedom at Issue*, September–October 1978.

———. *Out of Step: An Unquiet Life in the Twentieth Century*. New York: Harper and Row, 1987.

Hunter, Edith F. *Conversations with Children*. Boston: Beacon Press, 1961.

———. *Sophia Lyons Fahs: A Biography*. Boston: Beacon Press, 1966.

"Intelligence Agencies in a Free Society." *Freedom at Issue*, March–April 1976.

Kamenetz, Rodger. "What I Learned about Judaism from the Dalai Lama," *Reform Judaism*, summer 1994.

Kertesz, Louise. Introduction to *A Muriel Rukeyser Reader*. Edited by Jan Heller Levi. New York: W. W. Norton, 1994.

Klass, Rosanne, ed. *Afghanistan: The Great Game Revisited*. Lanham, MD: University Press of America, 1987.

Kolsky, Thomas A. *Jews against Zionism: The American Council for Judaism, 1942–48*. Philadelphia: Temple University Press, 1990.

Lapham, Lewis H. "Notebook: Washington Phrase Book." *Harper's*, October 1993.

"Leah Rabin Expresses Solidarity with Reform Jews." *Special Interest Report* (American Council for Judaism), May–June 1996.

Maldonado, Alexander W. *Teodoro Moscoso and Puerto Rico's Operation Bootstrap*. Gainesville: University of Florida Press, 1976.

Manet, Enrique Gonzales. "Issues and Development." In *International Information and Communication Order Sourcebook*, edited by Enrique Gonzales Manet, Kaarle Nordenstreng, and Wolfgang Kleinwachter. Prague: International Organization of Journalists, 1986.

Manglapus, Raul S. *Will of the People: Original Democracy in Non-Western Societies*. New York: Greenwood, 1987.

Mathiane, Nomavenda. *South Africa: Diary of Troubled Times*. New York: Freedom House, 1989.

McLean, Deckle. *Privacy and Its Invasion*. Westport, CT: Praeger, 1995.

Mihajlov, Mihailjo. "The First Dissident: In Memoriam Milovan Djilas." *Uncaptive Minds*, summer 1995.

Moynihan, Daniel Patrick, and Nathan Glazer. *Beyond the Melting Pot.* Cambridge, MA: MIT Press, 1970.

Neal, Steve. *Dark Horse: A Biography of Wendell Willkie.* New York: Doubleday, 1984.

Packard, Vance. *The Naked Society.* New York: D. McKay, 1964.

Pool, Ithiel de Sola. *Forecasting the Telephone: A Retrospective Technology Assessment of the Telephone.* Norwood, NJ: Ablex, 1983.

———. *Technologies without Boundaries: On Telecommunications in a Global Age.* Edited by Eli M. Noam. Cambridge, MA: Harvard University Press, 1990.

Qoboza, Percy. "South Africa: A Black View." *Freedom at Issue,* September–October 1977.

Richardson, Elliot. *Reflections of a Radical Moderate.* New York: Pantheon, 1996.

Rukeyser, Muriel. *The Life of Poetry.* New York: Current Books, 1949.

———. *One Life.* New York: Simon and Schuster, 1957.

———. *The Collected Poems.* New York: McGraw-Hill, 1978.

Saunders, Frances Stonor. *The Cultural Cold War: The CIA and the World of Arts and Letters.* New York: New Press, 1999.

Savimbi, Jonas. "The Horizon of Peace in Angola." *Freedom at Issue,* September–October 1988.

Shils, Edward. *Center and Periphery: Essays in Macrosociology.* Chicago: University of Chicago Press, 1975.

———. "Leopold Labedz." *Quadrant* (Australia), January–February 1996.

Fred S. Siebert, Theodore Peterson, and Wilbur Schramm. *Four Theories of the Press: The Authoritarian, Libertarian, Social Responsibility, and Soviet Communist Concepts of What the Press Should Be and Do.* Urbana: University of Illinois Press, 1956.

Margaret Chase Smith, *Declaration of Conscience.* New York: Doubleday, 1972.

Sussman, Leonard R. "The Sacred and the Profane in Judaism." *Religious Education,* May–June 1960.

———. *Mass News Media and the Third World Challenge.* Beverly Hills, CA: Sage, 1977.

———. "Who Controls Journalism? The London Information Forum." *Freedom at Issue,* July–August 1989.

———. *Power, the Press, and the Technology of Freedom: The Coming Age of ISDN.* New York: Freedom House, 1989.

———. "The New Press Law of the USSR." *Freedom at Issue,* September–October 1990.

———. *The Culture of Freedom: The Small World of Fulbright Scholars.* Lanham, MD: Rowman and Littlefield, 1992.

———. *Press Freedom in Our Genes: A Human Need.* Reston, VA: World Press Freedom Committee, 2001.

Suzman, Helen. *In No Uncertain Terms: A South African Memoir.* With a foreword by Nelson Mandela. New York: Knopf, 1993.

Tugwell, Rexford G. *The Stricken Land: The Story of Puerto Rico.* New York: Doubleday, 1946.

———. *The Art of Politics as Practiced by Three Great Americans: Franklin Delano Roosevelt, Luis Muñoz Marin, and Fiorello H. LaGuardia.* New York: Doubleday, 1998.

Watts, Duncan J. *Six Degrees: The Science of a Connected Age.* New York: W. W. Norton, 2003.

Willkie, Wendell L. *One World.* New York: Simon and Schuster, 1943.

Zubrzycki, Jerzy. "Edward Shils: A Personal Memoir." *Quadrant* (Australia), January–February 1996.

INDEX

www.ingramcontent.com/pod-product-compliance
Lightning Source LLC
Chambersburg PA
CBHW050232270326
41914CB00033BB/1879/J